Unbounded Practice

Unbounded Practice

*Women and Landscape Architecture
in the Early Twentieth Century*

Thaïsa Way

UNIVERSITY OF VIRGINIA PRESS

CHARLOTTESVILLE & LONDON

University of Virginia Press
© 2009 by the Rector and Visitors
of the University of Virginia
All rights reserved
Printed in the United States of America
on acid-free paper

First published 2009
First paperback edition published 2013
ISBN 978-0-8139-3482-2 (paper)

9 8 7 6 5 4 3 2 1

THE LIBRARY OF CONGRESS HAS CATALOGED THE HARDCOVER
EDITION AS FOLLOWS:

Library of Congress Cataloging-in-Publication Data
Way, Thaïsa, 1960–
   Unbounded practice : women and landscape architecture
in the early twentieth century / Thaïsa Way.
      p.   cm.
   Includes bibliographical references and index.
   ISBN 978-0-8139-2808-1 (cloth : alk. paper)
   1. Women landscape architects—United States—History—
20th century. 2. Landscape architecture—United States—
History—20th century. I. Title.
   SB469.9.W39 2009
   712.082'0973—dc22
                                        2008034281

Dedicated to Natasha, Adrian, and Marc

CONTENTS

ACKNOWLEDGMENTS

I offer my genuine thanks to many people for the support and encouragement given me as I researched, wrote, and rewrote this book. I begin by thanking those who offered their books, files, and photographs to me and spent time with me answering hundreds of questions. Interviewing Dean Perkins at age ninety-eight, after he had played tennis for two hours, remains one of the highlights of this project. So does sitting at Donna Caldwell's kitchen table, talking about her memories of Agnes Selkirk Clark and Ellen Biddle Shipman. Patricia Cautley Hill shared generations of her family with me. The Phipps Houses Foundation (John L. Fox and Owen Shakespeare) and the Radburn Association (Felice Koplik, Louise Orlando, and Herbert Reynolds) invited me to explore their collections of documents, tour landscapes, and hear many many stories. Art Wrubel spent hours with me at Oakcroft, in New Jersey, as did Thomas Williams at the Phipps Conservancy, in Denver. I thank all of these individuals and organizations, for without them this book would not be.

Of those who share my love of research and the hunt for knowledge, I want to thank Leslie Close and Catha Rambusch, who consistently surprised me with new sources of information. Catherine Brown's research files were shared with me by William Moorish, for which I am honored and grateful. Librarians are at the heart of research. Elaine Engst and Eleanor Brown, at the Kroch Library, Cornell University, and Linda Lott, at Dumbarton Oaks Library, were incredible librarians, as were their staffs. Archivists and curators are another stellar community. Waverly Lowell, curator at the University of Berkeley Environmental Design Archives, and William Whittaker, collections manager for the Architectural Archives at the University of Pennsylvania, helped me to track down a myriad of documents, images, and sources. Sherrill Redmon, at Smith College, allowed me to peruse materials the archive had barely had time to inventory. At Winterthur, Heather Clewell and Maggie Lidz hosted my visit to the libraries and gardens of the du Pont family. Lynn Laffey, at the Morris County Park Commission, was consistently helpful with the

Hutcheson materials. There are not enough songs about the work of such scholars.

The work of my mentors, Diane Harris, Ann Komara, Elizabeth Meyer, D. Fairchild Ruggles, and Gwendolyn Wright, inspired this project. Colleagues Elen Deming, Jean-Marie Hartman, Valencia Libby, and Rebecca Warren Davidson offered access to a breadth of sources, as well as support (and even some editing) throughout my adventure. I would like to thank the members of my dissertation committee, Herbert Gottfried, Claudia Lazzaro, Leonard Mirin, and Mary N. Woods, my chair, who remained steadfastly confident in the importance of my topic. Richard Hawks, at the SUNY College of Environmental Science and Forestry, provided incredible support to me as a teacher and scholar, all while opening new doors and providing fresh opportunities. Cheryl Doble, Robin Hoffman, Anthony Miller, and Matthew Potteiger were indispensable as mentors in my balance of teaching and scholarship, cheering me on as I struggled to think and write. I learned a lot about good teaching, relevant scholarship, and clear writing from my work with students, in particular graduate students at SUNY-ESF and the University of Washington. Joining this esteemed group of colleagues is my editor, Boyd Zenner, who found me early and kept the candle burning. As the community of landscape historians grows and matures, I am honored to be an active member alongside each of you.

Particular institutions and foundations have also supported first the research and then this book. I was privileged to be an Enid A. Haupt Fellow at the Smithsonian Institution and to work with the staff of the Archives of American Gardens. I was also fortunate to receive a Henry Luce Foundation/American Council of Learned Societies Dissertation Fellowship in American Art, which funded a year of writing. I was awarded a Citation of Special Recognition by the Graham Foundation for Advanced Studies in the Fine Arts, and the Clarence S. Stein Institute for Urban and Landscape Studies helped to fund research on housing projects. For the publication of this book, the Beverly Willis Architecture Foundation graciously awarded support for the color plates and additional black-and-white photographs. I am extremely grateful to Beverly Willis and Wanda Bubrinski for their hard work and large visions. The Foundation for Landscape Studies awarded this project a David R. Coffin Publication grant to meet the final expenses of publishing a work that depends on images for its narrative. The University of Washington, College of Architecture and Urban Planning, also supported the book, expanding its breadth and depth. The significance of this support for scholarship and publications in landscape history cannot be overstated. While I take full responsibility for the final project, I am indebted to every one of these people and organizations.

I am also grateful for the opportunity to draw on two previously published papers that were vital to the development of this book. Chapter

6 originally appeared as "Early Social Agendas of Women in Landscape Architecture," *Landscape Journal* 25, no. 2 (Fall 2006): 187–204, copyright 2006 by the Board of Regents of the University of Wisconsin System, reproduced by permission. A portion of chapter 8 entitled "A Practice Focused on the Public Realm" was first published as "Designing Garden City Landscapes: Works by Marjorie L. Sewell Cautley, 1922–1937," *Studies in the History of Gardens and Designed Landscapes* 25, no. 4 (2005): 297–316.

In the end it is my family that truly sustained me throughout the project. Brenda Way and Lori Laqua provided much-needed editing of the first and final manuscripts. Henry Erlich made vacations happen at moments of need. Niobe Way, Lucan Way, Justin Erlich, and Peter Way offered confidence and fresh air. My grandfather Victor Erlich taught me the power of daily writing, while my grandmother Rhoda Way shared her love of gardens and gardening. I am sad that neither lived to see the book in print. Marc, Adrian, and Natasha keep me going every day, and it is to them that I dedicate this work. May we all be a Force.

Unbounded Practice

Introduction

Central Park has been a New York City landmark for almost 150 years, revered by local residents, visiting tourists, and almost any landscape architecture student. Walking along the paths through woods and meadows, by creeks and ponds, many believe it to be a remnant of an idyllic landscape predating any modern urban civilization. But this, of course, is entirely wrong. Central Park was meticulously imagined and designed by North America's first professional landscape architects, Frederick Law Olmsted and Calvert Vaux, in the 1850s and 1860s. Every rock, tree, and grassy meadow was planned and placed. As Anne Whiston Spirn has written: "Many landmarks of landscape architecture are assumed to be either works of nature or felicitous serendipitous products of culture. Their very success prevents appreciation of their triumphs as artful answers to knotty problems of conflicting environmental values or competing purposes."[1]

Landscape architects have struggled since the nineteenth century to develop a vocabulary that could be used to define the practice and position the profession in the public realm. In part the issue was how to define a breadth of practice comprised of flower garden design, park systems planning, urban transportation development, suburb design, and university campus master planning, to name but a few of landscape architecture's concerns. The practitioners came from backgrounds just as diverse and wide-ranging. However, this range and diversity have rarely been acknowledged in the histories and narratives of the practice. Historians have instead primarily positioned landscape architecture only in terms of its relationship to architecture, dismissing its complex and rich depth and breadth.[2]

In 1899 the American Society of Landscape Architects (ASLA) was founded to make visible the work of landscape architects. Contemporary magazines and books attest to the range and depth of practice, even when the public did not necessarily understand the profession or its role in the landscapes they enjoyed. To the frustration of many, particularly those in the ASLA, the public frequently conflated landscape architecture and the craft of gardening. In 1909 a Boston architect recalled "an amazing number of otherwise sane, responsible business men [who came] to him every year, saying: 'I'm all worn out. I need a rest. Once upon a time, I dug a rose-bush and it got on famously. Do you know, I've a notion to go in for landscape gardening!'"[3] Practitioners grew increasingly frustrated and actively sought to disengage their practice from gardening and horticulture. In the 1930s Jens Jensen noted the call to disassociate with gardening, as if, he said, "that word smelled of cabbage."[4] Practitioners, writers, and educators soon described landscape architecture as the sister to architecture, more akin to artful engineering than a practice intimately engaged with the environment, nature, and the land. The historical narratives of the profession have supported this disengagement by sweeping aside the range of experiences and practices based in horticulture, gardening, and ecology, which have in fact been dynamic agents in the shaping of the practice.

In this process of sweeping aside diverse practices, practitioners were also discarded from the canon. Those who came to design through the garden or gardening because they had worked in a nursery (Warren H. Manning, Annette McCrea) or after having learned to love gardens as children (Fletcher Steele, Beatrix Jones Farrand), or those who advocated a horticulturally oriented design practice (Jens Jensen, Ellen Biddle Shipman), were frequently placed in the sidebars of historical narratives.

Such narratives remained essentially unquestioned by textbooks and the professional community until the 1990s, when increased attention was given to a few individuals, including Jens Jensen, Beatrix Jones Farrand, and Fletcher Steele. From this work a more interesting narrative of landscape architecture is beginning to emerge, telling of a diversity of practitioners from a breadth of backgrounds.

These narratives have generally focused on individuals, relying on the format of the monograph, presenting each practitioner as a star within the larger practice. I challenge this narrative and suggest, with all due respect to the importance and quality of the work, that the practitioners were members of larger constellations of professionals without whom the practice and the profession would be far inferior.

Understanding these larger constellations not only allows us to place the individual stars within a context but also promotes a broader and deeper understanding of the practice and its role in our culture, in the past and in the future. If we are to develop a new vocabulary for landscape architecture, as Elizabeth Meyer has challenged us, we must begin to try to describe the "in between" spaces and practices; the places of overlap; and the relationships among nature, land, and practice.

I have chosen to consider women who practiced as the profession emerged in the public sphere. A review of early twentieth-century magazines, journals, lecture series, and designed landscapes reveals a significant group of women who both actively signified and shaped contemporary landscape architectural practice. They engaged in the practice in ways unprecedented by women in architecture, engineering, or law. This was not mere coincidence; the practice of landscape architecture matured into a profession in the United States in the first four decades of the twentieth century, at the same time that women actively entered the paid-labor force and, in particular, the professions. Considering the practice of landscape architecture through the lens of women's praxis (both the practice and the theory or approach) opens avenues to better understanding how the profession came to be what it is today and the potential of what it might become tomorrow.

This narrative confronts a number of assumptions about both the profession and the role of women in practice. The primary assumption challenged is that in the early twentieth century a few wealthy women practiced garden design as a "hobby." They are frequently described as a few elite upper-class women leading "bedroom" offices, as Olmsted is reported to have described the practice of Beatrix Jones Farrand, whose work included designs for Princeton University, Yale University, the University of Chicago, the Santa Barbara Botanical Garden, and the town square in Oberlin, Ohio, as well as a number of large country estates. In fact hundreds of women are documented practicing during the first half of the twentieth century. Some practiced within their local communities, such as Edith Schryver and Elizabeth Lord in Salem, Oregon, while others, such as Annette Hoyt Flanders and Ellen Biddle Shipman, led offices with commissions across the nation.

Women were featured in professional exhibits, their work was published in professional journals, and they participated in professional organizations at both local and national levels. Popular garden magazines featured images of and articles about gardens and landscapes designed by female practitioners including Mary Parson Cunningham, Rose Ishbel Greely, and Isabella Pendleton. Martha Brookes Hutcheson, Ellen Biddle Shipman, Ruth Bramley Dean, and Mary Rutherfurd Jay were frequently invited to lecture to garden and art clubs, civic improvement organizations, and professional associations. Marjorie S. Cautley, Katherine D. Jones, Mabel Keyes Babcock, Florence Robinson, and Elizabeth May McAdams taught design, site planning, city planning, and horticulture in programs at Columbia University, the University of California at Berkeley, Wellesley, and the University of Illinois, among others. It is hard to imagine telling the history of the profession without including these practitioners, writers, and teachers.

The second assumption centers on a two-pronged description of practice: that women were commissioned exclusively for home garden design and that such garden design was an insignificant part of practice. Women did design flower gardens, as did their male colleagues. Residential design played a central role in most offices, including those of the Olmsted

Brothers, Charles Adams Platt, Warren Manning, and Thomas Church, among many others. Historians of the profession have chosen to ignore this aspect of early practice. Norman T. Newton, in his seminal history of the profession, published in 1971, suggested such work was secondary and only viable if balanced by significant public works. Residential work, according to Newton, was generally done with success by a few notable women (Beatrix Jones Farrand, Marian Cruger Coffin, and Annette Hoyt Flanders), as other professionals did not find it *workable*.[5] Such work subsequently was not considered important in the establishment of a larger canon of significant American landscape designs, which were predominantly public or quasi-public.

Women's practice ranged from university campuses to city parks to urban housing projects and highway systems. Marian Cruger Coffin designed the campuses of the University of Delaware; Elizabeth Lord and Edith Schryver were hired by the city of Salem, Oregon, to design parks and public spaces; Maud Sargent and Elizabeth Bullard worked for Robert Moses in New York City and for the state of New York; Iris Ashwell worked for the Federal Public Housing Authority; Marjorie Sewell Cautley designed and supervised the construction of ten New Hampshire state parks; Ruth Shellhorn was a landscape architect for Walt Disney's Disneyland; and Florence Yoch and Lucille Council were commissioned to design the country estate and movie sets of the film director David O. Selznick. This book begins to describe the variety and depth of the work and the role of women in shaping the profession. While at times its focus is on the specifics of a particular practice, it is the cumulative narrative that is significant.

The Story Line

While a general background is provided, the narrative of this history begins in 1893, the year of Olmsted's landscape for the Chicago World's Fair and of the publication of Mariana Van Rensselaer's book, *Art Out-of-Doors,* both of which marked significant moments in the establishment of the practice as a profession. The narrative ends in the mid-1940s, as the profession moved into a new phase of growth and definition. It is during these early decades that the practice of landscape architecture matured into a profession; this was also a time when women were most actively engaged and visible. This book weaves together these stories, of the profession and of the women who helped to shape its development.

The narrative is grounded in the concept of constellations, as developed by Martin Jay and Gwendolyn Wright. This approach considers how individuals remained distinct yet shared the experience of being women. As noted by Wright, Jay uses the term *constellation* to describe "a specific milieu, at once local, national, and transnational . . . to suggest elements (or people) at once juxtaposed and changing; a definite pattern unites them but it overlaps with other patterns and has no inherent or total-izing essence."[6] The idea of constellations suggests that difference can be discussed in broader terms to reveal trends, biases, and influences. The profession chosen by a group of women can be juxtaposed with their experience as women within a specific time period and a shared geogra-phy. The shared experiences of female landscape architects are explored in their differences from and similarities to those of male landscape ar-chitects. These experiences are understood within the social traditions and structures that place men and women in distinct relationships with social and economic powers through different modes of access to educa-tion, training, and authority.

The present narrative draws on these ideas by describing two primary constellations of women practitioners, one within the other. The larger comprises a community of approximately two hundred women whose work I have been able to identify. These women practiced, wrote about design, and photographed landscapes during the late nineteenth and early twentieth centuries. They fostered a dynamic and complex network among colleagues, mentors, teachers, and collaborators. This constella-tion includes those leading offices with a primarily local clientele; those focused on publicizing the principles of quality garden design; those with specific social agendas promoted through their design practice; and those who worked for transportation departments, park systems, plan-ning offices, and architectural firms. These women were educators in pri-vate and public institutions, as well as teachers of extension services and correspondence programs.

Wodell & Cottrell, a firm led by two sisters, served a local clientele in New Jersey, designing home gardens, neighborhood parks, and garden club exhibits, few of which still exist. Lois Page Cottrell and Helen Page Wodell had no formal training in design but learned to garden alongside their friends, attended lectures given by practitioners, and acquired draft-ing skills by copying plans from books. They called themselves landscape gardeners instead of landscape architects, since they did not view their work in the same light as that of those with more formal education and training. However, for the community in Short Hills, New Jersey, they were professionals.

Popular magazines and small books were increasingly available to an enthusiastic public. Madeline Agar, Hannah Champlin, Elsetta Gilchrist, Lucille Teeter Kissack, and Isabella Pendleton became better-known for their articles on the design of gardens and landscapes than for their de-sign work. Along with many other female writers and critics, they helped to educate a generation of home owners and gardeners in the principles of design and the horticultural sciences.

Rose Ishbel Greely (1887–1969) was born and raised in Washington, D.C. She attended the National Cathedral School for Girls, then the Abbott Academy in Andover, Massachusetts, and graduated from Finch School in New York in 1905. Greely studied interior decorating at the Art Institute of Chicago, then metalwork, and even traveled to Florence, Italy, to learn silver repoussé work and enameling on metal. Not yet finding her niche, Greely took courses at the University of Maryland in agriculture and finally enrolled at the Cambridge School for Domestic Architecture and Landscape Architecture, graduating in 1920 with certificates in architecture and landscape architecture. Her first position was as a draftsperson in Fletcher Steele's office in Boston. In 1923 she began work for Horace W. Peaslee, architect and designer of Meridian Hill Park. In 1925, after opening her office, she became the first licensed female architect in Washington, D.C. Greely led a small practice with a secretary, an assistant, and two draftspersons, first in downtown Washington and later out of her home in Georgetown, until her retirement in 1960. Iris Ashwell, Cary Parker, Edith Cochran, and Julia Andrews trained in Greely's office before launching their own practices.

Greely specialized in residential design, emphasizing the integration of house and garden. She worked on over five hundred landscape and several architectural designs. Her public projects in the 1940s and 1950s included military installations, secondary schools, suburban developments, government housing projects, embassies, and museums. She was the only woman to be a member of the ASLA Committee for the Williamsburg Restoration Project (1929–35) and was elected as an ASLA fellow in 1936. Despite all this work she was probably best-known for her writing. She was widely published in magazines such as *Landscape Architecture Magazine, House Beautiful, House and Garden, Country Life,* the *Garden Club of America Bulletin,* and newspapers including the *Washington Post.*

Elizabeth May McAdams (1881–1967) was born in Illinois, the daughter of a pioneer flower and plant breeder and operator of a greenhouse on the south side of Chicago. At the age of thirty-one she enrolled at the University of Illinois, graduating with Florence Yoch in 1917, and subsequently found work in the office of Warren Manning. McAdams joined the Illinois faculty in 1918 and taught there until 1929. Her courses included planting design, general design, and plant identification, and she led student tours of European gardens and landscapes.

McAdams helped to found the Landscape Gardening Association for professional women and was secretary for a Chicago-region club of landscape architects. In 1935 she went to work for the Chicago Park District, where she remained until 1946, after which she led an office in Northbrook, Illinois, focused on residential design in the North Shore area. McAdams was elected a member of the ASLA in 1938 and a fellow in 1955. She was influential as an educator, designer, and civil employee. The stories of such designers, small firms, writers, and advocates are woven into the history of the practice, highlighting the range of opportunities and potential embraced by landscape architecture in the first half of the twentieth century.

A smaller constellation of women in landscape architecture comprised Beatrix Jones Farrand, Ellen Biddle Shipman, Marian Cruger Coffin, Martha Brookes Brown Hutcheson, Annette Hoyt Flanders, and Marjorie Louisa Sewell Cautley. The histories of these women are largely accessible either because of their own efforts (Farrand donated her papers to the University of California, Berkeley) or those of their clients (du Pont collected many of Coffin's works) or because of the nature of prior research (Hutcheson's work was substantially uncovered by Rebecca Warren Davidson), which allows a more in-depth investigation into the particulars of training, education, practice, office management, and the design process.

The best-known early woman in landscape architecture was Beatrix Jones Farrand (1872–1959). Of the founding members of the ASLA, Farrand was the only woman. She opened a practice in the 1890s, working out of the top floor of the New York City house where she and her mother lived. Basing her practice on Olmsted's office, Farrand helped establish professional standards and procedures for landscape architects. Her client list featured some of the nation's wealthiest families, including the Rockefellers, J. Pierpont Morgan, Mrs. Woodrow Wilson, and the Whitneys of Oyster Bay, New York. She was responsible for a number of projects for university and college campuses and for the landscape designs of arboretums, botanic gardens, and observatories in New York City, Santa Barbara, and Washington, D.C. Farrand lectured from Maine to California for garden clubs, civic organizations, and educational institutions. She was a consummate professional, known as a grand dame of the profession by her colleagues and clients.

Ellen Biddle Shipman (1869–1950) came to landscape architecture late in life when, in 1911, her husband left her with children to support. Living in Cornish, New Hampshire, among artists and intellectuals, most of whom were avid gardeners, Shipman had also become an accomplished gardener. After noting what he believed were innate talents, Charles Adams Platt, a neighbor and an artist and architect, took Shipman under his wing, tutored her in design, and then hired her to create planting designs for a variety of projects in the 1910s. Her designs were featured in landscapes in and near Chicago, Cleveland, New York City, and Washington, D.C. She went on to develop her own practice, establishing an office in New York, and mentored dozens of women practitioners.

As women in the late nineteenth century considered the career options open to them, a number looked at the work of Farrand as proof that landscape architecture was a viable option. When she realized she needed to identify a career for herself, Marian Cruger Coffin (1876–1957) decided to follow Farrand's path. Unlike Shipman or Farrand, Coffin enrolled in the only existing landscape architecture program, at the Massachusetts Institute of Technology (MIT). As she told the story, on finishing her course work, she was unable to find an office that would hire her. Undeterred, Coffin set up her own practice in Manhattan. With the help of friends such as Henry Francis du Pont, Coffin established a practice that included small home gardens featured in popular magazines, country estates for many of the du Pont family members, and the University of Delaware campus. She mentored many women and wrote extensively in hopes of inspiring a second generation of both practitioners and well-educated clients.

Martha Brookes Brown Hutcheson (1871–1959) completed an art education and enrolled in the landscape architecture program at MIT a year behind Coffin. She set up an office and hired young women to work with her. Hutcheson's major contribution was less her design work than her role as a lecturer and writer advocating for the profession and pushing a social agenda. She believed that improved home grounds would improve the American culture and raise the standard of living for less privileged citizens. Hutcheson argued that professionals should be public servants and that the public should be well-educated in issues of nature and matters of taste.

The next generation of designers took advantage of a growing number of university programs and an expanding network of offices and practices. Annette Hoyt Flanders (1887–1946) attended Smith College and the University of Illinois, where she completed a degree in landscape architecture. She became the first women to be employed by Vitale, Brincker-hoff, and Geiffert, an established firm. Opening her own practice, Flanders worked out of New York and Milwaukee, often traveling between offices while addressing projects across the country. She was a prolific writer and served as garden editor for *Good Housekeeping Magazine* in the 1930s. While Flanders is most often noted for her exquisite estate plans, her design of model gardens for the public contributed significantly to the development of landscape architecture as a profession with a social purpose.

As the profession matured, a Progressive Era agenda continued to play a major role in shaping practice. Idealism was matched with increased knowledge and skills in city planning, new town development, and housing project design. Inspired by the English garden cities described by Ebenezer Howard, and the new towns of Letchworth and Welwyn Garden City outside London in the 1920s, Clarence Stein and Henry Wright gathered together a team of experts and planners to design American garden cities. Marjorie L. Sewell Cautley (1891–1954) was the landscape architect for four of these projects. She had completed a degree in landscape architecture from Cornell University and worked in a number of established offices before launching her own practice. Cautley focused primarily on public projects, collaborating with architects, planners, and visionaries to develop high-quality housing grounds for working-class families.

This group of six women constituted a professional norm and force during the first half of the twentieth century. They struggled to establish professional standards and practice and to expand the public's knowledge of the discipline and were recognized by their peers and colleagues as successful professional landscape architects. They were also viewed as leaders and mentors by the hundreds of contemporary women entering the field.

Retelling the stories of these early women in landscape architecture brings a more thoughtful perspective to the profession and to the development of the American landscape. Landscape architecture has been described as a hybrid activity that operates "in between," and in response this history explores the relationships between practitioners and practice, as revealed in the work of women.[7] In so doing, it proposes to expand how we understand the profession today and how we teach the designers of tomorrow. We have the opportunity to recognize how movements such as sustainable design draw on the work of H. W. S. Cleveland, Wilhelm Miller, Ruth Dean, Jens Jensen, Elsa Rehmann, and Marjorie Sewell Cautley, as well as that of Ian McHarg and late twentieth-century environmental planners. For those outside of the professional community, my hope is that this book might inspire a more thoughtful reflection on our place in the American landscape—what has been lost, what has been gained, and what might be our collective future.

1

Landscape Architecture Emerges as a Profession

In 1805 Thomas Jefferson wrote in a letter to his granddaughter Ellen that, of the fine arts, "many reckon but five: painting, sculpture, architecture, music & poetry. To these some have added Oratory. . . . Others again add Gardening as a 7th fine art. Not horticulture, but the art of embellishing grounds by fancy."[1] A century later it was not gardening per se but landscape architecture that had joined the fine arts and the professions. In 1900 the newly formed American Society of Landscape Architects described the art and profession in its purpose statement as "planning, designing, or supervising the development of land areas for the purpose of improving human environment, enjoyment, use, convenience, or welfare." While Jefferson's description of gardening as the embellishing of landscape was only a part of what would become landscape architecture, it is from such roots that the practice grew and a profession was launched, first in the United States and later in Europe. It may seem remarkable that such an old practice would become first recognized as a profession in a relatively new nation; however, this was the logical conclusion of two significant characteristics of early American culture: a deep appreciation for the landscape as vital to the nation's identity and culture and a desire to establish new professions that would be accessible to middle-class citizens. What is remarkable is the significant role that women played in this new profession, and that is the story of this book.

Women, Mother Earth, and the American Landscape

Women have long been associated with nature, earth, and land. For many this association arises from the very beginning, from the Great Mother Goddess Gaea. In Greek mythology Demeter, the earth mother, with her daughter Persephone's help, took care of the earth's vegetation and its seasonal nature. Cultures indeed have long worshipped goddesses as nurturers of nature and symbols of fertility and agricultural bounty.

These relationships between nature and women, whether as mothers or goddesses, have engendered a natural association in many cultures of women with nature and the land. By extension women were associated with gardens and gardening as appropriate spaces and activities.

Such concepts of Mother Nature accompanied European settlers in the New World, shaping how they described their relationship to the new landscape. For these explorers and dreamers, as historians including William Cronon and Carolyn Merchant have noted, the New World offered the possibility of a paradise that might be realized through the application of man's artistry to God's nature and Mother Earth's bounty and generosity. Despite clear evidence that Native Americans had cultivated and altered the landscape, Europeans often described it as natural, native, and otherwise untouched by civilization. Rather than exploring how the landscape had come to be, they looked toward the land's potential to create and nurture a new civilization. For leaders such as Thomas Jefferson, third president, farmer, gardener, and scholar, the nation's future rested on the land's potential productivity. This belief in the bounty of the American landscape, its pristine wilderness, and its unpolluted nature framed Romantic thinking.

Susan Fenimore Cooper (1813–1894), Ralph Waldo Emerson (1803–1882), Henry David Thoreau (1817–1862), and others in the Romantic movement noted the potential of the land. These writers joined naturalists in observing, recording, and describing American nature and landscape in evocative images and eloquent terms. While Emerson appreciated the act of gardening as a way to engage nature, Cooper promoted gardening as essential to a communion with nature. Her book *Rural Hours,* like Thoreau's better-known but later *Walden,* described nature and culture as intertwined elements of a larger ideal. She suggested that horticulture and landscape gardening were arts of much older and much higher civilizations and that American society would demonstrate its maturity by exhibiting evidence of such knowledge and tradition. As a botanist, naturalist, historian, folklorist, and gardener, she argued that the hand of a gardener improved the landscape by actively bringing together the arts and nature. She not only appreciated the appearance of a garden, where nature and art met, but treasured the act of gardening, suggesting that since the time of Adam, "it has always looked well to see man, or woman either, working in a garden."[2] Her focus was on the experience of nature through gardening, nature walks, and observations made during the course of daily life.

For nineteenth-century writers, intellectuals, and artists, nature was at the core of who Americans were and who they might be. Gardening and cultivating the land reflected active engagement with nature. Writers such as Cooper, Catherine Beecher Stowe, Andrew Jackson Downing, and Frederick Law Olmsted suggested that by stewarding the American landscape, by merging art with nature, the nation's culture would be intrinsically improved. The health of the American landscape thus both nurtured and reflected the health of the nation.

Designing Gardens and Landscapes

Garden design dates to the earliest records of civilization, from the gardens of Babylon to the Egyptian garden courts to the medieval courts of monasteries. Since at least the seventeenth century, artists, architects, and gardeners have been identified as the designers of significant and elaborate gardens and landscapes. Architects, hydrology engineers, and gardeners created the gardens of Italian villas. French gardens were designed by the country's head gardener, André Le Nôtre, and in England the landscape of Stowe was created through the joint efforts of Sir Richard Temple and the landscape gardeners Charles Bridgeman, William Kent, and later Capability Brown. Nevertheless, it was not in Europe but in the United States that the profession of landscape architecture was first established.

In the New World the practice of employing an individual to create a garden or landscape was rare. One of the only known early examples is Middleton Place in South Carolina, where in the early 1700s the family hired the Englishman George Newman to design and supervise the planting of their plantation along the Ashley River. By the beginning of the nineteenth century, the nation featured numerous estates laid out with a variety of gardens, woodlands, and wildernesses, but most had been designed by their owners, not by landscape gardeners or designers. These owners learned from books, as well as the advice of nurserymen and gardeners. Lady Jean Skipwith of Prestwould Plantation in Virginia (1748–1826) read books by Martha Logan and Bernard McMahon, as well as those she ordered from England, including Philip Miller's enormous *Gardener's Dictionary*. She applied the ideas to her flower and kitchen gardens and orchard, developing a landscape recognized for its magnificence. The main garden lay due south of the house and adjacent to the juncture of two rivers, where she introduced a landscape of orchards and native wildflowers. Skipwith kept meticulous notes of her observations and documented her collection of seeds and bulbs, corresponding with friends, including fellow garden enthusiast Thomas Jefferson, on a variety of gardening topics.

In time a community of practicing landscape gardeners emerged. They initially designed country estates and subsequently took on the design of rural burial grounds and garden cemeteries. André Parmentier (1780–1830), from the Austrian Netherlands, arrived on Long Island in 1824 as a trained nurseryman and was commissioned to design estate gardens and landscapes on Long Island and along the Hudson River. Others followed, but a distinct discipline was not defined until the work of Andrew Jackson Downing.

Andrew Jackson Downing (1815–1852) formally established landscape design as a discipline by way of his work as a designer and, more significantly, through his writing on design. As a young man he established himself as a nurseryman and designer. He planned gardens for Matthew Vassar's Springside estate in Poughkeepsie, New York, and the Daniel Parish house in Newport, Rhode Island. His best-known design was for the public grounds in Washington, D.C., which included a picturesque series of naturalistic landscapes for the Capital Mall, as he believed that while men needed to live in cities, "it is not . . . needful for them to live utterly divorced from all pleasant and healthful intercourse with gardens and green fields."[3]

In 1841 Downing published his first book, *A Treatise on the Theory and Practice of Landscape Gardening.* The treatise directly addresses issues of design and the layout of the American landscape, relying heavily on the work of the British authors and designers John Claudius Loudon (1783–1843) and Humphrey Repton (1752–1818). Regardless of Downing's reliance on these English writers, his book became known as a distinctly American work, responding to the climate, landscape, and social conditions and "taste" of the United States. His contemporaries recognized the book as "the first work of the kind, of any considerable pretensions, [to] come from the American press."[4] It went through four editions during Downing's lifetime, as well as many reprints after his death. Downing was also the editor of the monthly magazine *The Horticulturist and Journal of Rural Art and Rural Taste,* which featured an essay of his each month.

Downing both articulated a theory of landscape gardening and framed a broad practice of landscape design for the next century. His approach was founded on the idea of adapting landscape design (its forms, practice, and uses) to the language, manners, and customs of Americans, as well as to the "real character" of the nation's indigenous landscape.[5] Downing described a link between patriotism and the improvement of house and garden and consequently domestic life. His ideal republican village would celebrate the "power and virtue of the individual home," while simultaneously encouraging community activities. Parks were at the heart of his ideal suburbs in that they might provide "mental and moral influences" for all in the community.[6] Such places, he argued, reflected a more cultured and cultivated nation, having the leisure and disposition to appreciate the arts. Beautifully designed landscapes benefited American culture, increased patriotism, and improved the public image of the United States. In a similar light Downing supported reformist programs, many led and promoted by women, aimed at encouraging the establishment of publicly funded libraries, art galleries, and parks. These amenities would provide healthful recreational grounds within which there would be ample social opportunities for all classes of people.

Downing equated outdoor public spaces with libraries and museums in importance to the public and proposed the idea of creating a large public park in New York City. His park would embrace recreational and educational goals in a "naturalistic setting for the promotion of popular refinement."[7] The park would contain spaces allowing the passive contemplation of natural scenery, settings for public institutions, and the recreational uses of a pleasure garden. Unfortunately, Downing died in 1852, just before his idea was realized in 1853. He was a passenger on the steamer *Henry Clay*, which burst into flames and sank.

FREDERICK LAW OLMSTED AND CALVERT VAUX

Downing's advocacy for a public park was heard, and members of the Board of Commissioners of New York City were appointed to see the plan through. In 1853, after a rocky start and with no clear plan in place, the commissioners faced the dilemma of who to hire to design and supervise the construction of their new park, Central Park. The commissioners announced a competition for the design in 1857, and its 1858 award to Calvert Vaux (1824–1895) and Frederick Law Olmsted (1822–1903) officially launched landscape architecture in the United States as not only a practice but a potential profession.

While Vaux and Olmsted designed Central Park and other projects together, it was Olmsted who established a framework for the profession of landscape architecture. Like Downing, Olmsted firmly believed that landscape scenery would engender a restorative and civilizing influence on communities and that such works improved the daily lives of Americans. His projects included large urban parks, parkways, scenic reservations, university and college campuses, residential suburbs, and country estates. He is most recognized for his designs of city park systems, including Central Park, the Emerald Necklace, and parks in Buffalo, in Rochester, and at Niagara Falls, as well as the Riverside community, outside of Chicago, and landscape plans for the campus of California's Stanford University and North Carolina's Biltmore estate. Olmsted's designs recalled English landscapes composed primarily of large areas of grass and trees, highlighted by water features and laced with carriage drives and footpaths. These were integrated with public spaces through broad interconnecting thoroughfares, or parkways, often forming a ring or necklace of park-spaces throughout an urban landscape.

Olmsted was also widely recognized for his design of the 1893 World's Columbian Exposition in Chicago, a hallmark in the history of American architecture and landscape architecture and one of his last large projects. Olmsted demonstrated in his design how two approaches, formal and naturalistic, could be merged to meet the physical and aesthetic needs of the public and the wishes of artists. At a testimonial dinner Daniel Burnham, the supervising architect of the fair, offered this tribute to Olmsted: "Each of you knows the name and genius of him who stands first in the heart and confidence of American artists, the creator of your own parks and many other city parks. He it is who has been our best advisor and our common mentor. In the highest sense he is the planner of the Exposition—Frederick Law Olmsted. . . . *An artist, he paints with lakes and wooded slopes; with lawns and banks and forest-covered hills; with mountain-sides and ocean views.*"[8]

While Olmsted is the best-known early landscape architect, he was joined by others. Contemporary designers included H. W. S. Cleveland (1814-1900), Jacob Weidenmann (1829-1893), Robert Morris Copeland (1830-1874), Nathan Barrett (1845-1919), Samuel Parsons Jr. (1844-1923), Ossian Cole Simonds (1855-1932), and, near the end of Olmsted's and Vaux's careers, the first women to practice professionally: Annette McCrea and Elizabeth Jane Bullard.

ANNETTE E. McCREA

Annette E. McCrea (1858-1928), lauded by Mary Ritter Beard in her 1912 book on women's work in municipalities, was an important early woman designer of public and private landscapes.[9] Born in Cooperstown, New York, Annette E. Maxson married J. Franklin McCrea, the owner of the largest nursery business in the Detroit area. When Franklin died in 1892, she took over his wholesale nursery in Kalamazoo, Michigan. Although initially, she may have done this to support her two children, she had in fact begun a lifetime career as a landscape architect. She likely drew on the experience of her brother, Charles Maxson, who also worked in the nursery. She ran the nursery and was soon commissioned for residential design work, the first a project for Frank Henderson.

With several years of experience behind her, she moved in 1900 to Chicago, where she "convinced the Lincoln Park Board that the position of landscape architect should be created and that she should be given the position."[10] She was in that position from January to May of 1900, during which time she was responsible for tree and shrubbery planting for Lincoln and Chicago Avenue parks. In the ensuing years McCrea was increasingly enmeshed in civic improvement associations, including the American Park and Outdoor Art Association, and in landscape designs for railway systems and grounds.

By 1902, McCrea was working with the Chicago, Milwaukee & St. Paul Railroad, responsible for designing landscape improvements for railroad stations and depots. For the Illinois Central, in 1905, she was commissioned to plan a system of landscape improvements associated with the station grounds. McCrea served as consulting landscape architect for the Chicago & North Western; Chicago, Burlington & Quincy; Duluth South Shore & Atlantic; Southern Pacific; and other railroad lines. Her task was to "lay out grounds to stations, report artistic arrangement of colors for painting depots, design plans for improving unsightly points around station buildings, and in general to make the scenery of the system more attractive."[11] The designs likely used a simple palette of plants that would survive a relatively harsh environment. For many in the small towns where her work appeared, her designs may have been the first designed landscapes they had experienced and served as a model of good taste and culture.

McCrea was involved in promoting the importance of designing railway and other civic landscapes in addition to her design practice. Downing Vaux recognized her in 1900, when he wrote to O. C. Simonds to suggest, unsuccessfully, that she should be elected to membership in the newly formed ASLA (there is no evidence as to why this suggestion failed). McCrea was appointed chair of the Committee on Railroad Grounds for the American Park and Outdoor Art Association. In 1904, as the Art Association and the American League for Civic Improvements were merged to become the American Civic Association, she was named vice president of the Department of Railroad Improvements; she became a member of the executive committee in 1908, along with John Nolen, another landscape architect, and J. Horace McFarland, the president of the American Civic Association and a noted conservationist and national park advocate. (Others included the author and advocate for school gardens Louise Klein Miller; the journalist, writer, and professor of urban planning Charles Mulford Robinson; and the activist Jane Addams.) McCrea reported annually on the conditions, improvements, and potential of the railway system landscape to the association and its members, serving in the leadership position until at least 1913.

In Tomahawk, Wisconsin, a Chicago, Milwaukee & St. Paul company town, McCrea was hired to produce plans for civic improvements and a park. She drew plans for the Michigan College of Mines, a normal school, and designed gardens for private clients. In 1916 the State Board of Control in Wisconsin adopted her plans for landscape work in front of the reformatory in Green Bay. In 1917 she was given the contract for "beautifying" the new concrete road between Green Bay and De Pere and supervising highway improvement projects, working in collaboration with the Woman's Club City Beautiful committee in each city. The new road ran in front of the reformatory and may well have been considered an expansion of that program. Her other projects included designs for St. James Park in Green Bay and for Riverside Park in De Pere. McCrea moved to De Pere in 1917 and remained active in civic improvement associations and activities, as well as residential work. A January 16, 1913, article in the *Christian Science Monitor,* "Woman Landscape Architect," extolled her garden in the suburbs as a "striking example of this woman landscape architect's work. It is one of the most beautiful residences in Chicago."

McCrea also lectured and wrote extensively, as did many other practitioners. She promoted better taste in landscape design and improved civic planning, as well as women's suffrage and expanded access to education in landscape architecture for men and women. *The Chautauquan* and other magazines published her essays promoting good taste in railway grounds and in the homes and gardens of surrounding villages and towns. In an article in *Suburban Life,* McCrea cautioned readers to carefully consider color harmony in the home and garden, suggesting they use neutral and natural colors and natural plants. McCrea advocated for women in the profession and excelled at publicizing her work. She encouraged agricultural colleges to consider women's education in landscape gardening. She was frequently quoted as encouraging women to pursue a career in landscape gardening or landscape architecture, as noted by Frances Copley Seavey, another landscape gardener and writer.[12] She later returned to Chicago and then moved to Minneapolis, where she died at the age of seventy in 1928.

As McCrea was coming to the end of her career, women such as Shipman and Flanders were launching theirs. While she was acknowledged in the *Green Bay Gazette* as having "marked the evolution of the art of home beautifying," her work in the public realm reflected the practice of contemporary practitioners, including Olmsted and Vaux, as well as that of women in the Progressive movement, such as Jane Addams and later Marjorie L. Sewell Cautley.[13] Public landscapes were a major focus of the profession for the next century, and transportation routes significantly shaped the landscape of the nation.

ELIZABETH JANE BULLARD

Elizabeth Jane Bullard (1847–1916) was named one of the first two ASLA fellows in 1899.[14] Little is known of her work, although she was known to Frederick Law Olmsted Sr. and to her contemporaries. Bullard was born in Sutton, Massachusetts, in 1847. Her father, Oliver Crosby Bullard (1822–1890), was a farmer, a teacher, and later a park superintendent. He met Olmsted Sr. when he joined the newly formed U.S. Sanitary Commission in 1863. He worked with Olmsted first as a park inspector for Prospect Park and Tompkins Park in New York City and later on the Capitol grounds in Washington, D.C. In the 1880s Bullard's father was hired to execute the designs for Beardsley and Seaside parks in Bridgeport, Connecticut, and he was the superintendent of parks in Bridgeport from 1885 until 1890.

Bullard, a painter, assisted her father in his park work. When Oliver Bullard died suddenly, the elder Olmsted was asked by the president of

Bridgeport's city board, William Noble, whether Miss Bullard might replace her father: "I find that a single daughter of his, had, from natural taste, observation, and education under his eye, gained an extensive knowledge of the art; that Mr. Bullard was in the habit of consulting with her; that he trusted greatly to her judgment. She is an artist (painter) by profession, familiar with her father's ideas, especially as to our parks. How would it do to have her take up her father's duty?"[15]

Olmsted responded with an endorsement of Bullard's abilities to fulfill the requirements of the position:

> Fortunately I have some acquaintance with the lady, enough to justify me in warmly advising her appointment. There is some risk in it, mainly because of the difficulties of discipline, but my opinion is that it would have a wholesome effect on politics and patronage and stipulate the Commission to higher manliness. And most fortunately, I can cite a precedent. The plans under which the old burial grounds of London are being transformed into public pleasure grounds (under the influence of a Society there, of which I am an Honorary Member) are made by a woman and the keeping of these grounds is superintended by her.[16]

In a separate letter Olmsted acknowledged the challenges of hiring a woman: "Your Board should be prepared to trust much to her discretion and to support her against any possible prejudice due to the novelty of the situation in which she will be placed. It would, in my judgment, be more prudent to give her greater freedom of discretion in all matters of her duty, rather than less than you would be prepared to give a man under similar circumstances."[17]

Despite Olmsted's endorsement Bullard declined the position. She likely understood the political challenges and shared Olmsted's fear that, as a woman, she would not have the support needed to fully implement the park plans. Bullard went on to develop a design business and worked with John Charles Olmsted and with the Olmsted Brothers firm, the successor to Olmsted's practice, on the campus of Smith College in Northampton, Massachusetts. She was associated with Bushnell Park in Hartford and consulted on other projects. She was an active member of the American Park and Outdoor Art Association, as well as the American League for Civic Improvement. Bullard's obituary in the *Bridgeport Telegram* read, "Many of the gardens in this city are the result of her efforts, she having been a landscape architect of no mean ability."[18]

There were other women in practice as well. On September 22, 1901, the *Los Angeles Times* featured a story on women as landscape gardeners.[19] Frances Copley Seavey, its author and a landscape gardener, reported on the well-known Englishwoman Miss Fanny R. Wilkinson, whose work involved the Metropolitan Public Gardens Association and over four hundred projects in and around London. Miss Beatrix Jones (Farrand), Miss Kate Sessions, and Mrs. A. E. McCrea were featured as practitioners helping to establish and shape the early practice of landscape architecture in the United States. These were the pioneers, both for the profession and for women in the professions, who paved the way for the first professional association of landscape architects and for the development of training programs and schools.

Landscape Architecture as a Profession

Professions "provide the means for the organization and production of knowledge."[20] For a practice to become a profession, the public must recognize its claimed knowledge as distinct from that of other domains, serving a needed purpose, and fitting a professional status. To establish a profession, a group must articulate an identity, define a shared body of knowledge, and describe the education and training required of practitioners. Landscape architecture was first defined by practitioners and writers, an association was formed, and finally education and training were established.

Defining a Practice

An important advocate for the practice of landscape design and related disciplines was the weekly journal *Garden and Forest*, published from 1888 to 1897. The domain of knowledge landscape architecture embraced was widely described by the magazine as a "broad and catholic art . . . as useful in the preservation of the Yosemite Valley or the scenery of Niagara as it is in planning a pastoral park or the grounds about a country house."[21] The magazine's essays and editorials carved out an expanse of knowledge embracing the land, nature, and culture. The art critic Mariana Griswold Van Rensselaer wrote over fifty articles for the journal, including the series "Landscape Gardening."[22] She described landscape architecture as a fine art warranting the respect given painting, sculpture, and architecture:

> Some of the Fine Arts appeal to the ear, others to the eye. The latter are the Arts of Design, and they are usually named as three—Architecture, Sculpture and Painting. . . . But in fact there is a *fourth art* which has a right to be rated with the others, which is as fine as the finest, and which demands as much of its professors in the way of creative power and executive skill as the most difficult. *This is the art whose purpose it is to create beautiful compositions upon the surface of the ground.*[23]

Van Rensselaer emphasized the relationship between landscape design and landscape painting, rather than any similarity between the practice and gardening. As a member of the intellectual and cultural elite, she was a woman of stature and taste, and consequently, her opinions imparted to landscape architecture the status of an art. Her series of essays was later compiled into a book, *Art Out-of-Doors,* published in 1893, which defined the emerging profession for a public audience. The book was included in the landscape architecture curriculum at MIT, Harvard, and elsewhere well into the twentieth century.

Van Rensselaer was joined by others advocating the design of public parks as a national art. Mary Caroline Robbins, a writer for both *Garden and Forest* and the *Atlantic Monthly,* wrote that the "parks and park systems [were] the most important artistic work which has been done in the United States." In none of the other fine arts—sculpture, architecture, or painting—did Robbins find Americans had advanced the art. In park-making, she argued, the artist had the advantage of natural beauty "to stimulate the artistic imagination and few competitors to encounter." In America, she argued, pleasure grounds were planned to a large extent for the public, for the people at large. These public grounds educated the people in good taste and, in particular, inspired many to seek "more perfection in home surroundings."[24] According to Robbins, Van Rensselaer, and others, landscape designers' efforts to improve public spaces and individuals' efforts to increase the beauty of private landscapes were patriotic activities that improved American culture and society. Landscape designers were increasingly engaged in a patriotic activity, although they had barely defined themselves as a distinct professional body, and at the turn of the nineteenth century, professional recognition was essential if landscape architecture was to be considered distinct from the crafts (gardeners) and the trades (nurserymen).

Defining a Profession

In Great Britain a profession was an honorable pursuit for gentlemen, those of proper birth, who viewed it as an intellectual endeavor demanding expertise in a "professed" body of knowledge gained from a university education and experience. Gentlemanly status allowed the professional to serve the client's interests rather than to focus on acquiring an income. English professionals, distinguished by birth, gained recognition from association of class, and, ultimately, legitimacy from formal education.

Americans, however, defined professionalism more loosely. By the mid-nineteenth century an American profession was commonly described as a full-time occupation through which a man earned his principal income. The professions, in other words, were not limited to those born to the elite. Instead, members of the middle class earned a living in the professions and emulated those in the upper classes. The professions, as they were recognized, included sons of merchants, planters, and tradesmen. Ideals of professionalism thus "incarnated the radical idea of the independent democrat, a liberated person seeking to free the power of nature within every worldly sphere, a self-governing individual exercising his trained judgment in an open society."[25] American professionals did adhere to the English ethic of service: professionalism required that their commitment to a client's interest take precedence over any possible personal gain. The professional served as an expert on behalf of the client, rather than as the client's servant, craftsman, or tradesman.

Emerging professions gained legitimacy from the establishment of associations and organizations. These bodies determined a practice's standards and guidelines. One critical point in such efforts was the question of whom to include—that is, should amateurs and others interested in the discipline be allowed as members alongside those pursuing the field as a profession? Issues of class and possible associations with tradesmen and artisans were significant for emerging professionals: "Middle-class respectability was vital for any [artist] . . . who wished to appear professional, that is, as an artist rather than an artisanal limner."[26] This tension was reflected in the discussions of various art unions and clubs. While such groups advocated education of the public, promoting the profession of the fine artist was paramount.

Benjamin Henry Latrobe is credited with introducing architecture as a profession in the United States in the early nineteenth century. In the following years a community of architects formed and subsequently struggled with issues of professionalism and standards. The first architectural association, the American Institution of Architects, founded in 1837 and lasting only a year, included architects, master builders, and others associated with artisanal culture. This meant that many who once called themselves master builders or carpenters now believed it appropriate to adopt the title of architect, which linked practitioners to middle- and upper-class clients and distinguished them from trade unionists.[27] This was a source of frustration for those concerned with professional standards. In response, some twenty years later twelve New York architects established the American Institute of Architects (AIA) in 1857, limiting membership to self-defined professional architects. The Western Association of Architects, a professional organization established in 1884, admitted the first woman practitioner, Louise Blanchard Bethune, in 1885. Mindful of serving a national profession, these two organizations merged in 1889, with a membership of 465 practitioners. Like medicine, then, architecture developed from a craft into a profession, in part by disassociating itself from the crafts of building.

By the late nineteenth century there began to be "general recognition of the value to the public of designed and organized cities, and of parks, reservations, and other out-of-door spaces, and a greatly increased interest in private pleasure-grounds of various kinds."[28] The Olmsted office was a critical advocate for the emerging profession of landscape architecture, and many of the designers who apprenticed in the practice later became leaders in the field, including Charles Eliot and Warren Manning. Projects from the Olmsted office were consistently recognized as significant contributions to the American landscape.

The landscape architect Harold Caparn reflected later, in 1931, that the field's professionalization was the result of "modern specialization: for as knowledge and skill increase, the followers of an art, a craft a business or profession, find that its complexity or ramifications are beyond the capacity of one person, and so concentrate on one branch of it."[29] Landscape architects would distinguish their practice as a specialized study, separate from architecture, horticulture, and engineering, during the first half of the twentieth century.

The earliest association of landscape designers was the American Park and Outdoor Art Association, organized by practitioners and interested amateurs and patrons in 1897 in Louisville, Kentucky. This association embraced anyone interested in the advancement of landscape design and the promotion of public parks. Its name was changed to the American Civic Association, and it went on to realize a number of important projects, particularly in the area of town improvements.[30]

In Boston Warren Manning attempted to organize another association of landscape designers, but the professional community did not yet see a need. Charles Eliot suggested instead that a general association, rather than a professional one, should be formed, given the limited number of true professionals. Manning, joined by Eliot and John C. Olmsted, then established the informal Repton Club, which allowed interested practitioners to discuss professional work over lunch or dinner.

The Hillside Club was formed in 1898 by a group of North Berkeley women trying to protect the natural environment of Northern California from insensitive new development through advocacy and good design. In 1902 the women invited men to join their efforts, and Charles Keeler came to serve as president. The Hillside Club distributed a booklet, most likely written by Annie Maybeck and Bernard Maybeck, that suggested how gardens and the landscape should be designed: "In laying out a landscape, never take away what there is. Group with it what you add to it. This is the fundamental law of landscape architecture."[31] The club served to educate the public on appropriate landscape design, rather than to promote the profession of landscape architecture.

These various organizations, clubs, and associations reflected an enormous breadth of practices and values. Active practitioners held to different views of design, appropriate approaches, the relative importance of professionalism, and the role of landscape design in American society. Even the titles practitioners adopted and promoted revealed great differences of opinion—landscape gardeners, landscape designers, landscape architects, garden architects, garden engineers.

In 1899 a group of practitioners established a society to promote the discipline as a profession: the American Society of Landscape Architecture (ASLA). (Such associations were not formed in Europe until the second and third decades of the twentieth century.) The landscape architect

Samuel Parsons Jr. organized the first meeting of practitioners in the New York region in February 1898. After a number of meetings a group of Boston designers and Ossian C. Simonds, from Chicago, decided to join them. The first official meeting took place on January 4, 1899, held in the offices of Parsons and Pentecost, in New York. Ten practicing designers founded the association: John C. Olmsted, Samuel Parsons Jr., Warren H. Manning, Nathan F. Barrett, Daniel W. Langton, Charles N. Lowrie, George F. Pentecost Jr., Ossian C. Simonds, Downing Vaux, and Beatrix Jones (later Farrand). Its first president was John C. Olmsted, with Samuel Parsons Jr. serving as vice president and Langton, Lowrie, and Jones serving on the executive committee. A constitution and set of bylaws were drawn up and approved. Elizabeth Bullard and Frederick Law Olmsted Jr. had been elected founding fellows by December 23, 1899, and Arthur Shurtleff (later Shurcliff), E. Maitland Armstrong, and Albert B. Russell had been elected junior members. Of these practitioners five studied horticulture and/or worked in nurseries, two had been trained as park designers, three had backgrounds in civil engineering, and one was an architect.

One of the first orders of business was to state the association's purpose, outlined in the constitution as to increase "efficiency and influence of the profession, and to foster good fellowship among its members and to promote the public welfare." These intentions—focused on serving the profession and the public, not necessarily on making the public better informed—framed the development of the association and the profession. The new society's second important project was to define the practice and profession as distinct from other practices and professions. Thus, in 1900 the association published the following definition: "The practice of landscape architecture is performing . . . any professional service in connection with planning, designing, or supervising the development of land areas for the purpose of improving human environment, enjoyment, use, convenience, or welfare. . . . The practice of landscape architecture as herein defined is not to be construed or interpreted as including the normal practice of architecture or engineering."

The founding members shared with Olmsted Sr. the belief that landscape design should serve a significant role in the improvement of society. Olmsted had argued vehemently for the ameliorative effects of landscape scenery, purporting that appropriate landscape design could improve society if such scenery was accessible to all. He tied the land and natural scenery to the very heart of a working and healthy democracy. This commitment to landscape architecture as a social and civic activity would remain important to the profession through the 1930s.

The community of landscape architects shared a belief in landscape design as an art and a science and as a practice drawing on other disciplines, including architecture, gardening, and nursery work. Landscape architects described their profession as founded on the principles of a science, while simultaneously promoting the discipline as a fine art, as had Olmsted and his contemporaries.

While the profession was thus increasingly defined and described, the appropriate title for practitioners remained under debate. Olmsted Sr. and Vaux had adopted the French title "landscape architect," but this label remained unsatisfactory to many practitioners. "Landscape gardening," a title credited to Humphrey Repton, offered the idea of an established heritage and tradition. O. C. Simonds and Beatrix Jones Farrand, both founding members of the ASLA, always signed as landscape gardeners, as did Warren Manning later in his career. In an essay titled "Landscape Gardening—A Definition," in an early issue of *Garden and Forest,* Mariana Van Rensselaer called attention to the issue:

> Still another thing which prevents popular recognition of this art is our lack of clearly understood terms with which to speak about it. "Gardens" once meant pleasure-grounds of every kind, and "gardener" then had an adequately artistic sound. But as the meaning of the first term was gradually specialized, so the other gradually came to denote a mere grower of plants. "Landscape-gardener" was a title invented by the artists of the eighteenth century to mark the new tendency which they represented—the search for "natural" as opposed to "formal" beauty; and it seemed to them to need an apology as savoring, perhaps, of grandiloquence or conceit. But as taste declined in England, this title was assumed by men who had not the slightest right, judged either by their aims or by their results, to be considered artists; and to-day it is fallen so far out of favor that it is often replaced by "landscape-architect." French usage supports this term and it is in many respects a good one. But its derivative, "landscape-architecture," is unsatisfactory; and so, on the other hand, is "landscape-artist," although "landscape-art" is a good general term. Perhaps the best we can do is to keep both terms in use while recognizing that, in this country and I think in England also, the profession itself has definitely adopted, for its members and for their work, the names "landscape-architect" and "landscape-architecture.[32]

In 1915 members of the ASLA were asked to vote on the name of their profession and given the following choices: landscaper (1), landscapist (1), landscape architect (29), landscape designer (3), landscape engineer (1), landscape artist (0), landscape gardener (1), landscape man (0), garden designer (0), and landscapor (1).[33] These titles cut a wide swath across contemporary practice, from gardeners to engineers, yet none seemed to garner the support given to the title "landscape architect." While the official name of the profession did not change, the ASLA's bylaws were amended to include the titles "landscape architect" and "landscape gardener." Those associating their work most closely with horticulture, gardening, and botanical studies were most likely to use the label "landscape gardener." Those who believed their work was best aligned with architecture, engineering, and planning used the label "landscape architect." On the other hand, some used the latter title in deference to Olmsted Sr. and the reputation of his office. This ambivalence reflected the unease of the professional community in their relationship to architecture, gardening, and landscape design.

The Profession Expands

After 1900 the profession gradually came to be recognized in the public realm. During the Country Place Era, in the early twentieth century, many designers were commissioned to design elaborate private estates, but after the Depression public works predominated. City and town planning evolved as an important part of practice, as park and recreation planning continued to expand. By the 1940s the profession boasted a significant professional association, educational programs that met professional approval, established standards of practice, a code of ethics, increased attention to the licensing of practitioners (an important measurement of professional development), and practitioners serving diverse and far-ranging purposes across the nation. The process of the practice becoming a profession had truly begun in 1899, with the establishment of the ASLA, and by the 1940s it could be assumed that landscape architects were active members of the professional world.[34]

During this time of expansion and maturation, firms and practices came to be located in every major city, most led by men, but many by women. Too, women worked in a number of prominent male-led offices, including those of Warren Manning; Harold Hill Blossom; Fletcher Steele; Frost & Pond, Innocenti & Webel; and Vitale, Brinckerhoff, and Geiffert. Popular magazines such as *House & Garden* and *House Beautiful* featured landscape architecture as an art rivaling architecture. Women wrote, designed, and illustrated for these magazines, as did men. Landscape architecture was now open to a diversity of practitioners and, in particular, to a constellation of women unlike that evident in any other contemporary design profession. This period, which had begun with the work of women such as McCrea and Bullard, was a Golden Age for women in landscape architecture and an exciting and vibrant time for their male colleagues.

2

Learning a Craft

Launching a Practice

Landscape architecture as a new field of practice had yet to establish any formal training in the nineteenth century. Launching a design practice was thus a courageous act: it did not guarantee regular employment, nor was the profession fully regarded as respectable. For women the garden and the craft of gardening provided frameworks for training, education, and eventually professional legitimacy.

Learn to Garden, Practice Design

Gardens have played an important role in women's work from the earliest civilizations, as sources of produce, places of respite, or sites of pleasure. *Le Ménagier de Paris,* a medieval manuscript of household hints dated to circa 1393, relates the advice of an elderly husband to his new wife on getting rid of fleas, behaving in public, and planting a garden. The earliest-known garden book published specifically for women—William Lawson's *The Country Housewife's Garden* (1618)—emphasized the importance of a productive garden, attended to by an industrious housewife. In such gardens, the author suggested, women would find both value and pleasure, for they were providing for their family and cultivating the land, both worthy activities:

Every Good Woman Should Know How to Garden[1]

Wife, unto thy garden and set me a plot
With strawberry roots of the best to be got
Such, growing abroad among thorns in the wood
Well chosen and picked prove excellent food.

In March, May and April from morning to night
In sowing and setting good housewives delight
To have in a garden or other like plot,
To trim up their house and to furnish their pot

Good peasen and leeks, to make porridge in Lent
And Peasecods in July, save fish to be spent
Those, having other things plentiful then
Thou winnest the heart of the laboring men.

That the woman or wife should set out a garden plot to produce food for the table and to "trim up their house" was a familiar refrain, especially for working-class families. However, by the early eighteenth century in Great Britain, gardening was an ideal leisure pursuit for elite women. Charles Evelyn's *The Ladies' Recreation* (1707) describes how such women might pursue gardening interests without unnecessarily soiling their hands or overtaxing their intellects. Evelyn gives instructions on how to set out lawns and orangeries and how to place sculpture in the landscape. This focus on the ornamental pleasures of gardening was in contrast to the mundane activities of sowing, planting, and propagating common flowers, knowledge he assumed every "Country Dame" held.[2] By the mid-eighteenth century there were magazines devoted to female gardeners. *The Ladies Magazine* provided instructions for cultivating exotic flowers and bulbs and nurturing roses and peonies. Women in Jane Austen's novels appreciated a beautiful garden, took walks through picturesque landscapes, and named the flowers and shrubs within. These women did not garden to feed a family, but to practice the art of gardening.

Gardening in the New World presented new challenges and opportunities. Gardeners sent for books published in Great Britain, adapting the guidelines to their site. It was not until the mid-eighteenth century that the first garden books were published specifically for the New World. The schoolteacher, horticulturalist, and gardener Martha Daniell Logan (1704–1779), of Charleston, South Carolina, wrote one of the first American treatises on gardening, *A Gardener's Kalendar* (1756). She combined practical advice on the cultivation of a productive kitchen garden and encouraged gardeners to expand their horizons by trading seeds and plants with friendly neighbors and plant collectors. She celebrated native plants as well as European imports, as the New World landscape offered the opportunity to enjoy the best of both. Her book was soon followed by other books written by men and women for American gardeners, each emphasizing the beauty and the productivity of a garden.

Women in the eighteenth and early nineteenth centuries did not limit their gardening interests to horticulture but pursued studies in the emerging science of botany. In 1787 William Curtis suggested that his new *Botanical Magazine* was addressed to ladies, gentlemen, and gardeners who wanted to become scientifically familiar with the plants they cultivated. Women were encouraged to study botany, as it was the study of elegant and delicate elements in nature and, accordingly, seemed aesthetically concordant with feminine beauty. It was further argued that such study might make women better conversationalists, wives, and mothers. Maria Elizabeth Jacson's *Botanical Dialogues for the Use of Schools*

(1798) and Priscilla Wakefield's *Introduction to Botany in a Series of Letters* (1799) encouraged botany as an appropriate and worthy study for women, although these authors voiced concerns that such education not be taken too seriously. Jacson was firm that women should not "torment the world with their knowledge as they will be a bore. They must maintain a gendered dichotomy of the head and hand and a separation of occupations: *women's sphere is domestic.*"[3]

American women followed their European counterparts by pursuing interests in botany and horticulture, as well as agriculture. Eliza Lucas Pinckney (1722-1793) was the first to grow indigo on her South Carolina plantation. She promoted its cultivation, eventually boosting the region's fragile economy. From her mulberry trees she made silk cloth from which she created dresses, promoting yet another industry. She was noted for propagating and cultivating an extensive collection of trees, shrubs, and flowers. Her contemporary Jane Colden (1724-1766) was the first American botanist acknowledged for using the Linnaean system in a description of more than four hundred species of plants in the Hudson Valley. She corresponded with naturalists and botanists and published the first illustrated flora of New York. These women were actively engaged in the botanical discourses of the period.

While these were remarkable individuals, other women joined them on an amateur basis to pursue interests in botany and plant collecting. The Charleston Botanic Society and Garden was founded in 1805, offering a series of lectures on botany that "upwards of fifty young ladies" attended "for the purpose of acquiring a regular knowledge of this delightful science, many of whom were making the most flattering progress."[4] Botanical author Amos Eaton suggested in his *Manual of Botany* that by 1822 ladies made up more than half the botanists in New England and New York. To become conversant in botany, women collected plants, kept herbaria, read and wrote botanical Latin, studied handbooks about Linnaean systematics, learned botanical illustration, and used microscopes to study plant physiology. Women also wrote books on botany, addressed to their colleagues and peers. By the late nineteenth century women's schools and colleges included departments of botany, offering courses in botanical studies, horticulture, and sometimes landscape design.

While many authors chose to emphasize either botany or horticulture as distinct approaches more or less appropriate for women, Jane Loudon (1807-1858) pursued both. She wrote over twenty books on botany, gardening, and horticulture. Her earliest book, *The First Book of Botany* (1841), was well-received by the public and professional communities. Further, with a breadth that is not often credited today, her magazine, *Ladies' Companion,* included articles on science (among them essays by male scientists on geology, physical geography, and chemistry), as well as over a dozen of her own essays on botany. Unlike her predecessors, Loudon acknowledged that women might need to make a profit from their studies of botany and horticulture and believed they should be taught by professionals in order to assure the highest quality of education.

An American edition of Loudon's *Gardening for Ladies* was published in 1847, with a preface by the landscape gardener and author Andrew Jackson Downing, who wrote: "It is to be hoped, that the dissemination in this country of works like the present volume, may increase, among our own fair countrywomen, the taste for these delightful occupations in the open air, which are so conducive to their own health, and to the beauty and interest of our homes." The book was replete with useful information, including "how a lady, with a small light spade, may, by repeatedly digging over the same line, and taking out only a little earth at a time, succeed in doing, with her own hands, all the digging that can be required in a small garden."[5] Gardening was no longer merely an activity necessary for production but one meant to improve the health and beauty of women and of the home grounds. Downing deleted Loudon's chapters on the kitchen garden, for gardening should be, he argued, a leisure-time activity only. Nor did he refer to any possibility of an income from gardening activities.

While Downing's intent to describe gardening as solely an amateur activity would not prevail, he had clearly identified a growing audience. In 1854 Louisa Johnson's *Every Lady Her Own Flower Gardener* was published for an American audience (after fourteen printings in Great Britain), offering lessons in propagation, cultivation, and the arrangement of flowers. American books including Cornelia Randolph's *The Parlour Gardener* (1861) and Sophia O. Johnson's *Every Woman Her Own Flower Gardener* followed. The frontispiece for the 1869 edition of *The American Woman's Home,* by Catherine E. Beecher and Harriet Beecher Stowe, featured an illustration of a properly attired woman gardener, complementing chapters on gardening. Celia Thaxter's autobiographical book *An Island Garden* (1894) was an important contribution both to garden literature and to efforts to promote the craft of gardening as an art. Such books increasingly suggested that gardens were the domain of women, an appropriately feminine space where they could serve as horticultural experts with an eye for design.

Women pioneers, as they ventured west, were even encouraged to create garden spaces and look for beauty in the landscape. Catherine Parr Traill advised her readers, in *The Female Emigrant's Guide* (1854), "Do not allow the lusty teams and the broad acres, the grass, the grain and the trees to occupy all your time, but give a thought and an eye occasionally to the beautiful."[6] Such activity would establish culture within the wilderness and promote women's role as keepers of virtue and beauty.

By 1900 the home garden was a woman's domain. While not entirely accurate, the impression held by contemporary women was that this had always been the case. Mrs. Grant of Albany, New York, suggested in 1901 that, since colonial times, into the "garden, no foot of man intruded after it was dug in the spring. I think I see yet what I have so often beheld—a respectable mistress of a family going out to her garden, on an April morning . . . to her garden of labours. A woman in very easy circumstances and abundantly gentle in form and manners would sow and plant and rake incessantly."[7]

Nineteenth-century American publications advocated gardening as acceptable for women because it was a "further manifestation of the mothering instinct in woman, . . . [and] a widening of the housekeeping arts."[8] Women writers argued that gardening was a "universal feminine instinct," closely associated with the "unconscious expression of interest in bringing up children."[9] Domestic beautification was a symbol of good breeding and appropriate taste. Wealthy women were encouraged to take up gardening and horticultural interests to help them avoid numerous nervous disorders associated with the upper classes. Such were, at least, the most visible reasons used to encourage women to garden.

Despite this focus, of Downing and others, on the healthy aspects of amateur gardening, books and essays by women frequently encouraged their readers to lay a claim to the garden as personal space and to consider the potential for an income. *A Woman's Hardy Garden,* by Helena Rutherford Ely (1903), and *The Well-Considered Garden,* by Francis King (1915), centered on teaching the principles of good garden design, which, the authors believed, women might easily learn. Helen Albee's *Hardy Plants for Cottage Gardens* (1910) suggested that women were better suited to design and creative work than men, who "never actually make anything."[10] Such books on gardening by and for women connected the act of gardening with women's development of self-confidence, identity, and independence, with an escape from family and an opportunity to establish female networks.[11]

The potential of garden design and gardening to be lucrative was not overlooked by women authors. Anna B. Warner's *Gardening by Myself* (1872) suggested that every woman needed to have a garden space she could call her own, while her book *Miss Tiller's Vegetable Garden and the Money She Made by It* (1873) focused on the potential for a garden to generate an income. Ella Rodman Church's *The Home Garden* (1881), followed a year later by *Money-making for Ladies,* suggested that women might benefit financially from learning the womanly arts. Marion Cran's 1918 book, *The Garden of Ignorance: The Experience of a Woman in a Garden,* relates how she trained her daughter to be able to earn wages from house and garden labors. These were not mere musings of single women; rather, they reflected larger concerns for the plight (physical, emotional, and financial) of women, the aesthetic nature of the home, and the developing culture of the new nation. The garden became a middle ground where women might exist between nature and culture, between the private life of the interior of the domestic home and the public life of the city. By the turn of the century, garden design and gardening were considered by most advocates for women to be logical extensions of the gendered domain of domestic work. Writers such as Mary Ritter Beard, in her book *Women's Work in Municipalities* (1915), advocated that women pursue employment, as did pamphlets including *What Girls Can Do* (1926) and *Profitable Vocations for Girls* (1924). Landscape gardening was seen as a viable option.

Still, while landscape gardening was an option, gaining the necessary skills and knowledge was a challenge. In the late nineteenth century no schools offered a professional education in landscape architecture. None of the earliest offices accepted women as apprentices. Nevertheless, women launched successful practices. The earliest women to enter the field, like McCrea, began as gardeners and plantswomen. Beatrix Jones Farrand came from "five generations of garden lovers."[12] Her studies had been "directed along the lines of nature studies."[13] Ellen Biddle Shipman learned to design gardens in the artist's community of Cornish, New Hampshire. The narratives of such women illuminate the profession's history and the ways in which women were able to shape the practice of landscape architecture by applying their knowledge of the art and craft of gardening.

BEATRIX CADWALADER JONES FARRAND (1872–1959)

Beatrix Cadwalader Jones was born in 1872 to a well-established family in New York City. Her mother, Mary Cadwalader Rawle, served as the part-time literary agent for her sister-in-law Edith Wharton and was an active member of a sophisticated social circle that included Henry Adams, Henry James, Marian Crawford, and John La Farge, among others. This community of intellectuals took themselves seriously, and Farrand would reflect this attitude throughout her professional career.

Farrand's family shared a love of gardens and gardening. Her grandmother was the proud owner of an espaliered fruit garden and an extensive rose garden at Pencraig in Newport. Farrand fondly recalled watching her mother lay out the gardens and grounds at Reef Point, the family estate in Bar Harbor, Maine. Farrand later recalled exploring the woods in order to transplant some of the lovely woodland plants to the same gardens. Her enthusiasm for gardening and the arts became evident to her friends and family at a young age. Her uncle John Lambert Cadwalader recognized the young woman's interest, as well as her will, and is said to have observed: "Let her be a gardener or, for that matter, anything

Opposite page

Gardener's Calendar for July 1923 in *House & Garden* magazine, featuring Grace Tabor, Annette Hoyt Flanders, Ellen Biddle Shipman, Marian Cruger Coffin, Ruth Bramley Dean, Elizabeth Leonard Strang, and Beatrix Jones Farrand. (Courtesy of Condé Naste Publications Inc.)

The GARDENER'S CALENDAR *for* JULY

SUNDAY	MONDAY	TUESDAY	WEDNESDAY	THURSDAY	FRIDAY	SATURDAY
1. Peach curl develops about this time of the year. It is well to checkmate it by spraying with a combination of Bordeaux mixture and arsenate of lead. Pick off and burn immediately any leaves which are infected.	2. Don't neglect to protect the strawberries from the birds. An old tennis net properly spread will answer for small beds; special nets can be secured for protecting large plantings. Scarecrows may be helpful.	3. There is no cure for potato blight. It can be prevented, however, by spraying about once in three weeks with Bordeaux mixture. It is a good plan to put arsenate of lead in the mixture to destroy the destructive potato bug.	4. Spray the roses with arsenate of lead if they are infested with rose beetles. These drill holes in the leaves and, of course, weaken the plant. Topdress the bed with bone meal if you want quality flowers this autumn.	5. Most soils are partially deficient in humus. Cover crops of clover, vetch and rye are invaluable for restoring this element to the soil. Sow them now in the orchard and any vacant ground remaining.	6. This is a critical time in the garden. The ground bakes, and weeds are very persistent. The only remedy is frequent and deep cultivation. Don't believe the theory about deep cultivation destroying surface roots.	7. Blight is a very destructive disease to many garden crops. Cucumbers, muskmelons, celery and tomatoes are particularly susceptible. They should be sprayed with Bordeaux mixture every three weeks.
8. Take some chrysanthemum cuttings for flowering in small pots in the greenhouse. Don't neglect the carnation plants out of doors. The ground should be cultivated frequently and regularly.	9. Late cabbage, cauliflower, celery, kale and Brussels sprouts should now be planted out. Use plenty of water when planting, and a little fertilizer worked into the soil will start the plants growing vigorously.	10. A heavy mulch should be applied to the sweet peas. Any rough litter may be used for this purpose. Spray with a tobacco preparation if aphis appear. A little shade at midday will maintain the flower quality.	11. To insure plenty of fresh vegetables, you should now sow, lettuce, beets, carrots, beans, cucumbers, kohlrabi, corn, radishes, turnips and endive. Use early corn and saturate the drill before sowing if the soil is dry.	12. Select three or four of the best shoots on the tomato plants and support them by some means. Remove all other shoots and keep the lateral shoots reduced by occasional pinching. This makes larger fruit.	13. Hot, dry weather encourages the propagation of all kinds of plant lice. All plants are subject to attack, but more particularly soft foliage types. Inspect frequently, spray with tobacco or kerosene preparation.	14. Lettuce runs to seed considerably at this season. A board placed over the row, supported so it will be a few inches above the tops, will reduce the losses. The boards should be taken off during rainy weather.
15. There is still time to start a few flowers for fall. Sow in a frame or sheltered bed early asters, poppies, stocks, calliopsis, larkspur and candytuft. Use water freely when setting out, and have the ground rich.	16. Soaking seed to hasten germination is wrong in principle. Before sowing at this time of the year, soak the drill by letting a hose run into it. The moisture then penetrates and encourages downward root growth.	17. This is an excellent time to look over all trees for bark scars which should be cut back to live bark and thoroughly painted. Remove any stubs where branches have been improperly cut. Watch for fire blight.	18. Beets and carrots for winter use are always desirable. Sow several rows of each and if using ground that has been previously cropped, spade under some fertilizer. You can also start peas now for fall use.	19. After they have finished flowering, the climbing roses should be thoroughly pruned by removing a few of the old shoots and training the younger and more vigorous shoots in their place. Keep them in bounds.	20. The late potatoes should be swelling fast at this time. An application of fertilizer worked into the soil will increase the size of the crop and the quality of the tubers. Potatoes require attention.	21. Be very careful about artificial watering. Remember that the natural soil moisture is preferred if you can save it. If you must water, soak the ground thoroughly and after the surface has dried, cultivate.
22. Reduce the stems on the dahlia plants to three or four. Keep the lateral shoots pinched out on the flowering stems. Some sort of support should be applied now, to prevent breakage during storms.	23. This is an excellent time to sow rutabagas for next winter's use. New ground is preferred for this crop and the plants must never be allowed to suffer for want of water. Sow in drills and thin out to about 1".	24. Onions can be improved in size by partially breaking the tops down just above the bulb. This is best done by bending the tops over with the hand until the stem doubles. Do not loosen the roots.	25. It is now safe to sow peas for fall use. Other cool crops such as spinach, radishes and the large heading types of lettuce and endive may now be planted. This is the last call for beets, carrots and winter radishes.	26. Don't allow any newly set out plants to suffer for lack of water. All new stock should be marked and the plantings prepared beforehand, so the trees should never be allowed to lie around in the hot, drying sun.	27. Make preparations to move evergreens now. The bed should be marked and the plantings prepared beforehand, as the trees should never be allowed to lie around in the hot, drying sun.	28. Are you getting full value from your garden? Do you gather the crops daily, using those you require and putting the balance away in glass for next winter's use? If not, there is still time to do so much.
29. Weeds in the lawn are very conspicuous now and can be readily removed. A good method is to have some weed killer or gasoline in an oil can, dropping a little in the center of the weed. This is easier than pulling them.	30. Strawberries planted now will fruit abundantly next season. Be sure you order both staminate and pistillate varieties to assure fertilization. Prepare the bed by double digging, using well rotted manure.	31. Practice summer pruning on the fruit trees. Pinch back the most vigorous shoots and remove all thin, weak interior branches. This applies to trees of fruiting age. Others of smaller size need different treatment.				

This calendar of the gardener's labors is aimed as a reminder for undertaking all his tasks in season. It is fitted to the latitude of the Middle States, but its service should be available for the whole country if it be remembered that for every one hundred miles north or south there is a difference of from five to seven days later or earlier in performing operations. The dates are for an average season.

GRACE TABOR

Seven of the country's most noted landscape architects—they merely happen to be women—grace the Calendar page this month. Miss Tabor, an author, as well, has written several books on gardening.

ANNETTE HOYT FLANDERS

A graduate of Smith College, and of the University of Illinois in landscape architecture, Mrs. Flanders' training has included several years of study in Europe, the West Indies and through our Southern states

IRA L. HILL

BEATRIX FARRAND

Mrs. Farrand's very extensive practice has included the designing not only of many gardens and large estates, but also the planting of the Memorial Quadrangle at Yale and the grounds at Princeton University

ELIZABETH L. STRANG

One of our most frequent contributors, Mrs. Strang's interesting articles, illustrated with examples of her always splendidly designed work, are both helpful and familiar to House & Garden readers

ELLEN SHIPMAN

The work of all the women here has been shown at various times in House & Garden. Several views of the Croft garden, at Greenwich, Ct., designed by Mrs. Shipman, appeared in the March issue

RUTH DEAN

One of Miss Dean's many delightful gardens is her own in New York, in which she is standing. She has also written a book on design—The Livable House: Its Garden

MARION C. COFFIN

Some of Miss Coffin's most important gardens are those designed for Frederick K. Vanderbilt, Bar Harbor, Me., Lamont Dupont, Wilmington, Del., and Gordon K. Bell, Katonah, N. Y.

she wants to be. What she wishes to do will be well done."[14] To her friend Dorothy Elmhirst, Farrand wrote in 1943, "No one ever starts gardening either too late or too early, once it gets into one's blood it can never get out (like some insidious poison)."[15]

Farrand was a well-educated and avid reader and admirer of the arts, at one point considering a career in music. As was appropriate for a young upper-class lady in the Victorian period, she was privately tutored in French, German, Italian, and Greek, as well as music and art. However, landscape gardening and design soon dominated her interests. She met Mary Sargent and Charles Sprague Sargent, curator of Harvard's Arnold Arboretum, in 1892, and Charles suggested that she study landscape gardening. Although the "whole scheme seemed . . . so wild," Farrand enjoyed several long-term visits with the Sargents at Holm Lea between 1893 and 1895.[16]

Farrand launched her practice in 1896 in New York City. Over the course of five decades, she established an active practice with commissions across the United States, always limited to the number of projects she could personally oversee. Her repertoire included botanical gardens, university campuses, and public gardens. Between 1912 and 1946 she was responsible for the design and implementation of projects for Princeton University (1912–43), Yale University (1922–45), Hamilton College (1924), Vassar College (1926–27), the California Institute of Technology (1928–38), the University of Chicago (1929–36), the Pennsylvania School of Horticulture for Women (1931–32), Occidental College (1937–40), and Oberlin College (1939–46). Farrand designed botanical gardens in Santa Barbara, California, in collaboration with Lockwood de Forest (1938–59), and the Rose Garden in the Bronx Park for the New York Botanical Garden (1915–16). Four astronomical observatories featured landscapes designed by Farrand. Of her designs the best-known landscapes and gardens are Dumbarton Oaks, for Robert and Mildred Bliss of Washington, D.C.; The Eyrie, for Abby Aldrich Rockefeller of Seal Harbor, Maine; and the Willard Straight garden on Long Island.

In the midst of this career, at the age of forty-one, Beatrix Cadwalader Jones married Max Farrand to become Beatrix Farrand. Max Farrand was a distinguished historian and chair of the History Department at Yale University in New Haven, where the couple lived for part of each year. In 1927, when Max Farrand was appointed director of the Huntington Library in San Marino, California, they moved, and Beatrix established a small office. The California office never expanded significantly and was essentially closed when Max Farrand retired in 1941. Her only major project in California was the Santa Barbara Botanical Garden, and she maintained California letterhead throughout this project.

Throughout these moves the Farrands spent increasing time at Reef Point, the family summer home. After 1941 the Farrands retired and dedicated their time and efforts to establishing a learning institution, the Reef Point Gardens and Library. However, in 1946, before their dream could be fully realized, Max Farrand died. Beatrix Farrand continued to develop the institution until 1954, when she dismantled the project. She died in 1959 at Garland Farm, a cottage near the Reef Point residence.

Learning the Practice

To launch a practice, Farrand needed to learn the profession. While an education in landscape gardening was available through the land-grant colleges, a professional education was not yet a real option. When Farrand, like McCrea and Bullard, decided to pursue a career as a landscape architect, there were two routes generally open to women: mentorship and travel. Farrand took advantage of both.

The role of mentors was critical for many young practitioners. While the stories of women in landscape architecture are generally presented as heroic struggles of individuals who fought against many odds to succeed in a man's world, these women, like their male colleagues, were rarely entirely on their own. Indeed, some men actively supported women in their pursuit of a career. Charles Sprague Sargent served as a significant mentor for Farrand; Charles Platt mentored Ellen Biddle Shipman; and Warren Manning hired, mentored, and trained a number of important female practitioners, as did Jens Jensen and Bryant Fleming.

Charles Sprague Sargent (1841–1927) was a significant advisor for women in landscape architecture, although he was not always publicly supportive of their professional aspirations. As primary editor of *Garden and Forest,* Sargent published, in 1892, an essay titled "Taste Indoors and Out," suggesting that "women . . . are seldom great on an estate . . . [as] landscape-gardening on a large scale is, after all, a masculine art, and requires a certain manly vigor of treatment, an unhesitating despotism, that the gentler sex deprecate as cruel and unnecessary."[17] In fact, Sargent continued, "Women may be generally held responsible for the false details we so much deplore, because American men, as a general thing, are too much occupied to give much attention to their grounds and leave their arrangement to their gardener and their womankind."

Mrs. Robbins, a writer for *Garden and Forest,* took Sargent to task for his views, asking whether "we women [are] to be confined to the petty and the pretty forever, or may we not aspire to the loftier walks of landscape-gardening, even as some of us venture to try issue with senior wranglers in the higher mathematics?"[18] She acquiesced, however, by agreeing that "women are deficient in creative ability," wondering why there were as yet no schools for women in taste or landscape art. Sargent's published response was merely to note that one cannot easily teach taste. He admitted in a subsequent editorial that "if women develop capacity in this direction there should be opportunity for their employment in a professional way. . . . There is no reason why women should not enter callings that bring them into the healthy life of the open air, *if no hard manual labor is demanded.*"[19]

Instead of landscape design, Sargent proposed botany as appropriate for women. He published a glowing report of the new botany program at Barnard College for Women, suggesting that "the work of the botanist is such that a *woman* is specially fitted for it."[20] Sargent's comments suggest he believed that women generally lacked natural taste and that art would be less accessible to them than science, particular botany. The sciences did not require the heavy physical labor of gardening or travel to project sites. Nevertheless, Sargent observed and supported the successes of a number of women in landscape architecture.

Sargent's mentorship of Farrand shaped her approach to design and the design process throughout her practice. Sargent was both a teacher of arboriculture and horticulture and an admirer of art and beauty in the landscape. He advised Farrand that she should look carefully at great landscape paintings, to observe natural beauty and "learn from all the great arts as all art is akin."[21] Taking her to visit great gardens and landscapes, including the home and office of Frederick Law Olmsted and the 1893 Columbian Exposition in Chicago, Sargent helped develop Farrand's observational talents. From Sargent and his staff (including John G. Jack, a young lecturer in dendrology) Farrand learned the basic principles of design and the science of botany and horticulture, as well as the craft of gardening. Sargent introduced her to Professor W. R. Ware, dean of the School of Architecture at Columbia, who assisted her with enrolling in courses in mathematics and surveying. Farrand was also likely to have observed the design and construction process of Harvard's Arnold Arboretum, as Olmsted was working closely with Sargent to create what would become the preeminent arboretum in the United States.

From Sargent, Farrand learned to fit the plan to the ground rather than the ground to the plan. When she asked him how to approach her first plan, he told her to follow the wishes of her client. Mildred Bliss, in a tribute to Sargent and Farrand, described their relationship as an ideal match between student and teacher: "Never was a great teacher granted a pupil more ideally suited to his hopes. His knowledge was absorbed by her eager young intelligence."[22]

In 1895, with encouragement from Sargent, Farrand embarked on a grand tour of European gardens, carrying her journal and making extensive notes on what she saw. The resulting *Book of Gardening* frequently reads as if penned in response to conversations with Sargent and others, as Farrand began to articulate her own approach to landscape design. Such travel as Farrand undertook differentiated the designer or artist from the gardener or craftsman and provided a critical training ground for many designers. The gardener, Sargent suggested, "is naturally a good right arm, sometimes opinionated and lacking in that broad experience only to be obtained by travel and study. . . . It is not his business to be an artist."[23] Travel provided a broadened repertoire of experiences and images of works of landscape art, which Farrand or any artist could draw on as they created and designed new gardens and landscapes.

The most popular travel route was the grand tour of Europe, a traditional tour of Western civilizations and cultures. The diplomat, professional, artist, poet, teacher, writer, or physician was expected to be personally familiar with the culture and works of Italy. For potential architects and landscape architects, the study of European architecture, art, and landscapes was important as much to establish familiarity with contemporary European culture as it was to gain thorough historical knowledge.

Women engaged in the grand tour throughout the nineteenth century. After the Civil War increasing numbers of women artists ventured alone or in the company of friends and relations to Italy, France, and England to learn from the "old country." Mary Rutherfurd Jay (1872–1953), born into a family descended from John Jay, first chief justice of the United States, turned her grand tour into a resource for a career as both a designer and a lecturer. She went on to study architecture at MIT and Harvard's Bussey Institute and opened a practice in New York in 1908 as a garden architect. Her work, primarily residential, included designs for clients in New York, Connecticut, and Rhode Island, with some in New Jersey and Massachusetts.

Jay became best-known on the lecture route, speaking about gardens around the world. In 1912 she embarked on a long trip documenting landscapes with glass lantern slides, sketches, and copious notes. She used these to build a repertoire of illustrated lectures on international gardens. By the end of her career, she had amassed a significant collection of over two thousand photographs of gardens around the world, including in Japan, China, and India, accompanied by extensive notes. Her focus on international gardens was similar to that of Rose Standish Nichols, who established herself as a writer on gardens, publishing books and essays on Portugal, Spain, Italy, and England. Nichols also frequently used her travel photographs to create garden designs for clients in the United States. Clients often sought such imitation, wanting their garden art to create a visual link to established icons of culture. Jay and Nichols were part of a growing community of speakers whose lectures were noted for their rich content and images of landscapes around the world.

Tours of exotic, or at least less traveled, landscapes provided a breadth of scenes and perspectives for landscape architects, allowing them to build their inspirational repertoire. Annette Hoyt Flanders and the firm of Yoch & Council, for example, were particularly recognized for their use of foreign garden and landscape styles in their designs. The specialized knowledge gained from travel also contributed to designers' authority within the professional and client-based communities. Especially at a

MARY RUTHERFURD JAY

101 PARK AVENUE, NEW YORK CITY, ANNOUNCES

FIVE NEW GARDEN TALKS

ILLUSTRATED WITH COLORED LANTERN SLIDES

MONDAY AFTERNOONS AT THREE O'CLOCK

FORMAL GARDENS

DESIGN, PLANTING SUGGESTIONS

AT THE RESIDENCE OF

MRS. ARTHUR R. GRAY

178 EAST 80TH STREET, NEW YORK CITY

November 12th

COTTAGE GARDENS

ENGLISH INFORMAL TYPES

AT THE RESIDENCE OF

MRS. FREDERIC S. LEE

125 EAST 65TH STREET, NEW YORK CITY

November 19th

MODERN GARDENS

DUTCH SEVERITY, SIMPLICITY

AT THE RESIDENCE OF

MRS. ELON HUNTINGTON HOOKER

182 EAST 64TH STREET, NEW YORK CITY

November 26th

CHINESE GARDENS

DEVELOPMENT OF ROCK GARDEN

AT THE RESIDENCE OF

MRS. CHARLES D. DICKEY

37 EAST 51ST STREET, NEW YORK CITY

December 3rd

COURTYARD GARDENS

PATIOS OF SPAIN, CALIFORNIA

AT THE RESIDENCE OF

MRS. ARTHUR CURTISS JAMES

39 EAST 69TH STREET, NEW YORK CITY

December 10th

Announcement of five lectures on design offered by Mary Rutherfurd Jay featuring her knowledge of foreign gardens. (Environmental Design Archives, University of California, Berkeley) time when not everyone could travel, designers' ability to draw on exotic and exciting landscapes legitimized their role.

For those unable to travel abroad, visits to gardens and landscapes in the United States were justified as more "American." The firm of Wodell & Cottrell visited sites throughout the Eastern Seaboard and the Midwest, suggesting that they were focused on developing an American design style, based on native precedents. Visits to Arnold Arboretum and meetings with Charles Sprague Sargent were popular for students of design and horticulture.

Such travel was critical for professional landscape architects, particularly women, for many reasons. As noted earlier, it allowed practitioners to establish their credibility as knowledgeable critics and/or designers. This was true, for example, for Judith Eleanor Motley Low, who traveled extensively with her husband before establishing the Lowthorpe School of Landscape Architecture. For women such as Farrand, without a formal education, the cultural knowledge gained through European travel was critical to their future as designers. Graduates of the Lowthorpe and Cambridge schools were highly encouraged to travel, perhaps to supplement their resumes, which did not include a university degree. Even for those able to attend a school, by the 1920s, according to the Cambridge School model, a good education included "a well-rounded four-year college course, followed by a three-year graduate course in a well-recognized professional school, *to be followed by systematic travel and study in Europe* and a period of apprenticeship in a good office."[24]

Farrand's aunt, Edith Wharton, and her mother, Mary Cadwalader Jones, prepared her well for her travels, and she was able to visit an extraordinary number of gardens, landscapes, museums, and cities in Italy, France, Germany, and England.[25] Farrand used her garden journal to note her critiques of the gardens and landscapes she saw. She took her trip seriously as an educational venture and had prepared herself by reading extensively. Departing with a long list of appropriate references, she collected many more while traveling and referred to literary references and the histories of individual gardens and landscapes throughout her notes. She also compiled a significant collection of photographs of European gardens that, upon her return, she placed on the walls of her studio.[26] Farrand's trips were clearly a form of education, one that might replace the formal education of a college or university.

European tours also allowed the traveler to meet other landscape artists and writers. Farrand and Coffin visited William Robinson and Gertrude Jekyll, significant English writers and gardeners, during their sojourns in England, and many students of garden and landscape design called on Ellen Wilmott, an English garden writer. Indeed, Farrand forged relationships with European designers that she maintained throughout her professional career, including her friendship with Édouard André, the French landscape designer.[27] It is also possible that she enrolled in a course in drawing at a Berlin academy and in a few courses at Paris's Académie des Beaux-Arts.[28]

It was only when she returned to the United States that Farrand decided to commit to landscape gardening as a career. She subsequently hired private tutors from the Civil Engineering Department of the Columbia School of Mines to provide her with the technical training she needed to practice.

Drawing on her travels and studies, Farrand began submitting articles on landscape design for publication. Her first, a letter to the editor about landscape gardening with native trees in Maine, specifically in the Bar Harbor area, was featured in Sargent's journal, *Garden and Forest,* in the fall of 1893. Farrand wrote poetically about the landscape, noting that while "driving along the wooded roads in the district where the grounds lie which are to be developed, one who notes which are the handsomest of the native trees can get an idea as to which ones to plant and how these should be grouped." She cautioned that "the appropriate massing of foliage, so as to secure the best effect from soft harmonies or bold contrasts of color, requires much study and critical knowledge."[29] Her intuitive grasp of the landscape, and of how to apply the arts and sciences to its design, was evident in this early piece, as was the influence of Sargent. Two subsequent essays were published in *Garden and Forest:* one on design and one on horticultural aspects of design.[30] Farrand later wrote a long essay on Le Nôtre for *Scribner's Magazine* after researching and visiting his gardens near Paris.[31] This piece reflected her thorough research of historical prints and documents, as well as her ability to relate such descriptions to the present landscape. By 1896 she was as prepared as she might be to launch an office.

Opening an Office

Farrand opened her practice in 1896. Her first office was on the top floor of her mother's house, on East Eleventh Street in New York City. It was noted that as a *Society Girl* "Miss Jones does her design in a studio that she has fitted up for herself in her mother's home at No. 21 East Eleventh Street. There, surrounded by objects of art, she works hard over her drawing board, planning how to mould [*sic*] forest and lawn and shrubland so that they will simulate the wildest effects of nature or the fairest groves of antiquity."[32] An office at home was not unusual: Olmsted Sr., for example, had also located his office in his home. This meant that the lines between the domestic area of the house and the professional space were blurred as one moved back and forth between the two arenas. For women, particularly those in the upper class, an office in their residence did not risk their appearing too forward or otherwise inappropriate as they pursued a profession, a traditionally male pursuit. On the other hand, the combination was likely challenging, as they needed to keep distinct their roles as society member and professional.

To establish her professional office, Farrand looked to Sargent for advice and to the Olmsted office as a model. Olmsted Sr. had set the standards for professional practice in landscape architecture, although he had adopted his methods and procedures from architectural offices.[33] A primary concern of the Olmsted office was the need to make sure clients understood the role of a professional landscape architect, as few were familiar with the practice. A "Circular as to Professional Methods and Charges" was provided to any potential client, outlining not only the procedures of a design project but also which services would be provided. The office, the circular noted, was prepared to "undertake the arrangement and planting of public parks and squares. Of private grounds and gardens, of land sub-divisions and streets." Its professionals would serve as "advisors and designers only"; they were "not gardeners."[34] The distinction between the gardener and the landscape architect lay in the application of the art of design. As Olmsted wrote late in life to Mariana Van Rensselaer, "Nothing can be written on the subject with profit in my opinion in which extreme care is not taken to discriminate between what is meant in common use of the words garden, gardening, gardener, and the art which I try to pursue."[35]

Olmsted Sr. was one of the first landscape architects to insist that a topographical survey be made before he began to design a site. According to Stephen Child, a practitioner in the early twentieth century, earlier plans had merely responded to general impressions of the site, based solely on observation.[36] Olmsted's office was responsible for every step of a project, as Olmsted did not accept jobs where someone else would complete a design. When necessary, he hired a superintendent to oversee on-site construction and planting.

Upon visiting the Olmsted office in 1894, Farrand noted the design process, as well as office practices: filing, the use of note cards, billing methods. In her notebook she wrote:

> The office was interesting, the survey of a piece of ground is taken by the local engineer of the place, marking one foot contour lines & the principal land marks such as big trees, rocks, & of the streams wh[ich] there may be. The sketches are then made beforehand over the survey, of course on tracing paper. A card catalogue of all the shrubs in the market is very useful, with one column saying at which nurseries it is to be found, in what condition. That is size, & price, with a separate column for remarks. The planting plans are made first. The plantations are indicated in the sketch, as to size & shape, then the planter takes the shape & fills it out with the plants he thinks will go best in the soil, exposure, & give the best effect. He marks on the plan the size & shape of place that the shrubs are to be put in, & then labels the spot—first with a number wh[ich] corresponds to a no. on the edge of the plan, then with another no. which tells the number of plants to be put in. The scale is usually 20-40-60 feet to the inch. Outside on the left side of the house is a little lawn with shrubs planted about it & to my mind rather badly arranged.[37]

Farrand's office followed such practices. Farrand paid close attention to her office's professionalism, assuring clear accounting procedures, for example, and approached the design process using many of the same procedures, including surveys and site visits.

As the profession was establishing itself, issues surrounding payments, accounts, and profits were critical to codes of professionalism and ethics. Farrand was known for her scrupulous attention to every detail, providing account records for her clients that identified every dollar expensed. Her staff kept meticulous files and recorded all transactions for each project. Farrand established the practice of using shoeboxes to catalog invoices and records of employee work. As each employee worked on a project, she would slip a piece of paper, recording the project, time spent, and any expenses, into an appropriately marked box. At regular intervals Farrand would gather this information, create appropriate invoices for her clients, and pay her staff accordingly. Her invoices were detailed, specific, and always accompanied by a full report of any discussions, decisions, or other issues related to the garden and/or landscape.

Farrand maintained accounts for special clients, from which she would pay contractors, gardeners, and nurserymen. Clients would replenish the account as requested, and she would provide meticulous records of how the funds were being spent. She used such accounts for her work for the wealthy families of New York, such as the J. P. Morgans, and for her work for organizations and institutions, including the New York Botanical Garden and Princeton University. While such bookkeeping was time-consuming, it was good business, and it established her as a professional for whom art and practice were more important than "profits."

Farrand's first commissions included projects for William Garrison in Tuxedo, New York, and for W. H. Bliss, a New York banker. Her practice expanded relatively quickly: she told a reporter in 1897 that she had already designed a cemetery in Bar Harbor; was working at Chiltern, the property of Edgar Scott; and had submitted designs and suggestions to the New York Parks Department on work under construction.[38] She produced designs for two smaller schools in Fairfield, Connecticut, around 1896–97, and in 1899 it was noted that she often oversaw a crew of eighty to one hundred men at some of her larger projects.[39] Given the number of newspaper articles on her work, she was a success story. This success was to follow her through five decades of practice.

Farrand's practice grew, as did her reputation. She was invited to become a founding member of the ASLA only three years after opening her own office, notice taken of her work perhaps not only because of her early commissions but in particular because of a report she wrote on New York's city parks.[40] Samuel Parsons, then the superintendent of Central Park, probably read this essay, which he would have found in accordance with his own beliefs.

With her practice expanding, Farrand opened a dedicated office space in New York, at 124 East Fortieth Street, in a well-respected neighborhood. This both allowed her a certain gain in professional standards and maintained presence in the city. In 1926 Farrand acquired an apartment at 77 Park in New York City, while retaining her primary home in San Marino, California.

Farrand employed at least four to six draftspersons during the busiest periods of her career. Anne D. Baker had been hired by 1913, and soon thereafter Margaret Bailie was employed. In 1930 Ruth Havey joined the staff. Rosalind Spring LaFontaine, Helen Spaulding Phipps, Gladys Rose Seibold, Alice Orme Smith, Cynthia Wiley, Alice Bauhan, and Elizabeth Sears all reported working for Farrand. Many of these women later launched their own offices and remained involved in the profession.

Anne D. Baker (1890–1949), a 1912 graduate of Vassar, in 1934 was awarded a master's degree in landscape architecture from Smith College in honor of her completion of the program at the Cambridge School. She worked with Farrand for almost fourteen years, eventually leading the New York office and assigning Bailie, Havey, and others design tasks and specific gardens. From 1932 until 1934 Baker served as director of Lowthorpe, where she was expected to bring a practitioner's perspective to the curriculum and act as a direct link to the professional community. She was a member of the ASLA as of 1931, included in the 1934 edition of ASLA *Illustrations of Work of Members,* and served as secretary of the New York chapter in 1940. Baker was a landscape consultant for Simmons College, Boston, and advised the U.S. government's Procurement Division on the plantings at the Triangle Buildings in Washington and at the Post Office Department in New York. Smaller projects included estates in Illinois, Boston, Connecticut, New York, New Jersey, Maryland, and Kentucky.

Another notable Farrand employee, Ruth Havey, graduated from Smith College in 1920 with a bachelor's degree, and then the Cambridge School, in 1923 completing the work for a master's degree in architecture, awarded in 1934. She worked as a draftsperson for a number of small firms, including those of Henrietta Marquise Pope (1925) and Margaret Bailie (1929). In 1930 she began her work for Farrand, remaining until 1936. Farrand, Baker, and Helen Swift Jones later successfully proposed her for ASLA membership.

Farrand assigned individual employees to particular projects, although at times she called upon them to help on other projects as needed. Written correspondence confirmed the assignments and provided a record of the work requested, jobs assigned, and duties accomplished. The staff provided drafting, technical, and design skills, while Farrand provided the visionary and artistic leadership.

In addition to her design staff, Farrand employed secretaries and administrative assistants at each office. Mary Fulkerson was her secretary in the 1920s in New York. Anne Sweeney worked at Dumbarton Oaks as the librarian and was in charge of the educational programs. She also visited Farrand periodically at Reef Point to help with plans, memos, and other recording projects. Reef Point also hosted a separate staff. Isabelle Marshall Stover served there as the librarian, secretary, and office assistant. Marion Ida Spaulding, a graduate of the Rhode Island School of Design (RISD), worked primarily on the herbarium collection and in the gardens. Mrs. Clementine Walters ran the house, and Lewis and Amy Garland worked in the gardens.

Maintaining three offices at the height of her career (in New York City, Bar Harbor, and Santa Barbara), Farrand accomplished much work in transit, usually by train. A typical trip for Farrand might include a day each in Boston, New Haven, and New York; then two days at Dumbarton Oaks, in Washington, D.C.; then a stop in Chicago; and finally the journey back to her winter home in Santa Barbara. Letters, telegrams, and telephone calls with directions, inquiries, and confirmations of decisions would travel back and forth between Farrand, her clients, and her employees. Ruth Havey described such work: "I would bring the drawings being developed at the office and get on the train in New York and meet her on the train. She was usually on her way to do fieldwork in one of the jobs. We would review the plans, she would make suggestions and critiques or changes. As soon as the review was finished, I would get off at the next station, wherever that may be, and take a train back to New York."[41] Farrand expected her staff to be flexible and responsive to the requirements of the practice. They were often asked to produce sketches, research design details, and provide other materials at a moment's notice. Only much later in her practice did Farrand outsource some of the drafting to other offices, specifically to her former employees, including Havey.

Noting the challenges posed by such travels, Farrand wrote that landscape architecture "is a profession which no woman should attempt who is not above, rather than below, the average of physical strength and endurance, as the work swings from one extreme to another. . . . This not infrequently involves a week's continuous work in which the average day, including time spent in traveling, is twelve hours or over."[42]

While Farrand spoke of the physical challenges of the profession, she was also fully aware of the challenges presented by social protocol and professional standards. She was always very careful to maintain her status as both a woman of the elite class and a professional. Understanding this dual role, Farrand assured reporters, and thereby the general public, that society was a very agreeable part of her life and that her work was a "perpetual pleasure." Her portraits exhibit a well-dressed woman, although clients reported that she often wore bicycle outfits for fieldwork. Still, a sense of propriety infuses all of her correspondence, Farrand strenuously maintaining the appearance of a society lady in both her personal and her professional life.

Farrand repeatedly assured reporters that she was professionally on par with the men in her field. She claimed that her "professional point of view . . . [was] no different from that of any man's and I am thankful and proud to say that the men of my profession treat me as one of themselves. I have put myself through the same training and look for the same rewards. I no more expect special consideration because of my sex than any woman painter, or woman sculptor, or woman anything else ought to."[43] One reporter commented that there was "some feeling of surprise at first among workingmen who [found] that a young woman [was] to direct their work. But tact, courtesy, firmness, and good business ability are as quickly recognized in a woman as in a man."[44]

While tact and good business ability were certainly assets, professional respect also required attention to details, including Farrand's title. The appropriate form of address was important, particularly for women, as a title carried far more weight than a mere name. Writing to Yale on being appointed landscape designer in 1922, Farrand insisted that "when my name goes on the rolls . . . I am put down as Beatrix Farrand without any qualifying Mr. or Mrs. or Miss, as I regard Beatrix Farrand as a sort of trade name."[45] Many women considered this issue seriously, as a form of address established a particular relationship with clients and contractors. Annette Hoyt Flanders, for example, always maintained the title "Mrs. Flanders," despite the fact she had been divorced early in her professional life. As a married woman Farrand did not need to establish her status within the elite social classes, but as a divorced woman Mrs. Flanders needed to remain socially acceptable within her community of patrons and clients. Too, by the 1920s, when Mrs. Flanders was establishing herself, there was increased concern that professional women were not marrying at the rate of uneducated women, another factor that might have influenced her choice.

Yet another important element of professionalism, as noted earlier, was distinguishing the practice from the trades: a professional did not pursue commissions but offered them as a service. An 1899 report in the *New York Times* noted, for example, that while "it has been said that Miss Jones has made bids for work, . . . that is not so. All of her work has come to her unsolicited."[46] Farrand could not be perceived as begging or even asking for work. Instead, her professionalism required that she wait for clients to come to her to request her expertise and professional knowledge.

Similarly, Farrand, like many landscape architects, struggled to distinguish her role as a professional from that of an amateur or a gardener. In an interview in 1897 Farrand emphasized the importance of differentiating between amateur and professional work: "If I remained just an amateur, I might have studied and worked for years and never have had the least standing in my profession. No matter how good my designs might have been, they would have received little attention. Things are on a different footing when stamped with a recognized value."[47] The importance of charging for services was critical, as it clearly separated the amateur from the professional. "No one will be willing to accept your services for work of this kind without paying for them. If they pay for them the best professional work should be given," Sargent cautioned Farrand.[48]

Farrand, nevertheless, understood the importance of offering to do work pro bono as a way of introducing herself. When Farrand wanted to be named landscape consultant for the California Institute of Technology, for instance, she initially offered advice free of charge. In writing to the board, she made it clear that her work was a professional courtesy: "When the work increased to the point when it consumed a much greater amount of my time, an account was sent as a matter of professional practice, which was accompanied by a cheque as a present to the Institute so that my work would not mean a cost to the Institution."[49] She was neither acting as an amateur nor working as a social activity. In a follow-up letter she declined to continue providing advice: "As you have doubtless realized, I am not happy in the work as my present half-charitable, half-amateur status is not satisfactory. . . . It appears to me more professionally dignified to stop working at the Institute until the Committee decides whether or not it intends to employ me professionally."[50]

Despite Farrand's impeccable professionalism, many within the professional community remained ambivalent about her presence as a female. In an 1899 letter from the secretary of the newly formed ASLA, Downing Vaux, to Nathan Barrett, another founding member, Vaux wrote: "Miss Jones was at the dinner in a most becoming 'get up' and evidently carried the Fellows by storm. . . . The lady won."[51] Farrand was subsequently elected to the executive committee, serving through 1902, yet the distinct impression remains that the respect given her was tempered by the fact that she was "a lady."

Farrand, perhaps in response, remained aloof for much of her career. She supported the professional standards promoted by the ASLA, her fees, charges, and professional policies in line with those recommended by the association. She initially served on the ASLA committees to create a seal and to draft a constitution and amendments, and she regularly attended its annual meetings and dinners.[52] She responded to surveys and gave her opinions when asked. Still, the sense remains that she kept a professional distance from her colleagues. Farrand did not exhibit her drawings in the ASLA's exhibits. (Elizabeth Bullard also declined to exhibit at the ASLA meetings.) Nor did she share her work for discussion and review at informal meetings, as others did. She did submit photographs of her work at Yale and Princeton, as well as for the Willard Straight landscape, for the ASLA yearbooks in the 1930s, perhaps so that the public could view her as a member of the profession. She nominated only a few ASLA members, including Ruth Havey, and never served on the nominating committee. Further, while women looked to Farrand's practice as a model, none appear to have been mentored by her directly as a professional. By the 1910s and early 1920s, she was not listed as an active member of any ASLA committee. She did not serve as a critic or judge in professional competitions or reviews. Instead, Farrand focused on her own practice as a professional landscape architect.

In this role Farrand respected the profession of architecture and collaborated with many of the period's leading architects. As she noted early in her career, in an abstract of a talk given by H. E. Milner that she wrote for *Garden and Forest,* she believed firmly in the collaborative efforts of architects and landscape architects. She believed that the "arts of architecture and landscape gardening [were] sisters, not antagonists, and the work of the architect and landscape-gardener should be done together from the beginning, one supplementing the other, but not, as too often happens, one crowding the other out."[53] She worked with architects from the offices of McKim, Mead, and White; Ralph Adams Cram; and Aldrich and Delano, among many others. Myron Hunt designed the Farrands' home at the Huntington Library, known as the Director's Cottage.

During her career Farrand was acknowledged by an Honorary Membership in the American Institute of Architects, an Achievement Medal from the Garden Club of America, the Gold Medal of the Massachusetts Horticultural Society, and the Distinguished Service Award of the New York Botanic Garden. Smith College awarded her an honorary doctorate of letters, and Yale named her to the rank of professor and awarded her an honorary master of arts. She thus succeeded both in establishing her own practice and in furthering the profession of landscape architecture.

Decision Making and Design Philosophy

Farrand and Olmsted shared with the larger landscape design community the belief that the landscape architect's core aim should be to create beauty and to respond to the genius of a place. In describing her field to a reporter, Farrand explained that in landscape gardening one "takes Nature in the rough and tries to produce something beautiful by recombining her elements."[54] This approach reflected the contemporary focus on nature and art framing landscape architecture in the early twentieth century.

With her experience and expertise Farrand insisted on retaining control over the design process. She was solely responsible for design conceptualization and articulation. She reviewed drawings in progress, supervised construction, and dictated correspondence. Her design process involved a long and detailed series of decisions, alternatives, and further decisions that she herself orchestrated, always framed by the realities of the site.

In undertaking a project, Farrand first discussed ideas with clients and analyzed the site. To do so, she visited the site and sought to understand its genius loci. She requested surveys and other topographical information for every project, as had Olmsted Sr. With survey in hand she would walk the land, make notes, and perhaps sketch in order to understand the site's potential as a designed landscape. Her design intent was to reveal the landscape's strengths, rather than to treat it as an empty canvas.

Subsequently, Farrand would formulate a conceptual vision, which she would present to the client in broad and sweeping strokes. She frequently relied more on descriptive words than on drawings to convey her overall idea or concept for the landscape. Her practice relied on employees who could translate her verbal vision into visual presentations. A sketch or watercolor done by a staff member often enhanced her descriptions, giving a sense of the intended experience. Robert Patterson, a lifelong friend who took over at Dumbarton Oaks upon Farrand's retirement, recalled that "Mrs. Farrand always regretted that she never learned to draw."[55] While this statement implies that Farrand could not draw at all, there is evidence that it may more accurately suggest only that she could not draw as well as she would have liked. While only a few sketches were included in her *Book of Gardening,* and while no drawings can be indisputably attributed to her hand, sketches and notes she made on drawings throughout her career imply that she had at least rudimentary skills and could paint with watercolors.

Farrand's office produced numerous drawings on a variety of scales, used at every stage of the design process. Farrand's focus was not on a final plan as a work of art, but rather on the designed landscape itself. For a few select projects, including the Newbold estate, she had watercolor sketches of her design produced. (See color plate 1.) More typical were presentations in pencil on trace: full-size detail drawings produced on trace paper, with notes as needed to communicate materials and specifications. Study drawings were carefully detailed but not necessarily presented as works of fine art.

Regardless of who had produced a particular drawing, Farrand's florid signature went on all drawings, without the actual draftsperson's initials. This was not true of correspondence, which was often initialed by Farrand's secretaries, noted as to whether Farrand had actually signed a letter or merely approved its content. While she willingly acknowledged secretaries, however, she did not do so with her draftspersons, even women with whom she worked for many years, such as Baker or Havey. Instead, Farrand took full credit and responsibility for the projects completed under her practice. While typing a letter is understood as distinct from composing its text, the distinction between drawing and conception was perhaps not as obvious for much of the public. Still, most contemporary offices by the early twentieth century included the initials of the person who had actually drawn a plan or sketch.

Once Farrand and her client had decided on a general idea, Farrand would begin to design individual spaces. This was a long and detailed process of drawing, model-making, discussions, and decisions. Farrand

Full-size detail for ironwork on gate at Dumbarton Oaks, Washington, D.C., one of many such drawings produced as a part of Farrand's design process. (Environmental Design Archives, University of California, Berkeley)

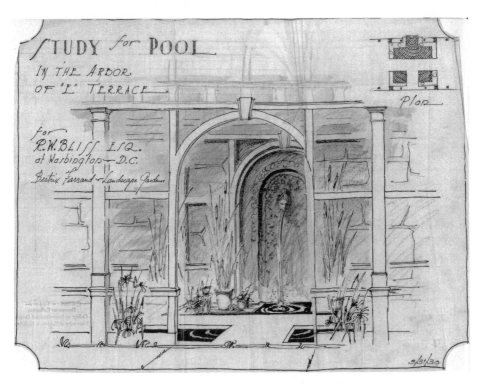

Sketch of arbor for Dumbarton Oaks landscape. Farrand signed all drawings and documents that were produced by her office. Farrand's signature signifies that it came out of her office and that it is her design concept; however, a draftsperson most likely produced it under Farrand's direction. (Environmental Design Archives, University of California, Berkeley)

would discuss an idea with a draftsperson and then assign that staff member to provide alternative sketches. She would initially review these options herself and subsequently go over them with her client. Farrand's decision process is evident in the Eyrie garden she designed for Mrs. Rockefeller in Maine. In doing so, Farrand explored several options for details including the gateway, the path, and the garden wall. The Chinese Moon Gate, for example, might have been incorporated into a variety of walls and finished in different manners, and the existing trees might have been kept or moved. At least three options were sketched, presented, and discussed.

Often alternatives were derived from earlier options, in an ongoing process of exploration and consideration. Even after a solution had been determined, comments were made on subsequent drawings suggesting changes and modifications. Once a choice had been made, more detailed drawings were presented before a design was implemented on the ground or otherwise constructed.

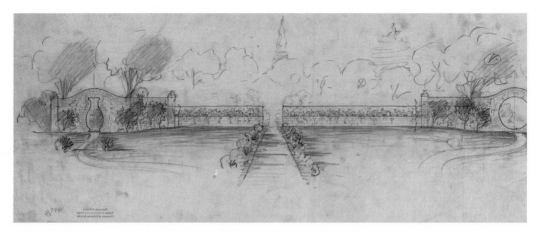

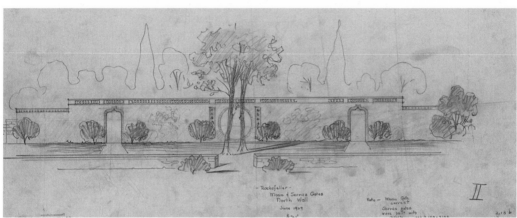

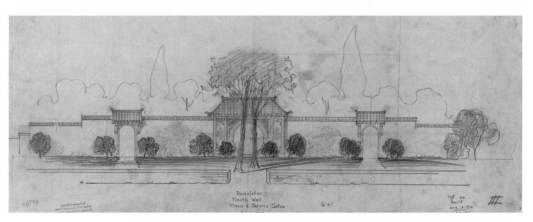

Farrand's three options for a Chinese Moon Gate, Eyrie Garden, for Mrs. and Mr. John D. Rockefeller, Seal Harbor, Maine. (Environmental Design Archives, University of California Berkeley)

Such attention, for Farrand, continued down to the smallest details. Over 1,226 drawings and sketches were recorded for Dumbarton Oaks alone. Where drawings might not provide the required information for a design detail, Farrand requested a full-sized mock-up. If she or a client could not be on site, she requested photographs for review. The documentation of her design process reveals entire walls, life-size sculptures, and framed views all constructed as "dummies" before design decisions were finalized. This reflects a clear emphasis on investing in the design process, prior to any more permanent construction or planting, and acknowledges the interplay of architecture and plant materials. Farrand's thoroughness, her attention to details, and her flexibility at each stage of the design process were always clear.

Architects used mock-ups in the process of either making design decisions or trying to describe the final design to a client. McKim, Mead, and White had a sample cornice of the Boston Public Library building erected on scaffolding on site, at actual height. Frank Lloyd Wright tested a column for the Johnson Wax administration building on site. Olmsted used a similar technique to determine the viability and impact of particular details of his design at the Biltmore estate. Farrand, too, used mock-ups with frequency, more so than most landscape architects. In a similar vein she also used full-size detail drawings more than most practitioners, insisting that these drawings be refined until they represented exactly what she wanted. The drawings were subsequently used to create or construct design elements. Farrand's use of alternatives, mock-ups, and full-size drawings reflects, yet again, her careful attention to detail. Each element of a design was vital both individually and in relationship to its site and context.

Farrand's planting designs were created in a similar process: first a concept, then a drawing, and finally on-site final decisions. Patterson described this process: "She preferred to prepare a planting plan alone in her sitting room, a landscape clear on her inner eye, arranging her palette by writing plant names on a half bushel of white labels. Sorted into bundles, the labels were taken to the job and parceled out to gardeners and assistants."[56] While Farrand produced planting plans, however, actual details were confirmed on the ground, thereby becoming a ground plan.

Opposite page
Full-size mock-up pieces produced for the Eyrie project, designed for the Rockefellers in Maine. Like the full-scale drawings, such samples were a vital part of the design process. Farrand and her clients might inspect the mock-ups, or photographs might be taken and sent to Farrand and/or the client for review. (Environmental Design Archives, University of California, Berkeley)

For her herbaceous borders Farrand drew on Gertrude Jekyll's use of color and the cottage garden style of planting. (See color plate 2.) Plants were identified within irregular spaces merging together as one whole plan. Evergreens, larger shrubs, and trees were identified by specific shapes such as circles, triangles, and squares. For larger gardens and landscapes Farrand frequently listed the plants to one side and placed corresponding numbers within the design next to each circle or irregular space identified as a plant. Rarely did she indicate the number of plants, nor did she seem concerned that their position be marked exactly. Again, this would be decided on site, often at the time of planting, depending on the individual specimens.

Farrand described this ground-design process to Mildred Bliss, suggesting that the "exact position of [the] different plantations is difficult to determine academically, and the most important groups should be placed on the ground as alterations of grade, root space, and exact angle of vision should be the controlling factors, rather than their exact position upon a planting plan." She advised that "the north slopes of the property should properly be studied from the ground itself rather than from any plan, as the contours and expressions of the ground will control the plantations more strongly than any other feature."[57] This approach focused on design as process rather than as product. Rarely did Farrand produce a full plan for an entire landscape with all of its details, as some might today. Instead, she worked with a vision and then implemented the details as appropriate for developing a landscape over time.

Farrand's process-oriented approach was also key to the construction and maintenance phases. As early as 1897 Farrand explained to a reporter that she worked with the laborers, overseeing the process of creating the gardens and landscapes she had designed.[58] An excellent example of Farrand's extensive involvement in this process was her work for Princeton University, which began in 1912, when Farrand was commissioned to design the landscape for the Graduate School. By 1915 she was Princeton's supervising landscape architect, and she remained with the university for over three decades.

Visiting six times a year at a fee of fifty dollars a day, Farrand oversaw the growth and development of much of the campus. She had roads moved, the golf-club house relocated, new roads and paths built, and an entrance court created at the base of Cleveland Tower. Plans were created for many of these projects, although for the final details Farrand provided on-site instructions in consultation with the head gardener.

In 1928 Farrand was instrumental in hiring the head gardener James Clark, who subsequently became Princeton's director of buildings and grounds. She worked closely with him to assure that her designs were carried out, as well as to implement needed changes as plants grew and matured. Letters, telephone calls, and telegrams sufficed when visits were not possible. As for meetings with her employees, each meeting with

Photograph of Farrand's work at Yale University, submitted by her for the ASLA *Illustrations of Work of Members, 1931.*

Clark was documented in a follow-up letter that assigned duties. Such a close relationship with a gardener—even a head groundsman—was unusual for landscape architects, who often remained aloof from laborers in order to distinguish themselves from tradesmen and craftsmen.

Farrand's practice, with all its idiosyncrasies, opened the field of landscape architecture to women as professionals. Farrand helped shape the field's standards of practice, which would be followed for much of the twentieth century. She maintained a strictly professional office, serving as a role model for young practitioners. Her lectures emphasized the struggles and challenges of her practice, alongside the grand nature of landscape architecture. Farrand's belief in the value of her discipline, as well as the inherent hard physical and mental work it required, helped to establish landscape architecture as an artistic profession.

Horticulture and Design; or, Science and Art

In addition to being a model professional, Farrand was instrumental in framing landscape architecture as an art embracing the science of horticulture and the craft of gardening. In all of her gardens Farrand's knowledge of botany and horticulture, as well as her skill as a gardener, was evident, often framing the design's success. Her designs, correspondence, and publications reveal multiple ways in which this knowledge formed a vital aspect of her design philosophy.

Farrand believed that "in order to have good gardens [the designer] must really care for the plants in them and know them individually as well as collectively . . . must know intimately the form and texture as well as the color of all the plants he uses; for plants are to the gardener what his palette is to a painter." Landscape artists, according to Farrand, should know

> the plants whose scent begins at dusk and those whose fragrance stops with the light. They must distinguish the flowers that are beautiful by night from those that are beautiful only by day; they must learn to know the sounds of the leaves on different sorts of trees; the rippling and pattering of the poplar; the rustling of the oak-leaves in winter, and the swishing of evergreens. And by noticing they will also learn that plants are only one of the tools, although to be sure one of the most important, with which a garden is made.[59]

Farrand's botanical knowledge was evident in her instructions to gardeners and nurserymen, her correspondence with clients, and her plant choices and descriptions. She knew botanical Latin and provided both the scientific and the vernacular names for plants. She could describe plants in botanical terms and understood plant taxonomy. For her work at Reef Point she amassed a significant collection of herbarium specimens, which she imagined would be used by students and practitioners. While a general knowledge was not uncommon among practitioners, Farrand's attention to exact varieties, and her knowledge of the characteristics of each, was far more extensive than that of many of her colleagues.

Farrand's knowledge of horticultural practices is consistently evident in the *Plant Book,* which she wrote in the 1940s for the Dumbarton Oaks landscape. She noted that *Ornithogalum arabicum* (star of Bethlehem) should be used with care as it might become rampant. She suggested *Hedera helix* (ivy) to replace *Vinca minor* (periwinkle) when a disease infected the latter. Considering the seasonal changes, Farrand allowed that *Fragaria chiloensis* (wild strawberry) be used, although she commented that it was not recommended "as it is deciduous and the planting of the Green Garden should be ever green, in order to be attractive through the winter when the garden is under frequent observation from the drawing-room windows and from the upper windows of the northeast part of the house."[60] Farrand observed her gardens throughout the seasons and from a variety of perspectives. She drew on her horticultural knowledge to create landscape paintings, vignettes to be viewed and enjoyed over many seasons and years.

As Farrand was well-versed in the horticultural facets of her landscapes, she often retained a supervisory position over gardeners as landscapes matured. She oversaw Princeton's head gardener for twenty-eight years, Yale's for twenty-three, and the University of Chicago's for fourteen. She consulted on the supervision of the gardeners at Dumbarton Oaks for decades. Her designs were not intended to be completed in one season but rather were to serve as frameworks for growth and maturation over the course of a lifetime. This meant that her initial design was just that—an initial design, a concept. In a letter regarding Harvard University's up-keep of Dumbarton Oaks, Farrand wrote to the curator, John S. Thacher: "It seems to me the whole difficulty in the relations between the 'heads' and you and me at Dumbarton is that they do not quite understand that a garden is not a static object, and that it must be constantly not only weeded and cared for, but that it must be replanted from time to time in order, like the Red Queen in Alice, to stay in one place, as otherwise it gets overgrown, untidy and as shabby as one is oneself if one does not wash one's face every day."[61]

Farrand's long-term commitments to her designs reflected the perspective of a gardener and an artist. Farrand established lasting relationships with most of her clients, returning to update and refine landscape and planting designs, often on an annual basis. This meant repainting views and vistas, as well as improving garden beds and addressing changes in the landscape over seasons and years. For example, she refined and redid the North Vista of the Dumbarton Oaks design numerous times to create the effect she sought. This approach was similar to that of Olmsted Sr., who continued to refine his designed landscapes as often as he was allowed.

Understanding the importance of healthy plants to the long-term success of a landscape, Farrand encouraged clients to establish plant nurseries. Such nurseries would allow clients to have their plants propagated and grown to appropriate size for transplanting into their gardens. The nurseries would guarantee the gardener had access to the specific varieties required, in the size needed, and already adapted to the local climate and environment. This was further advantageous for her institutional projects, as Farrand persuaded institutions to share their plants with each other.

As a designer Farrand understood that her intentions could not remain static, nor should gardeners adhere to her designs as if they had been created in stone. In writing to the curator Thacher about her garden record book, she noted that the report should "show the 'temperament' of the place [rather] than the actual position of each tree and shrub. When Bryce [the head gardener] said that he wanted the book so that he could abide by it, it made my blood run cold as nothing will so quickly kill the spirit of any place than to have planting slavishly repeated in certain places because it was originally put there."[62] She designed with seasons and years of growth in mind and considered landscape design a process.

In the 1930s, the same decade in which Farrand lost her mother, her aunt Edith Wharton, and her friends William Robinson and Gertrude Jekyll, she committed to creating the Reef Point gardens in Maine, intended to serve as a testimonial to the potential of horticulture and art through the design of a landscape and botanical collection. On seven acres of land in Bar Harbor on Mount Desert Island, bounded by the rocky Atlantic coast, Farrand hoped to "show what outdoor beauty can contribute to those who have the interest and perception that can be influenced by trees and flowers and open air composition."[63] Originally purchased by her family in 1883, Reef Point featured exhibit gardens and plant collections. To augment the gardens, Max and Beatrix Farrand compiled a significant collection of garden-design and history materials that might be used by students and professionals.

Farrand's design for the gardens reflected her botanical and horticultural interests. She arranged a vast collection of plants, retaining existing trees and shrubs as well as groundcovers. Plants that thrived in the region were used extensively, with an emphasis on native plants, "as the local flora is of incomparable beauty."[64] As a horticulturalist Farrand had learned "to cast aside [her] own fancies or preferences and to adapt [her] plans to what lay before [her] awaiting proper use."[65] She systematically placed the plants sections, with single species set individually, each within a microenvironment. Plants were labeled for reference, and a herbarium of almost eighteen hundred pressed plants was created. Sargent and other professionals in the field consulted and advised with Farrand on her collections and exhibits.

Between 1946 and 1954 Farrand produced a series of bulletins on Reef Point. Essays on its gardens, buildings, and library promoted the institution's educational purpose, and its collections of conifers, roses, heaths, heathers, vines, and plants native to Maine, as well as its constantly expanding herbarium collection, were featured throughout. Other pieces described Farrand's collection of garden prints and the books in the library, both reference works and historically important manuscripts. This combined focus on botanical collections, horticultural experimentation, and educational programs created a unique resource.

Reef Point reflected Farrand's breadth of interests and exhibited a disciplined design, encouraging visitors to "remember a certain harmony in plant grouping." As Farrand noted in her essay on Arnold Arboretum, Sargent had taught her to value "the various plant groups considered as an integral part of a harmonious picture." She recognized that his close observation and study of landscape composition had convinced him that plant materials could be displayed not only correctly, from a botanist's point of view, but also as a part of a design."[66] Reef Point reflected these values.

Reef Point might have been Farrand's greatest legacy, but she dismantled it at the end of her life. As the economy of the 1940s tightened, the location of her institution became problematic. With no successor it was

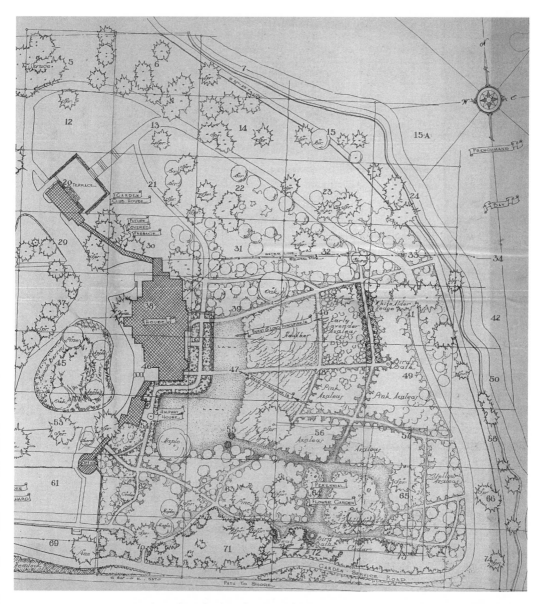

Portion of Reef Point plan, 1928, by Beatrix Jones Farrand, for the Reef Point gardens, Bar Harbor, Maine. The gardens were expanded and refined by Farrand as a showcase of plant collections and design principles. (Environmental Design Archives, University of California, Berkeley)

unclear how such an institution could be maintained to the standards Farrand believed necessary. Rather than leave it to an uncertain future, she completely disassembled the site so that no one could reconstruct it, dramatically demonstrating the passion with which she could both create and erase.

Farrand's practice of landscape architecture embraced the craft of gardening, the science of horticulture, and the art of design. Throughout her career Farrand used plant materials with a horticultural knowledge beyond that of many practitioners. She was a "dirt gardener" who appreciated the importance of the art and craft of gardening in the professional practice of landscape architecture.

Farrand's clear choice to call herself a "landscape gardener" revealed both her role in the profession and her praxis. This title emphasized the significance Farrand gave to the art of gardening. She objected to the use of the word "architecture" for the practice, as she believed it should be reserved for the designers of buildings, not landscapes. Architecture would always play a secondary role to plants and garden in her designs. Her choice of title did not cause any concern among the professional community, which had reacted vehemently to Manning when he altered his title—perhaps because Farrand was a woman, and some in her profession preferred that she have a different title, one more connected with the female world of gardening.

Her insistence on the title "landscape gardener" may also have been out of respect for her mentor Sargent, who considered it a folly to call a form of gardening "architecture." As an anglophile Farrand may also have appreciated the English title "landscape gardener" for its more picturesque connotations. In any case, "landscape gardener" was for Farrand the best description of her practice and her design philosophy.

Farrand's designs were grounded in her commitment to weaving together horticulture and art. Her horticultural and botanical knowledge did not just support her design practice; it was an integral part of her design process. In the essay "From the Ground Up," Selma Robinson suggested that "the modern landscape architect is one who combines in one profession horticulture, landscaping, architecture, and engineering."[67] Farrand's designs revealed the ability to merge the science of horticulture, the craft of gardening, and the art of design into aesthetically rich landscapes and gardens.

The range of Farrand's design practice reflected contemporary practice. Farrand's expertise in both residential and campus design allowed her to address projects on a variety of scales. However, while Farrand was known by her contemporaries, there is little record of her actively mentoring younger designers. She only participated minimally in the activities of the ASLA. She opened doors, but she did not usher in anyone behind her; rather, she took care of her practice and assumed others would do the same. Although no women remembered obtaining direct support or advice from Farrand, many commented that they had adopted her practices to establish their offices. Ellen Biddle Shipman adapted aspects of Farrand's professional practice, and Marian Cruger Coffin founded her office based on Farrand's. By exploring Farrand's praxis, we begin to understand the profession and practice of the time, for men and women. Turning attention to the practices of Shipman and Coffin, our understanding is expanded and enhanced, as we follow both similar threads and divergent paths and choices.

3

From Garden Craft
to Landscape Architecture

Thomas Jefferson spoke of gardening as a fine art, one that fostered great potential in the new nation. It is unlikely he envisioned women transforming this art of gardening into the profession of landscape architecture. He would likely have been taken aback by the headline in the *New York Times* in March 1938: "Women Take Lead in Landscape Art: Field Is Dominated by a Group of Brilliant Designers of Horticultural Vistas." By the early twentieth century women had in fact transformed interest in gardens, gardening, and horticulture into the practice of landscape architecture. They had thus translated the craft of gardening into an art of design on a professional level. Beatrix Jones Farrand, Kate Olivia Sessions, Ellen Biddle Shipman, Eleanor Roche, Edith Schryver, and Florence Yoch, like Jefferson and Lady Skipwith, were first gardeners, people for whom the plant world provided an abundance of materials with which to create beautiful spaces out of doors. Unlike Jefferson or Lady Skipwith, however, these women were born into a time when such an interest could be transformed into a career, one that women could pursue.

Women and the New Profession

As early as the 1830s there had been concern that "young ladies should make themselves the mistresses of some attainment, either in art or science, by which they might secure a subsistence, should they be reduced to poverty."[1] In the decades following the Civil War, industrialization, urbanization, and the growing population had compounded this concern, as increasing numbers of women had to fend for themselves. Women were often unmarried, widowed, deserted, or married to a man unable to appropriately provide for a family. Reformers responded by encouraging women to prepare themselves to join the labor force, albeit in careful and appropriate ways. Women responded, and the New Woman was born.

The New Woman emerged at the end of the nineteenth century, possessing the self-confidence, individuality, and independence of a generation ready to conquer the world. New Women included glamorous performers, strong athletes, committed reformers, and leaders of settlement houses, trade unions, and suffrage activities, as well as working girls in factories, offices, and stores, all of whom found a place in the public realm beginning in the 1890s: "Gone was the frail, pale woman and in her place was the strong, robust, red-cheeked outdoors person"—the Gibson Girl.[2] The New Woman gardened, took walks, rode bicycles, and sought adventures in nature. She was present in the city and on the farm throughout the United States.

Women entered the job market and the professional community in unprecedented numbers. They were increasingly visible in the professions of medicine, science, and of course teaching. By 1900, 7,387 women were physicians and surgeons, and 5,984 were literary and scientific persons. Teaching remained the largest profession, with 327,206 women employed, representing 76.2 percent of the total number of women in the professions. By 1920 the census reported that 24 percent of all women were "gainfully employed." In the Northeast the figure was even higher, at 37 percent of all women. There had been, then, an almost 40 percent increase in the total numbers of female professionals during the first two decades of the twentieth century. Women were active in a range of areas, including some in the "design" professions (architects, interior designers, draftspersons, inventors, and landscape architects). Outside of teaching and the decorative arts, women nevertheless remained a minority in the professions. Of 43,200 technical engineers only 84 were female, and of 10,581 architects 100 were female. Women were present, but not in significant numbers.

Landscape architecture and landscape gardening were included in the census as distinct designations only in 1930, and both were still listed under "agricultural proprietors and laborers" in 1940. (In comparison, architecture was listed under "professions" as early as 1900.) The 1940 census listed "agricultural" gardeners and groundskeepers as 1,852 women and 172,507 men and "professional" architects as 379 women and 21,621 men. A number of leaders saw the potential for women to practice as landscape architects. Catherine Filene's *Careers for Women* (1920) suggested that landscape architecture was an appropriate pursuit for women, one in which they might make a reasonable income. Charles W. Eliot, Harvard's president emeritus, suggested that landscape architecture was "a profession appropriate to women because, first it creates and preserves landscape beauty, and secondly, because it promotes good housing with pleasant surroundings."[3] On the other hand, Eliot also wrote, in a 1925 letter to *Landscape Architecture Magazine,* that women should "study landscape beauty, garden design, and planting rather than the engineering and architecture embraced in the general term 'landscape architecture.'"[4] Similarly, in 1928 Henry Atherton Frost and William R. Sears published a report, *Women in Architecture and Landscape Architecture for the Institute for the Co-ordination of Women's Interests,* which proposed that "the woman student has a tendency toward the more delicate side of design, the more intimate scheme." Nevertheless, building on such associations between women and beauty, design, and art, as well as gardens and gardening, many women went on to pursue the practice of landscape architecture.

Women took advantage of many opportunities, paving new paths across the nation. Kate Olivia Sessions (1857–1940) was first and foremost a horticulturalist and nurserywoman, who also practiced as a landscape gardener, designing public and private landscapes in southern California. A contemporary of Farrand, Bullard, and McCrea, she was born in San Francisco and raised in Oakland. She attended the University of California, Berkeley, graduating in 1881 as a chemistry major. Initially, she taught in the Oakland, San Diego, and San Gabriel school districts. In 1885 she left teaching to become co-owner, later sole owner, of the city's oldest nursery, as she had a love of and talent for growing plants.

Sessions introduced many native and nonnative plants into the nursery business. For example, she collected and popularized plants native to southern California, such as *Ceanothus cyaneus* (San Diego lilac) and *Romneya coulter* (Matilija poppy), and introduced plants that thrived in the San Diego environment, including varieties of palms, eucalyptus, bougainvillea, and aloe. She became known for her careful attention to

Advertisement for the Lowthorpe School, emphasizing the opportunities for women in the profession of landscape architecture.

selling the right plant at the right time to clients, refusing to sell a plant that would not survive.[5] In 1915 her nursery was identified as the primary source for the Panama Pacific International Exposition. Sessions also cofounded the San Diego Floral Association, with Alfred D. Robinson, and corresponded with major botanists and plant collectors throughout California and the United States. In 1939 she was awarded the Frank N. Meyer Medal by the American Genetic Association, the first woman to be so honored, recognized for her important work introducing new plants to Southern California.

Sessions served as a consultant on diverse projects throughout California. She was named the supervisor of agriculture for the San Diego school district in 1915, a position she retained for three years. She collaborated with the architect Irving Gill on many of his projects, including the Marston House and Lewis Courts.[6] She advised home owners, wrote garden columns for the local newspaper, provided over 250 articles to regional garden magazines including *California Garden,* and taught gardening classes for adults and children.

As her business grew, Sessions was offered the opportunity to move her nursery to City Park. In return for free water and the title of city gardener, she provided free trees, palms, ornamental shrubs, and other plants for city parks and streets. City Park later became Balboa Park, and Sessions became known as the "Mother of Balboa Park." She continued to care for the park, adding and replacing plants as she deemed necessary. She was also responsible for selecting and planting the *Cocos plumosa* (coconut palms) on what is now known as San Diego's Palm Plaza. Near the end of her life, she was involved in a small housing development overlooking Mission Valley.

Much of Sessions's career and life were spent advocating for the natural landscape surrounding San Diego, to "keep people from gardening and planting city flowers on this mountain."[7] However, little documentation of her designs remains: in the tradition of nurserymen, she rarely put a plan on paper, as she designed on-site. While Sessions did design parks and residences, her primary role was as a gardener, nurserywoman, and advocate for parks. She joined women such as the photographer Alice Hare and Alice Eastwood, the curator of botany at the California Hall of Sciences, in speaking out for the preservation of the native landscape and plants of California. While Sessions, Hare, and Eastwood exemplify the many early nineteenth-century women who studied botany and horticulture, they took their interests to a professional level. Ellen Biddle Shipman directed her similar interest and talent toward becoming a landscape architect, a profession very different from that of Sessions, although also focused on the arts and sciences of gardening. Shipman, however, did put her plans on paper, creating elegant plans for gardens throughout the country and helping to create the legacy of women in landscape architecture.

Ellen McGowan Biddle was born in Philadelphia to a career soldier and his wife, spending much of her childhood on the American frontier.[8] She attended private schools and was tutored so that she might fulfill her role as a young woman in the rising middle class. While book education was part and parcel of such an upbringing, Shipman spent many hours outdoors, exploring and learning. She would later recall the importance of natural environments in her childhood, in particular the special attention her father gave to trees in the arid landscape of Nevada, where he was stationed for a good portion of her childhood. Unlike her father Shipman was interested not merely in the horticultural aspects of her environment but in the artistic placement of plants and architecture in the landscape. The margins of her early schoolwork featured sketches and plans for gardens and houses. It would be decades, however, before Shipman would seriously follow her interests in any professional manner.

Of a generation and a family that valued education, Shipman enrolled in the Harvard Annex about 1892. Like many college women of the period, she was involved in Boston suffrage activities and developed lifelong friendships within her intellectual community. Two of these would be pivotal for Shipman: her friendships with Louise Emory (later the wife of Herbert Croly, editor of *Architectural Record*) and Marian Nichols (the writer and artist). These friends introduced Shipman to a community of intellectuals and thinkers. It was also at Harvard that Ellen Biddle met Louis Shipman, a struggling playwright, whom she married. When the Crolys moved to Cornish, New Hampshire, an artists' colony, they encouraged the new couple to join them. The Shipmans moved and were immediately woven into the community. Ellen Shipman became involved in social and progressive organizations offering companionship to women and promoting the arts and crafts industries.

Augustus Saint-Gaudens, a sculptor, artist, intellectual, and outspoken advocate for the arts, had early fostered Corning as an artists' colony. Rose Standish Nichols (1872–1960), his niece, lived in the community, as did her sister, the writer Marian Nichols. Rose had completed select courses at MIT as a nondegree special student in 1898, leaving just before the new landscape option was available. In Corning she opened a small garden-design practice and went on to design over seventy gardens and to write numerous books on European gardens and landscape design. While a garden Nichols designed was the only one by a woman to be included in Guy Lowell's *American Gardens,* she is recognized today primarily as an author.

Art was the heart and soul of the Cornish social community. Painters Thomas Dewing and Maria Oakey Dewing, and artist Maxfield Parrish, lived in this small New England village. The community was known as an "abode of artists . . . where gardens are plentiful."[9] Gardening was not only a hobby but a social and cultural activity leading to improved intellectual and physical health, as an art and a profession. Shipman wrote that "here was the renaissance of gardening in America." She learned from her neighbors and friends how to apply an artist's eye to the garden, for the residents were "all artists of one kind or another and great gardeners."[10] It was in this community and setting that Shipman became a friend and protégée of fellow Cornish resident Charles Platt.

Charles Adams Platt (1861–1933) initially practiced as a painter and etcher, having studied at the National Academy of Design in New York. After traveling in Italy, he published a series of articles that was compiled as a book in 1894, titled *Italian Gardens,* the first such book published in the United States. Italian gardens became a primary source of design inspiration for Platt, who went on to become an architect and a landscape architect. His practice of landscape design was clearly influenced by his understanding of the Italian gardens he had visited, his designs reflecting formal and architectonic approaches to the area surrounding the architecture and transitioning slowly to more naturalistic parklike landscapes further from the house. He sought to integrate individual garden spaces into a whole design through the use of simple geometries, an emphasis on site lines and vistas. His designs also featured an extensive use of stone and water, along with an abundance of plants. Although initially drawn from Italian villa landscapes, Platt's design approach eventually became recognized as a particularly American contribution to landscape architecture.[11]

The Shipmans lived in the Platt house during the winter of 1899, while their house was being renovated. Later, Ellen Shipman recalled how she had accidentally left her drawings on Platt's board, which he found on his return. For Christmas Platt sent her a note recommending that she continue to draw and attached a drawing board, T-square, and other drafting implements. Platt provided Shipman with training in drafting and design and encouraged the development of her skills as a gardener and landscape artist.

In the ensuing years Shipman worked on gardens at her homes, first at Poins House and later at Brook Place, both in Plainfield, a part of the larger Cornish community. Brook Place remained at the core of Shipman's practice and her life, in many ways the bridge between the two parts of her life. This was the garden that she cared for over the decades and retreated to each summer. It was a small place serving as both a showpiece and a retreat. It was here that Shipman refined her gardening skills and developed her distinctive style of design. Potential clients and friends might come to visit and, in enjoying her garden, learn to appreciate the art of garden design and the craft of gardening.

When her husband left her in 1910, Shipman, now forty-one, embarked more formally on a career in landscape architecture in order to support herself and her three children. She drew on Platt's knowledge and skills, as well as his contacts, to develop her practice. Her knowledge of gardens, gardening, and plants, as well as her eye for design, were clearly assets to Platt's practice. Platt was soon asking her to produce planting plans for projects, as he did not have the horticultural knowledge called for in his designs of country estates. Shipman moved from being an informal apprentice to a collaborator and colleague within a few short years. She was divorced in 1927, by which time she had moved her primary office to New York. She died in 1950, after practicing for almost thirty years. Shipman's legacy can be located not only in the gardens she designed but also, significantly, in the work of the many young women who studied under her before opening practices across the country.

A Garden Design Practice

While Farrand worked alone, the partnership between Platt and Shipman in its early years resembled that between Edwin Lutyens and Gertrude Jekyll, a partnership familiar to most garden enthusiasts. As Shipman collaborated with Platt on projects from Seattle to Philadelphia, their partnership, like that between Lutyens and Jekyll, reflected typical gendered roles, the man taking the lead in architecture and the woman in gardens and landscape. Like Lutyens, Platt was the better-known partner and established the first contacts and commissions, while Shipman developed planting plans to accompany many of his larger projects. A number of these designs—including those for the Mather estate, Gwinn; the Merrill garden in Seattle; and the Russell A. Alger estate, the Moorings—were revisions of earlier ones, an acknowledgment of her eye for the craft of planting design, in particular for flower gardens, which became a hallmark of her work.

While this partnership was important initially, however, Shipman rather quickly began working independently. She emulated her mentor and set up an office resembling his in both its physical layout and the procedures adopted. Shipman collected garden and landscape books and resources, assembling a notable library over the course of her career.[12] She also took on young apprentices, as Platt had taken her on in his practice. For Shipman mentoring became a focus of her practice, as she invited young women considering a career in landscape design to work in the office for a summer or a season, although little if any wages were provided.[13]

Shipman's practice thrived in part because she drew heavily on her social networks, only later establishing a professional network of architects, photographers, and landscape architects. Women and men pursuing a career in landscape architecture frequently began their professional careers in this way, identifying clients among family, friends, and acquaintances. Word-of-mouth remained a primary source of commissions, particularly among the elite families owning country estates and serving on the boards of institutions and corporations. For early twentieth-century professional women, social networks remained a critical thread throughout their practice, even as professional networks grew and opened to women.

Farrand, as noted earlier, similarly drew on her social networks, her practice almost exclusively with those within her large social network and her outside commissions often connected to someone she knew and considered a friend. When such social networks failed, women were often surprised. Farrand, for example, was confused when her close friendship with Mildred Bliss did not guarantee her the commission for the Santa Barbara Botanical Garden, whose primary patron was Mildred Bliss's father. Farrand had met with the garden's board of directors to discuss the site's landscape design, assuming her relationship to the Bliss family was sufficient for her to be hired as the professional designer. Yet she was not hired, in part as she had not directly asked to be hired or advocated her own work during the meeting, and therefore, board members had concluded she must not be particularly interested in the project. Farrand, in contrast, believed such self-promotion to be undignified, unprofessional, and inherently unnecessary, given her social connections.

This misunderstanding reveals Farrand's assumptions and the nature of upper-class East Coast culture, in which self-advertising was considered beneath the professional. On the West Coast such restraint was viewed as unnecessary and perhaps even evidence of snobbery. As the frontier, the West Coast fostered a culture that promoted a sense of adventure and self-aggrandizement that still remains a part of its identity. Farrand was never able to fully establish a practice in California, perhaps in part because the culture was so unlike that of the more traditional East.

While Shipman did not have Farrand's depth of familial connections, she created alternative alliances. She used her network of friends in Cornish to learn the skills and art of her profession and to establish her practice. She understood the importance of entertaining and hosted small parties and gatherings at her home, where anyone might admire the gardens. She hosted tours of her gardens with groups such as local garden clubs. Giving lectures to garden and civic organizations, Shipman promoted both the profession and her own practice. She was a well-respected lecturer, providing just the right balance of expertise, feminine decorum, and practical knowledge, in addition to inspiring and beautiful images of gardens and designed landscapes.

Cornish was an ideal community within which to begin a practice, but Shipman soon realized that an office in Manhattan was required to fully establish her practice and to ensure the needed commissions. In the early 1920s she moved her home and office to the corner of East Fiftieth Street and Beekman Place, in New York City. She thus joined the growing community of women landscape architects in the city—Nellie B. Allen, Agnes Selkirk Clark, Ruth B. Dean, Beatrix Jones Farrand, Annette Hoyt

Flanders, Louise Payson, and Isabella Pendleton. Shipman's townhouse was an older brick building in a neighborhood being gentrified by actors and writers, featuring views of the East River and a southern exposed garden area, perfect for a show garden. The office was designed to face Beekman Place, the reception room featuring a bay window looking over the neighborhood, a large drafting room, and a private office facing the river. The office was well-furnished, with art and garden books on the dining table.

Shipman's private residence was attached to her office, but she established a separate entrance for each domain, providing distinct identities for work and home. Her interior design was successful enough that photographs of her home were published in the November 1927 issue of *House Beautiful*.[14] Indeed, in the 1930s, when landscape business was sparse, Shipman offered interior design services. Throughout her practice the New York office was packed up each spring and moved to Brook Place, where she spent the warmer months working and socializing.

Shipman maintained a busy practice, eventually designing over six hundred gardens. Unlike many of her colleagues and employees, she never joined the ASLA, perhaps because by the time she was at the height of her career, it was expected that practitioners had completed some type of formal education. While many men and women without such degrees belonged to the ASLA, this was increasingly less the case for new members. By the 1920s, then, when Shipman would have felt most professionally comfortable applying for membership, her application might have been noted for her lack of formal education.

Shipman admired those who were able to gain more formal education and training in landscape architecture, hiring many graduates of the Lowthorpe and Cambridge schools. She lectured for schools including Lowthorpe, providing opportunities for young women to gain the advice of an established professional woman landscape architect.

Shipman's staff included five to ten draftspersons and two secretaries in the 1920s and 1930s, when her practice was at its most productive point. Many women gained the experience of working under Shipman's guidance, including, among others, Dorothy May Anderson, Dona Caldwell, Eleanor Hills Christie, Agnes Selkirk Clark, Mary P. Cunningham, Louise Payson, Eleanor Louise Roche, Edith Schryver, and Elizabeth Leonard Strang. These women, with the exception of Caldwell, who worked summers for Shipman, had all attended either Lowthorpe or the Cambridge School before entering Shipman's office. Cunningham, a 1910 graduate of Vassar, had studied at Lowthorpe (1918 certificate) and the Cambridge School and in 1923 was the first woman to receive a master's degree in dendrology from Radcliff College, through the Bussey Institute at Harvard University. She opened her own office in Cambridge and then Boston, focusing, like Shipman, on residential designs, and became known for her *House Beautiful* garden column. Cunningham taught at the

Cambridge School, Lowthorpe, and Smith College and was elected to the ASLA in 1924. She was the only woman member of the Boston chapter of the ASLA for many years. Frances McCormic quit her formal studies at Lowthorpe in the early 1920s, when she was hired by Shipman, and stayed until the 1940s, when she went to work for Condé Nast. She worked for Shipman as the head of the office, chief draftsperson, and model maker.

Reflecting Shipman's commitment to mentoring a new generation of women practitioners, her approach to her work was collaborative, and she frequently credited her employees for their work. In the foreword to her book manuscript, Shipman named many of her assistants and wrote, "Without them my work could never have been accomplished, and so when I say 'we,' you will know I am speaking of these great assistants to whom my gratitude is unending."[15] While Farrand was most interested in employees who would support her own work, Shipman focused attention on her role as a model and mentor, in many ways creating both a social and a family network.

As a designer Shipman was acknowledged by professional colleagues and the public. Her projects with Roger H. Bullard, Clark and Arms, Delano and Aldrich, and Alfred Hopkins were featured in professional journals and magazines. Jessie Tarbox Beals, Mattie Edwards Hewitt, and Frances Benjamin Johnston were commissioned to photograph her gardens. In 1923 the Architectural League of New York included Shipman's design for the Magee garden in its annual exhibition, and she was named "dean of American women Landscape Architects" by *House & Garden* in 1933.

Designing Gardens

Shipman, near the end of her career, wrote her first draft of a book on gardening, in which she described her process of designing gardens and landscapes. Although she never completed the manuscript, the remaining foreword, preface, introduction, and outline provide a framework for understanding Shipman's design praxis. The book was to feature chapters on design, construction, planting, maintenance, and a calendar of work. Shipman, then, did not move away from the craft of gardening to the art of design, but set the two on an equal basis. The book was to include a hardiness zone map; photographs of Shipman's work, as well as drawings and illustrations; and an introduction by her mentor, Platt. The content, thus framed between an introduction by an architect and a horticultural zone map, would reflect the breadth of Shipman's practice. The book itself was to be a "contribution, as one might give a friend the seed or root of some plant, with directions for its care that had brought beauty to her own garden."[16]

Shipman started the design process with a visit to the site to observe the existing landforms and vegetation. She documented these visits with photographs and notes. She requested survey plans to be sent to her of-

Fahnestock garden, designed by Ellen Biddle Shipman and photographed by
Jesse Tarbox Beals. (Ellen McGowan Biddle Shipman Papers, #1259, Division of
Rare and Manuscript Collections, Cornell University Library)

fice and then worked from these notes to produce rough sketches and a broad conceptual scheme. She did not create designs for any garden or landscape she had not personally visited. Asked to give advice on a garden unseen, Shipman would insist she could be hired for a consultation, as she did to Dona Caldwell's mother, who had met Shipman in Bermuda and hoped for some quick advice.[17]

Shipman worked carefully and closely with her assistants to produce alternative plans before any ideas were presented to a client. This allowed her to give her client choices, as she did not believe good design could be accomplished solely by the designer. It was critical that her designs reflect the desires and character of the client, as well as the existing landscape. She wrote one client that "each garden that I do is like a portrait of the person and should express their likes and dislikes."[18] It was only after Shipman and her client had agreed on a general design concept that the office would produce final drawings, plans, and construction details. By eliciting their participation, Shipman encouraged her clients' eventual ownership of the designed gardens.

Indeed, in her commitment to reflecting her clients' tastes and wishes, Shipman was not averse to using plants that she did not personally appreciate. While she encouraged designers to consider the plants already established, she was open to a client's particular tastes. For example, she did not like the blue spruce of Colorado, which was popular at the time: "Blue Spruce are beautiful in the mountains of Colorado . . . but not in our front lawns."[19] Nonetheless, she used it when requested.

Shipman developed an elegant style for the presentation drawings that were given to each of her clients. Most of her plans were ink on vellum and featured plans, elevations, and small vignettes or perspectives, the layout carefully composed on the page. The vignettes gave the impression of a stroll through the garden, highlighting specific views or focal points. Shrub borders were sketched with light lines implying loosely defined edges, while architectural lines were heavier and firmer. Path lines, which Shipman believed were critical to the overall plan, were clearly delineated. In part because these plans were on vellum, a durable and elegant paper, instead of the thinner and more fragile trace paper used for sketches and drafts, the presentation drawings appeared to be finished products themselves, rather than merely landscape plans. A similar attention to both the presentation's composition and the garden's design is evident, for example, in Shipman's plan for the Campbell estate.

Shipman provided her clients with the information they needed to assure the design's success. Once the design concept had been agreed upon, a general plan was created, the projects' scale ranging from small garden designs to larger landscape plans. By the time of construction the client would have a full set of drawings, including detailed planting plans and relevant horticultural notes on issues from soil preparation to staking trees.

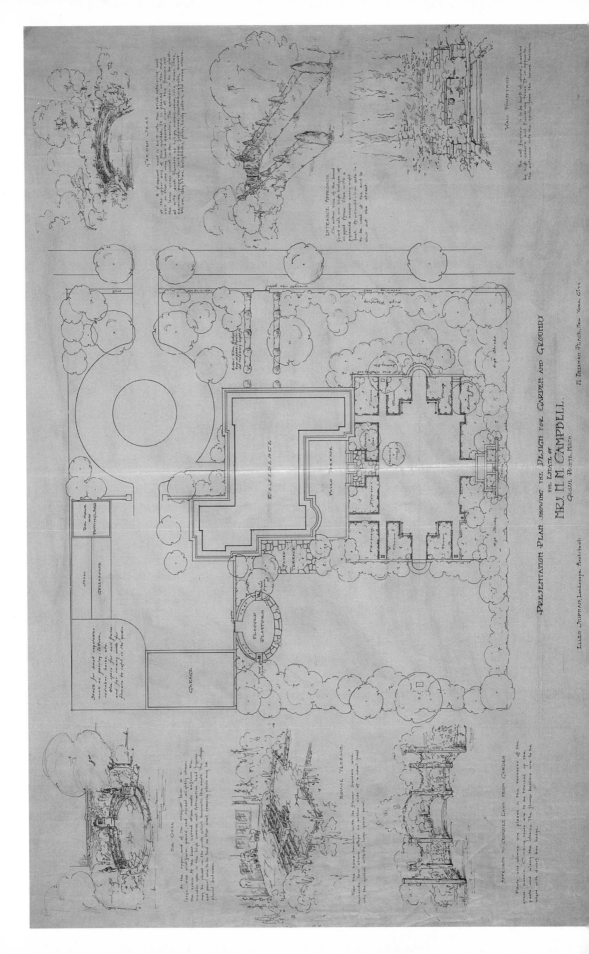

PLANTING PLAN showing the DESIGN for GARDEN and GROUNDS
for the ESTATE of
MRS H. M. CAMPBELL.
GROSSE POINTE, MICH.

ELLEN SHIPMAN, Landscape Architect.

21 BEEKMAN PLACE, NEW YORK CITY

Shipman encouraged her clients and employees to be good gardeners and to better understand garden design. In the draft of her book, she suggested that gardeners and designers observe plants in their optimum environments to determine their appropriate placement in the garden. Such observations should not be, Shipman noted, those of a botanist who considers the different parts of the plant, but those of an artist "seeing them as a whole and their artistic relation to other plants." With the same holistic thinking Shipman warned readers to consider the preparation of the soil as a required investment in the garden: "It is best to know from the beginning that a ten cent hole and a dollar plant will not give you encouragement or satisfaction. Rather buy a smaller, but good plant, and make a large and deep and well fertilized hole. You will then enjoy its beauty for years to come, and from one plant, well taken care of, you may grow to be a great and enthusiastic gardener bringing joy and happiness to yourself, your family and your community."[20] This was a tall order for a limited investment of time and funds, but it was the ground upon which Shipman built her practice.

With plant materials and soil conditions established, Shipman turned her attention to the planting and construction. While she preferred to be on site when plantings were placed, at times this was not possible, and she relegated the work to the resident gardener, understanding that this person might need to modify plans once construction began. With this in mind Shipman would outline her design priorities, creating a framework within which decisions on details could be made. She frequently instructed laborers to keep the paths to the exact measurements specified, allowing any extra space to flower beds. Any leeway in a design, in other words, was to favor a looser flower bed rather than a less exact path plan.

Shipman, like Farrand, maintained long-term relationships with her clients, overseeing the growth of her projects and visiting the gardens in a variety of seasons. She frequently stayed as a houseguest while working on the gardens and landscapes. Over the seasons and years she reworked some of her gardens as they matured and as clients' needs changed; it was not uncommon for her to suggest modifications to reduce the maintenance required or to serve a modified purpose. Shipman also sustained professional relationships with gardeners, most of whom were men de-

Opposite page

Plan for the Campbell estate, 1925, Grosse Pointe, Michigan, designed by Shipman. The composition of the page, with vignettes surrounding the ground plan, is typical of her presentation drawings. This was a style many practitioners used to help clients visualize the character of the proposed design. (Ellen McGowan Biddle Shipman Papers, #1259, Division of Rare and Manuscript Collections, Cornell University Library)

spite her wishes to hire more women. She wrote once, "I have never found any man who is able to keep a garden or place in the condition that I thought it should be unless I supervise it twice a year."[21]

Farrand and Shipman represent two approaches to professional practice. While Farrand was able to move easily within a network of clients who were members of her own social class, Shipman was reliant on her own deportment and her creation of new social networks. She also relied on professionals, including architects, to recommend her to clients. Shipman could not be as particular about her projects, as she depended upon the income generated by her practice. Further, although Farrand ran an office of four to six employees, she did not delegate any design projects to her employees, retaining full control. Shipman, on the other hand, had a slightly larger staff and was more willing to delegate specific jobs and projects to her employees, although she oversaw each project as the designer and primary supervisor. Farrand tended to take on much larger commissions, eschewing smaller projects or those where she would not be in control of the entire landscape. Shipman, in contrast, was willing to create small flower garden designs and to work as a team member with architects and other landscape architects. Farrand's office was responsible for approximately two hundred projects over the course of her career, as compared to Shipman's six hundred designs. While their offices are often paired, both practices run by women, their significant differences reflect the unbounded nature of women landscape architects at the turn of the century.

A Variety of Gardens

Shipman had learned to appreciate the beauty of gardens as a young girl, visiting her grandparents and watching her father create a garden in the Nevada landscape. Her interest was reignited when she visited Cornish, New Hampshire, in 1895 and stepped outside the home of Miss Annie Lazarus. Shipman later recalled this moment: "In the distance was Ascutney Mountain, the Fuji-Yama of the valley, and just a few feet below, where we stood upon a terrace, was a Sunken Garden with rows bathed in moonlight of white lilies standing as an altar for Ascutney. As I look back I realize it was at that moment that a garden became for me the most essential part of a home."[22]

This blend of a visual and a spiritual response to the viewing of a garden infused Shipman's designs. She believed that gardening is "an art of much more vital importance than most Americans realize. . . . [It] open[s] a wider door than any other of the arts—all Mankind can walk through, rich and poor, high and low, talented and untalented. It has no distinctions, all are welcome." For Shipman a house became a home when a garden had been created, and it was in the garden that the culture and democratic values of America were reflected and made evident: "If one can gauge the height of civilization by the beauty of the gardens, one can also judge the spirit of democracy in a people by the prevalence of gardens among all its classes."[23] This attitude was also held by both Downing and Olmsted, each of whom argued that domesticity was the finest expression of a culture.

While her mentor Platt had been inspired by Italian gardens, Shipman turned to English garden writers, including William Robinson, Ellen Wilmott, and Gertrude Jekyll. Robinson espoused an approach to garden design emphasizing a more natural or wild appearance, as compared with the bedding-out style of Victorian gardens. He encouraged respect for plant form, color, and foliage, along with concern for horticultural requirements and the establishment of appropriate ecological habitats. He promoted the use of permanent plantings, rather than bedding plants, and suggested mixing native and exotic plants in the garden. The resulting landscape was not a "natural" one, as when nature is left to its own devices, but rather one that drew on natural beauties in the massing of plants; the celebration of seasonal color; and luxurious mixes of perennials, shrubs, and trees. Robinson's ideas, adapted by Wilmott and Jekyll, became popularly known as the cottage garden style. While the plan of a landscape and garden might be quite formal, with symmetrically placed flower borders, allées of trees, and vistas of distant views, plant materials were used to soften, grace, and enrich the plan with color and texture. The intent was to create highly textured and colorful paintings using plants as the artistic medium and landscape as the canvas. This was the garden style that Cornish residents loved and that Shipman would celebrate.

As an artist Shipman applied her horticultural knowledge and gardening craft to creating hundreds of cottage gardens. These became artistic gems within larger designed landscapes, often placed close to the house. Shipman worked in the tradition of Jekyll, blending perennials and shrubs to create seasonal color and texture, though she did not copy Jekyll's emphasis on the massing of flowers.

Shipman was commissioned to create a number of such gardens, frequently for women clients—including Elizabeth Billings, Clara Ford, Elizabeth Mather, and Gertrude Seiberling. Women were frequently avid gardeners, and those of the upper echelons of society enjoyed their role as artists and craftspersons in the garden. Their gardens often included horticultural collections, while other gardens featured ferns (fernery) or cutting flowers. While many landscape architects avoided border beds, thinking them too fussy and small, Shipman enjoyed planning and planting such flower gardens. For these gardens she created brilliant mosaics of color and texture by using plants "as a painter uses the colors from his palette."[24]

While most of Shipman's gardens and landscapes disappeared over the decades, due to the high maintenance required and changing tastes, a few remain. The Causeway, in Washington, D.C., is one vibrant example of her work. In 1913 Shipman was brought into the Causeway project for Mr. and Mrs. James Parmelee, working with a general plan designed by Platt to develop garden and landscape areas throughout the estate. Located in Cleveland Park, a streetcar suburb in northwestern Washington, the Causeway estate was surrounded by other large homes and estates. Farmhouses were also a part of the mix near Cleveland Park, giving the landscape a rural air.

Gardiner Greene Hubbard, the founder of the National Geographic Society, had established Twin Oaks in the late nineteenth century, fashioning a grand summer estate of forty acres set on a wooded knoll, dropping steeply to two branches of Rock Creek at the northern and southern edges. Two large oak trees provided the estate's namesake. In 1911 James Parmelee, a banker from Cleveland, and his wife, Alice Maury Parmelee, bought a twenty-acre piece of the Twin Oaks estate from Hubbard's daughter. Avid art collectors and patrons, they then hired Platt to design a year-round country house. Their new home was to be placed within a varied and picturesque setting, the site composed primarily of woodland, with small areas carved out for pasture and barns. Old barns, an icehouse, and a small farmhouse remained from years past. An old bridle path, most likely established by the Hubbard family, swept around the edges of the estate, offering views of the landscape both from within the estate and beyond. Klingle Road, a part of the Olmsted Sr. plan in the late nineteenth century, followed one Rock Creek tributary at the southeast. The second tributary, which ran from the northern entrance of the estate to the southern end, merged with the first at the corner of Klingle Road.

The landscape was primarily woodland, with one farmhouse on its western edge, another near the top of the hill, and a cow pasture bordering Klingle Road. Platt drew on these elements, taking full advantage of surrounding views and vistas. He chose the summit of the hill for the new house, just south of the original farmhouse, and then designed a brick Georgian Revival mansion crowning the hill, in keeping with many of the District's larger homes. Leading up to the house was a long drive—the causeway for which the estate was named. This entrance drive began at Klingle Road, crossed a stream, and gracefully curved up the hill to the house (and later extended to the opposite edge of the estate). The house and terrace featured views of the grounds, as well as views out to metropolitan Washington in one direction and, in another, to the National Cathedral, to which the Parmelees were major contributors.

The 1915 book *American Country Houses of To-Day* includes a lengthy description of the Causeway as an example of a desirable lifestyle. The formal flower garden provided a place to walk and hold intimate conversations. The sweeping lawn, beyond the formal garden and embraced at its lower end by the woodland/pond garden, provided more dramatic views of the larger landscape and the distant city. Perhaps the landscape's most intriguing feature was the bridle path, winding along the eastern edge of the property, crossing under the southeastern end of the causeway, and then meeting the drive at the property's northern end, having originally circumvented the entire hilltop. By 1927 the Parmelees had expanded their holdings to include the northern landscape, on Macomb Street, and extended the drive, allowing for a back entrance to the estate. Experienced as a whole, the estate's landscape was more like that of an

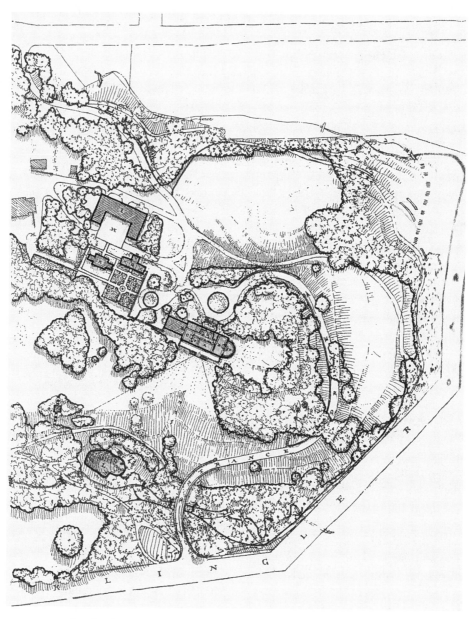

Plan for the Causeway landscape, ca. 1915, as illustrated in Samuel Howe's *American Country Houses To-Day.*

isolated country manor than of a house at the edge of the nation's capital. Indeed, the view of the pasture from the entrance gate established the site as a country place, while the formal mansion, glimpsed through the trees, implied the life of the gentleman farmer.

Shipman's formal flower garden, its design her first contribution to the Causeway estate, was positioned off-axis from the house, set just slightly farther north on the hilltop, announced by an exquisite arched gate set between tall piers. Here a garden, rather "stately in arrangement but promis[ing] to be gorgeously diversified in color and willful with its fragrance," replaced an earlier farmhouse (taken down in 1913).[25] Brick walls enclosed the garden on two sides, with dependencies and utilitarian gardens forming the remaining sides.

When one entered the garden, the view was carried along the axis toward a fountain set in the center of four quadrants. The symmetrical space was filled with bright flowering plants, edged with the deep green boxwood, and accented on the corners by dark yews. At the far end an evergreen-bordered path ascended the hill and culminated at an Italianate figurine, denoting Old World culture and New World wealth.[26]

Photographs taken three years later, by Frances Benjamin Johnston, show a garden recognizable as quintessential Shipman, relying on simple geometry, easy for the eye to take in and for the body to respond to. The core of the plan was symmetrical, emphasizing the entrance and the view down the center, while the second half of the garden was in fact only a narrow corridor. The garden beds balanced the architectonic symmetry, the graceful drooping flowers and arching stems bounded by the dense boxwood edge. The blooming calendar was focused on the spring and fall, the height of the District's garden season, and contained a mix of perennials and bulbs, planted in masses of color and texture, giving the garden temporality and seasonality.

While the view extended the axis from the entrance, the garden's main exit was on its western edge. Beyond, a landscape of trees, shrubs, and lawn provided views of the larger estate and the National Cathedral. From here paths either returned to the house or ascended to the terrace, where one could enjoy the vista or venture further, to the woodland garden. A rather exotic arbor offered an entrance to the woodland area, farther down the hillside.

This woodland garden was unlike Shipman's other known garden designs, relying on an informal composition of naturalized plants around a pond, similar to the wild garden described by William Robinson. Native and exotic plants intermingled. Masses of color and texture were blended to form irregular beds enhancing the undulating topography, the site's hydrology, and the existing trees. Shipman's design articulated the genius loci of the site by emphasizing the watercourse, celebrating the dappled sunlight through the trees, and calling attention to the rich seasonal color of the regional landscape.

Looking down the main path of the Causeway flower garden, past the fountain to the Italianate statue at the other end, ca. 1917. The flower beds are edged in boxwood, a hallmark of Shipman's style. The severe geometry would be relaxed in her later gardens, edges softened by overflowing flowers and plant materials. Photograph by Frances Benjamin Johnston. (Ellen McGowan Biddle Shipman Papers, #1259, Division of Rare and Manuscript Collections, Cornell University Library)

While Robinson was likely one influence on this garden, another, more immediate precedent might well have been the Billings estate in Woodstock, Vermont. The Billings family had been friends with Platt since the early 1890s, visiting him in Cornish and hiring him to help with the design of a series of Italianate terraced gardens at their estate, begun in 1894. The Billings family commissioned a number of landscape architects after Platt, including Martha Brookes Brown Hutcheson, who most likely laid out the entrance drive and shrubbery beds by the house, and Shipman, who redesigned planting beds in the Platt gardens in 1912–13. The Billings family also commissioned Shipman for a variety of local gardening projects, including improvements to the grounds of the Congregational Church (1913) and to the Woodstock train station, as well as a triangular park in front of the Elm Street Bridge.

The Woodstock estate also included a series of woodland gardens, developed largely by Elizabeth Billings beginning in the 1890s, adjacent to the formal landscape. These woodland gardens included a fernery with cascading pools, meandering paths, a woods drive with rustic stone walls, a stone bench, and a lily pond. Billings created these gardens in an area of mature trees and dappled sunlight, adding flowering shrubs and native and exotic plants and carefully thinning the existing plants. When Shipman visited the Billings family, first in 1911 and then repeatedly over the next few years, she was very likely treated to a walk through the fernery and the lily-pond gardens. Her design for the woodland garden at the Causeway appears similar, with existing trees and shrubs carefully thinned, the addition of native and exotic flowering plants, and the pond and stream as primary focal points. The stonework surrounding the pond may have even been similar to that along the Billings lily pond and woods drive.[27]

The gardens at Gwinn, near Cleveland, Ohio, offered yet another contemporary example of a landscape merging a range of garden types, from wild to more formal. There Platt and Warren Manning, beginning in 1906, had collaborated on an extensive estate for William Gwinn Mather, along the shores of Lake Erie. Platt designed the Georgian mansion, surrounded by formal Italianate gardens with an extensive view of the lakeshore. In 1912 Manning established a twenty-acre wild garden, offering a potent contrast to Platt's formal landscape and mansion. The two design approaches constituted parts of a dynamic and vibrant whole. Shipman had visited the estate in 1914, when she was asked to provide planting plans for the flower garden.

Shipman's wild garden for the Causeway revealed the development of her design sense as she honed her skills and became more familiar with the site. Her initial planting plan shows a conceptual design based on only limited site knowledge, without taking into account existing topography, vegetation, or trees. The final plan, however, dated "Christmas

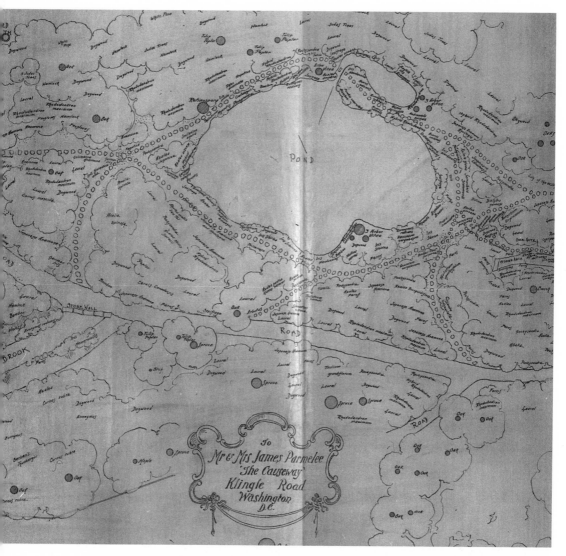

Portion of Christmas 1915 plan for the Causeway woodland garden, designed by Shipman. Note the how the existing topography and waterway are used to create a naturalistic woodland of native and naturalized plants. The path follows the course of the stream, with pockets of sun and water offering variety and interest. (Ellen McGowan Biddle Shipman Papers, #1259, Division of Rare and Manuscript Collections, Cornell University Library)

1915," incorporates the cow pasture, large existing trees, the stream, and the bridle path, the design carefully woven into the landscape.

Having entered the wild garden from the spacious lawn, the visitor would have been embraced by a high canopy of trees, with an understory of flowering shrubs, mingling with perennials, providing seasonal color and texture. Native and exotic plants were highlighted, including ferns, rhododendrons, and water iris, as well as an abundance of spring-flowering plants. Flowering trees provided further color and seasonal interest. A stone bench was placed in view of the pond, under dappled sunlight. The pond itself, surrounded by stones stepped along the bank, featured aquatic plants placed in small groups threading in and out of the water's edge. The atmosphere was of a natural or wild pond and garden, one that celebrated the existing topography and vegetation, improving on nature to create a beautiful place to enjoy sitting on the bench, walking, or horseback riding.

Platt's plan for the landscape centered on using the existing bridle path as a spine, bringing together the various parts of the landscape. Shipman designed the planting plans and gardens along this route, creating a series of garden spaces and experiences. The bridle-path circuit began in the wild garden, continued under the arch of the causeway, and ran along the edge of the stream, with small bridges making access easy,

The Causeway woodland garden with bench and pond, ca. 1917. A woman, likely Mrs. Parmelee, is walking under the dappled sunlight, enjoying the water garden. In contrast to the flower garden, this garden featured an "informal" or "naturalistic" plan, as if one had merely placed the bench in the midst of an existing woodland. The seasonal colors would have been remarkable, especially in the spring and fall, when clients were most likely to be at the estate. Photograph by Frances Benjamin Johnston. (Ellen McGowan Biddle Shipman Papers, #1259, Division of Rare and Manuscript Collections, Cornell University Library)

even on horseback. The path, with its stone walls and bridges, winding around the hill and among Shipman's mixed gardens of trees, shrubs, and perennials, framed a unique experience of the local and the regional landscape. It was edged with rhododendrons, mountain laurel, holly, and other shrubs, with rustic stone overlooks placed at strategic viewpoints to provide interest and variety along the way. The interplay of formal and informal elements, artistic and naturalistic settings, created a dynamic character. The experience of riding or walking along the bridle path encouraged a sense of being "out in the country" while remaining visually linked to the nation's capital.

The path continued downstream, along the contours of the land, exiting in a clearing facing Macomb Street. Shipman provided a planting plan for this area in 1927, shortly after the Parmelees purchased the land. Similar to that for the woodland garden, this plan enhanced the setting of existing mature hardwood trees, emphasizing a palette of medium-sized flowering trees, shrubs, and ground cover in a naturalistic composition.

The bridle-path landscape harkened to earlier pleasure routes, such as Thomas Jefferson's circuits at Monticello. However, this path's careful plantings marked it as a much more designed experience than most. This was a constructed landscape inviting the visitor to be actively engaged with the site and the setting: there was no single vantage point from which all views could be enjoyed. The Causeway, with its beautiful landscape of diverse gardens, in many ways exemplifies the nature of the partnership between Platt and Shipman.

While working on plans for the Causeway, Shipman also designed a series of garden and landscape spaces for other clients. In 1924 she was commissioned to design a Colonial Revival garden, Chatham Manor, in Fredericksburg, Virginia, the home of Mr. and Mrs. Daniel B. Devore. Photographed by a number of photographers, including Frances Benjamin Johnston, this garden represented Shipman at the height of her design skills.

Like the Causeway project, Chatham presented a complex challenge. Privacy and intimacy were tantamount for a good garden, in Shipman's opinion: the garden space should enclose a visitor and shelter him or her from the surrounding world. Yet many of her gardens had to serve multiple roles, as thresholds to the larger estate, or simply destinations for entertainment and relaxation. Shipman addressed this challenge by creating overlapping spaces through which the visitor might move, entering the house, wandering, or seeking shelter from the larger world.

Chatham's residence was a 1721 brick Georgian house important for both its early American and its Civil War history, and its gardens were to serve as a revival of a golden age and as a site for entertaining. These gardens also acted as a threshold to the residence, positioned between the entrance drive and the manor. Shipman's landscape design thus featured

The Bridle Path, ca. 1917. The Parmelees could ride horses or walk along the path, which began in the woodland garden following the edge of the hill to the opposite end of the estate. The path predated the Shipman/Platt design, having originally circumnavigated the entire hill. Shipman and Platt used the path to bring together the parts of this larger landscape, like gems on a necklace. Photograph by Frances Benjamin Johnston. (Ellen McGowan Biddle Shipman papers, #1259, Division of Rare and Manuscript Collections, Cornell University Library)

Chatham Garden in Fredericksburg, Virginia, designed by Shipman, ca. 1927. The refined placement of the trees, pots, and path reflects the increased elegance and grace of Shipman's design work. The use of pots and sculptures became a hallmark of Shipman's work. Photograph by Frances Benjamin Johnston. (Ellen McGowan Biddle Shipman Papers, #1259, Division of Rare and Manuscript Collections, Cornell University Library)

a traditional geometric layout, its central path on an axis with the house. Double rows of trees created an allée shading the path to the house itself and carrying the visitor's view beyond the house toward the river on the opposite side. This perspective was critical, as Shipman viewed the house and garden as integral parts of one whole design: neither should be considered dispensable or autonomous.

Chatham's garden court was enclosed by vine-covered walls and hedges and carefully divided into four primary rectangles on either side of the central path and allée, which were not identically sized or shaped. These four garden areas featured distinct characters and served different purposes. A wooden arbor provided a shaded and enclosed area for small intimate groups within the larger garden. Covered in vines, this was a cottagelike retreat. A gazebo and a larger gathering area, on the other side, described a more formal architectonic character. A small court area surrounded by boxwood on four sides provided a space more conducive to small talk and afternoon cocktails, while birdcages and a colonnade created a very different, perhaps more exotic, space on the garden's op-

Chatham house and garden as viewed from the main path from the entrance court. Photograph by Frances Benjamin Johnston. (Ellen McGowan Biddle Shipman Papers, #1259, Division of Rare and Manuscript Collections, Cornell University Library)

posite side. The gardens at Chatham were threshold spaces between the landscape and the architecture, as well as a series of distinct outdoor rooms to be enjoyed in their own right. They were designed with all the aesthetic senses in mind, allowing the visitor's experience of the garden to be holistic and entirely engaged.

This was not an old-fashioned Colonial Revival garden, but a new version embracing older traditions. Thus, while it made no pretense of being a colonial garden, it did draw on colonial interpretations, merging these with elements drawn from the English cottage garden and Italian villa styles. Architectural elements were much more prevalent here than in Shipman's smaller gardens. White columns and brick pillars created allées. (See color plate 3.) Pergolas were made by laying wood beams across these pillars and columns, while statues placed in niches and adorning the corners of a fountain gave the space elegance and style.

Shipman's planting plan featured flowers set in drifts of varying forms, scales, and habits of growth. The flowers themselves were planted so that no soil was exposed, and seasonal display was elegantly orchestrated, using both bloom and foliage. In the corners boxwoods were carefully trimmed, with flowers spilling around them. Strong foliage was placed among the flowers to create contrast and harmony. Irises lent vertical emphasis and grounded the flower beds, while baby's breath added volume and a sense of weightlessness. Climbing roses and clematis wove together the garden's architectural elements and nature. This balance, between a simple plan and an abundance of colorful and textural plant materials, gave the garden its "cottage" character. While this garden was in many ways reminiscent of Shipman's designs for Causeway, here she expanded her repertoire with a larger selection of plants and less formality and symmetry. The textures, color combinations, and seasonal variety seemed more complex at Chatham than at Causeway.

The Causeway and Chatham gardens were meant to be enjoyed by gardeners. Shipman's intimate horticultural knowledge allowed her to create diverse gardens that were rich in detail. She understood the growth habits of the plants she used and planned accordingly, sustaining her design throughout the growing season. She also knew how to carefully place architectural and water features to articulate axis and vistas. She used an artist's eye to create her compositions, as a painter uses paints. Shipman described her legacy for the *New York Times:* "Before women took hold of the profession, landscape architects were doing cemetery work. . . . Until women took up landscaping, gardening in this country was at its lowest ebb. The renaissance of the art was due largely to the fact that women, instead of working over their boards, used plants as if they were painting pictures. Today women are at the top of the profession."[28]

These gardens reveal the refinement of Shipman's garden praxis. As Shipman became more comfortable with a variety of scales and topographies, her designs reflected more complexity, while retaining certain key characteristics threaded throughout: a rich horticultural palette, an emphasis on garden rooms, and a balance between the architectonic nature of a design and the naturalistic character of plant growth. Shipman's designs reflect a period of history when landscape art was highly valued and horticultural vistas much appreciated. However, perhaps even more important was the network of young designers whom Shipman mentored, guided, and advised, just as Platt had tutored her.

From Craft to Art, from Coast to Coast

Shipman created a significant legacy by encouraging women to pursue practices across the country. Employees such as Eleanor Louise Roche and Edith Schryver went on to establish their own offices, as did others. However, an even more significant legacy was the increasing legitimacy given to garden and landscape design in the 1920s and 1930s—a legitimacy Shipman helped foster, built upon the work of her community of designers as well as many others. Shipman's influence was evident from coast to coast, in the work of Eleanor Louise Roche in New England and the Midwest and Lord & Schryver in Oregon.

Eleanor Louise Roche (1892–1975) was born into a family with long-standing gardening interests. Roche studied at the Lowthorpe School, graduating in 1917, and worked in Shipman's office. In 1926 she opened her own practice at 15 East Fortieth Street, sharing it with Mabel Parsons, a landscape architect and the daughter of Samuel Parsons, a fellow of the ASLA. Like Shipman, Roche specialized in residential work, particularly gardens for small and moderate-sized homes. She likely worked in the 1920s for the New York City Parks Department, which also employed Parsons. She became a member of the ASLA in 1926, and her work was later included in the ASLA's national and New York chapter yearbooks. Taking her professional membership very seriously, Roche served in a variety of roles within the ASLA, including as secretary and treasurer for the Detroit chapter. Acknowledging Shipman's leading role in the profession, in 1933 Roche and Ellen Payson organized a tour of Shipman's gardens for Lowthorpe students and alumni.

Roche moved her office to 295 Madison Avenue in 1931, still sharing the practice with Parsons. By 1934, Roche had moved her practice again, to 424 Madison Avenue, and within a year had moved to Grosse Pointe, Michigan, where a majority of her work was completed. Roche was also a frequent contributor to popular magazines and professional journals, including *Landscape Architecture Magazine*.

Roche's designed gardens brought together a formal and geometrical layout with an abundance of plant materials, much in the style of Shipman. Roche's gardens for Mrs. Peats, as illustrated in the 1931 ASLA *Illustrations of Work of Members,* featured flower beds, stairs, and statues, similar to what we might imagine Shipman would have designed. The

1932 ASLA illustrations of her work feature similar concepts. Roche also designed a courtyard garden for St. Luke's Hospital in New York City, the court paved and surrounded with densely planted flower borders and raised beds. A lattice covered in vines formed one side of the garden, and a small table with chairs and a stone bench was provided for visitors to relax as they enjoyed a green, cool respite from the gray, hot city.

Roche, like many of her colleagues, was also involved in civic improvement efforts. With Helen Swift Jones, Nellie B. Allen, and H. Stuart Orloff, Roche helped to organize a garden tour to benefit a school, the team offering to serve as professional consultants to tour participants. In all her endeavors Roche clearly drew on the expanding network of women in landscape architecture to both establish her own practice and promote the profession.

Another of Shipman's employees, Edith Schryver, also went on to form a long-standing practice, this one in Oregon. One of the first firms of professional women landscape architects on the West Coast, the office of Elizabeth Lord (1887–1976) and Edith Schryver (1901–1984) was active in and around Salem, Oregon, for over forty years.[29] Edith Schryver, who had grown up in New York's Hudson River Valley, had always had an

Garden in New York City for St. Luke's Home for Aged Women, by Eleanor Roche. Submitted for the ASLA *Illustrations of Work of Members*, 1933.

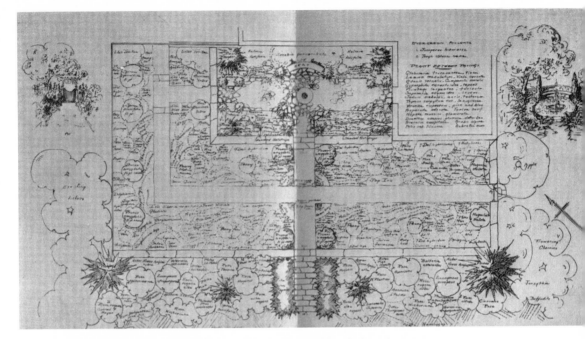

Portion of plan of Seaside garden, by Edith Schryver, created when she was a student at Lowthorpe School and included in the school's 1925–26 catalog. (Courtesy of Rhode Island School of Design Archives)

Opposite page
Plan of the garden for H. V. Greenough, Brookline, Massachusetts, drawn by Edith Schryver when she worked in Shipman's office, ca. 1926. (Ellen McGowan Biddle Shipman Papers, #1259, Division of Rare and Manuscript Collections, Cornell University Library)

interest in landscape design. She attended Lowthorpe School in the summers during high school and then enrolled at Brooklyn's Pratt Institute to study art. She eventually enrolled full-time at Lowthorpe, financing her schooling by working in the landscape architecture offices of Harold Hill Blossom, Elizabeth Pattee, and Elizabeth Leonard Strang (each of whom periodically lectured at Lowthorpe).

Schryver spent the summer of 1922 working for Shipman as part of her scholarship, remaining in the office until 1927, when she traveled to Europe. In the Shipman office Schryver received further training not only as a designer but also in the business of running an office. She corresponded with clients and nurserymen in addition to providing drawings and plans for Shipman's growing practice. Schryver's work drew on the design styles of Shipman and Platt, incorporating the Italian villa and English cottage garden influences that would remain evident throughout her career.

Elizabeth Lord, Schryver's partner, had been born in Salem, Oregon, her mother an avid gardener and garden-club leader. She traveled to Europe and Asia after her mother died, and upon her return, at the age of thirty-nine, she enrolled at Lowthorpe, where she likely met Shipman. She was finishing her studies when she took advantage of a second European tour in 1927.

Schryver and Lord met on this 1927 European trip, sponsored by the Lowthorpe and Cambridge schools, the only such summer program that was cosponsored, their "similar tastes and a fondness [for] gardening [bringing them] together."[30] They spent four months traveling, Lord likely revisiting sites while Schryver was seeing everything for the first time. After returning in 1928, Schryver and Lord opened their joint practice in Salem, putting in place the skills and business practices they had learned at Lowthorpe and in the Shipman office to build their own successful practice.

Lord & Schryver were known equally as plantswomen and as strong designers. They sought charm and elegance in their gardens, their design style generally formal, with garden rooms extending houses' living spaces. One important design principle for their work was the proper placement of a house and a responding division of garden rooms. In this way house, garden, and landscape were experienced as a whole, much as in Shipman's designs. Axes created by formal lines were given depth and softened by an abundance of informal plantings, merging the formality of Italian design with the abundance of the cottage garden style. These axes were accentuated with sculpture, specimen plants, and fountains or other water features. Lord and Schryver sought to create an informal formality, what one might term an Italian cottage garden. Schryver adhered to her own dictum that "order is beauty and beauty is order," with the caveat that "too much neatness without any careless grace will not produce charm."[31]

Privacy and intimacy were also integral to their garden designs, for like Shipman and their contemporaries, Lord & Schryver viewed the garden and home as a respite from the chaos of the larger community and world. An example of their style was established at their home, Gaiety Hollow, in Salem. A gardener's garden, Gaiety Hollow featured a Colonial Revival house and garden, designed as a pair. As the historian Liz Deck notes, this garden exhibited each of the design principles the partners had developed, serving as a model for their practice.

Lord & Schryver were also actively engaged in their community, participating in a range of organizations, including the Salem Park Commission, the Tree Commission, the Art Association, the Oregon Roadside Council, and the Capital Commission. Lord was a member of the Salem Garden Club and chair of the Willamette Valley Division of the State Federation of Garden Clubs. Schryver was a member of the Camellia Society for more than thirty years and taught briefly at the Oregon State

Agricultural College. Both women wrote articles for Portland's *Oregonian* and in 1938 participated in an imaginative radio series on Salem's KOAC *Home Garden Hour*. Over the course of their career, Lord & Schryver produced over 250 designs, primarily in the Northwest.

However, while their partnership enjoyed an extensive reputation in the Northwest, Lord & Schryver were rarely acknowledged at a national level, as Shipman was. This may be in part due to their isolation on the West Coast or to their apparent disinterest in establishing the larger social networks that Shipman worked so hard to maintain. Neither Lord nor Schryver joined the ASLA, nor did either appear in professional exhibits of landscape architects. Nevertheless, their practice carried on Shipman's legacy in their design aesthetic, their focus on smaller gardens, and their commitment to the practice of landscape architecture as a profession.

The West Coast was also home to other women in landscape architecture, influenced by the work of Farrand, Shipman, and Platt, yet establishing their own milieu, including Florence Yoch, Lucille Council, and Katherine Bashford. In Southern California in particular, the garden's potential to express cultural aspirations and the landscape's "natural bounty" was at the heart of regional landscape architecture. Paradise, many believed, was the California garden. Florence Yoch (1890–1972) and Lucille Council (1898–1964) are one of the better-known early landscape architecture firms in Los Angeles. Yoch had studied at the University of California, Berkeley; transferred briefly to Cornell University; and then received her bachelor's degree in landscape gardening at the University of Illinois, Champaign-Urbana, in 1915. After graduation she returned to Pasadena and began designing gardens. In 1921 she hired Lucille Council as an apprentice in her growing practice. Council had graduated from the Cambridge School and then returned to Pasadena, where her parents lived. After Council worked with Yoch for four years, the two women formed a partnership in 1925 and opened an office in Council's home in South Pasadena. Their partnership produced over 250 projects, primarily in the Pasadena, Santa Barbara, and Los Angeles areas, including a number in collaboration with such established Southern California architects as Myron Hunt and Roland Coate.[32]

Yoch & Council were commissioned for a range of projects, from a botanical garden to commercial landscapes to residential estates to movie sets. Their work was admired and well-publicized in magazines such as *California Art and Architecture* and Winifred Dobyns's *California Gardens*.[33] Their partnership won them an AIA award in 1930. However, their most famous work was done for movie sets, including their well-known designs for David O. Selznick's Tara, in *Gone with the Wind*. In 1932 they designed a project for one of the only women movie directors, Dorothy Arzner, and they also designed private estates for David O. Selznick, Jack Warner, and others in the Hollywood entertainment business. Yoch was the first woman to publish in *Landscape Architecture Magazine* in an article about her roof garden: "The Court Garden of the Woman's Athletic Club, Los Angeles."

Yoch & Council's designs shaped a regional approach embracing the Mediterranean landscape and climate's incredible potential to support the "California dream." This dream envisioned California as a place of bounty, a modern Eden, with a culture that might rival that of the Mediterranean. Yoch and Council's frequent trips to Europe and their extensive library of garden books formed the basis of their style. (See color plate 4.) They combined their knowledge with a deep interest in plants and in the potential of the regional landscape. While their gardens featured an expansive palette of plant materials, a gardener's delight, they did not create the intimate gardens of Shipman. Their gardens provided more dramatic settings, probably more appropriate to their entertainment-industry clients. Yoch & Council drew on Neoclassical styles, popular in California by the 1920s, layering a lush plant palette over a stricter geometry of spaces and highlighting architectural features as spatial definers.

Their practice was typical of many partnerships in its delineation of duties and responsibilities. Yoch was considered the primary designer, while Council managed the office, ordered plants, dealt with contractors, and often supervised design installation. By the late 1930s they had a staff of five or six people, with a large crew of outside workers. As with California firms, Yoch & Council retained a crew who could be hired to construct the landscapes it designed, a break with the professional standards advocated by the ASLA. While their work significantly shaped both the contemporary landscape and the impression many had of the life of the rich and famous in Los Angeles, with time their rich plant palettes, and the extensive maintenance and water required to support them, caused their projects to disappear.

Another member of the West Coast community was Katherine Bashford (1885–1953), who had studied at the Otis Art Institute and traveled in Europe in both 1920 and 1930. She worked for Yoch & Council for a period, and in 1923 she opened her own office, at the Architects Building in Los Angeles. She hired Fred Barlow Jr. to be her assistant and later made him a partner. Bashford designed estates and gardens and was involved with Barlow in the design of housing projects for the U.S. Housing Association in Southern California (Harbor Hills, Ramona Gardens, Rancho San Pedro, and Aliso Gardens). Since Bashford was a member of the ASLA (elected in 1930), images of her work were included in the 1930s editions of the ASLA *Illustrations of Work of Members,* as were those of Paul Thiene, one of the only other area practitioners who belonged to the ASLA. Bashford was also included, along with A. E. Hanson, Paul Thiene, and Yoch & Council, in Dobyn's *California Gardens.* These practitioners' gardens illustrated a loose regional style based on the landscape,

Garden by Katherine Bashford included in the ASLA *Illustrations of Work of Members*, 1932.

vegetation, climate, and, most important, social aspirations of Southern California and the entertainment world.

From Flower Gardens to Landscape Architecture

Warren Manning described Ellen Biddle Shipman as "one of the best, if not the very best, Flower Garden Maker in America."[34] *House and Garden,* somewhat differently, deemed her the "dean of American women landscape architects."[35] These descriptions might appear to describe two distinct practices. On the one hand, Manning appreciated Shipman for her ability to paint pictures with flowers and create beautiful gardens. For many this would be considered more closely related to gardening as a craft rather than landscape architecture as a profession. On the other hand, declaring Shipman the dean of women landscape architects emphasized the fact that she was a successful and professional practitioner. Nevertheless, Manning appreciated the natural landscape, and his compliment was genuine and flattering, while Richard Wright, the editor of *House and Garden,* clearly understood Shipman's role as a mentor, leader, and a consummate professional. For Shipman, then, both these descriptions were apt and appropriate. She was indeed a painter of beautiful garden landscapes and a leader in the field, especially for young women. This combination was her hallmark, positioning her work as the link between that of gardeners and horticulturalists, such as Sessions, and that of artists, such as Yoch & Council.

It is also critical to acknowledge the larger role of flower gardens in the profession. From 1931 to 1934 the ASLA's annual *Illustrations* featured one or two photographs of sites designed by a variety of member landscape architects. Flower gardens were the subject of the majority of these images, whether set in formal landscapes, such as those designed by Bryant Fleming, or in more natural settings, such as those designed by O. C. Simonds, James West, and Earl Blair. The work of many women was featured in these collections, including flower gardens by Mabel Keyes Babcock, Mary P. Cunningham, Rose Greely, Louise Payson, and Isabelle Pendleton. These flower gardens were considered representations of the profession's work, and it is noteworthy that so much of this, at least in the 1930s, focused on the design of gardens.

At the same time that gardens were in the mainstream of the practice, women struggled to be acknowledged as artists, as more than designers of flower gardens. They, like all in the emerging profession, wished to be considered legitimate artists and designers. An important route to legitimacy was a commission to design a public landscape or a very large estate, as Farrand did at Princeton and Dumbarton Oaks. For some, such as Yoch & Council, their work could be legitimized by being placed in the context of European landscapes, art forms that were clearly acknowledged. The publication of articles, photographic essays, and books on design was yet another route, as followed by Shipman and Roche. However, education and formal training became the most important means to legitimacy, for the profession as a whole and for women in particular.

4

The New Woman and a New Education

The earliest practitioners of landscape architecture, such as H. W. S Cleveland, Warren Manning, Annette McCrea, Beatrix Jones Farrand, and Ellen Biddle Shipman, were self-trained. For this reason they brought a variety of backgrounds and experience to their practices. Olmsted Sr. and Cleveland were writers, naturalists, and farmers; McCrea and Manning had been trained in a nursery; Farrand and Platt had focused on the fine arts and taken the European grand tour. By the end of the twentieth century, however, career paths were becoming more defined. While the founding members of the ASLA were trained or educated as engineers, architects, gardeners, and nurserymen, this was the last generation to reflect such diversity of preparation. From the first courses in landscape gardening offered in the 1870s to the accredited programs established by the 1950s, the focus was increasingly on setting standards to judge educational programs and evaluate graduates as potential professional practitioners. This was an essential step in the process of establishing the profession.

Educating Practitioners

Landscape architecture was a viable option for women, but it was not initially clear how they might gain the necessary training and education, especially in the increasingly standardized professional community. By 1900 three paths were by and large recognized for women wishing to pursue landscape architecture as a career. The first was training in the fine arts, the second was informal education through correspondence and extension programs in horticulture or landscape design, and the third and most formal was university education. By 1942 only the latter was recognized as legitimate preparation.

Art was one of the earliest foci of formal education open to women. The National Academy of Design accepted women as members from its inception, in 1825, when the leading artists Samuel F. B. Morse, Asher B. Durand, and Thomas Cole founded it to promote the fine arts through public exhibits and educational courses. Women were invited to show their work in the academy's annual exhibitions alongside that of their male colleagues. By 1831 enrollment in the academy's School of Fine Arts was open to women, and by 1847 they offered a life-drawing class for women.

In 1844 the first separate women's art school, the Philadelphia School of Design for Women, was founded by Sarah Worthington King Peter, who wished to "train professionals who could maintain their status as respectable women but gain enough skills to earn their living independently of men and the vagaries of the market."[1] Peter later went on to help establish a women's art school in Cincinnati. A decade later New York City's Cooper Institute of Design for Women was established. Other schools that accepted women were New York's Arts Students League (est. 1875) and the Art Institute of Chicago (est. 1879). The Ladies' Art Association became the first club to gather women artists together as a professional network, in 1866.

The New York School of Applied Design for Women, founded in 1892 by Ellen Dunlap Hopkins and incorporated as a charter member of the American Federation of the Arts, was notable for the number of successful women it graduated. Its curriculum offered instruction in textile design, interior architecture, fashion illustration, commercial art and posters, and historic ornament. A 1925 catalog claimed that the school had trained over ten thousand women to pursue careers in the design of textiles, posters, furniture, and fashion, as well as architecture, interior decoration, and other branches of the decorative arts. Certificates were awarded after two years by each department, with the exception of the architecture program, which required three years.

Although the New York School of Applied Design for Women did not offer a program in landscape design, the training it provided could be translated into the art of landscape design if a student also had knowledge of gardening and horticulture. Martha Brookes Brown Hutcheson enrolled in the school to study mechanical drawing, the history of ornament, and the design of book covers and fabrics. After developing the skills to design patterns for wallpapers, chintzes, and drawings, she successfully applied this training to her professional work as a landscape architect. The link between the school and landscape design is also reflected in the institution's community of patrons that included members of New York City's elite, many of whom commissioned important works by landscape architects. Mrs. Robert Woods Bliss, Otto H. Kahn, the Rockefeller Foundation, the Carnegie Corporation, Mrs. Russell Sage, and Mrs. Willard Straight all donated funds to the school, sponsored scholarships, or served on its board. Such art school communities provided a critical training ground for women who could bring gardening experience to their art.

But while art school was one option, not everyone could afford tuition or wished to concentrate on the fine arts. Correspondence courses, extension programs, and informal apprenticeships offered an alternative, providing training in horticulture, landscape design, agriculture, forestry, and botany.

Correspondence Classes and Extension Courses

Correspondence classes and extension courses were increasingly popular ways to gain the skills, knowledge, and recognition needed to launch a professional career. By opening their doors to less wealthy families, such courses allowed middle-class individuals to enter the professions, with women in particular constituting a new and growing clientele.

Correspondence courses were advertised in popular magazines such as *Garden Magazine, Horticulture Magazine,* and *Country Life in America,* the advertisements promoted both the new profession and the training programs. The American Landscape School, in Newark (est. 1916), declared that landscape architecture was a "dignified, exclusive, profession not overrun with competitors . . . [that is] easy to master under our correspondence methods," noted that a "diploma [would be] awarded" to successful candidates, and stressed that this was "a profession for men and women."[2] Some of its courses focused on the design of home grounds, while others taught students how to design golf courses, cemeteries, and small parks. As many middle-class men and women were seeking careers that were financially advantageous as well as socially acceptable, landscape design appeared a promising choice. Correspondence courses opened this path to those with minimal resources.

Lois Page Cottrell, who enrolled in correspondence courses at the American School of Landscape Architecture, later dropped out of the program in part, she said, because she had learned what she needed and because she "didn't want to do golf courses and cemeteries!"[3] Instead, she partnered with her sister, Helen Page Wodell, to create the firm of Wodell & Cottrell, based in Short Hills, New Jersey, designing gardens for middle- and upper-middle-class families, as well as a small botanical garden and neighborhood parks. Another practitioner, Agnes Place Lillington, completed a correspondence course offered by the National Landscape Institute in California: "Ornamental Horticulture and Landscape Gardening." This course was one of the more expensive offered, at one hundred dollars for fifty lessons. With little other professional training, Lillington went on to open a small, locally based practice.

College graduates also took advantage of such courses to enhance their skills or to study subjects not offered within the university curriculum.

Helen Bullard, after completing a degree in landscape architecture at Cornell University, took a correspondence course in salesmanship. Walter Holsbach, a Milwaukee-area landscape architect, supplemented his agriculture degree from the University of Wisconsin with short courses offered through the University of Illinois. Eunice S. Fenelon, who had received her bachelor's of science degree from the Department of Landscape Architecture at the University of Illinois, enrolled in a correspondence course in 1924 while exploring practice options on the East Coast. The course she chose served as an introduction both to New England plant materials and to the region's community of designers. Fenelon later left the East Coast to work for the firm of Alexander & Strong, in Cleveland.

Land-grant colleges also offered extension courses, taught by practicing landscape architects and faculty members in design and horticulture. Such courses provided a link to an established university without the admission requirements or financial commitments. Initially, extension programs were intended to be a source of education for the public, rather than a form of preprofessional training. In one case, Liberty Hyde Bailey, a professor of horticulture and rural art and author of the *Encyclopedia of Horticulture,* created a Cornell University extension program in order to raise community landscape standards. Bailey believed that "professionalism is essentially aristocratic; extension work is essentially democratic." He understood that many might use extension training to gain employment as gardeners and even garden designers, but not, he hoped, as members of the elite professional ranks. His aim was a program far more pragmatic and democratic than what he saw in the emerging professions. Nevertheless, extension programs became a legitimate and important means of training for aspiring landscape designers and landscape architects.

Indeed, many young women and men took advantage of correspondence courses and extension programs, which offered access to some of the best faculty members in the discipline. The Arnold Arboretum, for example, sponsored courses led by Harvard faculty, including Stephen F. Hamblin, who taught "Trees and Shrubs" in 1927. Elizabeth Leonard Strang, a Cornell graduate and professional landscape architect, led correspondence courses in landscape design for the Massachusetts State Department of University Extension. "The Landscape Garden Series," a popular ten-pamphlet course written by Philip Elwood Jr., a practicing landscape architect, a university professor at Ohio State University, and the author of the 1924 book *American Landscape Architecture,* focused on the planning, planting, maintenance, and design of home grounds, with additional information on country places and "the Home and the City." These courses offered students professional legitimacy, as they were taught by practicing architects, as well as a potential professional network.

Along with the white women and men who pursued such training and education, African American men and women also took advantage of extension programs. Booker T. Washington, for example, inspired the establishment of the Negro Cooperative Extension Service through his work at Tuskegee Institute. While it focused primarily on farming methods, agents expanded its program to include home-demonstration work. Over one year at least one hundred women of color served as home demonstration agents in the South, training local women in improving their homes and yards. In 1920 they helped complete over seventeen thousand demonstrations in the beautification of lawns and flower gardens. These agents, along with volunteers, sought to support less fortunate African Americans by modeling home improvements, particularly those visible to the public and thus open to judgment. One agent claimed that "practically every home has put forth some effort to have flowers around the place and much beauty has been added in the country-side by these patches of color."[4] These women worked closely with one another on the design and layout of gardens, as well as their care and cultivation; together, they believed, they could "uplift" the community.

In the early years of the profession, the lines separating amateurs, volunteers, agents, and landscape architects were porous and malleable. Informal training was available through correspondence programs, extension services, and the more traditional in-house training offered by nurseries or local gardens. For women, in particular, these less formal, more flexible, and less expensive training options were critical to professional success.

Despite their popularity, however, the ASLA did not support correspondence or extension courses as legitimate paths to practice, instead promoting them merely as a means to a more educated client base. Warren Manning was particularly concerned that instead of educating the public, such courses were being used to launch professional practices—which, indeed, they were.[5] The problem stemmed from the programs' lack of standards and, Manning claimed, from the fact that too great a range of knowledge was being covered, with little being done to maintain the discipline's status as a profession rather than a craft. This was in contrast to efforts in the field of architecture, in which home-study courses included an extensive series in the professional journal *The American Architect and Building News*. While landscape architects never condoned such a series in their professional journal, *Landscape Architecture Magazine,* the institutions offering the courses had no reason to close them, and they remained a popular, accessible resource.

The ASLA's disapproval nevertheless ostracized many who pursued such alternatives. Women without a college or university education or degree increasingly used titles such as "landscape designer," "landscape consultant," or "garden designer" to describe their practice, rather than "landscape architect." Helen Wodell and Lois Cottrell always signed documents as "garden consultants," as they believed they lacked "the experience, the training, or the college education" to be called landscape architects.[6] Despite the fact that she had received a European education, Louise S. Hubbard, an early Chicago practitioner, used the title "landscape designer," reflecting her lack of any specific training in landscape design. These women acquiesced to the professional community's growing conviction that only a college or university degree earned one the privilege to use the title "landscape architect." At the same time they were careful to avoid the designations "landscapers" and "gardeners," as these referred to manual laborers such as groundskeepers and caretakers, positions that were considered to be at the lowest levels of the hierarchy.

A Professional Education

While alternatives continued to be available, formal education remained core to efforts to professionalize landscape architecture. As early as 1897 an essay in the *Atlantic Monthly* suggested that with the appropriate formal education, the designer "ought not to commit any gross offenses against good taste in Landscape Art."[7] Formal education could provide a framework for standardizing good taste, establish a set of credentials, and serve as a filter to protect against those who might not share the community's values and visions.

Notwithstanding the concerns and obstacles, many women were willing to pursue the advantages of a college education even as the educational system was being transformed. By 1900 women made up more than a third of the college population, two-thirds attending coeducational institutions. At the same time colleges and universities were struggling to incorporate new fields of knowledge into the study of the liberal arts and sciences. By the turn of the century, new and traditional areas of study vied for a place in the curriculum. Engineering, calisthenics, and home economics were found in course catalogs next to classics, philosophy, and mathematics.[8] Each specialty struggled to be recognized as a legitimate subject in a liberal arts education, including landscape architecture, a discipline first aligned with agriculture and horticulture and later with the fine arts and architecture.

University education had become the standard for landscape architects by the 1920s. It was accepted that the proper course of training for a professional architect or landscape architect consisted of "a well-rounded four-year college course, followed by a three-year graduate course in a well-recognized professional school, to be followed by systematic travel and study in Europe and a period of apprenticeship in a good office."[9] For women there were two paths to a formal education: coeducational colleges (primarily the land-grant colleges) and private women's institutions. Coeducational colleges offered the earliest courses in landscape design and remain to this day at the core of professional education for landscape architects. Private women's colleges did not initially offer such programs, but three small institutions were established in the early part of the century to train women in landscape gardening, landscape architecture, and architecture. Together these programs educated thousands of women in the new discipline of landscape architecture, thereby launching generations of women in practice.

COEDUCATIONAL PROGRAMS. Land-grant colleges offered the first courses and programs in landscape gardening and design, and they were, by law, coeducational. The land-grant system, proposed by Senator Justin S. Morrill of Vermont and signed into law in 1862 by President Abraham Lincoln, provided funding for the establishment of state universities offering a curriculum in practical disciplines and, most important, required schools to admit women and minorities. The purpose was to establish colleges where faculty members taught courses in agriculture, the mechanical arts, and military tactics in order to promote the liberal and practical education of the middle class, who then might pursue careers and professions. The state universities of Indiana and Wisconsin were among the first to take advantage of the act and subsequently admitted women into their degree programs. Cornell University was founded in 1865, and state universities in California, Kansas, Indiana, Iowa, Michigan, Minnesota, and Missouri also accepted women, although some only from the home state. As these schools were coeducational, the first courses in landscape design were open to women and men, thereby framing a perspective distinct from that of any other emerging profession of the late nineteenth century.

Michigan Agricultural College offered the earliest recorded course in landscape gardening, in 1863—a half-year course required for all students at the college. The University of Illinois and Iowa State College were offering at least two courses in landscape gardening and design by 1871. Other early courses were offered at agriculture colleges including Kansas State University, Cornell University, Massachusetts Agricultural College, and Harvard's Bussey Institute. Women enrolled in all of these courses in small but significant numbers that increased dramatically in the early twentieth century. The University of Illinois announced that "ladies and gentlemen alike engage in the studies and exercises of the course."[10] The University of Wisconsin–Madison's School of Agriculture reported that approximately 33 percent of the graduating classes of landscape designers were women by the 1920s and 1930s.[11]

The Massachusetts Institute of Technology initiated a landscape architecture option in 1899 as a specialized route for architecture and engineering students, under the guidance of Guy Lowell. Lowell, now best known for his design of the Museum of Fine Arts in Boston, had been educated at Harvard College, graduated from MIT's Architecture Department in 1894, attended the École des Beaux-Arts, and spent a summer of study at the Arboretum at Kew, in England. His 1902 book, *American Gardens,* was one of the first to highlight designed landscapes in the United States at the end of the nineteenth century.

The MIT curriculum, like most late-nineteenth-century architecture programs, was based in the Beaux-Arts tradition. The landscape option built on this foundation, adding courses in horticulture, biology, topographical drawing, surveying, curves and earthworks, landscape design, and working drawings for landscape gardening. The program was intended to allow architects to specialize in landscape architecture, rather than to produce landscape architects, as the degree remained in architecture.

Lowell brought in Charles Sprague Sargent, the director of the Arnold Arboretum (and his father-in-law), and the horticulturist John G. Jack to teach classes. Together they drew extensively on the Arnold Arboretum as a primary resource for the horticulture courses. While the landscape option drew at least ten students in its first year, it had been terminated as an undergraduate program by 1904 and continued only as a graduate-level course until 1909, when all courses in landscape architecture were cancelled. In the meantime, however, a number of individuals gained a legitimate education in landscape architecture, including a small group of women who became leaders in the profession.

MIT had been coeducational since its founding, although the admittance of women was not always consistent. Ellen Swallow Richards, the first woman awarded a degree in chemistry, in 1873, became MIT's first woman instructor. By 1941 over 1,000 women had attended MIT, 307 of them awarded degrees (it was not uncommon for men and women in the early twentieth century to attend college without ever matriculating). The most popular courses of study for women were chemistry, biology, and architecture.[12]

The MIT architecture department was one of the only programs to grant women a professional degree, and its graduates often went on to excel in the field. Lois Lilley Howe (1888) established two architectural firms over the course of her career and was one of the first women fellows of the American Institute of Architects. Sophia (Hayden) Bennett (1890) won the design competition for the Women's Pavilion, built at the Columbian Exposition in 1893. Rose Standish Nichols designed gardens in and around Cornish, New Hampshire, and became a well-recognized writer on European gardens. Marian Cruger Coffin and Martha Brookes Hutchison established successful landscape architecture practices responsible for the design of small home gardens, large estates, college campuses, and public arboretums. Elizabeth Greenleaf Pattee, who completed an undergraduate degree in architecture in 1916, received a certificate in landscape architecture from the Lowthorpe School in 1918, later becoming director of Lowthorpe's program. Mabel Keyes Babcock, who received her graduate architecture degree in 1909, subsequently practiced as a designer, taught at Wellesley College, and served as the primary faculty for conservation courses at the Lowthorpe School. Babcock also designed areas of the MIT, Bates, and Wellesley campuses. Edna Stoddard worked for Hutcheson and then opened her own practice, focusing on small residential sites in the Mid-Atlantic region. Considering the obstacles facing women in the professional community, the MIT alumnae were a remarkable group.

In 1900 Harvard offered the first degree specifically in landscape architecture, under the leadership of Frederick Law Olmsted Jr. However, Harvard's program did not accept women. Kansas State offered the first land-grant landscape architecture degree in 1903; it was thus the first such degree open to women. It was followed by the University of Massachusetts (1903), Cornell University (1907), the University of Illinois (1907), Michigan State University (1907), the University of Michigan (1909), and Pennsylvania State University (1909). By 1921 seventeen professional programs and twenty-four nonprofessional programs were being offered by institutions across the nation.

The programs offered at land-grant colleges generally served two audiences: students of the profession and the general public. Essential "nontechnical" courses, Harvard's Professor James Sturgis Pray noted, "[spread] among those who are not going to practice the profession, familiarity with the principals for which it stands, and with the ways in which its service is of value; for such a course is a most direct and important means of increasing the profession's clientele and the number of appreciative votes on park, playground, and city-planning questions."[13] While the intent may have been to educate the public, however, the reality was that these programs also educated generations of women who would become professional practitioners.

While the curricula varied at the different colleges, all included core courses in the art of design and the science of horticulture. The standard education of a landscape architect included courses in "design, planting plans, engineering, horticulture, including knowledge of trees, shrubs and perennials, general knowledge of agriculture and insect pests, agronomy or chemistry of soils, architectural design and its proper application, construction covering road paths, grades, and drainage, a clear conception of business methods, and practical ability to apply the above knowledge."[14] In preparation, one writer suggested, women should take courses in charcoal perspective drawing, freehand sketching, mechanical drawing, mapping, and Latin, as well as business management. Landscape architecture, then, was considered both an art and a science, and the curricula reflected both areas of study. Elizabeth Pattee, then a faculty member at the Lowthorpe School of Landscape Architecture for Women, took a more concise view: "The training of a landscape architect should be composed of the artistic studies of architectural and landscape architectural design, drawing, perspective, etc., and the scientific studies of botany, horticulture, plant material, surveying, and construction."[15] Those teaching landscape architecture today continue to discuss the respective roles of art and science in the profession's pedagogy.

In response to the need for pedagogical and curricular standards, the first National Council on Instruction in Landscape Architecture (NCI-

LA) was founded in 1920, and one of its first orders of business was a re-view of coeducational programs.[16] Within a year the NCILA had adopted a series of resolutions, including one urging coeducational institutions to give equal encouragement to men and to women planning to pursue the profession of landscape architecture. In 1922 the NCILA Committee on Co-Education reported that coeducational programs were being of-fered at twelve institutions, and in 1924 *Landscape Architecture Magazine* reported thirty-eight programs, twelve offering a B.S. degree, one a B.A. degree, two a five-year course leading to a special degree, one a graduate degree only (Harvard), three certificates, and the rest one to four courses in landscape gardening.[17] Many of these programs were coeducational.

The report of the Committee on Co-education assured readers that "the existence of coeducation is in no way harmful. . . . Its effects appear beneficial." Women, the committee reported, "do not retard class pro-grams even when taking such strenuous field work as plan surveying." In fact, the presence of women might even increase the competitive nature of the studio classroom: "Being especially skillful in drafting their pres-ence in design classes makes for a high standard of plan presentation. . . . The possibility of having one of the young women win first place on a problem over the men, as sometimes happens, keeps the work of men and women up to a high standard." The report continued, "In consultation and criticism with other students, she receives something of the same experience that she is sure to undergo later when consulting with pro-fessional men and contractors." It was suggested that "by receiving her professional training in contact with men, a woman has the advantage of learning her place sooner than she otherwise would."[18] The question of the exact nature of that "place" was left open: was she to be subservient to men or an equal?

Women, according to the report, also served as social role models: "Their presence tends to curb the rough-house and horse-play spirit with-out destroying the social atmosphere." It was recommended that men and women work in the same drafting rooms and that the instructor "should imagine the sex line eliminated as far as possible." Instructors were advised not to discourage women and to give them equal opportu-nities for conferences and criticism.

The committee's report, despite its overall support for coeducation, nevertheless reflected cultural biases about the potential of women stu-dents. For example, it was suggested that while men and women should be given the same problems, women would benefit from extended op-portunities in modeling, drafting, and domestic design, as these were skills they were more "likely to use in office work later to a greater extent proportionally than men." In addition, the report suggested the study of stenography as useful. Such comments clearly hinted at a different role for women in the office, rather than as leader, designer, or even draftsperson. Still, the report concluded with a statement of support for both the education of women and the possibility of their success:

> Opposition to the training of women in landscape work has been offered by some on the ground that a woman may not use such training throughout her life in practice. The same might apply to men who take up the work. It is true that a woman's life is subject to more abrupt change than a man's life, but the fact in itself is an argument for herself to be self-supporting, as most normal minded women wish to be, even in the face of wealth. The fact that some women have made a name for themselves in landscape work is not proof that all women are likely to qualify as experts in the professional field even if they remain single, but they have a right to a chance at education in landscape work if they so elect at institutions conducted on coeducational lines. They must stand or fall on their merit, and because the test is even more severe for them than for men they are deserving of an added amount of credit if they succeed.[19]

Thus, there was institutional support for coeducational programs and for women to build a professional career. However, not all women wished to attend a coeducational institutions, many choosing instead to attend schools specifically for women.

SCHOOLS FOR WOMEN ONLY. Colleges for women were a significant mid-nineteenth-century response to the need for advanced education for women. Oberlin College, established in 1833, was the first coeducational college, while Georgia Female College, founded in 1839, was the first women's college. Private women's colleges such as the "Seven Sisters" were founded in the 1860s and 1870s to provide women with a liberal arts education equal to that offered to men. Teacher training was initially the only significant professional education these colleges provided. A committee of women including Mrs. Louis Agassiz and Miss Alice Longfellow, both members of an association called Private Collegiate Instruction for Women, founded the Harvard Annex, later Radcliffe College, in 1878, offering courses taught by Harvard faculty members. By the turn of the century, landscape architecture had emerged as a viable profession that required a formal education, and schools for women were subsequently initiated.

After visiting Lowthorpe School of Landscape Architecture for Women, Richard Kimball wrote: "What could be more appropriate to the sex than anything connected with horticulture, from the propagation of plants up to their final arrangement in lovely gardens? What could give better scope to the aesthetic sense inherent in woman, to her gentleness, delicacy, patience, intuition, her fostering care and maternal instinct?"[20] The programs established for women, however, emphasized a far wider domain of practice than Kimball imagined. Three programs in particular—the two most important in the Northeast, both connected to Harvard, and the third the influential program at the Ambler campus in Pennsylvania—educated and trained over a thousand women over the course of just four decades.

The Lowthorpe School of Landscape Architecture for Women opened in 1901, only a year after Harvard's program. In 1909 it was incorporated under Massachusetts law. Lowthorpe's three-year curriculum was intended to prepare women to take a role in the professional community of landscape architects and horticulturalists. Although the school never offered a university degree, as it was not accredited, it had matriculated approximately three hundred women by 1945, when it closed.

Judith Eleanor Motley Low (Mrs. Edward Gilchrist Low) founded the Lowthorpe School in 1901 at her country home in Groton, Massachusetts. Low came from a family committed to education in the natural sciences and landscape. Her great-grandfather Benjamin Bussey had bequeathed his estate, Bussey Park, to Harvard University in 1835, and in 1869 Harvard had established the Bussey Institute as a school of agriculture and horticulture, admitting women to study. Charles Eliot, son of Harvard president Charles W. Eliot, enrolled in the institution before he went to work for the Olmsted office. In 1908 Bussey shifted from being an undergraduate school to one devoted to advanced instruction and research, becoming part of Harvard's Graduate School of Applied Science. Charles Sprague Sargent, a professor of horticulture at Bussey, later helped to found the Arnold Arboretum, made possible through a gift from James Arnold, on what had been Bussey Institute land. Low had spent many of her childhood years at her grandparents' home Woodland Hill, the only tract of the original Bussey estate left to the family.

Low was also related to James Sturgis Pray, who led Harvard's program and would later support efforts to establish Lowthorpe. She corresponded with Sargent, at the Arnold Arboretum, and also knew J. F. Dawson and the Olmsted brothers, all of whom served as teachers and lecturers in the school's early years. Emeritus Harvard president Charles W. Eliot later served as honorary president of the Lowthorpe endowment fund and contributed quotes to the school's catalogs. Its patrons included the president of Mount Holyoke; Alice Freeman Palmer, president of Wellesley; and Harvard professor Charles Sprague Sargent. Contemporary practitioners Stephen Child, Loring Underwood, Rose Standish Nichols, and Amy F. Tripp (a 1908 Lowthorpe graduate) all served on the school's board of directors or as patrons. Its 1925 catalog featured endorsements from the writer Mrs. Francis King and from Miss Louise Klein Miller, the curator of the Public School Gardens in Cleveland, Ohio. A broad and deep community thus sustained the school and its efforts to educate and train women in landscape architecture.

In the 1901 announcement of the school's establishment it was proposed that the school would offer instruction in landscape gardening, elementary architecture, horticulture, botany, and allied subjects. Tuition was initially set at five hundred dollars, including living expenses;

" The Long Border "

LOWTHORPE SCHOOL
Of Landscape Architecture for Women
GROTON, MASSACHUSETTS

The Lowthorpe School was in a country house set among gardens, trees, and lawn, allowing students to learn a profession in a genteel setting. (Courtesy of Rhode Island School of Design Archives)

in 1902 it was set at one hundred dollars, plus living expenses—approximately thirty dollars a month. The 1902 courses included horticulture; arboriculture; botany; work in the greenhouse; work in the flower, fruit, and vegetable gardens; economic entomology; ornithology; agricultural chemistry; plane and solid geometry; surveying; freehand and mechanical drawing; landscape gardening; and garden design. The emphasis on the sciences is evident, as is the emphasis on drafting, with apparently little placed on the art of design.

Initially, Lowthorpe's catalog made no claims as to how women might use the education it offered, but by 1903 it was being suggested that they might find gainful employment in a number of areas, including the care and maintenance of rose and flower gardens; the supervision of country and suburban estates; the supervision of greenhouses and window boxes; hybridization and specialization in plant culture; the design and planting of flower gardens; work with school gardens; and the design and planting of small estates and village parks, as well as village-improvement work in general. The school's purpose was to train young women who wished to "enter upon any of the many lines of work in life appropriate to women comprehended under the terms Landscape Architecture, Landscape Gardening and Horticulture."[21]

The first women enrolled were housed in Mrs. Low's home, and the first to graduate, Elizabeth Hill, completed her certificate in 1902. Maude Chesley finished coursework in 1905, and Amy F. Tripp graduated in 1908. There were likely other students, but many left without completing the full term required for a certificate, as was common at the time.

Within a few short years the curriculum became increasingly focused on educating women to work in professional offices. The 1911 catalog stated: "The purpose of the instruction given at the Lowthorpe School is to provide students with sufficient horticultural training to enable them at graduation to take charge of gardening operations and to become assistants upon private estates. Instruction in drawing, engineering, and design is added to the course in order to familiarize the students with the more elementary phases of landscape architecture, and to fit them to solve simple problems involved in playgrounds, small estates, village improvements, and other rural matters."[22] The faculty included four instructors and five visiting lecturers. Most were practicing professionals or faculty members at Harvard University, including the landscape architects Arthur A. Shurcliff and Edna Stoddard and Robert Cameron, the head gardener at Harvard's Botanic Gardens. Courses in landscape gardening and plant materials were taught by J. F. Dawson, an employee at the Olmsted office, while courses in design were taught by Stephen Child and Loring Underwood, both practicing landscape architects.

In the first decade Low and the Lowthorpe faculty assumed students should gain a broad education in both the science of horticulture and the art of design. This approach, however, did not adequately attract students, in either number or quality. In 1914, then, the faculty offered two programs, one in design and one in gardening and horticulture, each with a distinct curriculum, although significant overlap remained. At the end of two years of coursework, students received the appropriate certificate.

LOWTHORPE SCHOOL
LANDSCAPE ARCHITECTURE

HORTICULTURE

Cover of Lowthorpe School catalog for 1943–44 school year, showing the emphasis on drafting skills and design, with a small insert exhibiting fieldwork. (Courtesy of Rhode Island School of Design Archives)

For those students interested in horticulture, the curriculum focused on practical gardening and applied sciences. Like Lowthorpe's earliest students, those focused on horticulture generally aspired to be florists, nurserywomen, or gardeners, and the curriculum offered lectures and laboratory (greenhouse) courses, along with field trips to Arnold Arboretum and other botanical collections. No design courses were required, the students instead studying plant materials, gardening, and greenhouse management. Lowthorpe's greenhouse, gardens, and fields served as laboratories for practical horticultural training, surveying, sketching, and the study of ecology and plant identification. In the winter the students used a facility in Boston at 491 Boylston Street, on loan from the MIT architecture department, to complete research at Arnold Arboretum and MIT's horticultural libraries. In 1935 Lowthorpe introduced the Dawson Course in Horticulture, attracting even more new students. Enrollment was at its highest in 1936, with twenty women as first-, second-, and third-year students.

For those students interested in design, Lowthorpe offered a core curriculum that reflected the influence of Pray and the Harvard faculty in its emphasis on engineering and architecture, featuring courses in construction, surveying, engineering, architectural drafting, and drawing. Drafting was an especially important component of the program, and large desks were provided for students, as was an area for model-making. In the design studio problems were assigned to emphasize critical features of construction, architecture, and/or landscape architecture, the projects given titles such as "A Private Estate," "A Farm Group," and "A Subdivision." Faculty lectures addressed a particular project, and individual supervised study then commenced. Each student made a final presentation, critiqued by peers and faculty, including visiting lecturers. Since Lowthorpe's only admission requirement was a high school diploma or its equivalent, this program proved rigorous for many students.

In 1915 Lowthorpe dropped "Gardening and Horticulture" from its name, becoming the Lowthorpe School of Landscape Architecture for Women, and the program was lengthened to three years of coursework, leading to a diploma. By 1917 the school was no longer concerned with landscape gardening, instead focused exclusively on landscape architecture. Its courses focused on four general divisions: fine arts, design, elements of construction, and horticulture.

In preparation for the rigors of practice, Lowthorpe students participated in the national Landscape Exchange Problems program from 1924 to 1931. An informal association of landscape architecture faculty organized these annual problems and competitions, led by Stanley H. White of the University of Illinois. The competition's judges frequently recognized Lowthorpe students for their high-quality design work and craftsmanship. The quality of its students was also recognized in 1924, when the ASLA Committee on Education listed Lowthorpe, alongside the Cambridge School, as having "technical courses sufficiently broad and thorough to admit their graduates as junior members of the society."[23] A 1939 article in *House & Garden* titled "Women in Landscaping" described Lowthorpe's curriculum in more detail:

> The importance of excellent design is stressed throughout the entire three years of the course. This is studied from the theoretical, historical and practical angles, and it is, of course, linked with practice in drafting, perspective and freehand drawing. The big basic problems of Landscaping are handled in courses in geology, topography, road making, drainage and grading and the social responsibilities of the profession are considered in Community and City Planning. . . . And finally, in preparation for the hard realities of dealing with clients and contractors, there are courses in estimation and problems of professional practice.[24]

The rigor of the program was vital to the school's success. Design students were expected to graduate ready to enter as an assistant in an established office and eventually to open a practice of their own. Highly skilled in the horticultural aspects of design, Lowthorpe alumnae were also highly valued as garden designers and writers. For example, Ellen

PLATE 1. Newbold estate, watercolor drawing produced by Beatrix Jones (Farrand). Farrand did not produce a lot of watercolors, but those that she did create are beautiful evocations of the designed landscapes. (Beatrix Jones Farrand Collection [1955-2], Environmental Design Archives, University of California, Berkeley)

PLATE 2. The Farm House in Maine, a flower garden designed by Farrand. This garden is full of color and texture, similar to those designed by Jekyll and known as cottage gardens, with added elegance in the combinations and composition, a hallmark of Farrand's design work. (Smithsonian Institution, Archives of American Gardens, Garden Club of America Collection)

PLATE 3. Chatham gardens, as photographed for a glass lantern slide by the Garden Club of America. Shipman's composition of plants, particularly flowers, vines, and shrubs, grew increasingly refined as she developed as a designer. In addition, her skill in combining architectural elements such as pergolas and gazebos as well as sculptures became a feature of her best gardens. (Smithsonian Institution, Archives of American Gardens, Garden Club of America Collection)

PLATE 4. The Boswell Garden in San Marino, California, designed by Florence Yoch and Lucille Council. The dramatic style and Mediterranean flavor of the garden became a hallmark of Yoch and Council's work. (Smithsonian Institution, Archives of American Gardens, Garden Club of America Collection)

PLATE 5. Brick House terrace and garden, ca. 1930. The designers included Ruth Bramley Dean, Mary Deputy Lamson, and Martha Brookes Brown Hutcheson. Glass lantern slides, often hand-painted, were frequently used to illustrate lectures by speakers such as Shipman, Flanders, Farrand, and Coffin. (Smithsonian Institution, Archives of American Gardens, Garden Club of America Collection)

PLATE 6. Old Acres, ca. 1930, designed by Martha Brookes Brown Hutcheson, featuring flower gardens set along the edges of woodland with an informal path trailing through the landscape. Photograph by Edward Van Altena. (Smithsonian Institution, Archives of American Gardens, Garden Club of America Collection)

Opposite page, top

PLATE 7. Sunken Orchard, or the McCann Garden, on Long Island, designed by Annette Hoyt Flanders, ca. 1930. Flanders was awarded the AIA Gold Medal in Landscape Architecture for this garden in the French style. (Smithsonian Institution, Archives of American Gardens, Garden Club of America Collection)

Opposite page, bottom

PLATE 8. Watercolor of garden, painted by Harry Sutton, illustrating an article by Helen Koues, "Good Housekeeping Exhibition: Classic Modern Garden and Pavilion at a Century of Progress—Chicago," in *Good Housekeeping*, August 1934. The severe geometry of the garden contrasts with the transparencies and light textures of the trees, creating a complex layering of design elements.

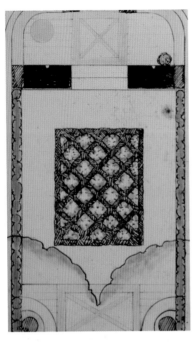

PLATE 9. A glass lantern slide of a "modern garden" by Flanders, which she used for her lectures. This garden, in its use of cubes and diagonals, can be compared to those Fletcher Steele described in France, but it does not have the sophistication of the French modern gardens. (Annette Hoyt Flanders Papers, Sophia Smith Collection, Smith College)

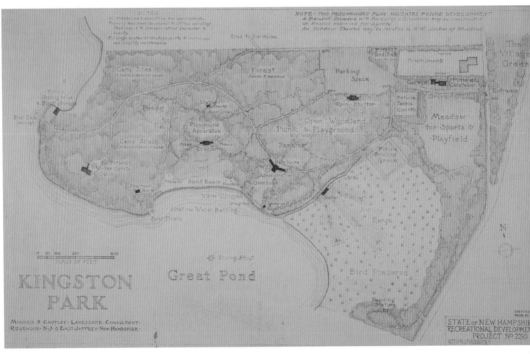

PLATE 10. Landscape Plan for Kingston Park by Marjorie Sewell Cautley, Landscape Consultant to the State of New Hampshire CCC Projects, 1934. This state park is designed to include active recreational spaces along with more passive scenic areas. Natural areas such as bird sanctuaries are fit in along with athletic fields, as Cautley tried to meet the varied demands and desires of the 1930s public. (Marjorie Sewell Cautley Papers, #4908, Division of Rare and Manuscript Collections, Cornell University Library)

Louise Payson (1894–1977) had been born in Portland, Maine, to a prominent family, many of whom pursued professional careers. She enrolled at Lowthorpe and graduated in 1916, along with Isabelle Pendleton, who went on to become a well-respected landscape architect and prolific writer. Payson initially worked in Ellen Shipman's office, learning the business and refining her design skills. Shipman later recognized Payson for her good work: "Louise Payson came fresh from Lowthorpe, so young and full of ability, and after twelve years with me, started out brilliantly for herself."[25]

Payson opened a practice in New York at 22 Beekman Place, near Shipman's office, specializing in designing the grounds of country estates in the Northeast, including several in Maine. Her work was featured in publications such as *House Beautiful, House & Garden,* and *Home and Field,* and she was also recognized in the 1933 *House & Garden* Hall of Fame as a leading landscape architect. Despite her success, Payson, like Shipman and her classmate Pendleton, never joined the ASLA.

The success of Lowthorpe students was also enhanced by the faculty's embrace of the breadth of contemporary practice. The 1915 faculty included practitioners Elizabeth Leonard (a 1910 Cornell graduate), Elsie D. Varley (a Swanley Horticultural College graduate), and Arthur C. Comey (a Harvard graduate). In 1932 landscape architects Anne D. Baker, Mary Parson Cunningham, Henry B. Hoover, Frederick Kingsbury, Elizabeth Greenleaf Pattee, and Robert H. Walter were teaching under the supervision of James Sturgis Pray, of Harvard University. In 1940 Harvard professors Norman T. Newton, Stephen Hamblin, and Walter Chambers all served on the faculty of Lowthorpe, bringing contemporary ideas and discourses to their studio courses, while Josef Albers offered basic exercises in design and drawing that would lead, he argued, to an appreciation of the functional qualities of the relationship between form and space.

Elizabeth Greenleaf Pattee, another important member of the Lowthorpe faculty, held a degree in architecture from MIT (1916) and a certificate in landscape architecture from Lowthorpe (1918) and was a member of both the AIA and the ASLA. She was hired in 1916 to serve as Lowthorpe's assistant principal and to be an instructor in design, planting design, surveying, and the history of landscape architecture. As the curriculum grew, her courses expanded to include architecture. Like many of her contemporaries, Pattee based her practice and teaching on the belief that the both disciplines—architecture and landscape architecture—were better served by being addressed in a collaborative manner. Pattee also continued to practice, often in collaboration with Constance Peters, and their work was represented in the 1934 ASLA *Illustrations of Work of Members.* In 1942, when Lowthorpe was absorbed by the Rhode Island School of Design, Pattee moved to the Providence campus. She became head of the department in 1952 and retired in 1959. While schools such as Harvard were establishing firm boundaries between architecture and landscape architecture programs, schools such as MIT, Lowthorpe, and later the Cambridge School were instead blurring the boundaries.

Judith Eleanor Motley Low, who had founded this important institution, remained a supporter until her death in 1922, having given the school grounds to the Lowthorpe corporation in 1916. Her vision of an alternative approach to the education of women, and of the potential for women to serve as landscape architects and landscape gardeners, remained a vital component of Lowthorpe's mission. By the 1930s the school was well-respected by the professional community, and in 1932, for example, its board included the practicing landscape architects Fletcher Steele, Robert M. Tappan, Bradford Williams, Isabella Pendleton, and Constance E. Peters, with Anne Baker at the helm. Patrons and friends continued to support the school, the Garden Club of America (GCA) donating twenty thousand dollars in 1931. Other garden clubs, including those in Rochester and Buffalo, sent students to Lowthorpe with all expenses paid. Despite all of this support, however, the school's financial instability finally caused its demise, as it never attracted the numbers of students required for financial solvency or gained the necessary support from endowment funds.

Lowthorpe had tried to initiate new programs and collaborate with other schools to establish a broader and more stable base. In 1923, for example, it offered a course for amateur gardeners in the summer, but with tuition set at one hundred dollars for the six-week program, it did not enroll many students. The next year it offered the same program for fifty dollars and continued to do so for a number of years afterward. Further, in 1924 and 1925 Lowthorpe's board agreed to combine resources with the Cambridge School, offering a travel program and allowing students to enroll in classes at either campus. Nevertheless, with a faculty of eight and a student body of eleven, Lowthorpe could not make ends meet. John A. Parker, holding a master's degree in architecture from MIT, was hired to run the school in 1934, but he faced an uphill battle, as Lowthorpe's lack of college accreditation continued to plague student recruitment.

Finally, as noted above, in 1942 Lowthorpe merged with the Rhode Island School of Design, and by 1945 RISD's "Lowthorpe Department" offered a bachelor's of science degree in landscape architecture to both men and women. Lowthorpe's books, resources, and equipment were moved, the building that once housed the school sold. RISD, with the addition of landscape architecture, initiated a Division of Planning to encourage collaborations among the disciplines of architecture, landscape architecture, and interior design, and a graduate degree was added to the program in 1948. In 1964 the designation "Lowthorpe" was dropped from the department's name, becoming a part of the program's lost history.

The financial crisis at Lowthorpe reflected broader trends in higher education. During World War II enrollment in colleges decreased overall,

Work by Elizabeth Pattee and Constance Peters included in the ASLA *Illustrations of Work of Members,* 1934. Members submitted photographs of their work, with one or two published in annual catalogs from 1931 to 1934.

while women's schools faced increasing emphasis on accredited degrees and licensing requirements. Lowthorpe's decision not to offer degrees put it at a disadvantage for attracting enough of the best students, eventually leading to its closure.

Another key institution focused on the education of women was the Pennsylvania School of Horticulture for Women, which trained students to work in the areas of horticulture and landscape design. While it never developed the professional curriculum or reputation of Lowthorpe or Cambridge, it nevertheless remained influential. Founded in 1910 by Jane Haines (1869–1937) near Philadelphia, this residential school for women offered practical and scientific training for outdoor work. Haines believed women would live healthier, happier lives, and gain greater economic independence, if they sought employment in areas such as horticulture, garden design, farming, and estate management.[26] The emphasis of this program was clear from the school's title, which stressed the horticultural arts and landscape management rather than design. Several hundred women eventually graduated with a certificate from the school, finding employment in both public and private venues.

Jane Haines had grown up on her father's fruit- and shade-tree nursery in Cheltenham, Pennsylvania. As Quakers, the Haines children were all educated, Jane attending Bryn Mawr College, where she received a bachelor's degree in history and economics and subsequently a master of arts degree She also obtained a certificate from the Library School in Albany, New York, in 1899. After traveling to visit schools for women in practical horticulture and design, including the Lowthorpe School and the Horticultural College at Swanley, Haines and fellow GCA member Eleanor Percy Stewardson purchased a seventy-acre farm in Ambler, outside Philadelphia. The school's first board of trustees included members of the Garden Club of Philadelphia and Byrn Mawr college alumnae. Beatrix Jones Farrand and the writers Mrs. Francis King and Mrs. Rutherford Ely were also invited to join.

The school offered a two-year diploma course of ten months' duration, for which a high school diploma and a minimum age of seventeen were the only prerequisites. Initially, its catalog was sent to local garden clubs, and in 1911 five students began study. The curriculum centered on horticultural topics, including floriculture, fruit and vegetable growing, and soil science, alongside courses in beekeeping, canning and preserving, and farm carpentry. The program also emphasized business courses to encourage students to develop the skills to be economically self-sufficient. For every lecture hour students trained for two hours in the school's gardens, fields, and greenhouse. This combination of "theory" and "practice" was admired by locals, as evidenced in a 1911 article published in the *Public Ledger,* "Farm and Garden School for Women: The Pennsylvania School of Horticulture at Ambler Combines Theory and Practice in Its Curriculum," which noted the program's practical and educational strengths. It was considered rigorous, not for the dabbler or dilettante.

Leaders of the school included Elizabeth Leighton Lee, the first woman to professionally practice landscape architecture in Philadelphia. She had studied at the Practical School of Agriculture and Horticulture at Briarcliff Manor, England, and had taken a course at Harvard in the theory of pure design before starting her practice in 1903. In 1913 Lee was invited, with Farrand, to serve as a landscape consultant to the Garden Club of America. In 1914 she came to the Pennsylvania School to teach design, and by 1915 she was the school's principal. A strong advocate of education, she consistently promoted both the school and women's role in the profession.

Another notable member of the Pennsylvania School's faculty, the landscape architect James Bush-Brown, initiated the school's first paraprofessional program in 1924, which allowed women to focus on practical courses that would prepare them to work in a landscape architecture office, rather than to lead one. James Bush-Brown's future wife, Louise Rogers Carter, a writer and teacher, became the director of the school in 1924 and remained at the helm for twenty-eight years. In 1933 Louise Bush-Brown took a brief sabbatical to write the first of the many books she and her husband would pen together: *America's Garden Book*. Before her retirement in 1952, she was instrumental in gaining the school the much-needed provisional accreditation from the American Association of Junior Colleges.

The Pennsylvania School had been established in part in response to larger concerns about the plight of contemporary women, particularly the sedentary life of the office worker. Contemporary newspaper accounts remarked on the dreary life of women confined to desks on a daily basis, suggesting that horticulture was perhaps more appropriate for up-and-coming women who did not want to submit to office-bound drudgery. The school continued to address the broader role of women as part of its mission, hosting a national horticulture conference in 1914 at which the Woman's National Agricultural and Horticultural Association was founded. More broadly, it not only educated hundreds of women who worked in a variety of positions but was also instrumental in promoting women's economic independence and professional status.

In 1958 the Pennsylvania School of Horticulture merged with Temple University, Temple's new Department of Horticulture subsequently offering an associate of science degree to both men and women. Like the Lowthorpe program within RISD, the Pennsylvania program eventually became subsumed within the larger university system, essentially invisible until historians such as Valencia Libby began to take note of it.

The third women's school—like Lowthorpe, based in the Northeast and connected to Harvard—was the Cambridge School of Architecture and Landscape Architecture for Women. Founded in 1916, the Cambridge

School, by the time of its 1942 closing, had graduated over four hundred professional landscape architects. While Cambridge offered a three-year program without a professionally accredited degree, its graduates were accorded a professional respect that was not extended to graduates of either Lowthorpe or the Pennsylvania School. In part this may have been because many Cambridge students, primarily college graduates, came from elite Eastern colleges such as Vassar, MIT, Smith, and Abbot Academy. The school's urban setting, in addition to its direct association with Harvard, lent it a further form of legitimacy that was more elusive for rural schools. Finally, Cambridge's emphasis on architecture and landscape architecture, rather than on horticulture, led the professional community to consider it more seriously, as it reflected broader trends in the development of professional practice.

The Cambridge program had begun in response to one young woman appealing for instruction. In 1915 Katherine Brooks requested permission from James Sturgis Pray, head of Harvard's landscape program, to study architectural drafting. As Brooks could not attend courses at Harvard, Pray asked Henry Atherton Frost, a colleague, to tutor her privately. Within a year other women had joined the small tutorial, and a small school was founded, with Frost and his colleague Bremer Whidden Pond serving both as its directors and as primary teaching faculty.[27]

Although Pond supported the school throughout his life, other professional commitments, including leadership of the ASLA and chairmanship of Harvard's landscape architecture program, eventually drew him away from direct leadership. Frost, on the other hand, continued as the Cambridge School's director and leader until the school's closure in 1942, eventually becoming a major advocate for women in practice, as he believed that the professions of architecture and landscape architecture were particularly appropriate for women.

By the spring of 1916 Cambridge School students were being taught in the professional offices of Frost and Pond, at 209 and 211 the Brattle Building, on Harvard Square. This move was advantageous on several counts, both convenient for the teachers and key to establishing a professional framework for the students. This alone fixed the Cambridge School in a very different vein from either Lowthorpe or the Pennsylvania School.

Further, the Cambridge School, unlike Lowthorpe or the Pennsylvania School, was a graduate program, requiring a college degree for admittance. Women without a college degree were asked to qualify for admission by demonstrating knowledge gained from travel, study, and office work. The school was intended to prepare women for independent practice in architecture and/or landscape architecture, teaching them the art of design, the sciences of engineering and horticulture, and the management of a business and professional practice.

The Cambridge School's leadership and faculty were impressive. In

1930 the school's General Educational Council included the presidents of Radcliffe, Smith, Wheaton, Wellesley, and Mount Holyoke, while its trustees included John Nolen, Albert D. Taylor, Ferruccio Vitale, and Walter H. Kilham—all well-established practitioners. In 1935 the practitioners Clarence Fowler, Eleanor Raymond, and Fletcher Steele joined the school's trustees, along with the sculptor Amelie Peabody and the lawyer Romney Spring. The program also drew on senior and junior Harvard faculty members, including Pray, Henry Vincent Hubbard, Herbert Langford Warren, and Norman Newton. Faculty members in the 1920s and 1930s included Carol Fulkerson, Robert Swan Sturtevant, Stephen Hamblin, Jean Jacques Haffner, Morley J. Williams, Kenneth John Conant, Mary P. Cunningham, Charles W. Killam, Edith V. Cochran, and William Sears. G. Holmes Perkins, on the faculty of Harvard's architecture program and later dean of the University of Pennsylvania, began his teaching career at the Cambridge School. In addition, women increasingly served as full-time faculty and/or special lecturers and critics at the Cambridge School. By thus integrating established Harvard faculty members and practitioners with women professionals, the school enhanced and expanded women's opportunities for mentoring and validated their work as professionals and teachers.

From the school's initial years its curriculum was thorough, focused both on design and construction and on practice and providing instruction in in horticulture, history, modeling, and office practices. In May 1916, a school announcement described the Cambridge School's approach: "The method of training is by lectures, conferences, observation, tests and desk work. The number of students admitted will be small in order to insure personal instruction."[28] In 1916, in addition to standard coursework, the Cambridge School offered guest lectures by Harvard professors on town planning, wood finishes, architectural history, stained glass, construction, and plant materials. The course of study was designed to cover a three-year period, depending on the individual student.

The 1916–17 Cambridge School "Bulletin" specified the nature of the courses then offered, focusing on " (a) the theory and practice of domestic architectural design, (b) the theory and practice of landscape design with particular reference to domestic work, or (c) the combination of these two in the study of the house and its garden." Subjects taught in 1917 included design, construction, and drainage (six courses); horticulture (five courses); history (five courses); graphics; freehand drawing; and modeling. The school's broad focus, as articulated in the 1927 catalog, was on preparing students by teaching them the fundamental principles underlying good design and construction and providing training that was as practical as possible without sacrificing theory—"not so much a fund of technical facts, which are changing constantly, as . . . the principles which will help her later to derive the facts during an office apprenticeship." The goal was to assure that the school's graduates would be of "immediate

Students at work in the drafting room at the Cambridge School. Similar images were used in many of the catalogs, emphasizing the role of design in the curriculum. (Cambridge School Collection, Smith College Archives)

use in the offices of architects and landscape architects, [and] . . . to make their training broad enough so that their point of view will become that of the independent practitioner." By 1935 the school offered certificates in architecture, landscape architecture, and interior architecture. A thesis was required for the completion of a degree, correlating the Cambridge School with Harvard's program and positioning its graduates within the growing field of landscape research. By this time arrangements had been made to allow a student to be recognized, upon completion of her degree, by a recommendation for a master's degree in architecture or landscape architecture, to be conferred by Smith College.

In 1928, with the help of an alumna, a new home for the school was located, and everything was moved to 53 Church Street in Cambridge. As the Colonial house was not quite large enough, studios were added on, the addition in a more modern style, with large windows, unadorned white walls, and a flat roofline. The interior featured two drafting rooms, each holding desks for thirty students. The main house included offices, ample exhibition space, a library, and two lecture rooms, while the yard provided space for outdoor classrooms. The Cambridge School was close to Harvard Square, the Fogg Museum of Art, the Boston Museum of Fine Arts, and the Isabella Stewart Gardner Museum. Its 1930s' catalogs emphasized easy access to the Arnold Arboretum, the Boston Public Library, the Widener Library of Harvard University, and the Library of the Massachusetts Horticultural Society. The school, in other words, clearly took advantage of its urban setting.

Further, not only did the Cambridge School offer its students an impeccable education, but it gave Harvard faculty an opportunity to teach architecture and landscape architecture as an integrated program, challenging the specialization of schools like Harvard, Cornell, and the University of Illinois. From the beginning the curriculum designed by Frost and Pond wove architecture and landscape architecture into a cohesive pedagogy. The school was thus widely recognized as the "only school to offer the two complete curricula to women under a single faculty of architects, landscape architects and engineers working in close association."[29]

Cambridge School at 53 Church Street. The new studio addition can be seen on the left. (Cambridge School Collection, Smith College Archives)

Indeed, students did not differ in their coursework until their last year, when they specialized (and some chose to specialize in both areas). Frost and Pond believed that any practitioner who understood both fields enjoyed a significant advantage, noting that "the best domestic work has usually been done where both branches of the design are in the hands of one individual, or at least under the direction of designers closely associated, each one keenly sympathetic in the other's field. It is realized that the proper sympathy can exist only when there is an understanding of the entire problem."[30] This "combined" approach to education, then, was both an important asset offered to students and a key to the respect the professional community held for the school's education and training.

Initially, the Cambridge School concentrated on domestic architecture and landscape architecture, as reflected in the 1919 decision to change its name to the Cambridge School of Domestic Architecture and Landscape Architecture. This focus on domestic work encouraged students to establish an important niche within the professional world, and as the 1930s brought an increased focus on smaller homes and planned communities with integrated landscape designs and architecture, those experienced in designing such projects held a distinct advantage. Even so, Frost grew worried that the "domestic" label might limit the graduates' professional roles, pigeonholing the program by attaching too much importance to the domestic arena—the private domain—as opposed to public landscapes and municipal projects. This label, in other words, was too easily understood by the public to refer merely to training in designing flower gardens. Frost thus decided in 1932 to eliminate the word "domestic" from the school's title and to increase its requirements for classes in mathematics, engineering, and structural knowledge, most likely to combat the perception that women were not as skilled in these areas.

Regardless, Cambridge's program maintained its emphasis on diverse domestic environments, including small homes and gardens, large housing projects and landscapes, and residential communities with public and private spaces. Frost argued that the school prepared graduates to attend to the needs of future livable communities, as it was the "duty of the schools to lead in progressive thought in design and construction."[31]

The curriculum at the Cambridge School, like that at Harvard and MIT, reflected a Beaux-Arts approach to teaching, with a conservative emphasis on classical design and historical precedent. In the 1920s and 1930s, as architecture began to feel the influence of European modernism, the Cambridge School shifted to a more modern approach to design education, reflected in both student designs and lectures. In 1930 the school sponsored its first traveling lecture series, delivered by two longtime friends, Fletcher Steele and Jean Jacques Haffner, the new head of the Harvard School of Architecture. Their lecture, "Modern Trends in Architecture, Decoration and Garden Design," considered the house and garden of the future and its relationship to modern living. Closer to home, Cambridge projects included "Middlesex Village" in 1933 and Glaston in 1935, both intended to reflect modern principles of town planning and architecture.

In 1940 the Cambridge lecture series featured Cynthia Wiley and Ilse Frank Gropius, their presentations entitled "Experiences in Modern Architecture" and "Modern Trends in Landscape Architecture." These were also the keynote lectures for the "Houses and Housing" exhibition, originally created by the Museum of Modern Art and brought to Boston by the Cambridge School in honor of its twenty-fifth anniversary. The Cambridge School incorporated both student and faculty projects into the exhibition, demonstrating the application of new design approaches. Significantly, the choice of two women to address urban planning issues for a major museum exhibit also reflected Cambridge's consistent efforts to recognize women practitioners.

In 1932 the school published a small brochure recognizing its achievements, including a total registration, over sixteen years, of 674 students from thirty-nine states, as well as from England, France, Canada, and Mexico, and from forty colleges and universities. Graduates of the school included Eleanor Raymond (1919), who practiced with Henry A. Frost until 1935. Recognized by the journal *Architectural Forum* in 1933 for constructing the first modern house in Massachusetts, she was well-known professionally for combining industrial materials with historical motifs. She became head of the drafting room at the Radar School of MIT and was elected to the AIA's College of Fellows in 1961. Another notable Cambridge graduate, Helen Swift Jones (1924), worked for Robert Moses in New York City. She later became a supervisor in the city's park department, with Gilmore Clark, and hired Maud Sargent (1934) to work in the department as well. Dorothy May Anderson (1933) practiced in New England and taught at Lowthorpe for many years, including serving as codirector for one year. Eloise Anderson Ray (1928) led an independent practice focused on civic projects, including planning and supervising highway plantings and reclaiming land for public parks.

During World War II, Cambridge School alumnae served in remarkable breadth of roles, from Emergency Housing, to the Soil Conservation Service, to an army report center, to victory gardens. After the war these alumnae continued to be actively engaged in the profession. Janet Darling Dixon, for example, worked for the Federal Housing Authority, while Faith Jones was an architect for the New York City Bureau of Architecture. Virginia Perry was employed by North American Aviation Incorporated, while Frances Loring was hired to help design an alternative airfield for the U.S. Navy on Long Island. Maud Sargent served as a landscape architect in the office of Manhattan's borough president, working on East River Drive and on the Battery and Lincoln Tunnel approaches. Cambridge School alumnae formed an influential constellation of professionals at the time.

The Cambridge School, however, struggled for almost thirty years, never attaining an enrollment or endowment adequate for it to qualify as an independent graduate school empowered to grant academic degrees. As many of its students already held undergraduate degrees, tuition for further education was a significant investment of funds to prepare for a professional career, further limiting the number of students. Nevertheless, of the three schools for women, Cambridge was the most successful. Incorporated under Massachusetts law as an educational institution in 1924, in 1934 it became affiliated with Smith College as a graduate school. Only then was it able to offer master's degrees in architecture and landscape architecture. Two years later bachelor's degrees in both fields were introduced, and in 1935 the school added interior architecture as an option, although it never gained the breadth of the original two areas.

In 1938 the Cambridge School became a part of Smith College, and it closed officially in 1942, due to insufficient funding and student enrollment. At the same time Harvard, out of desperation for students during World War II, agreed to allow women to enroll in its programs in architecture and landscape architecture. Eighteen Cambridge School students including Cornelia Hahn Oberlander transferred to Harvard, along with three who enrolled specifically in a course taught by Walter Gropius.

These three schools successfully educated and trained large constellations of women to become landscape architects as well as garden designers, informed patrons, and civic volunteers. They did not pursue these goals alone, but garnered the support of other institutions, with faculty from Harvard, Cornell, and MIT offering courses and lectures and serving as guest critics. This academic community fostered the emergence of landscape architecture as a viable and respected profession that embraced women as practitioners.

From Education to Practice

Women initially accessed landscape architecture by means their contemporaries considered appropriately feminine. They began as gardeners, nurtured interests in botany and the sciences, studied to be artists, and with time merged these interests and skills into a productive profession. Women also took advantage of opportunities once designated for men. They enrolled in courses, attended colleges, traveled, and launched practices. Their opportunities remained more limited than those available to male colleagues: fewer practitioners were willing to take them on as apprentices, fewer schools offered them a degree rather than a certificate, and social restrictions limited how and where they could travel. Nevertheless, women did not define their work by nonexistent opportunities but followed new paths and broke new ground.

Henry A. Frost, in his introduction to the *Alumni Bulletin of the Cambridge School,* noted the following in 1930:

The professions of architecture and landscape architecture have been, until very recent times, entirely in the hands of men. At present, women are not welcomed in many offices [even] as draughtsmen, and not a few practitioners are sincere in advising women not to attempt either profession. Therefore, a student entering the Cambridge School has to some degree the pioneering instinct [as well as] a modern viewpoint. She must realize that success in a field where men are receiving their training in long-established schools requires for her a training as good . . . and that with this training, because she is of necessity a pioneer, must go a high enthusiasm and an unusual tenacity of purpose. Our students do not drift into their professions along the lines of least resistance, nor do they drift through this school.

The financial returns for women in the profession were adequate, given other opportunities, although it was suggested that while a comfortable living could be made, the field was not one in which to become rich. The typical salary for a draftsperson was approximately fifteen dollars per week, barely a living wage. For a Lowthorpe student the first year of practice brought in between eight hundred and fifteen hundred dollars; those practicing over four years could earn up to twenty-five hundred dollars. However, if one was drawn to the arts and horticulture, and had the physical ability to stand the manual labor, the supervisory skills, and the requisite training and education, landscape architecture might prove, many argued, a good career choice.

Successful women shaped their opportunities to fit contemporary ideas of what it meant to be a professional landscape architect. They chose diverse paths and forged links within the professional and amateur communities. As they followed these opportunities, their paths diverged, creating significant constellations of practitioners.

5

Professional Legitimacy

Speaking, Writing, Photographing, and Designing

While education was an essential part of becoming a professional, practicing landscape architects struggled to gain and sustain legitimacy. The ASLA was formed in large part to establish and promote the profession. Members were expected to support efforts to publicize the profession, its attributes, standards, and potential. In 1923 the ASLA Committee on Publicity encouraged members to write one article a year for either *Landscape Architecture Magazine* or a popular magazine or journal such as *Vogue, Ladies' Home Journal, Country Life in America, National Builder, Golfer's Magazine, American City, American Magazine of Art,* or *Architectural Forum.* Practitioners were encouraged to join civic groups, lecture for amateur groups, and associate with professional organizations. The profession needed increased visibility, and it was up to practitioners to encourage such attention. Women, who had to establish themselves both in a new profession and within a new professional community, understood that legitimacy determined their potential for any level of success.

Professional Legitimacy

Women sought to promote landscape architecture as a legitimate profession in a variety of ways. They were involved in associations, engaged in specialized activities, and created professional networks. Many women joined the ASLA, lectured, wrote for popular and professional publications, and commissioned photographs of their designs. For women, in particular, these were acceptable means to promote their practice and simultaneously advance the profession.

Lecture series or circuits were a standard part of many of the landscape design practices. Clubs and associations organized lecture series and short courses as a way to educate the public and expand professional networks. In response, practitioners developed repertoires of lectures and talks, frequently illustrated by glass lantern slides. Olmsted, Platt, Manning, Nichols, and Farrand lectured extensively for public and private audiences, sometimes to discuss a specific project, other times to promote the broader importance of quality in landscape design. Others, such as Fletcher Steele and Annette Hoyt Flanders, addressed civic organizations and college courses on design principles. By the 1930s the ASLA had a committee focused specifically on guest lectures, and lecturers' names circulated among associations, clubs, and educational institutions, establishing a regional, and sometimes national, audience for individual speakers.

Such lectures advanced the profession, raised the standards of public taste, and promoted individual practices. As such, it was standard for a lecturer to receive a fee in addition to travel expenses. Indeed, those who chose to lecture without fee ran the risk of being viewed as unprofessional—as Sargent had warned Farrand when he told her not to provide her design services pro bono. Many lecturers' fees were listed in the 1920 *Garden Club of America Bulletin,* along with a list of possible topics. Cautley and Coffin charged fifty dollars per lecture, while Farrand and Flanders required seventy-five dollars. Wodell & Cottrell often lectured at no cost, reflecting their discomfort at considering themselves full professionals.

Speaking engagements and lectures provided an ideal way to instruct an audience in design principles, especially if the speaker chose to illustrate the ideas with beautiful images and simple, straightforward language. And audiences expected to use the information lecturers provided, whether as professionals or amateurs. Young women wishing to pursue a career in landscape design often depended upon such lectures to learn the landscape-design canon, while amateurs wanted both to expand their design vocabulary and to be able to make informed decisions in their personal gardens. A lecture audience might learn how Le Nôtre used axes at Versailles and then how the technique was used by Martha Brookes Hutcheson at her home in New Jersey. Or Coffin might teach them how an assortment of trees could be used in a variety of settings to create garden rooms and take them to visit gardens designed by Ruth Dean. Mary Rutherfurd Jay might explain the different approaches to design in Japan and China. References to famous gardens emphasized the potential of a professionally designed landscape, while modest projects underscored the universality of design principles. Social events following lectures might enable personal contact between lecturers and potential clients or future employees.

In spite of its effectiveness, however, lecturing did not allow practitioners to reach the audience made possible through the increased availability of popular magazines and publications, which catered to a potentially much larger and broader audience, offering practitioners the opportunity to expand their sphere of influence by thousands of individuals. Horticulture and garden design had entered a golden age in the United States, and the related market for periodicals flourished in the early twentieth century. Writers such as Elizabeth Leonard Strang, Mary P. Cunningham, and Isabelle Pendleton became better-known for their essays than for their actual designs, while other articles were written by such well-established designers as Rose Greeley, Flanders, and Coffin. While most middle-class families could not afford to hire such a designer, they could read the articles they wrote for popular magazines like *Garden and Forest, Scribner's Magazine, House & Garden,* and *House Beautiful.*

Writing had long been deemed an appropriately female occupation. Contemporary writers included Louisa May Alcott, Edith Nesbitt, and Mariana Van Rensselaer, and writing a book about gardens and garden design might easily be seen as an appropriately domestic activity for educated women. Indeed, since women were deemed experts in the domains of home and garden, it seemed natural that they would understand the principles of gardening as a fine art. And magazines with broad and far-reaching audiences, including *House Beautiful* and *House & Garden,* frequently hired women as garden editors and writers, such as Flanders and Ruth Dean, who saw such work as a way to expand the public's knowledge of landscape architecture as a profession and as an art.

While a plethora of books on gardening and garden design was available in the nineteenth and early twentieth centuries, Van Rensselaer's *Art Out-of-Doors* had firmly established a place for women in the field. Gertrude Jekyll's reputation was based almost entirely on her books about garden design. Others came to writing as amateurs, including Ella Rodman Church, the author of *The Home Garden* (1881), and Helena Rutherford Ely, the author of *A Woman's Hardy Garden* (1903)—a book specifically applauded as an American work on American gardening. Numerous other books by successful amateur gardeners followed, including Louise Shelton's *The Seasons in a Flower Garden* (1906), Louise Beebe Wilder's *Colour in My Garden* (1918), and Nellie Doubleday's *American Flower Garden* (1909) (written under the pseudonym Neltje Blanchan). These books and essays by women on gardening "contributed to the formation of a network of women's specialized knowledge and support."[1]

By writing a book, a practitioner established her expertise in a more substantial manner than she could in an ephemeral weekly or monthly magazine. Books were used in the education and training of young practitioners, as well as the instruction of potential clients, and they were often reviewed in *Landscape Architecture Magazine,* thereby establishing them as possible additions to a professional library. Interestingly, in the first decades of *Landscape Architecture Magazine,* a vast number of the books reviewed were about gardening and flowers, many by women. In 1912, for example, Grace Tabor's *The Landscape Gardening Book* (1911) was favorably reviewed. *Landscape Architecture Magazine* also published articles by women, including Amy F. Tripp's description of the Lowthorpe School program (1912), Catherine Koch's piece on wild marsh plants (1916), and

Elma Loines's essay on garden plants (1916) (both Koch and Loines were botanists).

An important woman in this world of design magazines and books was Theodora Kimball Hubbard (1887–1934), the first librarian of the landscape architecture collection at Harvard. She served in a variety of roles, including writer, critic, historian, and coauthor of the first textbook on landscape architecture. Beginning in 1912, she wrote an annual review of city-planning reports for *Landscape Architecture Magazine,* as well as book reviews, reflecting a broad range of interests. She remained one of the few women to contribute articles to the professional magazine until 1921. In 1917 Kimball collaborated with Henry Vincent Hubbard to write the first textbook on landscape architecture, *An Introduction to the Study of Landscape Design.* She was named contributing editor of *Landscape Architecture Magazine* in July 1918 and became associate editor in October 1921, holding this position until her death in 1935.

In 1918 Kimball served as consulting librarian to the U.S. Housing Corporation in Washington, D.C. Becoming increasingly interested in city planning, she also wrote articles for *City Planning Magazine* and collaborated with Hubbard to found the journal *City Planning* in 1925. She was the first woman to serve as a member of the American City Planning Institute, and, with James Sturgis Pray, wrote a city planning guide that provided a comprehensive contemporary analysis of the subject.

Kimball was also a significant historian of the profession of landscape architecture and the design of public landscapes. While Van Rensselaer's publications focused on Olmsted's life and work and on defining the new profession, Kimball wrote more broadly about related issues. For example, she reviewed the work of H. W. S. Cleveland and wrote a brief history of modern landscape architecture. She also served as an editor for the two volumes of *Forty Years of Landscape Architecture: Frederick Law Olmsted, Landscape Architect,* her history of the design of public parks before Central Park providing a context for Olmsted's essays. She was also a vital proponent of researching in the discipline and practice of landscape architecture and its history.

Kimball's library work was also significant, as hers was the first effort to organize and classify knowledge of landscape architecture. By organizing the texts and resources of the profession, and identifying gaps and potential research areas, Kimball, along with her collaborators Pray and Hubbard, established a framework for the development of landscape architectural knowledge. When she developed an interest in city planning and zoning, she applied similar methods to establish this new area as a research-based discipline.[2]

A second notable figure in the world of landscape letters was Katherine McNamara, who became a librarian at Harvard after Kimball and then served as the contributing editor to *Landscape Architecture Magazine* from 1929 until 1962, when the next Harvard librarian, Caroline Shilaber, took over. Another important librarian was Sarah Lewis Pattee, the director of the Landscape Gardening Library at the University of Illinois. She used Kimball's classification system to organize and catalog the books in her library's collection, developing a significant collection by the end of her tenure. In 1924 she also published an article in *Landscape Architecture Magazine* titled "Landscape Architecture in American Colleges." Such librarians, scholars, and critics were vital in framing landscape architecture as an intellectual discipline.

Other women came to writing by way of a professional design career, seeking to articulate the design principles used by a professional landscape architect. One such book was Martha Brookes Hutcheson's *The Spirit of the Garden* (1923), which focused on architectural design principles. Rose Standish Nichols authored a series of books illustrating the typical gardens of cultures around the world. Mrs. Francis King introduced the "Little Garden Series" in 1921 in response to growing interest in the design of smaller, suburban lots. This series, which included Fletcher Steele's *Design in the Little Garden* (1924), offered readers practical advice with a professional stamp of approval. Marjorie Sewell Cautley's book, *Garden Design: the Principles of Abstract Design as Applied to Landscape Composition* (1935), was another significant contribution to the literature.

Many books by landscape architects sought to teach home owners about residential-garden design, including Grace Tabor's *Gardening Book* (1911), *Making the Grounds Attractive with Shrubbery* (1912), *Suburban Gardens* (1913), and *Planting around the Bungalow* (1914) and Ruth Dean's *The Liveable House, Its Garden* (1917). Helen Morgenthau Fox's *Patio Gardens* (1929) featured Spanish and Mediterranean influences, while plan books such as Eugene O. Murmann's *California Gardening* (1914) provided gardening advice, planting plans, and plant lists for home owners according to local climate and growing conditions. Mary Rutherfurd Jay compiled *The Garden Handbook* (1931), a pocket-size book of images and descriptions of historic and modern examples of a variety of garden details. Drawing on her extensive travels, Jay presented a range of examples and possibilities. While not widely distributed, the book reflected growing interest in foreign garden and landscape style.

Elsa Rehmann, a designer and author, advocated the careful selection of plant materials and the application of ecological concepts to the practice of landscape architecture. She initially had attended Wells College and then graduated from Barnard with a B.A. degree. Perhaps drawing on the knowledge of her father, the architect Carl Rehmann, she opened a landscape architecture office in Rockport, Massachusetts. Her first book, *The Small Place: Its Landscape Architecture* (1918), analyzed fifteen garden-design problems, focusing on site, plant materials, and seasonal interest. Each chapter focused on a small garden designed by a professional landscape architect, including Pray, Hubbard, White, Manning, Arthur A. Shurtleff, Coffin, the Olmsted brothers, Elizabeth Leonard

Strang, and Elizabeth Bootes Clark. Rehmann, like Mrs. King, validated the quality of such professional designs, drawing her examples from the work of recognized practitioners, while simultaneously translating their work into layperson's terms for the home gardener. She was particularly knowledgeable about Coffin's designs and would later work with Coffin to supervise the plantings for the College of Delaware in 1919.

Rehmann's second work, *Garden-Making* (1926), was done in collaboration with her sister Antoinette Perrett, who had become a well-known garden photographer. This book sought "to give garden-making its place in the realm of art and to discuss garden design in its simplest forms." Rehmann noted that this text "dwells upon plant material . . . not so much for their individual beauty as for the way in which they embody the garden's design and interpret its character."[3] Similarly, Rehmann's work with Edith Adelaide Roberts, *American Plants for American Gardens* (1929), served as an important resource for designers and for those interested in more "natural" designs. Roberts, a professor of botany at Vassar College, had earlier published a pamphlet for the Conservation Committee of the GCA advocating the conservation of native plants, and this joint work with Rehmann featured chapters on a variety of ecological associations, from juniper hillsides to bogs. For each such association the plant materials and ecological development were explained and the design characteristics described. This book, in other words, did not advocate clearing a piece of land to create a garden but working closely with the existing site and vegetation, reflecting growing interest in ecological design.

In 1931 Frank Waugh's "Ecology of the Roadside" became the first article about ecology published in *Landscape Architecture Magazine*. Two years later, in 1933, Rehmann published an important follow-up article, "An Ecological Approach," addressing the growing interest in plant ecology (organized as a science in 1895 and used to varying extents by Manning, Waugh, and Jensen) and its role in landscape architecture. Rehmann here clearly explained the science of plant associations and argued for the important role they could play in landscape architecture, articulating a growing argument for the use of native plants. She expressed her fervent belief that better designs would result from a "keener appreciation of the relationship inherent between native vegetation and the landscape" and suggested ways in which student investigations might be incorporated into studio projects.[4] Rehmann's written works, taken as a whole, reveal her significant concern for the landscape architect as both scientist/ecologist and artist/sculptor of the land, the breadth of her concerns reflecting the range and depth of contemporary practice.

Books on landscape architecture were often written for both public and professional audiences, authors describing the principles of good design in the home garden and addressing the planning of larger estates. These authors frequently emphasized the composition of the landscape over collections of plants. Further—and significantly here—they introduced the work of their colleagues and peers, many placing the work of women alongside that of men, others featuring women's work primarily. For amateurs, then, these works served as introductions to both the language of design and the community of designers. For students they served as texts that would frame both their practice as landscape architects and their professional networks. For practitioners they served as both a design resource and an aid in communicating design principles to clients. Regardless of the individual reader, their overall message was consistent: the landscape should be carefully and artistically designed to assure that its inherent beauty was revealed, and this was best achieved by a professional landscape architect—many of whom were women. Such works confirmed not only the importance of garden and landscape design but also the presence of women as a force in the profession.

Photographs played an essential role in these publications, serving as an important professional link for landscape architects and providing yet another career option for women. In *Careers for Women* the photographer Jesse Tarbox Beals suggested that photography was a vocation that fell naturally within the capabilities and talents of women. She noted only three or four specialists in garden photography, observing that the demand for more was great. To pursue such work, she cautioned, a woman "must be strong," as the equipment was heavy and the work outdoors. The chances of success, however, were great: "Practically every owner wants lovely pictures of his garden, and if they are successfully made, beautifully finished and mounted, they will be the best advertisement that the photographer could possibly have."[5]

By the 1910s and 1920s garden photographs were a staple of popular publications, and many of the garden photographers were women, including Jessie Tarbox Beals, Mattie Edwards Hewitt, Frances Benjamin Johnston, Antoinette Perrett, and Clara Sipprell. Photographs by Johnston, Hewitt, and Beals were featured in Louise Shelton's *Beautiful Gardens in America,* and Hewitt's and Sipprell's images were frequently used for ASLA member exhibits and in design books and magazines. Significantly, Sipprell's cityscape *New York—Old and New* was one of the first photographs acquired by the Museum of Modern Art, in 1932. Hewitt photographed the work of essentially every significant landscape architect of the period, her romantic photographs of Shipman's gardens appearing in such popular household magazines as *House & Garden, House Beautiful,* and *Garden Magazine,* as did her photographs of the work of Coffin, Hutcheson, and Flanders. Hewitt's photographs were also essential to the books written by Coffin and Cautley.

Photographs were also vital on the lecture circuit. Annette Hoyt Flanders compiled over a thousand slides, many hand-painted, in order to illustrate her lectures on the principles of good design. Beatrix Jones Farrand amassed a collection of glass lantern slides and photographs of gar-

The Frick garden, Clayton, on Long Island, designed by Marian Cruger Coffin, ca. 1925. The severity of the image reflects many of the photographs, which emphasize the garden as a work of art, rather than its horticultural characteristics. Photograph by Samuel Gottscho. (Courtesy, The Winterthur Library: Winterthur Archives)

dens throughout the world that she used to lecture and to illustrate her ideas for clients. She also kept an extensive assortment of Jekyll's photographs, integrated into her own collection of images. Mary Rutherfurd Jay also established a career as a lecturer, drawing on the thousands of lantern slides she had acquired during her travels to illustrate design principles.

Photographs also illustrated the speaker's breadth of knowledge and experience. When Farrand, Jay, or Flanders spoke of gardens they had visited in tropical or exotic lands, this established them as informed and experienced practitioners. At a time when not everyone could travel, these designers' firsthand experiences on the grand tour and visits to other remote locales served as important signifiers of both their status in society and their dedication to the profession.

For the typical audience member, then, these illustrated lectures provided a way to see the world vicariously. For many in the audience, images of India, China, and other far-off places enhanced their own repertoire of sceneries and cultures, allowing them to feel conversant about a range of cultural landscapes without having to visit them in person. Women such as Jay and Nichols were particularly responsive to such audiences, eventually developing a collection of lectures, essays, and books focused more on introducing the landscapes of different cultures than on the broader principles of landscape design.

Landscape architects, increasing both their own knowledge base and the viability of their professional network, collected these books, essays, and photographs by and for women. An inventory of Farrand's collection, for example, revealed at least 50 books written by women between 1800 and 1925—books that were also found in the collections of Alice Orme Smith, Coffin, Flanders, and Shipman. Of approximately 150 books Henry Francis du Pont held in his horticultural library prior to 1927, at least 55 had been written by women. Books authored by women were frequently recommended in landscape design programs and in the bibliographies of textbooks, both providing an educational resource and shaping women's networks in first decades of the twentieth century. Such networks were essential for landscape architects, helping them to develop design expertise, build a practice, and establish professional legitimacy.

MARIAN CRUGER COFFIN (1876–1957)

Marian Cruger Coffin is an example of a practitioner who actively pursued each of these paths to enhancing her professional status—participating in the activities of the ASLA, lecturing for civic groups and organizations, writing essays for popular magazines, publishing a book on design principles, and commissioning photographs of her work from women photographers.[6] Born in Scarborough, New York, Coffin was a member of a well-connected family that included both artists and engineers. Jonathan Trumbell, a distant uncle, had been a Colonial-era painter; another uncle, Benjamin Church, had been one of the engineers responsible for Central Park in Manhattan. Her father, Julian Ravenel Coffin, came from a well-established Nantucket family that had owned a plantation on St. Helena Island until the Civil War. Her mother, Alice Church Coffin, came from a large family based in upstate New York.

When Julian Coffin died in 1883, he left his family with insubstantial funds. Mother and daughter moved from New York City to Geneva, New York, to stay with John Barker Church, Alice Coffin's uncle. Thus, while her family was established within the upper echelons of society, Coffin still needed to pursue a career to earn a living for herself and her mother. She had, as she explained in an interview, "cherished the idea of being a great artist . . . but that dream seemed in no way possible of realization, and though my desire to create beauty was strong, I did not seem to possess talent for music, writing, painting or sculpture, at that time the only outlet a woman had to express any artistic ability she might have."[7]

Coffin claimed years later that she had long "been hearing of Beatrix Jones' novel profession and the success she was making of it, so on further investigation ... [she] found by far the most worthwhile course being offered was at the Massachusetts Institute of Technology, and off [she] went gaily expecting to be welcomed with open arms."[8] Despite initial discouragement from faculty members, Coffin enrolled at MIT in 1901 as a special student in the landscape architecture program, along with Edna Stoddard and Martha Brookes Hutcheson. "Special student" status, referring to a common practice in architecture schools, meant she would enroll in a shorter program, the typical four-year curriculum reduced to three, focused on core courses and lacking general courses in the arts and sciences. After being tutored in mathematics and geometry, Coffin took courses in botany and horticulture, as well as technical and architectural courses in drafting, engineering, and grading.

Coffin's description of the studio vividly captures its atmosphere: "In the drafting rooms and in our classes the four women students of my year (two were studying straight architecture and we other two in landscape . . .) were thrown in, all our work in competition with the men, and the invasion of their province as well as our specialty (what was a new and untried architectural development), put us on our mettle to prove that we too, were serious students and competitors. This association with many types of boys and men I found very helpful as we had a fine spirit of camaraderie in the drafting room, and many a helping hand was given me at a critical moment, though one had to steel oneself to hear many a severe criticism, which was perhaps even more valuable!"[9]

Coffin completed the courses she needed within three years by studying during the summers and supplementing her education through studies at the Arnold Arboretum. Like Farrand, Coffin studied with Charles Sprague Sargent and his staff, including John G. Jack, and she also took advantage of the resources of the Bussey Institute. Coffin was fully aware of the precedent she and her fellow students were setting: "We were pioneers, and moreover pioneer women in a new-old profession and one in which all one's ability to see and interpret beauty out of doors taxed all our resources, and we were determined to show what enthusiasm and hard work could accomplish."[10] Nonetheless, Coffin did not complete the degree, instead leaving to launch her own professional practice.

Henry Francis du Pont (1880–1969), a full-time student at the Bussey Institute while Coffin was at MIT, formed a lifelong bond with Coffin, based on their shared love for landscape architecture and horticulture. The two knew each other from youth, as their mothers had been friends since childhood. With both of them in Boston attending courses and lectures, their friendship deepened. Du Pont shared with Coffin the list of texts required for his courses, including Gertrude Jekyll's and E. T. Cook's books, and the two exchanged garden and horticultural books each Christmas, beginning in 1903, when du Pont gave Coffin the four-volume set of *Cyclopedia of American Horticulture,* by Liberty Hyde Bailey.[11] They wrote each other of their botanical finds, as well as their horticultural observations, often in great detail. It is tempting to speculate that du Pont may have wished to become a landscape architect as well but that, because of his social status, such a profession was out of the question for him.

Chaperoned by her mother, Coffin traveled through Europe with du Pont. The postcards and letters they sent home reveal their approach to seeing gardens, similar to that of Wharton and Farrand: they admired the plants, valued the art and architecture, and assessed the designs as they experienced them. Later Coffin returned to Europe to meet Gertrude Jekyll and others in the English garden community. In 1907 Coffin and her mother toured the Dalmatian Coast of the Adriatic Sea, noting the "wild, lonely, and impressive" landscape, visited by few other tourists. They traveled by packhorse, rowboat, and horse-drawn cart and also walked for miles. Coffin wrote about this trip for *National Geographic Magazine,* illustrating her essay with thirty of her own black-and-white photographs of the people and landscape, as well as a sketched map of the geography.[12] She was entranced by the drifts of wildflowers and the bright colors of the Dalmatian hills, writing of the colors of the sky, land, and vegetation. These scenes might well have been the inspiration for some of Coffin's later designs, which featured broad swaths of bright colors viewed against the sky or a body of water.

In 1904 Coffin began to search for employment. As she noted many years later: "On leaving school one expected the world would welcome newly fledged landscape artists, but alas, few people seemed to know what it was all about, while the idea of taking a woman into an office was unheard of. 'My dear young lady, what will you do about supervising the work on the ground?' became such a constant and discouraging query that the only thing seemed to be for me to hang out my own shingle and see what I would do about it."[13] She thus launched a practice out of her home. By the 1920s she was an established and well-recognized practitioner with commissions across the nation.

Like Farrand, Coffin received her first commissions from acquaintances within her circle of family and friends, many from the elite New England social world. The Church family, her mother's relatives, provided important connections in and around New York and the Hudson River Valley, and Henry Francis du Pont was also very helpful. In fact, a recommendation from the du Pont family likely led to Coffin's first important commission, for William Marshall Bullitt at his estate Oxmoor, in Louisville, Kentucky (1909-10). When du Pont inherited Winterthur, the family's one-thousand-acre estate, in 1928, he turned to Coffin for design help, and he continued to recommend her for numerous projects across the Eastern seaboard. By the 1920s Coffin had become one of the country's preeminent landscape practitioners, her clients including the Fricks, the Vanderbilts, and members of the du Pont family. She was commissioned for designs for Marjorie Merriweather; for Edward F. Hutton, at Hillwood, in Wheatley Hills, New York (1922) (now a part of the C. W. Post Long Island University); for Marshall Field (1920–23); for Stephen H. Pell, at the King's Garden Fort in Ticonderoga, New York (1920–26); and at the Winter Cottage Garden, at Caumsett, Lloyds Neck, New York. Over the course of her career Coffin designed at least fifty large estates in the Northeast, in addition to numerous smaller projects and gardens. A garden by Coffin, like one by Farrand or Shipman, was a point of honor.

While public gardens did not constitute a substantial portion of her practice, Coffin was commissioned to design a small number. She created gardens for the New York Botanical Garden (1942–57), including the Robert Montgomery Conifer Collection, the Havemeyer Lilac Collection, and a pavilion for the Rose Garden. She was also consulted on the design for school landscapes, one of her largest and most long-term projects done for the University of Delaware.

Coffin was recognized for her work by both professional and amateur organizations. Her design for the Bassick estate, in Fairfield, Connecticut, was awarded the Gold Medal of Honor for Landscape Design by the Architectural League of New York in 1930. In 1946 she was awarded the honorary degree of doctor of letters from Hobart and William Smith colleges, in Geneva, New York. Maintaining an active practice until the end, Coffin died in 1957.

A Legitimate Office

Coffin was determined from the first to establish herself as a professional landscape architect. She immediately set about creating a professional office, methods of practice, and a list of fees. Her first office, opened in 1903, was at the National Arts Club, 15 Gramercy Park, New York City, where she and her mother also lived. Coffin insisted on the title "landscape architect," as she felt it established her professional status. She firmly believed that the discipline embraced architecture, art, and horticulture: "[The] landscape designer should . . . have the architect's sense of form and line . . . the artist's perception of color and texture, . . . [and] be sensitive to the play of light and shadow on his composition."[14] In 1906 she was elected a junior member of the ASLA, the first young woman to be so recognized. She continued to be engaged in ASLA committees and activities throughout her career.

As her practice quickly expanded, Coffin moved with her mother to a larger home, at 73 East Ninety-second Street. To manage her practice, Coffin hired as her secretary Selina C. Appleyard, who took care of the correspondence and office files and records until Coffin's death. For her home Coffin hired housekeeper Mary Meher to oversee the entertaining of clients and colleagues, a role Meher held until her death during World War II.[15] By hiring a staff to manage both her office and the her home, Coffin could easily blend with both the social elite and the professional communities.

Primarily women were hired to work in Coffin's office, which included probably no more than three to five staff members at any one time. After only a few years on her own, Coffin hired Elizabeth F. Colwell in 1910 to help with the drafting and office management. Colwell oversaw early work at Winterthur, corresponded with du Pont, and made frequent site visits to the estate for consultations. She left in 1913 to open her own office, although she continued to work for Coffin on a consulting basis. In 1913 Coffin hired an associate architect, James Scheiner, to provide technical expertise. By associating with an architect, Coffin strengthened her position, as architecture was already well-established as a professional domain. In addition, by associating with a male practitioner, Coffin likely validated her own work, which could no longer be discounted as merely that of a female garden designer. Scheiner left to serve in World War I, but he returned afterward to partner with Coffin throughout the rest of her practice.

In 1917 Coffin opened a larger office, at 830 Lexington Avenue, which she called "a real little office."[16] This dedicated office space allowed her to clearly separate the professional and private arenas of her life and to significantly expand her practice. She was elected a fellow of the ASLA, along with Fletcher Steele, in 1918—the same year Scheiner returned to the office. By 1930, Coffin had moved her office to One East Fifty-third Street, and Scheiner had opened a practice in Pelham, New York.

Clara Stimson, later Coffey, joined the practice in 1923 and soon became Coffin's close associate and friend. Coffey and Scheiner continued to work for Coffin even after setting up separate practices, charging hourly rates as consultants. By 1946, Scheiner noted, they were sharing a third of the work and proceeds of the Coffin practice, although Coffey's name never appeared on the letterhead. Ethel D. Nevius also joined Coffin's practice, her name added to the letterhead around 1928. In 1941, when Coffin closed her New York office, Nevius established her own successful practice.

Throughout her practice Coffin established collaborative partnerships with other practitioners, particularly architects. She was frequently asked to recommend an architectural firm or other professional consultant. In 1931, for example, after Connecticut College asked her to provide a list of possible architects with whom she could work on a campus design, the architects she recommended were uniformly grateful. Harry Milliken wrote: "I do not believe that it is possible for an architect alone to work out such a plan in a thoroughly satisfactory manner. I believe the questions in which the topography enters in, to the extent that it does in this case, should be studied by the architect and the landscape architect working in consultation from the very beginning."[17] Whether or not architects generally supported such a collaborative approach, Coffin's professional success was evident in the fact that architects did wish her to recommend them for projects.

On the other hand, concerned about architects' tendency to control landscape architecture, Coffin was careful to delineate the role of each professional in any collaboration. For a project for du Pont, Coffin asked him to confirm in writing that as landscape architect she was to "take entire charge of the landscape grading, dune building, soil preparation, planting, as well as any paths not already under the contract for the roads."[18] Clearly, then, while Coffin understood that architects might help legitimize her work and contribute to its quality and extent, she was careful to assure that her practice remained autonomous and distinct.

Coffin's own gardens provided an indispensable resource for her practice, functioning as exhibits of her skill as a designer and gardener. This was particularly true at her summer home, Wendover. Coffin had purchased Wendover, in Watch Hill, Rhode Island, in 1921 and had immediately begun to transform it from a dilapidated cottage into a showplace. She frequently entertained, as Shipman had in Cornish and Olmsted in Fairsted. Potential clients, family members, and friends were regularly invited to relax at the summer house, and each spring Coffin hosted a large party. She designed Wendover's gardens to be at their best during the entertaining season—primarily the spring, early summer, and at the height of autumn. She also used the house to exhibit her paintings of flowers, gardens, and landscapes. Scheiner and Coffin wrote about Wendover in "Our Substitute Castle in Spain," published in the September 1922 issue of *Country Life in America*. The house, they noted, was furnished with antiques and works of art, providing an excellent space for professional and social entertaining.

In 1927 Coffin and her mother moved to New Haven, Connecticut, where they bought a large house and garden at 165 Bishop Street, just blocks from the Yale campus. Coffin still maintained her office in New York, traveling to the city on weekdays and visiting her clients, while simultaneously building up her New Haven practice. Her New Haven gardens, while not large, were carefully developed, filled with flowers, shrubs, and trees and enclosed with a picket fence—providing the setting for her annual May garden tea parties, as well as less formal gatherings. While the picket fence allowed Coffin the privacy she wished for to control the views, her neighbors were not pleased, as they were used to the property's large, open, parklike yards. Coffin responded by planting a plethora of flowering trees, which might be enjoyed by the whole neighborhood. The large clapboard house itself was furnished with family antiques and arranged to allow boarders to rent rooms—yet another shock to her neighbors. Coffin's boarders included the scientist Francis Crick and Warren Hunting Smith, who became a lifelong friend (and bought the house after her death, donating it to Yale University in 1989).[19] Coffin officially moved her office to New Haven in 1932, when her mother passed away, although she kept the New York office operating until 1941.

In New York, Coffin had clearly separated her professional from her personal space, but in New Haven the quarters were closer, and the space needed to be used more efficiently. Coffin and her boarders thus lived on the first two floors, while she maintained space for drafting and offices on the third floor. To help her maintain her professional identity, Coffin had Grace Boulard serve as secretary in the city office from 1935 to 1937, while Mrs. Appleyard led the New Haven office.

Indeed, Coffin, like Farrand, was widely noted for her exacting professionalism. She maintained a strictly businesslike relationship with clients while addressing a project, even if she might otherwise be a friend and colleague, distributing a "Schedule of Professional Charges" during her initial consultation, as recommended by the ASLA. Clients were subsequently given contracts that they were asked to sign, outlining the exact duties and obligations of both the landscape architect and the client, as well as those of possible contractors and others who might be involved in the project.

Coffin's charges, like her procedures, were guided by the ASLA, and she adjusted them as she gained more experience and as the ASLA increased the standard levels. Coffin set the initial fees for a consultation according to a project's complexity, importance, and distance from New York. The fees for the subsequent development of a plan were based on "the creative and constructive services rendered, including an overhead charge for all office work of drafting, ordering, directions, etc, that may have to do with the undertaking." For a preliminary plan these charges ranged from $250 to $500, which could be detailed in a report to the client upon request. If a client wanted working drawings, the fee ranged from $50 to $350 for each plan, again depending on size, as well as complexity and the number of drawings required. Personal supervision of construction or planting cost $50 per day for time and $25 to $35 per day for Coffin's assistants. Coffin's fees for public or institutional work were based in part on a percentage, as recommended by the ASLA. For private clients or smaller projects, Coffin allowed a lump-sum payment, again in accordance with ASLA guidelines.

Coffin also carefully delineated the roles in her office, retaining artistic control over all commissions. Lead employees acted in Coffin's stead only as requested, as was true in most professional firms. Colwell and Coffey, for example, visited construction sites, reporting back to Coffin on the matters at hand. Colwell corresponded directly with du Pont on the gardens at Winterthur, as she was maintaining a planting plan that needed to be updated every time he changed the beds, even the annual flower beds. When Coffin was out of the office, she informed du Pont, they had to wait until her return to make final decisions, in spite of the fact that du Pont had specifically hired Colwell through Coffin's office for a particular project at Winterthur—creating a key for the entire garden, identifying each planting bed by code and each plant within each bed. While Colwell was drafting such a key and supervising the planting of some of the beds, and had produced drawings for du Pont, she could not commit to her next visit to supervise work until she had spoken with Coffin.[20] Coffin's close control of her firm, she believed, allowed her to maintain the standards and process she believed represented the best practice.

Design as Collaboration

Coffin's praxis, as noted earlier, was based on a collaborative approach to the design process. She began a project with a visit to the proposed site with the clients, assessing their desires and needs: "In taking up the problem the first step was to ascertain the wishes of the owners." She would walk the site and discuss its potential with the clients, listening carefully and making great efforts to assure that the "design [would] be in scale not only with the house and grounds but also with the means and taste of the owner."[21] Like Shipman, then, Coffin did not believe that the artist necessarily knew better than the client what would work best for a specific landscape.

Coffin worked with the existing landscape, although she was not averse to altering it dramatically in order to reflect a site's genius loci. She might, for example, modify topography or vegetation to realize a concept or a practical request. Through the process of responding to both the client and the site, Coffin considered the character of the landscape on many levels. When, for example, the Sabin family commissioned her to design their estate, she advised that they purchase a nearby farm so that the topsoil could be moved to their garden to create a terraced landscape leading down to the waterfront, the final view to the ocean and the natural slope optimally realized through terraces and the garden's placement on a slope. In many respects this approach was not significantly different from Olmsted's work in Central Park, where an average of four feet of soil was added to the entire site. And Olmsted would have similarly argued that he had expressed the character of the landscape through his design.

Once a general idea had been agreed upon, Coffin requested a professional survey and inventory to document the site's topography, as well as detailed information on boundary lines, buildings, roads, or other items that would influence the design of the landscape. After reviewing these documents, notes, and sketches, she drew preliminary plans for review, showing the "layout of the property, the outlines of existing or proposed structures and the general disposition of gardens, plantations, roads, etc."[22] These were discussed either on site or at Coffin's office. Written correspondence followed every meeting and confirmed all decisions. Cof-

The Sabin gardens, during (*top*) and after (*bottom*) construction of terraces
leading to the ocean view. Photographs by Mattie Edwards Hewitt. (Courtesy,
The Winterthur Library: Winterthur Archives)

fin described her process to Edward Byer, a potential client, explaining the various ways in which her expertise might be used:

> My professional procedure is as follows: I make a preliminary visit to the ground, go over all the points with the client getting their ideas and giving them mine. This is called a Consultation and is the first and most important step in the proceeding. Sometimes it is all that is required and my suggestions can be carried out without further aid from me, but usually it leads to making sketches for the garden scheme, which after approval are turned into working plans. If the Consultation is all that is needed I charge $100 in the vicinity of New York . . . but if further services such as sketches, plans, supervision etc. are required I charge for these though the original consultation fee is credited as a first payment on the account. After seeing the problem and understanding your requirements I can usually give a fairly close estimate of what my services will amount to, and can procure you estimates for the cost of carrying out the undertaking.[23]

Coffin, accomplished in sketching, drawing, and painting, used each medium to help convey her design ideas and her intent. She believed that drawing helped her to perceive a site's potential, and thus, each project elicited multiple sketches that provided options, ideas, and explanations. Her initial drawings were generally in pencil, on either trace or light paper, while presentation drawings were either in ink or watercolor, on linen or other durable paper. Exhibit drawings were done on large vellum boards. Coffin provided plans as well as elevation drawings, as they allowed the background that lay beyond the landscape to be "brought into the picture."[24]

Coffin attributed her talent as an artist to her ability to "see" clearly and intuitively. She was, in fact, an accomplished painter, exhibiting her paintings in New York galleries and selling her work through Arden Galleries on Fifth Avenue.[25] At the time of her death, Coffin was writing a book tentatively titled "The Seeing Eye," intended to teach others how to cultivate their perceptive vision through painting, drawing, and observing, learning to see the landscape as it existed and as it might be transformed.[26]

Coffin's attention to the composition of her paintings and presentation drawings was equaled by her attention to the working drawings. Planting plans were created for new gardens, specifying species and varieties of plants as well as quantities and including instructions on how plants should be planted, transplanted, and otherwise cared. When Coffin was called in to revise a garden, on-site supervision replaced such detailed planting plans, as noted in her "Method of Practice": "In new projects general and detailed planting plans and planting lists are furnished. . . . To revise an existing property it is often impossible to make planting plans as the work of reconstruction will consist of moving existing trees and shrubs and the use of the axe in thinning out over-grown plantations. For this type of work personal supervision is essential."[27]

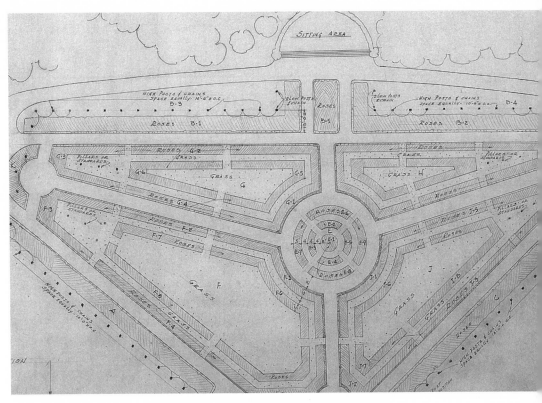

Portion of preliminary plan for the Rose Garden at the New York Botanical Garden, by Marian Cruger Coffin, 1953. This is similar to many preliminary plans Coffin would present to clients as she developed a design. (Courtesy, The Winterthur Library: Winterthur Archives)

When Coffin decided that a design needed to be a "ground plan" (with the plants actually placed on the ground), a planting plan would not be made. The du Pont home in South Hampton, Long Island, demanded such a plan:

> For this new part of the work which is solely landscape and which will consist of gardening, soil preparation, dune building, planting, paths and steps not taken up under the road contract, I understand we are to handle in a different way. As this is distinctly a ground job it will require a good deal of supervision. It will be necessary to give one or two visits a week to the job. . . . My charge for supervision is $50.00 per day for me and $35.00 per day for Mr. Scheiner or assistants. . . . The dimension or working plan we will check as we go along and only charge you a nominal sum for the work on this. When we get as far as doing the actual planting I will be able to tell you whether it will be more advisable to do it as a plan job or as a ground job. When we do work on this per diem basis I take no commissions whatever.[28]

Coffin ordered plant materials and passed on the wholesale rates, as was customary. Unlike Farrand, she did not maintain an account to pay nurserymen but instead had the invoice sent directly to the client, with a copy for her office files sent to her. "The Landscape Architect," she noted in her "Method of Practice," "is not a gardener nor a dealer in plants, takes no commissions on purchases, assumes no responsibility for errors of nurserymen, for miscarriage or damage of plants in transportation, or for their failure to grow." Landscape architects were struggling to distinguish themselves from tradesmen in general and nurserymen specifically, and the middle-man role was not one Coffin appreciated.

An Artist's Mastery of Plant Materials

Practicing at a time when women were increasingly associated with flower garden design, Coffin emphasized the need to master the horticultural requirements of a garden and draw on a larger plant palette that included trees, shrubs, and ground covers. The landscape architect, she wrote, "knows and uses . . . plant material to develop his plan, always keeping in mind its value to the composition at maturity, but the landscape architect is a highly trained professional who is (or should be!) a master of his materials. . . . For it is after all the *right plant* in the *right place* that will give that sense of restfulness and permanence that good plantings should have, beautiful in themselves and in harmony with their surroundings."[29] It is noteworthy that here she refers to the landscape architect as "he": this can be read as Coffin's associating herself with male professionals, emphasizing her position within the larger community of professionals instead of the smaller community of women in landscape architecture. Or it was a simple shorthand.

Coffin believed that the maturity of a given landscape was particularly important and that good design required a long time. She explained to her clients: "As the development of the property may take several years it is essential to retain the services of the Landscape Architect in order to complete the design according to the original conception. Even where the design is practically completed at once, annual supervision is advisable to preserve the design, to control the proper growth of trees and shrubs, and to maintain the color scheme and succession of bloom in the garden."[30] She reminded her readers, assumed to be women, that a property owner "must remember that it takes from one to three years for her executed plans to grow into full perfection, depending upon the kinds of trees and shrubs the place has been beautified with. Then the place must be carefully watched, to see that growth proceeds in accordance with the plans."[31] Gardens and landscape designs, according to Coffin, required regular attention and decision making over the course of many years, if not decades. This approach defined her work for the University of Delaware, a project she was involved with for over three decades.

Coffin was commissioned in 1919 to bring together the landscapes of the two Delaware colleges—the men's and the women's—into one campus. The men's college had been established in the early nineteenth century, while the women's college was new. The two colleges were now to appear linked without actually being merged, since campus life would in fact remain separate. Initially, only the library, placed at the edge of the men's campus with a front facing the women's, served as a coeducational space, but students, while maintaining distinct spaces, were to have a meeting area in the middle.

Coffin's office produced a "General Plan for Layout of Delaware College at Newark, Delaware," in 1919, and Coffin remained the university's landscape architect until 1952. She developed designs for each campus, as well as the shared middle space, working closely with the architectural firm of Day and Klauder. Coffin wrote that the plan "should afford a unique example in the Eastern States of what a College can be when planned from the outset as a complete whole." She went on to argue that "good planning . . . is bound to express in the most economical as well as in the most beautiful manner (as beauty logically develops from a well ordered plan) the life and aims of the institution."[32]

Coffin's plan for the men's campus called for ordered rows of elm and oak trees surrounding the central green, which extended from the entrance on Main Street to the men's side of the library. A cross-axis was also planned, with a double row of trees leading from the theater to a second major campus entrance. The allée of tall stately trees emphasized the order and austerity of the men's campus. Coffin also placed *Taxus baccata repandens* (spreading English yew) at the base of the campus buildings, marking the intersection of architecture and landscape. She used *Juniperus virginiana* (red cedar), *Ilex Opaca* (American holly) *Crataegus pyracantha* (thorn tree), and *Pyrus japonica* (Japanese quince) in their tree forms to break the line of yews and accent the architecture's verticality. As these trees were primarily evergreen, the campus remained green throughout the year. She put little emphasis on flowering trees, although the *Ilex* bore bright red berries in the winter and the quince bloomed in the early spring. Coffin also avoided using vines on the buildings, adding to the austerity and firmness of the architecture.

Coffin's plan for the women's campus, on the other hand, called for flowering trees and shrubs to soften the architecture and create a romantic atmosphere. She chose a floral scheme of yellow, pink, and white,

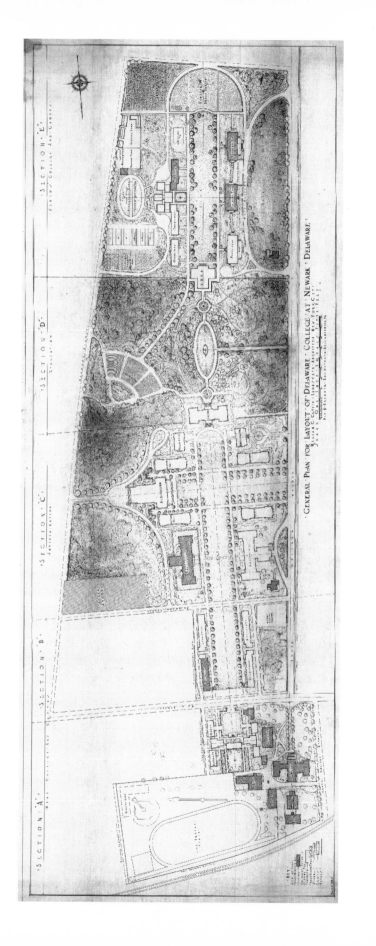

· GENERAL · PLAN · FOR · LAYOUT · OF · DELAWARE · COLLEGE · AT · NEWARK · DELAWARE ·
MARIAN C. COFFIN · LANDSCAPE ARCHITECT · NEW YORK CITY ·

as opposed to the predominant green with red highlights of the men's campus. Flowering trees included a variety of *Magnolias, Cladastris lutea* (yellowwood), and *Gleditsia tricanthus* (honey locust), seemingly scattered as if they were in a grove, although they in fact formed two rows that extended the length of the campus. The resulting much more informal landscape encouraged meandering walks, with little emphasis placed on the axis with the library, although it stood at the edge of the women's campus.

Gardens were placed in front of each women's dormitory, emphasizing the theme, the dormitory walls cloaked in *Schizophragma hydrangoides* (Japanese climbing hydrangea) and *Hedera helix* (English ivy). Shrubs were also used far more extensively, including deutzia, roses, lilacs, and laburnum. The overall atmosphere evoked more of a campus within a garden, as opposed to the more architectonic men's campus landscape.

Coffin also designed a central recreation area for women and men to use as a common space, featuring a circle of pink-flowering magnolia trees surrounding an oval lawn. This served as a transitional space, where men and women could meet and relax without leaving the university grounds. The space also drew attention away from the bend in the axis between the men's and women's campuses, giving the impression that the two extended out like balanced arms on either side.

A naturalistic grove was also planned for the northern part of the middle landscape, with a theater set to one side. This grove was reminiscent of Downing's plans for the mall in Washington, D.C., with paths meandering among large native trees. Coffin suggested that this small grove should be "mostly of a native character . . . which will afford from early spring until autumn a variety of beauty and interest."[33] The trees specified were *Cornus florida* (dogwoods), *Amelanchier* (shad bushes) set under a grove of *Fagus sylvatica* (beeches), *Liriodendron tulipifera* (tulip poplars), and *Liquidamber styraciflua* (sweet gum). In 1925 she specified *Paulownia tomentosa* (princess trees) to be set in rows on either side of the grass oval—special trees planted in tribute to the du Pont family, who had planted it throughout their estates in Wilmington, recognizing their generous support of the university. The trees also added a colorful display of blooms in summer and filtered sunlight throughout the spring and fall. It was as if this naturalistic middle landscape generated the two campuses—one for the men, with its strict allée, and the other for the women, with its colorful grove.

The primary entrance to the campus was designed as a straight path leading to the southern end of the oval garden, serving both the men's and the women's colleges. Unfortunately, as a result of the Great Depression and the growth of the campus, many of the elements of Coffin's plan were never fully realized, including the entrance path, although recent building projects at the university have generated renewed interest in the design.

Coffin clearly delineated the various gendered spaces on campus, separating and clearly distinguishing the areas accessible to men, women, or both. The library had two fronts, one facing the men's college and the opposite side facing the transitional middle space. The YWCA building was designed to be placed at the end of the women's college, visually separating the women from the men and even from the central area. Unfortunately, this building was never constructed, and the central area remained barren for decades, planted only in the 1940s, with a library built on it in the 1960s.

Coffin not only provided initial plans for the university's plantings but also worked closely with the staff to maintain the landscape. Her attention to details was evident in her extensive correspondence, for example, with Rodney Sharpe and Henry du Pont (both of whom served on the university's board of directors) and with the university leadership. Coffin hired Elsa Rehmann to supervise the initial plantings at the university, as Rehmann's knowledge of plant ecologies and attention to the plants' horticultural requirements assured a high-quality implementation of the plans. Once the initial plantings had been established, Coffin worked closely with Lee Rose, the university's superintendent of grounds, to maintain and update the landscape. Through this project Coffin established her ability to successfully address the complex issues inherent to an educational institution, and her plan's success is perhaps most clearly evident in its ability to grow with the changes commonly undergone at universities over the past century. At a time when work in the public realm was increasingly important, Coffin's work at Delaware was an important professional contribution.

Although the university was one of the few institutional projects Coffin undertook, she continued to explore a variety of design approaches in her designs for private estates. Her growing interest in native plants and naturalistic designs, for example, is evident in her designs for the Bassick family in Bridgeport, Connecticut, and the Wing estate in Millbrook, New York. Indeed, the Architectural League of New York awarded Coffin the 1930 Gold Medal of Honor for the Bassick and Wing landscapes.

For the Bassick estate Coffin designed a woodland landscape featuring a small body of water, drifts of daffodils echoing the swale, and boulders woven among existing and newly planted trees. Coffin encouraged the use of native trees and shrubs, as "they will fall imperceptibly into the character of the countryside."[34] The seasonal nature of the landscape was also an important element in the design, as the woodland glades would be full of bloom in the spring, quiet and cool in the summer, and brilliantly colored in the autumn. Shaping her design around the native trees already thriving on the site, Coffin described designing the woodland, clearing extra growth to define a feature. Years later, when the family needed to simplify the landscape, Coffin worked with them to retain the daffodil beds and woodland areas, while removing most of the annual flower beds. This

Bassick estate landscape featuring the woodland garden area. This area was retained for many years even when the clients could no longer maintain the more formal flower gardens. Photograph by Amemya. (Courtesy, The Winterthur Library: Winterthur Archives)

woodland landscape was reminiscent of Thomas Jefferson's vision of the American woods merely trimmed up in order to allow dappled sun and a plethora of flowering shrubs and herbaceous plants.

The Wing garden drew on a more dramatic landscape of water and trees, characterized by an irregular-shaped lake, edged by willows and water-loving plants. A white willow tree growing on the bank dominated the view, while flowering shrubs provided a sense of balance and unity. Native flowers, shrubs, and trees established the landscape's natural character, while stepping-stones formed a bridge across the lake's shallow end, on an axis with a small garden bench, which marked the landscape as peopled as opposed to untouched. Coffin's use of native and naturalized trees and shrubs, water features, and topography, and her

Wing estate, pond and willow tree. The caption in Coffin's book reads: "A water garden made to feature a large White Willow at the edge of an existing lake. Stepping stones form a causeway across a shallow end. All the planting is carefully kept subordinate to the superb old tree." Photograph by Amemya. (Courtesy, The Winterthur Library: Winterthur Archives)

careful placement of rocks and boulders, created a garden that might easily be mistaken for an ideal "work of nature" rather than a designed landscape, as was her intent.

Overall, Coffin's designs consistently reflected a deep concern for encouraging an appreciation of nature and the outdoors and reinforcing the potential of the American landscape and culture. Coffin was committed to educating both clients and the public in good design, expanding her sphere of influence beyond those who might be able to hire her by publishing in popular magazines and writing a book. Her work was featured in Rehmann's *The Small Place,* Richardson Wright's *House & Garden Book of Gardens* (1921), P. H. Elwood Jr.'s *American Landscape Architecture* (1924), and Louise Shelton's *Beautiful Garden in America* (1924). Coffin gave a copy of *The Small Place* to a client (Mrs. Bassick) so that she might subsequently donate it to the Fairfield library. Further, Coffin's own book, *Trees and Shrubs for Landscape Effects,* and her numerous articles for magazines, including *Country Life in America,* helped to establish her as an artist, a professional, and an advocate for the American landscape.

Trees and Shrubs for Landscape Effects was intended as an inspirational resource for gardeners and designers who wished to use plant materials in a thoughtful and tasteful manner. Coffin noted her frustration with the book's publisher, Scribners, which wanted her to include more horticultural information, declaring that she was not interested in writing a "gardening dictionary." Rather, the book was meant for "nature lovers and plant lovers . . . who wish to add their quota in creating outdoor beauty," as well as for anyone who would like to encourage growers and nurseries to expand their stock of interesting plant materials.[35] Coffin may well have imagined her book on a shelf with works by Rehmann, Hutcheson, Cautley, Steele, and Hubbard, rather than those by King or Ely. Her focus on trees in particular emphasized her interest in the landscape's form and structure, as opposed to its decorative or ornamental details. Coffin treated trees as architectural elements in the creation of a visionary design, a work of art.

Coffin organized her chapters as one might approach a landscape: first the entrance to the site; then the house and its setting; then the lawn and terraces; and finally the details of backgrounds and ground covers, walks and woodlands, green and other gardens, and planting fundamentals. Each chapter considered a variety of circumstances, illustrated by images of Coffin's garden designs. Coffin explained how design relationships established in large landscapes could be emulated in smaller-scale gardens. She responded to requests for specific planting recommendations by including an extensive list of plants appropriate for specific sites and purposes at the end of many of the chapters.

Coffin began the book by discussing the importance of considering the existing site—much as she would begin a design project with a site visit. She told a reporter: "The important thing is to find the distinctive note and make the theme complete. I must study the ground contour and become familiar with the plans for the house. This cannot be properly done by 'board work' in the office or by adapting well-known examples. Each problem is distinct."[36] The plan should respond to the natural lay of the land and should be thought of in terms of elevation, for it must be, "or seem to be, primarily a part of its surroundings, and the beauty which lies beyond must be brought into the picture." Once the plan had been developed, the home owner could begin to consider the planting scheme, "provided he is blessed with a natural gift for proportion, a sense of suitability, a love of nature, and an interest in making landscape pictures."[37] Coffin thus made it clear to the reader that without some real talent the amateur might be better served by a professional designer.

A highlight of Coffin's book was its beautiful black-and-white photographs. Mattie Edwards Hewitt, Harry G. Healy, George H. Van Anda, Amemya, John Wallace Gillies, and Samuel H. Gottscho had each documented Coffin's designed landscapes, hired by Coffin or by clients. These photographers returned in different seasons or years to capture a garden as it matured and changed. Gottscho in particular photographed many of Coffin's later gardens, including Winterthur. By drawing on the work of these photographers, whose work was often published, Coffin both increased the visibility of her designed landscapes and associated her work with that of other respected artists.

Coffin's articles and essays were also illustrated by such photographs; many, in fact, took the form of photographic essays with little text, including a series in *House & Garden* between January and May 1920 and a piece in *House Beautiful* in 1926. Coffin also used photographs in her exhibits for the Architectural League of New York and for the American Institute of Architects, as well for as the annual ASLA exhibits. In the 1927 *Index of Exhibits for the Architectural League of New York,* Coffin was listed as showing six garden projects, more than any other woman landscape architect, including Cautley, Dean, Flanders, and Eleanor Roche. Coffin also provided images of her gardens to advertisers. An advertisement for E. W. Howell Col, Builders of Country Homes and Gardens, for example, featured an image of a Coffin landscape, and a book published by the Cyclone Fence Company in 1928, titled *Beauty in Gardens: A Tribute,* featured images of Coffin gardens photographed by Hewitt and others, alongside the gardens of Charles Downing Lay, Ruth Dean, John Russell Pope, Jens Jensen, Charles W. Leavitt & Son, and the Olmsted Brothers.

In her own book Coffin used photographs to illustrate design principles and the key elements of carefully composed garden spaces. The images visually describe the gardens' massing, form, and lines, highlighting the features making up her compositions. Many feature trees and lawn set against the sky, while others feature plants set within formal architecture. While her gardens frequently included an abundance of flowering plants, the images, in black and white, emphasize light and shadow as

Photograph by Mattie Edwards Hewitt for Marian Cruger Coffin's book, *Trees and Shrubs for Landscape Effects,* New York, 1940. (Courtesy, The Winterthur Library: Winterthur Archives)

opposed to color. Indeed, the architectonic nature of Coffin's designs is particularly evident in these photographs.

The images rarely contain a person, traditional for exhibiting a designed landscape or building. By thus presenting the given work without people, the focus remains on the work of art rather than the function of the space, highlighting the design's artfulness rather than its practicality. Sharp shadows and distinct references to scale emphasize the depth of the space in these images, allowing the garden's spatial character to dominate the details of plants or furniture. The images of Coffin's work persuasively convey the power of good design to highlight the beauty of a specific site, its spatial and aesthetic character. By so emphasizing design principles and spatial characteristics, Coffin associated her work with broader trends in landscape design in the late 1930s and 1940s—the increased interest in geometry and space rather than plant materials and vignettes.

Whereas early in Coffin's career it had been advantageous for her to be associated with the community of wealthy patrons, by 1940, when the book was published, Coffin was increasingly protective of her clients. None of the photographs in the book is identified by estate, owner, or location; only the photographer's name and a general caption are provided in each case. This was not the case for Coffin's earlier photographs appearing in magazines or in Elwood's and Shelton's 1924 books. Her increased loyalty to her clients was particularly important where the du Pont family was concerned, Coffin frequently promising in her correspondence to use the images without any hint of identification. She held true to this promise.

More broadly, sensitivity toward the privacy of upper-class clients often required landscape architects to avoid too much publicity, even though they might otherwise wish to promote their work. Farrand, for example, almost never had her work featured in magazines, and she rarely hired photographers to document her gardens for publication. Coffin instead chose to use images without identifying her clients, maintaining the careful balance between the professional realm and the private world of the upper class that was clearly a concern for practitioners.

Coffin was nonetheless well-aware of the importance of visibility in her professional and social communities. She was an active member of the ASLA, joining committees and attending chapter and annual meetings. From 1917 to 1921 she served on the ASLA's exhibition committee and from 1924 to 1926 on its traveling exhibition committee, her involvement ensuring that her work was often included in both annual and traveling shows. Indeed, three of the five images printed in the *American Architect* in 1926 to illustrate the third annual ASLA exhibition were of Coffin's work. Coffin also became a member-at-large of the GCA in 1920 and later regularly lectured for this group. She did pro-bono work for the Beach Club at Watch Hill, where she owned a summer house, and Henry F. du Pont appointed her to the horticultural committee of the New York Botanical Garden.[38]

Like many of her colleagues, Coffin understood that to hold public authority, she had to be viewed as a professional and landscape architecture had to be viewed as a legitimate profession. She also understood that landscape architecture had to be perceived as a public service—a practice that would improve the lives of American citizens, rather than a luxury item for the wealthy. Her book was in part, then, a description of the landscape architecture as a service meant to improve the home of the average American citizen. Coffin believed that the benefits of a well-designed garden were within the means of many. In an article in *Country Life in America* entitled "A Suburban Garden Six Years Old," Coffin wrote: "A garden that is well planned, well constructed, and well maintained is a luxury, but a luxury that need not be beyond the means of even the moderately well-to-do. . . . The same principles must be observed as in designing any other garden; that is, the design must be in scale not only with the house and grounds but also with the means and tastes of the owners."[39] Coffin was not interested merely in creating works of art for art collectors, but in creating beautiful spaces for any who wished to enjoy such places. Underscoring this vision, nevertheless, was her wish to establish the profession of landscape architecture as equal to that of architecture: while by the 1920s it had been accepted that architects were required for tasteful and good architecture, landscape architects had yet to firmly establish themselves.

Partners in the Professions

Partnering with an architect was a particularly successful way for a landscape architect to legitimate his or her practice as well as the profession itself. Such partnerships were not uncommon, allowing participants to address a wide range of design projects and expanding and enhancing their work. Notably, these partnerships frequently reflected the contemporary gendering of the professions, the man often serving not only as the architect but also as the business manager, at least publicly, while the woman addressed the gardens and landscapes. Coffin and Scheiner are one important example of such a partnership; an even more typical configuration was the married team: Janet Darling and Richard Webel, Agnes Selkirk Clark and Cameron Clark, Helen Morgenthau Fox and Mortimer Fox. In each of these partnerships the wife served as the landscape architect and the husband as the architect.

Ruth Bramley Dean and Aymar Embury II (1880–1966) worked as partners while also leading autonomous practices, much like Scheiner and Coffin. Ruth Bramley Dean was born in Wilkes-Barre, Pennsylvania. She took courses at the University of Chicago from 1908 to 1910 but dropped out to work for Jens Jensen, whose work in conservation and efforts to found Friends of Our Native Landscape—a preservation organization that worked to conserve natural areas throughout the Midwest—provided the training ground for numerous young men and women, many of whom carried on his conservation efforts. Dean left Jensen's office in 1915, worked briefly for Rand McNally, and then opened an office at 137 East Fifty-fifth Street in New York City, drawing on Jensen's work to frame her own practice. For example, in her 1917 book, *The Livable House, Its Garden,* published as part of a series edited by Aymar Embury II, Dean outlined an approach to design celebrating the potential of the American residential landscape, although Dean paid more attention than Jensen would to fitting the gardens to a house's architecture.

Dean married Aymar Embury II, later partnering with him on a number of projects while continuing to practice separately. Aymar Embury II, a prolific author of books on American homes, churches, and country houses, served as the editor of the "Livable House" series, which featured Dean's book, and also wrote the series' companion book, *The Livable House: Its Plan and Design.* He designed numerous buildings in the public and private sectors, primarily in New York and on Long Island. His designs were predominantly revival styles, in accordance with the tastes of his clients. His interests overlapped with Dean's, however, in their mutual desire to create an American style of design, based on the American culture and its landscape.

Dean established her professional work relatively quickly. She published a series of articles on garden design in 1915 in *Garden Magazine,* and the *Christian Science Monitor* published an interview with her titled "Landscape Architect—A New Vocation for Women." In this interview Dean suggested that anyone wishing to become a landscape architect would "need practical experience in both an architect's and a landscape architect's office, and must start as draftsmen. . . . A knowledge of engineering and architecture, horticulture and art, is requisite."[40] Dean described the long process involved in her work, from surveying the landscape to overseeing construction, emphasizing her belief in the value of fitting home and garden into one composition. The *Christian Science Monitor* interviewed her again in 1917, this time on foundation plantings.[41]

Dean was also a prolific writer for home and garden periodicals, including *House & Garden, House Beautiful,* and *Country Life in America,* and served as garden editor for the *Delineator,* a 1920s women's magazine. Her writing style was straightforward, featuring rules, examples, and illustrations, and architecturally oriented. The projects she addressed ranged from a "place developed along strictly utilitarian lines," to a campfire circle, to gardens in a naturalistic style.[42] Dean, particularly interested in rooftop gardens in New York, wrote one article suggesting that they were "one of the by-products of the zoning law, which provides that upper stories of tall buildings shall step back so as to establish a certain angle with the street."[43] While she admitted to the need to sacrifice plant

materials in such gardens, as few large plants could survive for more than
a season or so, on an annual basis, her interest in pushing the boundaries
of conventional design was clear. The city garden at the rear of her office
in New York, for example, relied on the architectural elements of walls,
fountains, benches, and sculpture, with turf, trees, and vines providing
minimal vegetation.

Dean led an office in New York, as well as working out of her home
and office in East Hampton on Long Island. Her garden on Long Island

Rooftop garden designed by Ruth Bramley Dean and published in the ASLA
Illustrations of Work of Members, 1931. Dean spoke about this garden in a number of
early interviews.

Ruth Bramley Dean and Aymar Embury's home garden as photographed for the ASLA *Illustrations of Work of Members*, 1932. The garden was a showpiece for Dean, an example of her approach to Colonial Revival styles. It is a simple plan outlined with boxwood plants and filled with seasonal flowering and fragrant plants. Next to the three-hundred-year-old saltbox house, the garden appeared to be an update of a much older garden.

was a showpiece, as was the three-hundred-year-old saltbox house, which Embury had restored. Dean's staff was composed of women, including her niece Marianne Dean McMasters, who had taken courses at the University of Chicago and the Carnegie Institute of Technology. Vera Poggi Breed also worked in the Dean office after taking agriculture courses at the University of Massachusetts. She later worked for the Department of Parks in New York (1934–38), designing, drafting, and supervising projects while maintaining an individual practice. Mary Deputy Lamson, a writer and designer, joined Dean's office in the early 1920s. She had completed a bachelor's degree in English literature and received a master's degree in fine arts from the University of Indiana, as well as a master's in landscape architecture from the Cambridge School. She had taught in Minnesota before joining Dean's office. Lamson went on to launch her own practice in 1927 and later published a number of books, including *Landscape with Shrubs and Flowering Trees* (1946), which went through four printings.

Dean, elected to ASLA membership in 1921, served on New York City's ASLA executive committee. In 1929 she was awarded the Architectural League of New York's first Medal of Honor in Landscape Architecture for three gardens, described as "informal in feeling," and one termed "distinctly naturalistic." The plant palette for the "naturalistic" landscape included shadbush, black alder, arrow-wood, hawthorns, ironwood, bittersweet, beeches, elms, and oaks—all native plants. Reviewing the garden, one writer claimed, "The visitor is inclined to give to nature the credit which really belongs to the landscape architect."[44] This review commended Dean for her knowledge of both architecture and landscape architecture.

In 1930 Dean and Embury undertook a design for the Guild House, in East Hampton. Embury's building was designed with a modernist vocabulary, while exhibiting the craftsmanship characteristic of arts and crafts architecture. Dean's landscapes similarly reflected a modernist approach to the period's favored Colonial Revival style, featuring increased

A garden featuring native plants in an informal setting designed by Ruth Bramley Dean for Hiram Walker and published in the October 1929 issue of *Architectural Forum*. Architecture magazines frequently covered landscape architecture, including the more informal or naturalistic approaches of many designers. Dean's work, as well as that of Annette Hoyt Flanders, was covered in a number of architecture journals.

simplicity and geometry in the garden's layout and plant materials. Unlike many of her contemporaries, Dean did not use an abundance of flowering plants. Rather, she relied on a palette of green plants to shape the spaces of the garden, using color only to highlight a specific spot or note in her composition. Unfortunately, Dean died in 1932, before this project was completed, although a fountain was placed in the garden to memorialize her contribution both to the project and to the town of East Hampton. After Dean's death Embury continued to practice in the New York metropolitan area, including working for Robert Moses and designing houses and buildings, until his death in 1966.

In each of these partnerships—between Coffin and Scheiner and between Dean and Embury—the partners established distinct practices in addition to collaborative work. These partnerships underscored the increasing complexities of projects, the need for architects and landscape architects to work together to create a unified whole, and the benefits for women of partnering with a male colleague. Not everyone jumped on the collaborative wagon, of course, but such partnerships diversified the range of practitioners' projects, because of the breadth of expertise and experience partners could bring to the table. That women could both act as partners and remain autonomous reflected significant societal changes over the course of the first decades of the twentieth century.

Raising the Standards of Professionalism

By the 1910s and 1920s there were a number of practices, led by men and women, where young women could learn the art of design as well as the business of a professional practice. Women, indeed, were taking the lead, as an article in the *New York Times* declared. The members of the second generation of women who entered the field were so successful in part because of their forebears—the men and women who opened their doors as mentors, teachers, and colleagues. They nevertheless had to contend with rising standards of professionalism as they sought legitimacy and success.

Professional legitimacy was in part reflected in the protocols and procedures individual practitioners adopted and adapted. Fees, in this respect, were critical. What amount to charge, and associated costs, were a constant source of debate within the professional community. Early and well-established practices, such as the Olmsted Brothers and Farrand's, Coffin's, and Flanders's offices, charged rates as detailed in the ASLA guidelines, and their clients could afford these fees. Others based their charges on what they believed their clients could afford. For example, Alice Orme Smith, a Connecticut landscape architect, charged less than the ASLA guidelines as she was concerned that, otherwise, local families would not be able to afford her assistance.[45] Eunice Fenelon charged hourly and for mileage: "That was it, and that was very cheap.

... I charged what I felt was right for myself."[46] Wodell & Cottrell also charged less than the recommended fees and for the same reason referred to themselves as landscape consultants rather than landscape architects. They did not believe their work warranted the full professional fee.[47]

Compounding the challenges of professionalism was the issue of pro-bono or reduced-fee work, which was frequently viewed as a public service. Lois Cottrell, for example, primarily designed residential landscapes, although in the thirty-five years she practiced part-time, she also completed projects for numerous public grounds and business sites. She did not charge the full fee for these public projects, as she viewed this work as a public service.[48] Cottrell's sister, Helen Page Wodell, also provided design services for public institutions at a minimal fee. Indeed, it was not uncommon for women to offer their services to the public at a minimal fee—or for no fee at all. In the cases of Cottrell, Wodell, and other smaller designers, their willingness to work for no or minimal fees may reflect both their belief in public service and unease with women designing public landscapes—on the part of both the designer and institutional clients.

Staffing was also a significant issue for practitioners, especially if they needed an income. Hiring extra staff, including secretaries, was often unaffordable. Cautley, for example, at the height of her career, handwrote most of her own correspondence.[49] Eunice Fenelon worked on more than ten plans per year, her files indicating continued correspondence and supervision over long periods of time; "I was working on them all the time; doing my own typing and all my own ordering for them," she later stated.[50] Having a secretary was simply not an option for many from the middle and working classes.

On the other hand, in order to increase income, practices had to take on more projects. And more projects required staff, particularly draftspersons. Larger, more established offices hired draftspersons to produce drawings, plans, and other documents as required. While Cautley, for example, did not hire a secretary, she almost always had at least three draftspersons on staff as her practice expanded into housing projects and state parks. Flanders and Farrand were able to cover a geographical breadth not common among their colleagues by having staff in place in two geographically distinct offices. Coffin maintained an office staff in addition to hiring private practitioners on a project basis, including Coffey and Scheiner.

These women were pioneers in an emerging profession, forming a cornerstone for the women who would follow in their footsteps. Each contributed differently; together they opened doors. Farrand established a professional model, while Shipman created a legacy of practitioners. Coffin engaged in professional activities as neither Shipman nor Farrand had. The level of legitimacy all achieved both shaped and reflected contemporary practice.

BLAZING NEW TRAILS IN THE FIELD OF LANDSCAPE ARCHITECTURE

Mrs. Annette Hoyt Flanders

Times Wide World

Miss Helen Bullard

Pach Bros.
Miss Helen Swift Jones

WOMEN TAKE LEAD IN LANDSCAPE ART

Field Is Dominated by a Group of Brilliant Designers of Horticultural Vistas

COUNTRYSIDES MADE OVER

Mrs. Ellen Shipman

Bradley

Eric Stahlberg
Mrs. Beatrix Farrand

sible for much of the beauty of design developed in the city's parks in recent years; and directed the annual program for flower planting for two years. Designs for the five boroughs called for 300,000 Spring

share his interest in growing things with his daughter on trips here, and later in Europe and South America. Following her graduation from Smith College, she studied landscape architecture at the Uni-

Charles H. Sabin at Southampton, L. I. Topsoil from an entire farm bought for this purpose was brought in to make the soil fertile on the site overlooking the sea; and the plans Miss Coffin designed called for a large, sandy dune to be constructed to give the landscape the proper seaside atmosphere.

Her design for the grounds of Mrs. Edgard Bassick at Bridgeport, Conn., won her the gold medal of the Architectural League.

Among the designs she has executed during the last twenty-five years are Mrs. Irving Brokaw's place at Oyster Bay, L. I.; a huge estate near Wilmington, Del., and a number of show places at Watch Hill, R. I., as well as Southern gardens in Kentucky and Virginia.

"Women Take Lead in Landscape Art," *New York Times,* March 13, 1938. This article featured many well-known women in landscape architecture, suggesting that this profession was relatively open to women. Like the magazines' calendars and halls of fame, this article makes the point that women were not merely participating in the profession but shaping it. (Copyright © 2009 The New York Times Co. Reprinted with permission)

By the 1920s the possibilities open to young women had expanded significantly. In 1921 a Smith alumna wrote that while she appreciated the opportunity to work for an established office, "the ability to run one's own peanut stand, with the attendant independence of action and also some gain in originality of ideas in working independently, . . . impelled

[her] to strike out for [her]self."⁵¹ She did not view the launching of an office as the last resort of a woman with no other options, as Coffin had. Instead, she believed she could choose whether to work for an established practitioner or to set up her own practice.

While McCrea and Farrand had opened the possibility that women might pursue landscape architecture as professionals, Shipman had modeled how to transform a talent for gardening and art into a landscape architecture practice. Shipman and Coffin had mentored and trained a generation of practitioners, and Coffin, alongside authors, librarians, and photographers, had positioned women squarely within the professional community and the profession within the fine arts.

Martha Brookes Brown Hutcheson, Annette Hoyt Flanders, and Marjorie Sewell Cautley followed. They formed a second constellation of women in landscape architecture, sharing a social agenda focused on improving the daily lives of Americans across the nation.

6

Designing a Social Agenda

Landscape and Culture

The practice of landscape architecture was shaped as much by the contemporary culture as it was by the community of practitioners. American culture at the turn of the twentieth century was a society in search of a new order. This period, known as the Progressive Era, embraced populism, reform efforts, and social gospel movements in response to increasing industrialism, expanding urbanism, and corollary changes in social structures. Progressives believed in progress as a sustained upward movement of the human race. Their focus was not only on intangible cultural issues; the progressive temperament understood "social politics in terms of form as well as function," suggesting that architecture and landscape reflected social values.[1] Progressives, then, argued that society as a whole, as well as its individual members, were shaped by the environment. Thus, the built environment was both an agent of social change and a signifier of contemporary culture. Progressive efforts, consequently, focused on improvements in the built environment both to inspire change and to reflect a culture worthy of the nation. Women were critical players in these efforts, as amateurs, professionals, artists, and civic leaders, and landscape architecture and architecture provided powerful means to attain these goals.

The Progressive Landscape

The American landscape, as idea and reality, played an essential role in progressive thought. Early twentieth-century progressives believed that to improve the American character, the nation's citizens must experience the native landscape; in fact, each citizen, to be a real American, must have access to nature. Thus, if one had no access to nature on the frontier, in the wilderness, or in open lands or forests, then nature should be brought home in the form of parks, gardens, and common greens. Home and community gardens should be cultivated and maintained, in part for their productivity but also for their relationship to American nature.

The nation's moral fiber depended on citizens having access to a garden that they could cultivate as they would their families.

Progressive Era activists, whether city planners, members of village-improvement societies, or involved with extension-service programs, advocated for improved conditions and public access to parks, open spaces, and common greens. They argued for significant physical improvements in public spaces and landscapes on behalf of the general good of society. The contemporary conservation movement, then, equated a healthy environment and ready access to nature with a prospering and healthy culture.

A second important goal for progressive thinkers was improvement of the home. For city planners this issue was framed by zoning ordinances, efficiency studies, tenement laws, and the construction of housing projects. For village-improvement advocates the focus was on the home and garden and its relationship to the community landscape. Extension programs focused on teaching citizens how to beautify their domestic environments and use their space efficiently and productively. All shared the belief that enhanced living conditions would mean an improved social reality.

Gardening, during the two world wars, had also become a patriotic act, the war gardens of World War I and the victory gardens of World War II linking patriotism and gardening in increasingly potent ways. President Woodrow Wilson encouraged such efforts in 1917: "Everyone who creates or cultivates a garden helps, and helps greatly, to solve the problem of the feeding of the nations; every housewife who practices strict economy puts herself in the ranks of those who serve the nation."[2] Magazines such as *Garden Magazine* and *House Beautiful* proclaimed the importance of sowing seeds for victory. These patriotic gardens were to be not only productive but also ornamental, featuring plants and flowers that would meet the physical, spiritual, and emotional needs of the community.

This progressive agenda—increasing public access to nature, promoting healthy public landscapes, and improving the home environments in which the masses lived—was critically important to landscape architects. And women worked within both these realms—the primarily volunteer reform movement and the professional city-planning and landscape architecture community.

Commonly viewed as guardians of virtue and morality, women were "naturally" associated with efforts to cleanse and purify the municipal, state, and federal spheres and to upgrade quality of life for their brother and sister Americans. Women, indeed, served as civic housekeepers and mothers for the public in their roles as social workers, teachers, nurses, and volunteers for a breadth of social causes. Warren Manning argued that women's work "can be known only to those who can appreciate with what moral courage, enthusiasm, and self-denial women will take up new interests, and how often one woman's persistency and persuasiveness is the impelling force behind important movements for the public good."[3] Many, untrained in any type of design or related profession, nonetheless assumed the burden of critiquing their urban, suburban, and rural environments. Their colleagues commented on "the extent and variety of women's interests and activities in cities and towns . . . [and] the spirit in which women have approached some of their most important problems."[4] By the turn of the century, many referred to the late nineteenth century as "the woman's century."

Women approached these challenges with the skills learned within the confines of home and family. Through the work of women such as Catherine Beecher, for example, scientific investigations of domestic duties eventually transformed housekeeping into a domestic science, forming a natural bridge to municipal housekeeping. By viewing community work as an extension of their housekeeping role, women became involved in the broader community in ways that might otherwise have been seen as unseemly or overtly political.

The efforts of individual citizens to improve civic landscapes for the public good burgeoned in the early nineteenth century. In 1831 one young woman, Maria Edgeworth, wrote to her aunt: "What do you think is my employment out of doors, and what it has been for this week past? My garden? No such elegant thing, but making a gutter, a sewer, and pathway in the streets of Edgeworthtown, and I do declare I am as much interested about it as I ever was in writing anything in my life."[5]

Mary Hopkins Goodrich founded the Laurel Hill Association in 1853 for the purpose of beautifying Stockbridge, Massachusetts. The association embraced efforts to improve and ornament streets by planting trees, grading and draining roads, establishing sewerage systems, and "generally doing whatever may tend to the improvement of the village as a place of residence."[6]

Writers and leaders acknowledged women's dominant role in such efforts. George E. Waring, in his 1877 book *Village Improvements and Farm Villages,* wrote:

> [At] the outset it is to be said that the organization and control of the village society is especially woman's work. It requires the sort of systematized attention to detail, especially in the constantly-recurring duty of "cleaning up," that grows more naturally out of the habit of good housekeeping than out of any occupation to which men are accustomed. Then, too, it calls for a degree of leisure which women are the most apt to have, and it will especially engage their interest as being a real addition to the field of their ordinary routine of life.[7]

In the 1890s Mary Caroline Robbins, a writer and activist, argued for the importance of village and public improvements. In an essay titled "The Art of Public Improvement," she contended, first and foremost, that "only in controlling Nature does [America] find a congenial way to express its profound sense of true beauty, and to line out grandly for itself a bold and characteristic picture."[8] While she acknowledged America's debt to English landscape designers and gardeners, especially the passion for landscape, she firmly believed that in the art of public improvement, Americans would excel:

> Amid sylvan surroundings, separated by oceans from all that has artistically gone before, our fresh young race, if it is to achieve an artistic development, must do so on lines where there is still room for advance, with an art intelligible to the people to whom it must appeal, and in ways in *which large participation is possible to produce a general result*. It is in dealing with nature that we can best find our opportunity to gratify our need for a great art, an art the people want, an art they can love, one that will give them true joy, that will appeal to the humblest and the wisest alike . . . an art in which the simple can bear a hand, and yet which will afford scope to the highest artistic gifts; an art which will educate while it gratifies, and will uplift while it rejoices.[9]

While others emphasized the beauty of the land, Robbins noted the importance of such efforts for less privileged, working-class families, concluding that "in the end its good moral effect must be seen upon many of those people who are most in need of sweetness and light to brighten their hard daily existence. Proceeding as it does from the most highly civilized members of a community, it is a reform which can be shared in by all, and which must tend towards cheerfulness and content wherever it is accepted with enthusiasm."[10]

While Robbins acknowledged the significant role of men in such projects, particularly as leaders, she firmly emphasized the importance of women: "Everywhere that village improvement takes active form we find women connected with it, for there is something about it congenial to the feminine temperament, even as the intimate connection between a woman and a broom-handle is an obvious and natural fact."[11] Robbins's letters and essays to *Garden and Forest* reflected wider societal appreciation of the need for women's involvement in civic-improvement associations and organizations. Robbins linked such work to patriotic national pride and to women's duties as housewives and mothers. Civic-improvement work was viewed as vital to the American character and culture and, specifically, to women's culture.

In 1904 the landscape architect Warren Manning narrated a history of village-improvement efforts, linking the work of the pioneers with that of early twentieth-century professionals. He saw the roots of village improvement in the New England common: early "Societies for Promoting the Art" had spawned agricultural societies that gave their attention to improving home grounds, planting trees, and caring for forests.

Promoting such rural-improvement associations, Manning argued that the aim of their work was to "cultivate public spirit and foster town pride, quicken intellectual life, promote good fellowship, public health, improvement of roads, roadsides, and sidewalks, street lights, public parks, improvement of home and home life, ornamental and economic tree-planting, improvement of railroad-stations, rustic roadside seats for pedestrians, betterment of factory surroundings."[12] He addressed improvements to the grounds of railroad stations in the same paragraph as he promoted improvements to home grounds and the establishment of school gardens, suggesting that these efforts must depend on each other if the culture as a whole was to be uplifted. Manning was not alone in his views: such efforts were also promoted in *Country Life in America, Park and Cemetery, American Gardening, House Beautiful, House & Garden,* the *Youth's Companion,* and horticulture magazines.

Despite all the enthusiasm, however, not everyone appreciated the generic and sometimes static standards promoted by many involved in village improvement. By the turn of the twentieth century, as landscape architects were establishing themselves as members of a profession, some, like Martha Brookes Hutcheson, expressed concern about the ubiquitous "front lawn." Many landscape architects and writers thus encouraged home owners to create individual, distinct gardens; interesting and diverse street-tree plantings; and well-designed, nongeneric public open spaces. They also promoted the design of small intimate spaces for families out of public view. This emphasis on privacy, individuality, and diversity in the landscape established new guidelines for village-improvement efforts, and women again assumed a significant role in defining such new standards and expectations.

Housekeepers for the World

In the mid-nineteenth century women had come together in clubs and associations, first to socialize and later as civic-improvement advocates. Initially meeting as amateurs and volunteers, women, by the early twentieth century, gathered as professionals, practitioners, and leaders. Their associations often mirrored those of men, who had similarly shaped communities of tradesmen, craftsmen, and later professionals. In 1873 the Association for the Advancement of Women was convened in order to discuss women's issues and underscore the power of women as a collective force. The General Federation of Women's Clubs was formed in 1882 to bring women together from all parts of the country to exchange ideas and successes.

Diverse groups and organizations sponsored discussions of social reform and community development, from the need for more district nurses to the problems with tenement housing or the eight-hour law. Club members actively participated in advocating and signing petitions and spoke with members of local government. Self-improvement, in other words, became civic reform, as women moved from learning more about art and gardening for their own edification to sponsoring museums and planting trees for the public good.

Similar organizations were being established in a variety of communities. African American garden clubs formed to bring order and beauty to rural and urban areas, encouraging women to plant and share flowers, learn new methods of cultivation, experience self-expression through neighborhood leadership, and thereby improve their communities. Historically black colleges and universities promoted nature study, school gardening, and the formation of garden clubs from 1898 to 1948, these pursuits considered critical to the economic development of rural areas in the Southeastern United States.[13] Such groups shaped the local landscape and provided participants a position of social power.

Two women's organizations in particular took leading roles in addressing public landscapes as part of broader reform and improvement efforts. The Woman's National Farm and Garden Association and the Garden Club of America, founded within a year of each other, shared many of the same goals and members, even as they approached common issues differently.

The Garden Club of America (GCA) was established in 1913, when the Garden Club of Philadelphia hosted eleven garden clubs that then founded the national organization. The landscape architects Beatrix Jones Farrand and Elizabeth Leighton Lee were subsequently invited to serve as professional garden consultants, the organization's stated purpose to engender knowledge and love of gardening, to assist in the protection of native plants and birds, and to encourage civic planting. GCA women supported their vision through three significant movements. First, they addressed the issue of women's role as protectors of domestic life and the home and defenders and teachers of values, morals, and patriotism. Second, they promoted the preservation and narration of the nation's history as revealed in the homes and gardens of political, social, and cultural leaders. History thus became the history of domestic life: homes were idealized, the garden playing a starring role as a place of respite, a source of beauty, a productive part of the household, and an appropriate space for women. Finally, they encouraged higher standards for private and public landscapes. The homes and gardens of club members should, club members argued, serve as role models, just like public parks and open spaces. These three focuses of concern fell easily within the purview of women, who commonly saw themselves as defenders of family values, protectors of the home, and advocates of an American history reflecting an ideal culture. The roles GCA women adopted, however, broke the ties that had kept them within the confines of the home, moving them into the community at large.

Reflecting this breadth of purpose and confronting the question of what roles were appropriate for women, garden clubs struggled to determine an overall vision. One controversial issue was whether clubs should pursue horticulture as a fine art or pursue civic improvements. Martha Brookes Hutcheson expressed concern, wondering "whether in finding billboards to suppress, rubbish to pick up, national parks to protect, Congress to influence, nurserymen to endorse, wild flowers to save, school children to inspire and towns to plant, we were not in danger of losing sight of our original object, to set a standard in the finest gardens America can produce."[14] One specific direction could not be agreed upon, and each club was thus instructed to choose among projects and priorities, allowing for regional differences as well as increased individual leadership.

While specific activities thus varied from club to club, as an association the GCA addressed a breadth of issues related to the nation's landscapes, supporting efforts to promote the profession of landscape architecture as essential to both the nation and the progressive vision. GCA members founded a fellowship in landscape architecture at the American Academy in Rome (although women were not allowed to apply for it until many decades later) and a two-year graduate scholarship in botany at Vassar College in 1923. The club contributed twenty thousand dollars to the Lowthorpe School for Women, contributed funds to preserve a portion of the redwood forest in California, and supported efforts to ban billboards along Virginia highways. The GCA also fought for a reasonable plant-quarantine law and organized educational programs on the value of native plants and the need to protect wildflowers—important projects that continue to shape our environment today.

While the Woman's National Farm and Garden Association (WNFGA) shared the GCA's commitment to civic housekeeping and utilizing the professional and amateur communities, its ultimate aim was more pragmatic: helping working-class women. Elizabeth Lee and Mrs. Francis King had launched the first meeting of the Agricultural and Horticultural Association in January 1914, as a support group for the Pennsylvania School of Horticulture for Women. The association's purpose was to further the school's interests and to stimulate involvement in the conservation of natural resources and the appreciation of country life. Mrs. King, named president, would serve until 1920. In 1916 the association changed its name, becoming the Woman's National Farm and Garden Association. Unlike the GCA, the WNGFA was focused on efforts "to create a clearing house of information on farming or gardening," as well as employment opportunities for women. It advised state and national government entities on the challenges facing women in the workforce, representing a more middle-class perspective, and was responsible for establishing the Woman's Land Army Units (the "Farmerettes") during World War I.

The WNFGA supported women landscape architects as role models, providing a link to the professional community and supporting the association's vision and growth. The landscape architects and writers Mary Rutherfurd Jay and Elizabeth Leonard Strang were active members of the organization's directors' group, while *Farm and Garden,* the group's periodical, promoted the profession, encouraging women to pursue a career in the field. Julia Lester Dillon, the city landscape architect for Sumter, South Carolina, wrote "Municipal Landscaping for Women" in 1922, emphasizing the value of women designing public spaces. After describing some of her early trials and errors in her municipal position, she noted:

> This is a field of endeavor for women that is entirely uncharted. It has limitless possibilities for public service, it is exceedingly interesting and it should be fairly well paid. It is a splendid field of work and women are particularly well fitted for it. . . . As there comes—and there will come—a gradual awakening to the stupidity of the present situation and as women come more and more into view as city housekeepers, their popularity and their opportunities in this field of service will rapidly increase.[15]

Dillon was a landscape architect and the author of *The Blossom Circle,* as well as many magazine articles. She had studied informally at school in New York City and Boston before returning to Augusta, Georgia, where she launched an active practice and served as the Southern garden editor for *House & Garden* magazine. In 1920 she moved to Sumter, where she was appointed the city landscape architect and later the superintendent of parks.

Women already in the profession lectured for the WNFGA on career potential and the need for involvement in civic improvements. Farrand gave a lecture entitled "Landscape Gardening for Women" in which she described the profession "as an agreeable [one] for women," one in which "an increasing number . . . have therefore been studying and starting professional work."[16] Despite this optimistic introduction, she discouraged anyone faint of heart from pursuing the discipline. Helen Deusner, a Chicago landscape architect, encouraged young women in her lecture "Landscape Architecture as a Profession for Women," and Strang frequently addressed the topic "Women in Landscape Architecture."[17]

The Garden Club of America and the Woman's National Farm and Garden Association both supported improvements in the environment that would, their members assumed, subsequently engender advancements in the moral and physical health of the populace. Both organizations thus assumed the need for collaborative efforts between professional designers and amateur advocates. King might have been commenting on the goals of either association:

> The Garden Club of America has, with such distinguished . . . landscape architects . . . , the rare privilege and prospect of raising the general standard of taste on our side of the Atlantic . . . [so] we may become the finest of amateurs. . . . By combining their energies and experience with their wealth and visibility, these women generated an enormous influence over the civic

designs and municipal improvements in the country's public landscapes. They recognized the need for collaborations between not only professionals and amateurs but also women in a variety of spheres of influence. . . . Let us make of this Association a great democratic band of women, valuable to each other and their communities, representative of our whole country, women engaged in those noble out-of-door occupations for which no man is too high or too low.[18]

Landscape architects were indeed engaged in such public efforts. Jay noted as much to a journalist in 1924: "I have always believed that everyone is under obligation to be a producer of one kind or another, and not a mere consumer. To profit by the activities of others but to do nothing oneself to make the world better and more beautiful is wrong."[19] Civic engagement was not a mere pastime, but a social obligation. Practitioners thus served as lecturers, writers, and consultants, their topics ranging from the use of color in the garden, to saving native plants, to the gardens of foreign nations, to city planning and housing projects in the United States. Marjorie Sewell Cautley listed a series of lecture topics in her professional brochure, including housing projects in Europe, the planning of city parks, and the design of home gardens. Farrand also presented lectures on a variety of topics and wrote on garden design and on "City and Town Planning and what the Garden Clubs Could Do Toward This Movement." These designers articulated their vision of the American landscape, rural, suburban, and urban, while encouraging volunteers to become educated advocates.

Club members realized the potential of good landscape design not only through such presentations but also through the groups' annual meetings. Shipman's, Coffin's, and Farrand's landscapes were often sites featured as part of the GCA's annual meetings. For example, one year in Grosse Pointe, Michigan—a wealthy Detroit suburb and a regular annual meeting destination—club members visited over a dozen gardens designed by Shipman, including her public projects on Lake Shore Drive. GCA members also visited Winterthur to see the work of Henry Francis du Pont and Marian Cruger Coffin. Such visits allowed women to develop both a visual and a verbal vocabulary for describing and critiquing designed landscapes.

As noted earlier, professional women and volunteers worked collaboratively toward these organizations' lofty goals, and this relationship was fundamental to women's effectiveness in the Progressive Era. Professional women were often politically aware and extremely active in reform work within their purview. Women in landscape architecture interjected professional attitudes and knowledge into volunteer organizations, expanding their sphere of influence. Through their involvement as club officers, speakers, and contributors to popular publications, and via visits to landscapes they had designed, they established a level of discourse that encouraged amateurs to mature as effective observers and as critics of public and private spaces. Amateur women thus expressed increasingly sophisticated critiques of social issues related to the landscape.

In 1912 the National Municipal League acknowledged the strength of women in civic improvement, commissioning Mary Ritter Beard to document their work in civic reform as volunteers, amateurs, and professionals. Beard's resulting book, *Women's Work in Municipalities,* documented the breadth of the work in which women were involved, its survey grounded in the belief that "women by natural instinct as well as by long training have become the housekeepers of the world, so it is only natural that they should in time become effective municipal housekeepers as well."[20]

Beard was adamant about the vital nature of city planning and the role of women in promoting such work, in particular their advocacy of facilities to substantially improve the lives of mothers and children. She commended Annette McCrae, of the American Civic Association, for her work for the Chicago and Northwestern Railways, writing that such work was the result of a "recognized demand on the part of the people, and of women as an aggressive element among the people, for attractive and inviting front and back doors to their urban dwellings." Women, Beard declared, were "largely instrumental in initiating the playground work, [and] they ... followed it ... by service on appointed commissions, and as paid city playground employees, and in other cases they ... held positions on state recreation commissions." Prior to the involvement of women, she argued, the City Beautiful movement had ignored the alleys, filthy side streets, and tenements in efforts to provide a "more ostentatious display of mere ornamentation. . . . No provision was made for playgrounds and well-located schools and social centers."[21]

Women, according to Beard, "were everywhere found active along the new lines of development" in housing. Octavia Hill of London had focused on better housing, as had Ellen Collins of New York and the Octavia Hill Association, a branch of the Civic Club of Philadelphia. Beard acknowledged such women for having "attacked the evil where few in their day had the courage ... to meet it." Women were also actively affiliated with the National Housing Association "and cooperat[ed] with the men in the great work of arousing the nation to a knowledge of the deadly peril of low standard homes and to a sense of the immediate urgency of reform.["22]

Indeed, women's organizations undertook extensive studies on housing and other issues pertinent to improving urban areas. Florence Kelley and Mrs. V. G. Simkhovitch, for example, studied causes of congestion. Women, according to Beard, understood individuals' need for light, air, warmth, sanitation, and freedom from overcrowding. They believed, then, that a war on bad homes was a war on poverty.

Beard also recognized the ability and willingness of women to address the specific needs of mothers and children in the urban landscape. She lauded the work of Jane Addams at Hull House and of others who were starting child-care centers and improving playgrounds. In the design of cities, she noted, "women who have worked for shade trees so extensively have not been unmindful of the fact that mothers have to push baby carriages up and down through the hot sun, often times to the detriment of both mother and child, and they have taught us that mothers should be considered in city plans."[23]

Women in landscape architecture shared this interest in the urban landscape. In 1899 Farrand published a letter in the *Journal of the Committee on Municipal Administration* arguing that New York should support a larger system of small public parks. She was, she declared, against the "costly plantings and ornamental fantasies" of London or Paris parks, as these were inappropriate for an American city and most likely unfeasible in budgetary terms.[24] Farrand argued that European parks were intended for a homogeneous population that knew how to respect authority; American cities, on the other hand, needed parks that could serve a wider variety of peoples, of many classes, backgrounds, and ethnicities. She promoted the creation of formal designs with direct paths for travel, resilient playgrounds for children, and a system of open spaces linked throughout the city. New York City should, according to Farrand, increase the amount of open landscape accessible to the general public, as envisioned by Olmsted Sr. and Charles Eliot. Further, Farrand suggested, this open landscape should serve multiple purposes, including both recreational areas for children and more picturesque landscapes that could be passively enjoyed.

Farrand, as a professional, was joined by other women in the profession. Martha Brookes Brown Hutcheson used her role as a landscape architect and as a member of both the Garden Club of America and the Woman's National Farm and Garden Association to advocate for landscapes that would serve the general public and improve the daily lives of average Americans. She promoted the home garden, drawing on the resources of her social and professional positions.

MARTHA BROOKES BROWN HUTCHESON (1871–1959)

Hutcheson's initial interest in landscape architecture arose out of a desire to inspire improvements in the urban landscape.[25] Hutcheson had grown up in a Unitarian family of farmers, outdoor enthusiasts, and gardeners, her mother encouraging her to learn the craft of gardening as a source of pleasure and a healthy pastime. Spending time with her uncle John Pomeroy at Fern Hill in Burlington, Vermont, Hutcheson learned about contemporary agriculture, the horticultural sciences, and the value and pleasure of a beautiful landscape. She took watercolor painting lessons from Rhoda Holmes Nichols (1858–1930), a celebrated painter, writer, and teacher at the Art Students League in New York. With this training Hutcheson turned her attention to the School of Applied Design for Women, where she studied the decorative arts. Decorative arts, however, did not fully satisfy her curiosity, and she went on to pursue the study of native flora at the University of Vermont in the late 1890s. She supplemented her studies with the European grand tour, which her parents hoped would suffice as training for both a young lady and an amateur gardener.

Hutcheson, however, was determined to pursue a professional career. She recalled later that in 1898 she had come upon the landscape of New York's Bellevue Hospital and, with a gardener's eye, had been frustrated by the "terrible waste of opportunity for beauty which was not being given to the hundreds of patients who could see it or go to it, in convalescence."[26] Upon inquiry, as she described, she realized that little could be done in that particular case but that the emerging profession of landscape architecture might prepare her to do such work in the future. This avenue would also allow her to combine her artistic training and her gardening knowledge to establish herself as a serious professional. Hutcheson spoke with practitioners, including Farrand, and, after much investigation, enrolled in MIT's new program in the Department of Architecture.

Hutcheson was enrolled at MIT from 1900 to 1902, alongside fellow students Stoddard and Coffin. Hutcheson, however, was disappointed in the program's lack of emphasis on the public benefits of design and its cursory coverage of the plant world. Frustrated by the insufficient instruction on "what must be known of the plant world,"[27] she attended Professor Watson's horticulture lectures at the Bussey Institute and regularly visited the Arnold Arboretum, making exhaustive notes for an expanding card catalog she would use throughout her career. She also visited commercial nurseries and sought out experts to learn about tree and shrub cultivation. Her early publication "The Garden Spirit," in a 1901 issue of the *Cosmopolitan,* reflected the depth and breadth of her thinking. That same year she was interviewed in the *Outlook* as a representative of the discipline.

Hutcheson left the program at MIT to open her practice, without having completed the requirements for a degree. As noted earlier, it was not uncommon for students to leave such programs once they had the required skills, as the degree did not yet hold any particular clout nor did practice require its completion, since no registration or certification was required. In Hutcheson's case, while she may have withdrawn because of finances, MIT's faculty certainly did not share her vision of landscape practice: she was not solely interested in the aesthetics of design, instead embracing a desire to "bring about positive social changes through landscape design."[28]

In 1910 she married William Anderson Hutcheson, and subsequently limited her practice to consultations, writing, and lecturing, as well as improving the landscape of the couple's own new home. In 1911 the

Portrait of Martha Brookes Brown Hutcheson by Jane de Glehn, 1922.
(From the Collections of the Morris County Park Commission)

Hutchesons moved to Merchiston Farm, a one-hundred-acre farm and eighteenth-century farmhouse in the village of Gladstone, New Jersey. It was here that she designed and refined her own garden and landscape and wrote *The Spirit of the Garden,* which featured numerous images of gardens she had designed. While not practicing as a designer, Hutcheson continued to expand her role as a writer, lecturer, and advocate for the profession. Upon her death at age eighty-eight, she was lauded for her professional and volunteer work as a landscape architect, garden club member, and active community advocate.

When she opened her office at 60 Chestnut Street in Boston in 1902, Hutcheson had already been commissioned to design the Massachusetts estate Prides Crossing for Charles Head, and she soon took up the design work for Maudesleigh in Newburyport, Massachusetts, for Frederick S. Moseley. Hutcheson's early success may be in part have resulted from her social and professional networks, initially provided by her family and subsequently developed as a student at MIT and through her contacts with Sargent at the Arnold Arboretum. Hutcheson was also a member of the National Society of Colonial Dames and of the Cosmopolitan Club, each of which offered an extensive network. Hutcheson's professional practice consisted primarily of designs for large country estates, farms, and flower gardens in the New England and New Jersey regions. Engaged in professional activities, through her writing she became widely known as a spokesperson for the art and practice of landscape architecture.

Throughout her work Hutcheson used the title "landscape gardener," although she spoke of the profession as landscape architecture. Like Farrand, Hutcheson seems to have used this title for multiple reasons. She agreed with Farrand that landscape architecture was an art and a science, merging the areas of gardening, horticulture, and the fine arts, but she had rejected the architectural emphasis of MIT's program, and her use of the title "landscape gardener" reflected her belief that architecture played but a minor role in landscape design. In a 1909 interview Hutcheson noted that "landscape gardening is not . . . an architectural craft, although of course it embraces some of the principles of architecture." She suggested, further, that the title of "architect" had been adopted only to give landscape architecture a "sort of dignity in the popular mind."[29] She may have also appreciated the history contained within the designation "landscape gardening," which dated back to the eighteenth century. Finally, her choice of title reflected her dual role as a professional member of the American Society of Landscape Architects and as a leader in the Garden Club of America.

Although her commissions were primarily located in the Boston region, after only a few years Hutcheson joined the professional community in New York, opening an office at 146 East Thirty-ninth Street. During the 1910s she designed, according to her calculations, eighty-three landscapes. In 1912 she withdrew from active design practice and focused her attention on her social and professional agendas, retaining just a few select clients for whom she served as a consultant. In time she moved her New York office to an apartment at 45 East Eighty-second Street, and by the 1930s her office was at 1211 Park Avenue, in the hub of the city. Hutcheson's career can be divided into two phases: the first as an actively engaged designer and the second as an advocate, writer, and spokesperson for the profession and for improved standards in the nation's designed landscapes.

Hutcheson, who participated in the ASLA throughout her career, was frequently asked to contribute to professional discussions and decisions. In 1922 she was one of seventy-seven landscape architects asked to provide guidelines for professional practice. Successfully nominated by Marian Cruger Coffin and Arthur Shurcliff for ASLA membership in 1930, she submitted extensive landscape plans, grading plans, and construction drawings for the membership application, demonstrating her broad knowledge of the practice and her role as designer and supervisor. Photographs of Merchiston Farm were submitted for the ASLA *Illustrations of Work of Members* in the 1930s, and in 1935 Clarence Fowler nominated Hutcheson as an ASLA fellow in recognition of her design practice, writing, and lectures. For this application she provided copies of her many publications and the plans and images of four designed landscapes: Moseley Estate in Newburyport, Massachusetts; the Charles Head estate in Manchester, Massachusetts; Old Acres in Westbury, Long Island; and the Stout landscape in Red Bank, New Jersey. These were large private estates featuring formal and naturalized areas of water, woods, and lawn. That each had been completed many years earlier did not deter the nominating committee, which quickly recognized her role as a standard bearer for the profession.

Hutcheson was also simultaneously engaged as a gardener and a garden club member. In 1913 she was a founding member of New Jersey's Somerset Hills Garden Club, which soon became affiliated with the Garden Club of America. Hers was an enthusiastic community of gardeners and garden designers. To nurture it, Hutcheson served as a mentor for young women who visited her gardens at Merchiston Farm. Through her status as an established member of the upper class and a professional, she successfully bridged the realms of amateur "lady gardeners" and professional landscape architects.

Design as Praxis

Hutcheson's professional practice followed the protocol and procedures established by Olmsted, Farrand, and the ASLA. Hutcheson managed her practice in a standard manner, providing potential clients with a statement regarding professional methods and charges, including fees, services, and limitations. Her services could be commissioned in phases, from initial advice through construction supervision, as evidenced in her brochure, which offered "advice given for treatment of country places as a whole or in part; the rendering of plans for such treatment, and the supervision of the work at necessary periods while in process of construction . . . [in consultation] with the owner, the Architect, or the Engineer as to the placing of buildings, the laying out of roads, changes in grades, etc."[30] Unlike Coffin, who insisted on determining the layout of roads and grade changes, Hutcheson was willing to work in consultation with engineers and architects.

Hutcheson argued that a good relationship between architect and landscape architect was essential to a project's success. This collaborative relationship, Hutcheson proposed, should begin with the "very first planning and placing of a house and its surroundings," as there "are parts of the house which essentially belong to the garden and parts of the garden which are as essentially parts of the house, and there is no separating them if a successful scheme of the whole is to be realized."[31] With this belief as a framework, Hutchenson's focus was on the design of both house and garden as a whole. This might mean, in one case, designing the axis of the garden in accordance with the central axis of the house, its entrance and/or major windows. (See color plate 5.)

Hutcheson demonstrated a similar concern with establishing collaborative relationships with those participating in a landscape's construction, planting, and maintenance, commonly overseeing the employment and supervision of contractors and gardeners. She strove to implement professional standards at each phase of contractual work, as well as during a landscape's maintenance and maturation. Hutcheson frequently persuaded her clients to agree that she would perform annual visits to revise and update planting plans, for which she charged a small fee and expenses. These visits, she argued, insured the successful implementation and maintenance of the original design.

Through her early training in the decorative arts, Hutcheson had acquired a gift for artfully composed sketches and drawings and become an accomplished photographer. Over the course of her career, she accumulated a vast collection of photographs and images of gardens and landscapes, both her own and those she visited while traveling. She used drawing and photography to communicate her design principles to clients, students, and the public. In 1930, for example, she hosted a tea for young women in landscape architecture at which she showed images that might encourage observation of design principles in the landscape. She then took the women through her own garden, describing the principles as they were found in place and comparing them to those in the images. She hosted similar talks and tours for garden club meetings and potential clients.

If the public's taste in garden art were to improve, Hutcheson suggested, design principles must be laid out in a clear and concise manner. Of these principles the most essential was understanding the relationships among the house, its garden, and its surrounding landscape. These elements—house, gardens, and landscape—should be tied intricately together. This belief was in essence the core of Hutcheson's design philosophy, as described in *The Spirit of the Garden,* a compilation of essays she wrote over a twenty-year period. Dedicating the book to "those with a progressive spirit in their concern for the fine art of garden making," Hutcheson also explicitly linked the art with the period's reform activities. She proposed in the foreword that her book would help to teach "good taste" and, simultaneously, encourage American "appreciation of all phases of the 'great outdoors' such as has never existed."[32]

Hutcheson wrote her book to help average readers understand the principles of comprehensive planning and design, thereby improving their judgments, tastes, and perceptions. Specifically, she wrote for those in the middle class who wished to culturally associate themselves with elite society. The design principles underlying larger estates, in particular those designed by landscape architects, were not difficult to learn, she asserted. As Andrew Jackson Downing had suggested in the early nineteenth century, Hutcheson argued that the average home owner could learn good taste if instructed simply and clearly. Encouraging middle-class home owners to emulate such taste, she argued, would improve their lives and raise the general level of garden and landscape design.

Hutcheson began her instruction on design at the scale of the flower garden. (See color plate 6.) This garden, she wrote, should be a secluded place, where calm and peace preside. It should be a place to find delight in the act of gardening and to enjoy flowers for their colors, textures, fragrance, and seasonal nature. It should not be a place to display the collection of exotic plants offered by the nurseryman; rather, it should reflect the nature and character of the home and of the owner/gardener. For many it was the flower garden within the larger landscape that lent an American character to early twentieth-century landscape design, despite the fact that such gardens often emulated English cottage gardens.

Hutcheson's reliance on her knowledge and understanding of Old World gardens, particularly Italian gardens, was most evident in her description of design principles and elements: in her use of axes, views, and vistas; her definition of outdoor spaces set within an architectural framework; and her emphasis on the importance of a tasteful transition between architecture and the surrounding landscape.[33] Her design for Merchiston Farm was grounded in these principles and elements, especially the use of terracing, axes, and the transition from the architectural nature of the house to the natural landscape.

A primary design element at Merchiston Farm—and, according to Hutcheson, in any a good design—was the strong relationship between the house and the garden. This relationship, she argued, should be emphasized at any scale and in any setting. In particular, it should be expressed in the primary approach to the house. The main axis should lead from the entrance to the property, through the garden, to a specific and distinctive point of the house, creating a unity between the house and the garden. In a more formal landscape this axis might be a straight line—directly connecting the house to the property's entrance and to the garden in between. In such cases the primary axis should also be used

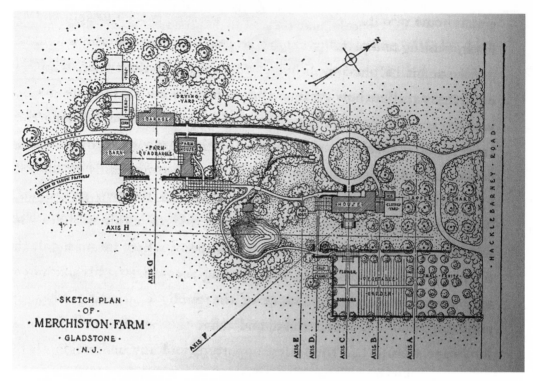

Merchiston Farm, plan by Hutcheson, used to illustrate her use of axes. The entire landscape was designed and planted by Hutcheson over the course of her life. It is currently being rehabilitated and is open to visitors. (From the Collections of the Morris County Park Commission)

in the architecture of the house—thus becoming an essential defining character of the whole site.

For informal gardens and landscapes the approach might be less direct. Main pathways might flow out from the entrance and through the garden to a vantage point of the house. Such pathways should not meander needlessly but reflect the character of the garden and the house by tying the two together visually and physically. In formal or informal designs the house and its placement in the landscape were critical to the whole composition. Using images from the gardens she had designed, Hutcheson showed how a pathway might take on a less formal feeling as it moved away from the house.

Hutcheson appreciated the garden rooms that composed a typical Italian villa landscape. Like Platt and Wharton, she believed that the terracing and roomlike organization of such gardens were key to the transition from the house's architecture to the surrounding landscape. She suggested that such rooms were created by drawing on the natural character of the Italian landscape of rolling hills, easily fashioned into individual valleys, terraces, and niches. Suggesting that a similar approach might be taken in the United States, she described how garden rooms could be created from the natural topography of the land or by making simple alterations. The smallest changes in grade, she suggested, could be used to create steps, setting the garden as a place apart. A second characteristic of garden rooms, their enclosure, might be accomplished through the

The path leading into the garden from the house at Merchiston Farm, demonstrating Hutcheson's emphasis on making a graceful transition between the house and the more informal landscape in the distance. A similar image was submitted by Hutcheson to the ASLA yearbooks in the 1930s. (From the Collections of the Morris County Park Commission)

use of walls and the planting of hedges and trees. Within such enclosures each garden might feature a simple water element or an elaborate flower garden. Vistas might be framed through openings in the walls or along the paths intertwining the gardens. In this way the Italian garden could serve as an inspiration for American gardens.

As garden rooms served as critical transitions from the house to the more natural landscape, the character of the rooms should follow a logical sequence, from the formality inherent in the area immediately adjacent to the house to the informality of the surrounding landscape. Hutcheson carefully explained how woodland might be brought into the design of the gardens for a formal house by allowing elegant transitions among the elements. At Merchiston Farm, for example, she had used pergolas to lead the eye, while in other gardens she might use a stone path with a rustic gazebo set in the woods to direct the gaze toward the house. These small interventions would gracefully move the visitor from natural woodland to formal gardens. The guiding principle was always that design must spring from its surroundings—that is, formality must spring from formality, and informality from informality. This principle of transitions, Hutcheson implied, was critical for rural home owners, who had to make their place within a landscape that was more wild, perhaps more natural. To state the obvious, the wild landscape should not come up to the door of the house, any more than the farm landscape should dominate the residential spaces.

These simple principles, Hutcheson proposed, could be learned and emulated by the average American home owner. She advised readers to "not only to dream dreams, but to make the dreams comfortable to live in—such is the demand upon her who makes beautiful compositions out of home grounds."[34] None required a large estate or a significant investment; they might be followed on the smallest and simplest scale and site. The same principles and values were a part of her lectures for the Garden Club of America, the Federation of Arts, the Federated Garden Clubs, the City Garden Club, and the American Civic Association. Her lecture at the Metropolitan Museum, "The Fine Art of Landscape Architecture," promoted the profession as necessary to the progress of American culture and society.[35] It was this speech that inspired Clarence Fowler to nominate her as an ASLA fellow.

Hutcheson considered landscape design a force for civic betterment. Through designs, essays, drawings, photographs, and lectures, she shared with her audience her belief that landscape gardeners could play an important part in the "social as well as the aesthetic development of the United States."[36] Her widely published essays emphasized the importance of the landscape in fostering the social and aesthetic development of the nation: "Better Front Dooryard Treatments for Rural Towns," "Co-operation of Citizens, Trained & Untrained in Beautifying our Rural Towns," "Plants for City-Use."[37] Her article "Trees for School Yards," published in the *New York Sun,* caught the attention of many in the profession, emphasizing the need for landscape architecture in public spaces.[38]

Hutcheson's advocacy also embraced the role of women. She argued that women should actively participate and take leadership roles in reform movements. She believed in their power to serve as advocates and activists in a variety of efforts that would advance American culture through improved environments. For example, she was a founding member of the Woman's Land Army of America, a collaborative effort between the Garden Club of America and the Woman's National Farm and Garden Association, formed to identify jobs for women on farms during the labor shortages of World War I, thus expanding employment for women and increasing farm production to serve the public. Over 260,000 women worked on farms through the Land Army. Hutcheson also hosted groups of women at her farm, thus providing young women with both support and mentorship.

The successful mobilization of women during World War I further inspired Hutcheson and her peers to strengthen the call for action among their professional colleagues and amateur peers. Through garden club activities women thus undertook or financed every conceivable form of support. They had, Hutcheson noted, "tasted the fruits of achievement in national helpfulness," and now stood "hundreds strong, stirred with a patriotic sense, impatient for a new program which will lead to greater

Women's Land Army at Merchiston Farm, ca. 1918. Hutcheson hosted a number of Land Army projects at her farm in New Jersey. (From the Collections of the Morris County Park Commission)

achievements—a formed membership of the finest, most influential womanhood of the whole country!"[39] Hutcheson wished to see the energies and talents of these women harnessed for the good of the entire nation.

In her role as writer and lecturer, Hutcheson strenuously promoted her social agenda—one that held that the future of American culture lay in efforts to improve and enhance the environment, specifically the landscape. In her lecture for the American Civic Association, "Co-operation of Citizens, Trained and Untrained, in Beautifying Our Rural Towns," Hutcheson focused on the relationship between urban landscapes and rural towns. This lecture was soon followed by an article in the *Garden Club Bulletin* that enthusiastically called "for a wider program" promoted by individual clubs. Hutcheson argued that the Garden Club of America was in a critical position to "help redeem the sordid, ugly, neglected rural villages of our entire country."[40] Farrand agreed with Hutcheson, and at a 1916 meeting at Sewickley, she encouraged individual clubs to seriously consider their civilizing influence on the community. She noted that the suburbs are "too often uncared for and piled with tomato cans, so that the whole scheme leaves one with a feeling of restlessness because of its very condition of chaotic lack of finish."[41] Louisa King agreed in a letter she wrote to the president of the GCA, Mrs. J. Willis Martin, purporting that the GCA has "with such distinguished societies of architects and landscape architects as exist in this country, the rare privilege and prospect of raising the general standard of taste on our side of the Atlantic."[42]

While many of her contemporaries were also concerned about the quality of life of many of the nation's citizens, Hutcheson focused on the role of home gardens rather than public parks. She believed in the importance of model gardens and the individual's ability to influence others through the example of a private garden—in essence a trickle-down theory of aesthetics. If the upper classes provided examples of "good design," then, this argument ran, those less fortunate would learn from these examples and apply the principles to their own residential spaces and/or landscapes. This argument, of course, assumed that the importance of beauty was a commonly shared value (if not immediately then eventually learned) and that the principles of good design were applicable at all scales.

Hutcheson asserted in her writing that the "greatest good achieved [would be] that of arousing a sense of need for a garden as a part of a home in its beauty and its restfulness." Noting that "in no country are there uglier villages than in America," she argued that garden club members should work to "bring to life a standard of home embellishment which would find its way to more than one class of society." She suggested that those with the means to do better had not risen to the challenge: "It is the unthinking indifference and lack of personal pride in our villages on the parts of those of larger estates which seems unfortunate at present and which suggests new lines for the efforts of garden club members toward learning of good planting and finding a way to help the villages to redeem themselves."[43]

Within garden clubs and established social networks, Hutcheson argued, individuals could "throw a magnetic co-operative and competitive interest into all the garden clubs in the new-found scope of their work." Women had already "by exchange of ideas and interest [raised] our own standards of our own gardens and places" and should now apply their new knowledge and elevated standards to the rest of the community: "We owe the coming generations both the useful and the beautiful. It is now that the cry should go out for lovely, simple naturally planted villages."[44]

Gardens, then, were not merely private spaces for the pleasure of the gardener, but part of the larger public landscape. Front yards and gardens were visually open to the public. "Nothing is more powerful than fashion," Hutcheson wrote, "and people have unconsciously emulated that which lay about them in the most blatant form. They have learned to adopt the meaningless lawn, the nurserymen's horrors, the lumps of shrub planting, and the bald, conspicuous paths and drives."[45] Home grounds were critical elements of a residential community's public image, which was in turn perceived as both an agent of change, influencing each of its individual residents, and a reflection and signifier of the community's social status. The gardens of diverse individuals within a village, town, or city needed to be framed in order to create a cohesive public image. A "sordid" front yard soured the image of an entire community.

Hutcheson nonetheless understood the danger of forcing a particular agenda on others, in particular the less advantaged. She suggested that garden club members and others of the wealthier classes—the "summer people" for many villagers—should be careful not to be patronizing, instead opening the doors of information and cooperation to those of any means. She advised club members that they could "never improve towns by imposing our suggestions or help in a patronizing way on the owners. Model house plantings have been tried in some places already, but there has, I believe, always been a form of patronizing connected with it. It was given by one class to another."[46] Hutcheson suggested that good garden design was valued by everyone and that efforts to share knowledge should cross class and cultural boundaries.

Instead of merely exhibiting and modeling good designs, Hutcheson contended, clubs could become meeting points for anyone interested in improving the landscape. Clubs, she asserted, might establish community centers or houses to serve as gathering places for club activities, as well as a cooperatively maintained model garden, kept as beautiful as possible along simple lines. She proposed that clubs should no longer hold private house meetings and should consider an organized program to benefit all clubs, thus opening the door to multiple influences and agendas. Women of diverse backgrounds should be encouraged to attend meetings and share their knowledge.

Home of Mrs. Elon H. Hooker, Greenwich, Connecticut. An ideal home and garden, with the front yard presented as a cottage garden, the house embowered in vines, and the back garden remaining entirely private. Photograph by Frances Benjamin Johnston. (Library of Congress, Prints & Photographs Division)

This tolerance for diversity and acknowledgment of the skills familiar to working-class individuals were significant. By allowing the potential of an exchange of knowledge between elite garden club members and working-class women, Hutcheson demonstrated her allegiance to Progressive Era reformers such as Jane Addams, Florence Kelley, and Dr. Alice Hamilton. Her idea was to create a place where a variety of people would come together to learn from each other and cooperatively improve the residential landscape. Such tolerance, however, was not shared by many of her garden club colleagues. Increasingly, many understood public education as a means to teach immigrants how to be "good" American citizens, rather than as an opportunity to share.[47] Public spaces were strictly regulated to encourage behaviors deemed appropriate for those aspiring to become good citizens. Such ethnocentrism and classism, in fact, permeated much club work, and Hutcheson was not successful in opening up access—to membership or knowledge—to those traditionally excluded.

In addition to encouraging fine gardens and shared knowledge as patriotic, Hutcheson promoted the use of native plants and landscapes. American enthusiasm for cultivating native plants was growing, as wild gardens became fashionable during the first decades of the twentieth century, considered a means to improve the physical and psychological health of the nation's citizens. Around 1900 two advocacy organizations—the Society for the Protection of Native Plants and the Wild Flower Preservation Society of America—were launched. For nineteenth-century landscape architects native plants seemed an ideal way to blend designed landscapes with existing vegetation, thus encouraging the individual's direct experience of nature and bringing gardens into the natural American landscape. Jacob Weidenmann, H. W. S. Cleveland, and Charles Eliot had all practiced this approach. Warren H. Manning also advocated for the cultivation and use of native plants, as did Wilhelm Miller and Ossian Cole Simonds, who encouraged the use of native plants in naturalistic landscapes. Jens Jensen, Ruth Dean, and Elsa Rehmann also argued that American plants should be the primary material of any American landscape.

Hutcheson's views, then, placed her in the mainstream of the native plant movement. She declared the need to conserve the country's "vast natural beauty with its amazing variety in scene and in plant life" and advised garden clubs to establish native-tree and -shrub study groups whose members could in turn teach others. Study-group members might thus learn to see their home landscapes with new eyes, perceiving "the countryside, not just a blur of jungle green . . . but differing individuals. . . . And in reward for that increase of knowledge and that greater accuracy of observation, there [would be] . . . a dozen beauties in each place where a single beauty was visible before."[48] Hutcheson must have been enthusiastic about garden club efforts to save parts of California's redwood forest and to limit the harvesting of holly and creeping pine for holiday greens, as these species were becoming endangered.

Native plants, Hutcheson argued, were inherently beautiful, well-adapted to the landscape, and able to provide all that a garden needed if used appropriately. She suggested that active members might create door-yard gardens composed of native trees and shrubs, with minimal areas set aside for lawns, to serve as models in the neighborhood. In particular, she wished to see the ubiquitous lawn, which she described as "a national blight" caused by the lawnmower, decrease in popularity.[49] American gardens featuring American plants, she believed, celebrated the nation's beauty, its powerful relationship to the land, and such gardens would play a role in preserving the endangered wildflowers that were slowly disappearing. Hutcheson's own gardens at Merchiston Farm featured numerous native plants around her ponds and in the woodlands.

Merchiston Farm, its pond and garden planted with native plants and cultivated to grow "naturally." This rather wild-looking pond was just to the side of the more formal entrance into the house and garden area. Nonetheless, it appeared in keeping with the larger landscape design. (From the Collections of the Morris County Park Commission)

Hutcheson's use of native plants did not only reflect ecological concerns; she was also addressing a second agenda—the need to create economically feasible gardens for working-class and immigrant families. She understood that less fortunate families could create gardens with native shrubs and plants, whereas exotics might be beyond their financial reach. While she appreciated the model gardens featured at garden club events, such treatments were generally too costly for the average gardener. Instead, she suggested, the "general structure in the background, foreground, privacy, incidental shadow, and decorative feature in form of twig or leaf, can be created with our most commonly found native shrubs and plants great and small, and . . . these could give the same value in general composition, if not better than plants of foreign origin."[50] Members could thus model gardens that were both ecologically superior and economically affordable.

Hutcheson's emphasis on native plants also acknowledged the expertise of farm and rural women, who had traditionally cultivated local plants in their gardens. Without saying so directly, Hutcheson framed a role for "country" women, who could teach "educated" women about gardening and horticulture, while the latter could perhaps guide the former in the fine art of design. Women writers frequently alluded to such an exchange of information between women, suggesting that the garden and home landscape might become a site of shared authority. Helena Rutherford Ely, an author of garden books, told a potent story of her experience trading seeds with a rural woman she referred to as a "mammie"—one with whom, she made clear, she might not otherwise have associated.[51] Just as she promoted the ideal of community centers where gardening expertise would be shared, Hutcheson suggested that gardeners might individually share their knowledge of native plants and landscapes.

A Taste for Beauty

Hutcheson's social agenda was founded on the assumption that an exhibition of good taste would raise the standards for all citizens and that with improved homes and gardens the poor, the working class, and the middle class would become more satisfied and better citizens of the nation. Hutcheson used her positions as a professional landscape architect, a garden club member, and a woman of the upper class to promote her vision of a more cultured and cultivated nation and a more beautiful America. She believed that landscape architects had no greater calling than "saving. . . rural villages through some ordered program. . . . Perhaps in the near future a large group of professionally trained people will assume the task and be the inspiration for a program which will lead to better towns in America."[52] Hutcheson served as a role model for women involved in the patriotic work of reforming and refining American landscape and culture. Having seen women rise to the challenge during World War I, she wanted to harness those same forces to realize her vision of a better nation.

Hutcheson established her sphere of influence through her designs, publications, and lectures. Annette Hoyt Flanders, on the other hand, created two important model landscapes, open to the public, in order to demonstrate the design principles for home gardens shared by Hutcheson, Flanders, and the larger design community.

7

Model Gardens

Public and Private

According to contemporary reformers, the home was a sacred landscape that both shaped and signified society. Home gardens were the focus of reform organizations, garden clubs, and extension programs, all of which struggled at one level or another to try to improve the visual characteristics of residential landscapes, as discussed in the previous chapter. Home gardens were featured in popular magazines and professional journals. Professional photographers published pictures of homes and gardens, some large, some modest, many reflecting the hopes and aspirations of American citizens. Garden clubs sponsored educational programs and competitions to try to improve the design and care of home grounds throughout the nation. Landscape architects, including Olmsted, Shipman, Coffin, and Manning, designed home gardens with the same aspirations. The American home and garden were the heart and soul of the culture and thus the focus of an outstanding number of organizations, associations, and individuals in the first half of the twentieth century.

This significance placed on the individual's personal space stemmed from an older American emphasis on ownership. Harriet Martineau, a British visitor, wrote in 1837 that in the United States "an artisan works, that he may die on land of his own."[1] The landscape architect Frank Waugh described domestic grounds in 1928 as representing "something permanent, general and significant," having grown out of a tradition of pioneers faced with the task to not only "make a living, but to make homes."[2] The American ideal had evolved to embrace the vision of each family living in an independent and detached home, surrounded by a landscape planted with trees, shrubs, flowers, and grass.

Ellen Shipman wrote: "If you are planning to build a home, you are embarked on man's greatest achievement—it is for its protection that wars are fought; and for its beautification that other arts have been developed. It was the building of a home, one stone upon another, and the cultivation of the surrounding land that differentiated man from beast more than any other one thing. . . . Do not take this great experience casually—give it all the consideration such a momentous undertaking should receive."[3] For many landscape architects it was the home landscape that held the potential to radically improve American culture—to help it achieve its potential. The private residential garden was the most direct means of influencing individual members of a community.

Critics' voices were also heard. Some viewed efforts to improve the taste and habits of citizens as "patronizing, technocratic social engineering"[4] to benefit the elite classes, as well as national and industrial economic interests—a viewpoint Hutcheson had tried to address. Despite critics, however, reform efforts were at the core of many volunteer groups and governmental programs, from the mid-nineteenth century through the Works Progress Administration (WPA) projects of the 1930s.

Designing Home Gardens

For landscape architects practicing in the mid-nineteenth century, such as Downing, Olmsted, and Cleveland, the home garden signified the values and tastes of a home's residents and users. Olmsted Sr. believed that "manifestations of refined domestic life were unquestionably the ripest and best fruits of civilization."[5] If Americans could be taught to evidence taste in their domestic setting, then culture and taste in public matters would follow, as would the social graces. These early practitioners were as much social thinkers as they were designers of the landscape.

During the Country Place Era many landscape architects could direct their attention to the fine art of design, and the resulting elaborate estates and extensive designed landscapes revealed the practice's potential as a fine and high art. Practitioners had the resources to create outstanding works, exhibiting clarity of spatial relationships; close attention to issues of classical scale and proportion; and exquisite details of construction, materials, and form. This era's works, indeed, were exemplars of design and good taste. But with the advent of World War I came significant social changes, and this period of abundance came to an end. Social concerns for the middle class came to the forefront, and landscape architects could no longer depend on large, well-funded commissions to fully support, and define, the profession.

They thus returned to earlier concerns: the challenge of improving the average American's home garden and landscape. Realizing that they could not persuade the vast population of middle-income home owners to hire landscape architects, many pursued alternate avenues to teach Americans taste in home garden design. Books and magazine articles remained an efficient, economic, and effective way to educate the middle class. In 1870 Frank Jessup Scott wrote a public-oriented treatise on the advantages and care of small home grounds, titled *The Art of Beautifying Suburban Home Grounds of Small Extent.* Frank Waugh's *Landscape Gardening: Treatise on the General Principles Governing Outdoor Art* also advised home owners on the design of home grounds, as well as providing gardening tips. Samuel Parsons, a founding member of the ASLA, wrote yet another guide for the home owner in 1899, *How to Plan the Home Grounds*, while Herbert J. Kellaway's *How to Lay Out Suburban Home Grounds* (1907, 1915) turned the focus specifically to smaller-scale suburban gardens. Brochures on the topic included Elias A. Long's *Landscape Gardening*, first available in 1891.

Others took a more actively engaged approach, including offering consulting services at a reduced price. Warren Manning, for example, hired women such as Helen Bullard to produce a guidebook and provide consulting services for small home owners. The guidebook, titled *A Handbook for Planning and Planting Small Home Grounds*, addressed home owners as well-meaning people who would benefit from professional consultation yet might not be able to afford it. Expertise was thereby offered as a community service for a minimal fee. It is significant that Manning hired women to carry out this plan. Similarly, he employed female designers to oversee the community days and pageants for which his office was commissioned. Women of the period were considered accustomed to community service projects, and it was believed that the uneducated public would take more easily to a woman's aid in the garden and home. Women could be seen as naturally nurturing the home and community environment, and Manning drew on these associations among home grounds, domestic landscapes, and women in his practice.

By the 1930s, designs for small residential landscapes were a significant component in the practice of landscape architecture. Some suggested that as the era of the country estate ended, the small-home landscape would become the primary focus of professional practice. The ASLA president noted, in his 1925 annual report: "While we may almost say that the day of the large country place is passing, the call for our service on the home grounds of moderate scope is increasing. The home-maker is getting to realize his need of us. He is gradually evolving into that laudable state when he says, what is home without a designer."[6] Clearly, the profession would be seen as more important if the average- or moderate-income family might avail itself of its services on a regular basis.

Interest in the small home was also linked to issues of housing on a larger scale. In a 1914 letter to Lockwood de Forest, Warren Manning suggested that the ASLA's annual meetings be combined with those of other associations, such as the National Housing Associates, the American Civic Association, the National Conference on City Planning, and the Society for Preservation of National Parks. The professional organization for architects, the AIA, also set up a small-house bureau at this time and suggested a similar focus on city planning. Such collaboration among professional groups was increasingly viewed as a necessary part of practice, as the complexities of city planning and addressing the diverse housing issues became more evident and urgent.

Schools responded to the increased interest in home landscape design by offering courses for home owners, as well as classes in garden design for young professionals. The schools for women turned a professional and practical eye on the topic, their administrators realizing that increased attention to critical housing issues and calls for improved living conditions created an apparently natural role for women as designers and consultants.

In the 1935 Cambridge School bulletin, the director Henry Frost wrote: "General housing conditions are deplorable. . . . There is a steadily growing appreciation of the necessity for more intelligent planning of living conditions, and in this work, architects and landscape architects, as well as regional planners, have an opportunity to play important parts."[7] Frost envisioned the school taking a leadership role in addressing these challenges and opportunities. From 1918 to the early 1930s the school was officially named the Cambridge School of *Domestic* Architecture and Landscape Architecture (my emphasis), and its future—and that of its alumnae—seemed set for success. The assertion that women might lend expertise to such work provided a powerful incentive for women to become actively involved as professionals and amateurs.

While many women landscape architects, probably all, designed residential gardens and landscapes at some point in their careers, some also embraced a broader social agenda than is generally recognized. Hutcheson's work is one example, as are the courses and model gardens of Annette Hoyt Flanders and the housing projects of Marjorie Sewell Cautley. Together the work of these practitioners covers a breadth of practice, reflecting shared values related to homes, domesticity, and the importance of responding to women's needs within the residential landscape.

ANNETTE HOYT FLANDERS (1887–1946)

Born in Milwaukee in 1887, Flanders grew up in a wealthy family that valued education, the arts, and great gardens. Her father, Frank Mason Hoyt, was a well-known attorney, as well as a plant enthusiast, who never missed "an opportunity to share his interests in growing things with his daughter on trips here, and later in Europe and South America."[8] Hettie Pamela Jones Hoyt, Flanders's mother, was a member of the Daughters of the American Revolution and the Mayflower Descendants. She was also an accomplished painter and short-story writer, having studied painting and sculpture in Italy. During Flanders's childhood the family spent summers at a fashionable resort on the shores of Lac LaBelle in Oconomowoc, Wisconsin, and also traveled abroad. Flanders was married in 1913 to Roger Yale Flanders, although they were separated and divorced by 1920. Nonetheless, she retained the name "Mrs. Flanders" throughout her professional career.

Of a later generation of women in landscape architecture, Flanders was able to take advantage of the formal educational opportunities offered by colleges and universities. Her initial education consisted primarily of private schools and tutoring in the natural sciences, literature, and painting. She graduated in 1914 from the Botany Department of Smith College with a bachelor's degree in the liberal arts. Smith College, founded in 1871 with a gift from Sophia Smith, had become one of the finest women's colleges in the nation by 1910, offering a liberal curriculum emphasizing the humanities, the fine arts, and the natural and social sciences. It had high standards for admission, particularly for students not educated in New England schools. Flanders took Smith's required courses in mathematics, English, physics, and art, as well as a number in elocution. She also played on the basketball team and acted in Shakespeare plays.

After considering a career in research in plant hybridization and propagation, Flanders enrolled in a summer program at Lake Forest, which introduced her to the field of landscape architecture. By the end of the summer she had decided to enroll in the University of Illinois's program (the same one from which Florence Yoch and Elizabeth May McAdams had graduated the previous spring), and she received her bachelor's degree in landscape architecture in 1918. Flanders followed up with courses in civil engineering at Marquette University. Later, while serving with the American Red Cross in France in 1918 and 1919, she took courses in design, architecture, and the history of architecture at the Sorbonne, Paris. She argued throughout her career that women had to be competent in engineering, surveying, and the technical aspects of design. She continued to travel widely in Europe and the West Indies tropics.

Flanders valued the credentials that were by the late 1920s an established part of a formal education. By 1934 she was signing articles with her degrees noted: A.B., B.S., M.L.A.[9] This last degree (a master's in landscape architecture) had been self-awarded, as she never enrolled in a graduate-level degree program. It is likely she believed her experience warranted such recognition. Her emphasis on formal degrees—even to the point of adding one based on self-evaluation—reveals the level to which such affiliations legitimized expertise.

In little more than twenty-five years, Flanders had established a major practice based in the Midwest, with commissions throughout the United States. She was a designer, writer, lecturer, and active participant in the Chicago chapter of the ASLA. She died of cancer on June 7, 1946, at the age of fifty-eight, still practicing in Milwaukee. In her obituary in *Landscape Architecture Magazine,* she was credited with having done "much to further interest in landscape architecture by lecturing on landscape design, construction, and planting before horticultural and botanical societies, schools, and garden and women's clubs."[10]

Professional Practice

As a graduate of the University of Illinois, Flanders found her first professional employment in the offices of Vitale, Brinckerhoff, and Geiffert in New York City, put in charge of design and supervising planting projects. This firm, led by three male designers, specialized in estate work, and Flanders worked on two important projects, both of which were published under her name: the Myron C. Taylor gardens, on Long Island; and the Oasis, the garden of F. E. Dury, in the heart of Cleveland, Ohio. Flanders opened her own first office on East Fifty-seventh Street and soon thereafter employed Helen Swift Jones as an associate.[11] Unlike Farrand and Shipman, Flanders lived in a separate apartment, across the street. She had moved to a more prestigious address, at 381 Park Avenue, within a few years, and in 1935 she moved to 540 Park Avenue. Here she joined several other landscape architects and architects, including Mary Rutherfurd Jay (whose office was at 100 Park Avenue, Suite 601), Ellen Shipman, Marian Coffin, Ruth Dean, and Martha Hutcheson. Jay and Flanders often presented their travel lectures for similar groups and may well have known each other through the lecture circuit.

In 1923 Flanders was elected to membership in the ASLA and honored by *House & Garden* as one of a small group of women who were nationally recognized leaders in landscape architecture (the others were Coffin, Farrand, Strang, Tabor, Dean, and Shipman).[12] Flanders was also included in the *House & Garden* "Hall of Fame" in 1933, recognized for her "broad grasp of horticulture, landscape design, architecture and practical engineering, and her ability to apply them to the creation of lovely gardens. And for that essential which no training gives—native genius."[13] She was elected an ASLA fellow in 1942.

Flanders maintained her New York office until 1942, simultaneously heading a second office from her summer home in Wisconsin. This arrangement allowed her to establish herself with both the New York elite and established Chicago families. In 1943 Flanders left New York to open a primary office in Milwaukee. Each office was staffed with employees, including a secretary and draftspersons.

The scope of Flanders's work included private estates, real estate subdivisions, recreational developments, and exhibition gardens. She worked on projects from the Canadian border to North Carolina, Texas, Colorado, and New Mexico, as well as a project in Hawaii and another in France. On Long Island alone she designed at least twenty-two landscapes for private clients. Flanders participated in professional committees, exhibited widely, and was often included in exhibitions of the New York chapter of the ASLA. She was awarded the medal in landscape architecture by the Architectural League of New York in 1932 for her McCann Garden, on Long Island. (See color plate 7.) During the 1930s several women were awarded this medal, reflecting both the number of women in practice and their standing within the mainstream of professional practice. Further, its inclusion of women alongside men revealed this organization's focus on quality and its interest in design rather than gender.

Flanders hired many women to work as designers in her office, including Helen Elise Bullard, Gertrude Deimel Kuh, Margaret Eaglesfield Bell, Dolores Hoyle Richardson, and Jeannette Schroeder, each of whom later established practices. Many of the women hired were graduates of Lowthorpe and Cambridge, where Flanders lectured periodically. In 1932 her office employed four staff: a landscape engineer, Herbert H. Cutler; Betty Lipman, who served as secretary and bookkeeper; Irving Dorman, the chief draftsperson and designer; and Betty Sprout, a draftsperson who also produced the planting plans.

Men, then, clearly played a role in Flanders's office. Herbert H. Cutler, hired as a landscape engineer and technical draftsperson, had graduated in 1930 from the New York State College of Environmental Science and Forestry at Syracuse University, with a degree in landscape engineering. Irving Dorman, Mr. Watson, and Mr. Clark all served as draftspersons and planting supervisors for a number of projects.[14] When Flanders needed to assign an on-site supervisor for a distant project—what she called a "Clerk of Works"—she generally sent a male employee, perhaps because a man might best be able to oversee the work of nurserymen and gardeners, who might not respond as well to a female supervisor. In the project Flanders did for Senator Lawrence C. Phipps in Denver, she frequently had to ask for his support in the face of disgruntled gardeners and nurserymen.

The quintessential professional, Flanders treated each aspect of her practice as an opportunity to display her good taste and professionalism. She presented her designs as works of art in bound books or framed photographs, led a professional office, published and lectured regularly, received commissions throughout the country, and was a respected member of upper-class society. Her work also served as a bridge between the more traditional Beaux-Arts approach to design and early modernist explorations. While improving society was critical to Flanders, the artistry of her work was also essential.

Flanders, who had a reputation as a demanding employer, expected her staff to gain the knowledge and skills to become excellent landscape architects. She was said to be difficult to work for, and rumors—probably stemming from territorial issues—suggested that she used methods "to acquire jobs which were not acceptable to others in the profession."[15] One can only speculate as to why women such as Flanders and Farrand had such harsh reputations. They were not described as approachable or friendly, like Shipman, nor were they deemed generous hostesses, like Coffin. Instead, they were often portrayed as accomplished but overly ambitious; even if well-respected, they were feared and rarely liked. These two women were clearly consummate professionals and driven practitioners, and perhaps they did not feel it necessary—and even thought it detrimental—to also be viewed as naturally gracious or accommodating, as this perception might interfere with their role as professionals. Farrand and Flanders wished to be judged purely on the basis of their professional work and did not appear to give much credit to other venues of social acceptability. But how different was this approach, after all, from that of their male colleagues?

Despite their reputations, however, Flanders—and to some extent Farrand—reached out to guide young women who wished to pursue careers as landscape architects. Flanders mentored her employees and taught them the skills necessary to launch successful practices. She trusted them to cultivate new clients and to identify new projects and provided clear guidelines for maintaining the office practice when she was not available. Her remarkable collection of source material was also available to her employees, including books, photographs, plans, and reports on botany, horticulture, engineering, and design. One Flanders employee, Alice Upham Smith, recalled a lecture Flanders gave to her students and employees, which Smith quoted years later:

> Landscape Architecture requires far more of a woman than the knowledge of when flowers and shrubs bloom and an artistic eye for color. To build a parapet on a country estate, to supervise the construction of a bridge or turn a barren tract into a land of haunting loveliness demands a knowledge of Architecture and Engineering as well as Botany. It is folly to take it up as a part time interest for it demands so much energy and time. Landscape Architecture demands physical endurance. The hours are long and irregular. Work must be done under all kinds of weather, for it includes not only the drawing of plans, but the laying out of roads, swimming pools, etc. A woman has to have an artistic eye for color, mass and line, and be able to handle clients and laborers pleasantly and smoothly. She must be extremely adaptable and possess tact as well as training. Few people would try to paint without study, yet many plant gardens because they like flowers.[16]

Flanders believed that women should never delegate the technical aspects of design and production to others: they should be knowledgeable in all aspects of design and construction. She had studied engineering, lectured on construction techniques and grading, and was recognized for her extensive knowledge of the technical elements of her work. Her attention to such details, evident in her correspondence with the Phipps family, was consistently noted by other clients. Not one detail or plant choice was left to the discretion of a construction crew or a gardener. Flanders insisted that either she or Mr. Clark, her "Clerk of Works," approve every phase of construction and planting, from the building of walls and pool, to the planting of perennials and large elm trees. This level of control allowed her to complete projects to her standards.

The professional relationships Flanders had with her clients were similar to those of her contemporaries. She offered a series of consultations and working plans, clients signing contracts agreeing to the described professional standards. In a 1929 letter to Helen Bullard, Flanders outlined her approach to new clients. She charged $100 for a first consultation if she could travel to the site and back to New York City within one day, $50 extra per day if it were farther away. Half of this charge was credited to the client's account if he or she chose to continue to work with Flanders's office. She then provided her "Professional Contract Charge Form," based on ASLA standards. A formal flower garden on the scale of a large country estate cost $350, while a rose garden or a cutting garden would cost between $200 and $250. A plan for an entire estate, on the other hand—which Flanders often provided—ran from $1,000 to $1,500, according to the size and amount of work.

Should any staff member meet with a potential client, he or she was to provide the "Professional Contract Charge Form," appropriately notated as to type of work, size, and fees. The client was expected to sign the contract before any further work would commence: "In taking this up with a client, explain that it is a standard form contract which is used for all work and they are kept on hand already typed and that the client's name and the fee for the general design are inserted as each piece of work comes up. I want them to thoroughly understand that it is not a special contract drawn up just for them, but that it is a standard form on which all of our work is done."[17] Clearly, Flanders was concerned that her clients understand the nature of a professional relationship and did not expect her to serve as a friend or casual consultant. She also insisted that for any project she be commissioned to oversee planting and construction until the work was complete.

Flanders took a similar approach in her projects for corporations, including her work for the 1934 Century of Progress exhibition in Chicago, for which she was hired by *Good Housekeeping* to design and supervise construction of a "modern garden." Meticulous about her role as designer and supervisor, she insisted that other professionals and laborers respect her position.[18] Flanders thus built a reputation as a strong and forthright professional who maintained high professional standards in all of her dealings with clients, employees, and colleagues.

Flanders's presentation drawings were similar to Shipman's in their detail and composition. They were often done in pencil on trace paper, composed on the sheet, as a painting might be. Flanders illustrated her intentions through the use of vignettes—which portrayed small scenes, as if the viewer were walking through the garden—elevations, and perspectives, though she rarely used all in one presentation. Instead, she carefully chose the appropriate medium and worked within the confines of a sheet of paper to present her design idea. These presentations were meticulously drawn and beautifully composed, highlighting the design principles appropriate to the specific project. Flanders's vignettes were particularly persuasive, presenting appealing "close-up" images of the

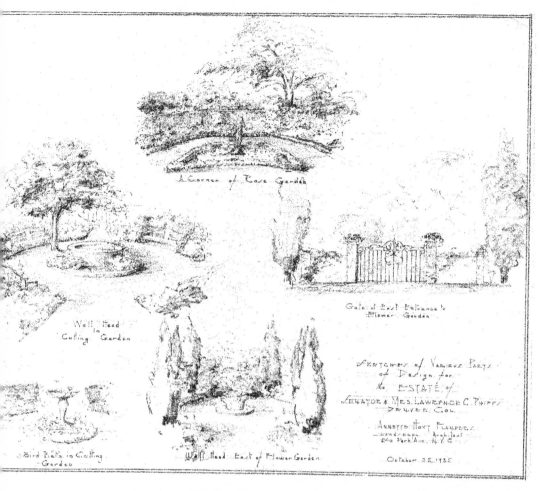

Flanders's sketches for the Phipps Garden, Denver, Colorado, ca. 1934. These vignettes expressed the experience of the intimate spaces within the garden, as well as the character of the designed landscape. (Image courtesy of the Phipps Conference Center at the University of Denver)

spaces within a garden, drawn to human scale. From her presentation drawings the client might also learn, along with Flanders's specific intentions, the broader design principles she believed most important.

Teaching Design

Flanders exhibited a strong commitment to teaching the public, clients, and younger designers throughout her career. She was a frequent guest on the lecture circuit, speaking for botanical societies, schools, and garden clubs. She presented a series of lectures on the plant materials suitable to the area for the Milwaukee Art Institute and at one point indicated interest in a faculty position at the University of Wisconsin–Madison.

She was known as a good teacher and appeared to enjoy the role. Flanders also wrote extensively on design for magazines, including *House & Garden, Country Life in America,* and *House Beautiful.* She served as *Good Housekeeping*'s consultant garden editor in 1933 and 1934, a four-part *Good Housekeeping* series featuring Flanders's design philosophy for small suburban gardens.

Flanders taught courses in landscape design in New York, Milwaukee, and many other cities in the Midwest and Northeast. A variety of students attended these lectures, although most were women. A well-designed brochure, from around 1932, describes two typical Flanders courses, each consisting of three classes. The first course was "The Designing and Building of Gardens," presenting a foundation of information on landscape design, construction, and the "theory of planting." This course focused on the basics of landscape development for large and small sites, simple construction, soil preparation, and planting-design guidelines. The second course, "Plant Material and How to Use It," focused—as its title implied—on plants appropriate to the landscape. The course addressed trees and ground covers, shrubs and vines, and perennials and bulbs.

While the settings for Flanders's courses (the Waldorf-Astoria, for example, for the New York lectures) and the sources of the quotations included in her brochure (Richardson Wright, editor of *House & Garden,* and the author Mrs. Francis King) might suggest an elite audience, further investigation reveals a much broader outreach to middle-class women, some pursuing an interest in landscape design as a career.[19] Flanders offered her courses to garden clubs, civic associations, and other smaller groups for a course fee of $7.50, which was quite reasonable at the time. Though Flanders might have gained some commissions through these courses, it is unlikely that they amounted to enough to cover the time and effort she put into her lectures. She was genuinely interested in educating middle-class home owners.

Flanders's lectures featured numerous glass lantern slides, illustrating design principles and process. She often began her lectures with a slide comparing the design of a garden to the composition of a symphony, other images also illustrating the various elements of design and composition. Flanders emphasized the challenges of designing with an eye to scale, balance, axis, sight lines, and the use of the best plant materials available.

Flanders did not promote a particular style in her lectures, nor did she insist that a professional was necessary for the design of any garden or landscape. Rather, her lectures presented a range of approaches to the garden and to styles of landscape design. Her slides featured design and horticultural principles that she described in clear and simple language, allowing even those with little or no background to learn the basics, while others might appreciate the finer points. Flanders, in other words, seemed as interested in educating the home owner new to the principles

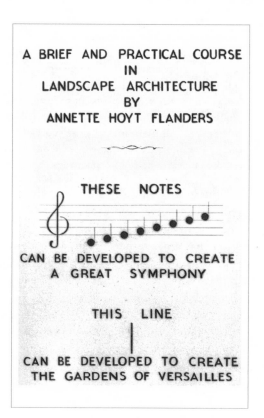

A BRIEF AND PRACTICAL COURSE
IN
LANDSCAPE ARCHITECTURE
BY
ANNETTE HOYT FLANDERS

THESE NOTES

CAN BE DEVELOPED TO CREATE
A GREAT SYMPHONY

THIS LINE

CAN BE DEVELOPED TO CREATE
THE GARDENS OF VERSAILLES

Glass lantern slide used by Flanders to introduce her courses on landscape architecture. She drew many similarities among music, art, and landscape architecture in her lectures and essays. (Annette Hoyt Flanders Papers, Sophia Smith Collection, Smith College)

of design or art for their own home gardens as she was in explaining the finer points of the art of design.

Flanders took a firm approach to educating her clients, both emphasizing the importance of a professional designer and suggesting that good taste in landscape design evidenced culture. She presented an elegant copy of her portfolio as a book, *Landscape Architecture,* to each client upon the signing of an agreement. This book—which illustrated Flanders's work and explained the aesthetic value of her designed landscapes—also served as her "Exhibition of Landscape Architecture Catalogue" for the Milwaukee Art Institute in 1932. In addition, clients such as Mr. and Mrs. Charles E. Van Vleck Jr. received a bound book of the drawings and sketches Flanders had produced for their own landscape, informally presented yet carefully composed with plans, vignettes, and perspectives.

Similarly, Flanders also took care to explain her work to each client through her letters. In her correspondence with Senator and Mrs. Phipps in Denver, for example, she was careful to describe the importance of the professional landscape architect to the success of a landscape. When the Phippses suggested that their gardener could use her planting plans to complete the project, rather than having Flanders or her assigned staff member oversee the work, Flanders responded quickly and decisively:

Planting composition is a fine art which can not successfully be left to the judgment of nurserymen and contractors. . . . A planting plan can only be a guide. The artist who is creating the garden must be free to adjust it as the planting proceeds. It is no more possible to definitely and finally specify planting than it would be for an artist to specify in advance exactly the manner in which he wants to apply paint to his canvas. If this could be done Sargent could have drawn a portrait and written a report for any painter to apply the color. . . . It is because of close supervision that other ranking landscape architects and I have achieved our reputations for creating landscapes that rank as fine art and not as "plantings."[20]

Flanders also carefully addressed the challenges faced by owners of small, urban homes and gardens, focusing on the potential of any site to be well designed. Her lectures and essays convincingly conveyed the notion that any site had potential if its owner took the time to learn design principles. This approach to promoting good landscape design in suburban and urban settings was different from that of many of her male colleagues. For example, Manning's response to the needs of small home owners was to provide professional expertise at a reasonable price, the expertise thus remaining with the professional rather than being conveyed to the home owner. Indeed, many members of the ASLA promoted the profession rather than trying to educate the public.

Flanders believed it was her obligation to educate the lay public in the art and science of good landscape design. She began lectures with her "Ten Commandments of Garden Maintenance," giving an overview of the kind of work involved in caring for a landscape or garden; the practical topics she addressed including planting, disease control, pruning, and weeding. She thus focused equally, in even the simplest plans, on the site's aesthetic nature and the appropriate choice of plant materials. This choice set her apart from many of her contemporary male colleagues, who increasingly deemphasized the role of horticulture and plant materials in design. Mary Black of Illinois later recalled being inspired to open her own nursery business by one of Flanders's lectures.[21]

Flanders promoted her vision of America as a nation of small gardens because she wanted to "make a more permanent contribution to the cause of beauty." According to her students, she was careful to teach the average home gardener the "logical sequence in which things should be done to develop property practically, beautifully, and economically."[22] Addressing both urban and suburban sites, Flanders frequently included slides in her lectures on designing "An Average City Lot," generally depicting a site with a small outdoor space. She also specifically addressed the challenges of small homes and gardens, which usually featured a lawn and gardens with trees and shrubs, her plans guided by her concern with symmetry, balance, and the creation of distinct spaces. She also presented her audiences with alternative plans, showing the functions of each area and how the areas related to one another and illustrating movement through the spaces. She emphasized both form and function as two parts of a larger whole—again, like the parts of a symphony.

In addition to lecturing, Flanders exhibited her work, ASLA exhibits providing her with one exceptional venue. Another special opportunity came when the Milwaukee Art Institute invited her to exhibit her work in 1932, the show featuring photographs and models, as well as a small catalog.[23] Organized first by presentation style and then by theme, this exhibit demonstrated the breadth of approaches that might be taken to a variety of sites. Beginning with a group of pastel portraits, the hand-painted images of her gardens featured a range of garden elements or moments: a doorway to a garden, small seating areas, walled gardens, the corner of a sunken garden, a friendly terrace garden. The photographs' sense of familiarity suggested a modest, intimate scale. Indeed, Flanders had deemphasized the size of her projects, focusing instead on particular aspects to which the average home owner might respond. She thus featured smaller garden rooms, intimate spaces, and nooks that might be "fit" into a more modest home.

The second section of the exhibit featured colored porcelain models of two of her designed landscapes, along with thirty-five models of small English cottages and gardens, linking Flanders's gardens to traditional cottage gardens and vernacular landscapes—or, read another way, illustrating the fact that the design principles Flanders used for estate landscapes could be found even in the most simple cottage gardens.

Another section of the exhibit was devoted to urban roof gardens, which were functional and pleasurable and also made use of otherwise "wasted" space. Such gardens responded to the needs of urban families, providing safe, private space that was both outdoors and protected and enclosed. The general popularity of roof gardens had increased in the 1920s and 1930s, as urban dwellers sought to expand their useable space.[24] Shipman, for example, designed a roof garden for the Aetna Insurance Company, while Dean designed a number for New York clients. Flanders similarly had created several rooftop and small urban gardens, her most noted design for a playroom rooftop garden, the image included in her exhibit showing a teacher and children playing in their "bird cage."[25] This particular rooftop garden illustrates Flanders's experiments in architectural elements. The garden space is defined by the "cage," a chimney, and the floor—or sky roof. Whereas in most gardens the sky serves as a "ceiling," here a pergolalike structure covered the area, framing the sky. No plants are visible in the image, only metallic replicas of shaped potted trees set on the ledge. Brightly colored metal "birds" fly above, as if the space were really a traditional garden.

The rooftop garden further reflected Flanders's experimentation with modernist sensibilities and new materials, its design emphasizing a space that is both a garden and an extension of the house. The green floor, a synthetic material, suggested mossy stone. The iron grille walls

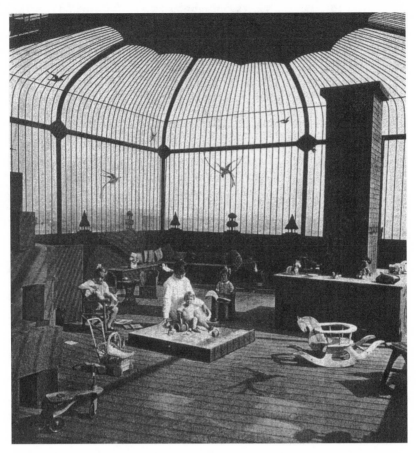

A "Playroom in the Sky," as illustrated in *An Exhibition of Landscape Architecture,* New York, 1932. This design was innovative in its use of the roof for terraces and gardens and its use of color and architectural elements. (Annette Hoyt Flanders Papers, Sophia Smith Collection, Smith College)

were painted green, in contrast with the blue sky. The furniture and architecture took clear geometrical forms, like building blocks. The sturdy chimney, with its surround of a toy box, grounded the garden, humanizing the space, especially given its location on a roof. The chimney also provided verticality to balance the roof's horizontal lines. The garden's "plants" were made of metal, shaped into triangles and circles that balanced the square and rectangular boxes for play.

Flanders's photograph of this rooftop garden clearly acknowledges that it was created for children and their caregivers, thus emphasizing the importance and potential of the domestic space. Its colors were bright lemon-orange and aquamarine blue, pillows thrown in the corners. The tricycles represented a new child-centered technology, while the wooden and wicker rocking horses and chair harked back to an earlier age. The wood and wicker furniture also provided some of the garden's only real pieces of nature: when it rained, according to a reporter, they sprouted grass.[26]

This "bird-cage" garden was one of three terraces Flanders created for this particular client, whose dining and living rooms featured their own terraces, each space designed with new materials, simple forms, and bold colors. The furniture, described as "simple and distinct," was constructed of square chromium metal tubing with a dull satin finish.[27] Flanders's designs were here reduced to essential elements, frequently formed from one continuous piece of metal, the colors minimized to shades of green and blue. The living room terrace also featured living plants in clusters, placed where they would not interfere with the space's overall design, which emphasized its architectural character. These design choices revealed significant experimentation for Flanders: an architectural rooftop garden emphasizing form, space, and technology was rare in 1932.

Plans, sketches, and scale models rounded out the Milwaukee exhibit, illustrating Flanders's artistry—the clear authorship of a professional. These gardens, clearly, had not simply been created by well-meaning home owners; they were the work of a very talented professional landscape architect. The contrast between the photographs, which made the gardens appear simple and natural, and the drawings, which were strikingly elegant and detailed, must have been obvious to the average viewer. The drawings clearly demonstrated that the professional could go beyond good taste to create a beautiful and unique design appropriate to a specific site and specific clients. Flanders subsequently presented a version of the exhibition catalog to clients at the start of her projects, as noted earlier, perhaps to insure that they would thus immediately understand the breadth and depth of her work.

Model Gardens

Model homes and gardens were key to the design professions and related popular publications. Magazines sponsored exhibits at fairs, while the Better Homes Campaign promoted models to be displayed in cities across the nation. For many such models were far more persuasive than books or magazines, because they were more tangible and real.

These models initially promoted specific images of the American Dream—a one-family home painted white, with a picket fence and cottage garden. The details were different, the orientation sometimes responding to a particular site and the materials varying according to the region. All suggested, however, that the average citizen could easily construct such designs with only a little guidance. The role of the designer-architect or landscape architect remained vague, as on the one hand these models were designed, yet the services of a professional were rarely a major element of such promotional materials. Nonetheless, many designers participated in model projects as a way to both encourage certain design approaches and promote their own practices.

By the 1930s model homes and gardens were introducing modern living to masses of visitors and guests. Modernism in this venue was about technology, privacy, and clean living. The modern house and garden encouraged the client or consumer to embrace a better, more modern living, and model homes and gardens were used as a means to educate the public about such modern living as the rooftop garden had suggested. Magazines, along with corporations such as General Electric, sponsored model homes in Chicago and at the New York World's Fair. Model homes were exhibited at the 1937 Paris Exposition, and the Better Homes Movement sponsored demonstration homes in Massachusetts, New Jersey, New York, Maryland, Virginia, South Carolina, Georgia, Tennessee, Alabama, Arkansas, and California. In a different venue, but with a similar agenda, Sears, Roebuck and Company promoted and sold over one hundred thousand homes through their mail-order Modern Homes program between 1908 and 1940. After World War II, from 1945 to 1966, the Case Study Houses project, sponsored by *Arts & Architecture,* commissioned major architects of the day, including Richard Neutra, Craig Ellwood, Charles and Ray Eames, and Eero Saarinen, to design and build inexpensive and efficient model homes to meet the residential housing boom. Together these exhibits, models, and catalogs promoted a view of family life and the home-and-garden aesthetic that would permeate all levels of residential life in the United States, in the early and mid-twentieth century and beyond.

Flanders participated in two model home and garden projects, one in Chicago and one in New York City. She used these opportunities as she had used lectures and publications—to teach her audience the principles of good design, using plant materials wisely while also introducing new ideas to the public.

As noted earlier, Flanders designed a "classic modern" garden for the 1934 Century of Progress exhibition in Chicago, sponsored by *Good Housekeeping.* In fact, the "home" on this site was only a pavilion, portrayed as the extension of an assumed house. Flanders's design drew on ideas of the modern, as reflected in her use of materials, plan, and details, and stressed the modern home's emphasis on privacy, the streamlined character of forms, and clear divisions among functional spaces. Specifically intended for public viewing, Flanders's model epitomized an appropriately modern landscape within a domestic setting.

Flanders's experiment in modern style here exhibited a much simpler and more geometric form than many contemporary suburban garden plans. Formal pools, hedges, terraces, and stonework provided the model's primary structures, highlighting the simple plant materials. Rather than emulating the style of a cottage garden, the design relied on a limited palette of green foliage and white flowers. To retain this simple color scheme, the brick paths were painted green. There was no space available for abundant flower beds, and the productive kitchen garden was to be placed at the side of the house, out of view of any of the private spaces. (See color plate 8.)

To emphasize the garden's spatial character, Flanders used changes in level. While the garden's terraces were an architectural feature, they were visually defined by plant materials and a limited use of bricks and concrete, the latter a relatively new material in a small residential garden. The intimate seating areas overlooked the sunken lawn and pool, shaping the garden as a scene to be passively viewed rather than walked through or enjoyed through gardening. This elegant garden focused on creating atmosphere and experience, with few materials and few distractions.

This model garden was in keeping with the general emerging modernism in landscape architecture. Its plan relied on direct geometries and clear articulated lines, although its symmetry was traditional. Its colors (green and white) and textures were reserved and subordinated to the plan. This approach set Flanders's project apart from other model gardens of the period, which often featured exotic specimen plants and plenty of gardening space. While gardens such as Shipman's flower beds and Farrand's rose garden emphasized the plants themselves and the idea of a garden-oriented space, the focus here was on the spaces defined by the terraces and plant materials, rather than on individual plants. A highlight of the garden was its statue, a modernist piece by Wheeler Williams titled *Maya*.[28] This white marble piece was set on an axis with the pavilion, with a backdrop of a high, dark green arborvitae hedge.

The garden was to be viewed while sitting in front of the pavilion or on one of the small patio areas. This was not, in other words, a gardener's garden. The major axes overlapped, one from the pavilion to the statue and the other across the rear of the garden. However, unlike the modernist designs of the late 1930s and 1940s, this model did not play with diagonal axes or abstract geometries. Flanders's exploration was far simpler, its emphasis on plants as architectural elements rather than features and on the clarity and crispness of the designed spaces.

In keeping with the fair's extensive electrification, Flanders's garden also featured night lighting by General Electric—again promoting modern technology and modern design. The idea that a garden could be visited at night was relatively new to landscape architecture, and the entire garden was bathed in white lights. In particular, the white lighting of the sculpture against the dark hedges created a distinctly modern look. Even the pool was lit, with bulbs set under ten of the metal lily pads, also reflecting light on the elm trees lining the border behind the statue. The fountains were lit from below, making each jet of water appear to drip iridescence, and the poplar allée was brushed with diffused lighting.

While the lit garden statue fit in with the electrical theme of the exhibition, it varied from the multicolored approach seen elsewhere. Here the light on the white statue against the black-seeming hedge emphasized the sculpture's form and lines. Together, sculpture, garden, and the pho-

Night lighting for Flanders's "classic modern" garden at the 1934 Century of Progress exhibition in Chicago highlighted the modernist statue. This image was used to illustrate an article by C. M. Cutler and G. R. La Wall, "Garden Lighting Brings Magic by Night," *Good Housekeeping,* September 1934.

tographs of both stressed a view of modern design that was more widespread in architecture, evident in many of the period's nighttime photographs of skyscrapers in New York and of other modernist architecture.

At the end of the exhibit, *Good Housekeeping,* with Flanders's permission, gave the model garden to the Chicago City South Park Board to maintain as a model suburban garden, although it did not last and was eventually deconstructed. Flanders later went on to construct a garden on the same lines as this model for the Phipps garden in Denver. The pool here was intended to highlight a copy of the same statue, although the Phippses chose not to purchase the piece.[29] Still, this garden's simple color palette and allée of trees established a different vocabulary than the rest of the landscape did, and while minor elements differed from the Chicago model, the overall effect—of a modern space within an otherwise relatively traditional designed landscape—was noteworthy.

The *Good Housekeeping* model garden was widely presented to the public in easily digestible views. The magazine itself featured both watercolor images of the garden and striking photographs of it at night. These images—one in light watercolors and the other a black-and-white photograph—initially appear at odds with each other, but the text accompanying the images made it clear that this garden was "classic modern"—that is, both classic and modern. This approach is particularly interesting, as indeed, the garden's pavilion and interiors seem far more traditional. Too, the garden as a whole, including the sculpture, especially when lit at night, could be viewed as classic in the sense that early modernist architects understood "classic"—as denoting a clean, simple, and expressive approach. Coming only a few years after Henry Russell Hitchcock and Philip Johnson's International Style exhibit at the Museum of Modern Art, Flanders's work here is playing with new ideas—as if in the garden one could experiment with a new way of viewing space and experience, especially within the safe zone of a classic pavilion and house.

Flanders could easily have chosen to design a garden more in keeping with the traditional cottage garden look, promoted in so many contemporary books and articles. Indeed, many of her gardens were just such celebrations of flowers and the potential of beds of perennials. However, here she chose to break the mold and show the public something different.

The long view of the pool garden at the Phipps estate in Denver, designed in 1935 just after the Century of Progress garden was closed. Photography by Hyskell. (Image courtesy of the Phipps Conference Center at the University of Denver)

Flanders also explored these ideas in other gardens, which can be compared to the work of French landscape architects of the period and of Fletcher Steele in the United States. Four of the lantern slides she used for her lectures evidence her interest in modern design. (See color plate 9.) By using a slightly altered vocabulary for her model gardens and presenting images of modernist gardens to her audience, Flanders brought modernist ideas and conceptions into public view, suggesting that residential gardens might respond to contemporary ideas in art, just as such notions were beginning to be explored in more academic private settings. In essence Flanders invited the public into the debate taking place within the professional community about modern ideas as they related to landscape architecture.

Flanders, notably, did not discount the role of plants and horticultural expertise in garden design, as later modernists did. Instead, like the modernist Garrett Eckbo, she considered plants carefully as part of her design experiments, attempting to use them in conjunction with her own understanding of emerging ideas about geometry and structure in the garden. In this light Flanders's work might be compared with Fletcher Steele's work for Mabel Choate at Naumkeag, in Stockbridge, Massachusetts. Steele similarly used plant materials, emphasizing the use of green and white, and merged his plants with architectural elements such as stairways. He also, like Flanders, used water to reflect movement, as well as to give life to the blue steps at Naumkeag.

Soon after the Chicago exhibit, Flanders was involved in yet another model garden—the design of "America's Little House." This was a project initiated by the Better Homes Campaign in 1922, sponsored by the Butterick Publishing Company's household magazine, the *Delineator*. This campaign promoted home ownership and beautification as ideals for American citizens. In cities and towns across the country, annual campaigns—or "better homes demonstration weeks"—encouraged citizens to own, build, remodel, and improve their homes and distributed advice on creating home furnishings and decorations. President Calvin Coolidge served as the honorary chair of the campaign's advisory council, and Secretary of Commerce Herbert Hoover was president of its board of directors. In *Better Homes in America: Plan Book for Demonstration Week October 9 to 14, 1922*, Mrs. Meloney, the president's secretary, noted that "the President feels that as many millions of dollars and the best minds of this generation have been devoted to improve factory conditions, the home is deserving of its share of the same intensive consideration. . . . It is felt that altogether too little attention has been paid to lightening the labors and bettering the working conditions of these women."[30]

Not built until 1934, "America's Little House" was the first model home in New York City. The house had been designed by Roger H. Bullard, and its interior included a kitchen created by Lillian Gilbreth for the New York Herald-Tribune Institute. This model home and garden were to promote family life, particularly convenience and economy. Pearl Buck described this house as a model of what "can be done with the moderate means we possess. There is room in the house for all of the life of the family. . . . Labor is incredibly lightened, and beauty of living seems made almost inevitable."[31] Flanders's garden was an integral part of the model's success, visited by over 145,000 guests in its first year. The garden was a fenced yard, an "oasis among the towering skyscrapers, . . . [created by placing] simply a layer of top soil . . . two feet thick . . . over discarded bricks, broken bottles and other rubbish."

With the help of New York commissioner Robert Moses and the American Association of Nurserymen, a garden was created that would entail a minimum of expense in execution and upkeep and allow a maximum of "beauty and usefulness."[32] Flanders's design was thus used to advocate a practical approach to garden design. The garden's plan was straightforward and clear. Surrounded by a white picket fence, it gave the impression of a traditional garden and home. To the rear of the house lay the garden rooms, not on an axis with the house, but as if they were interlocking puzzle pieces, the whole a simple rectangular city block. The garden's

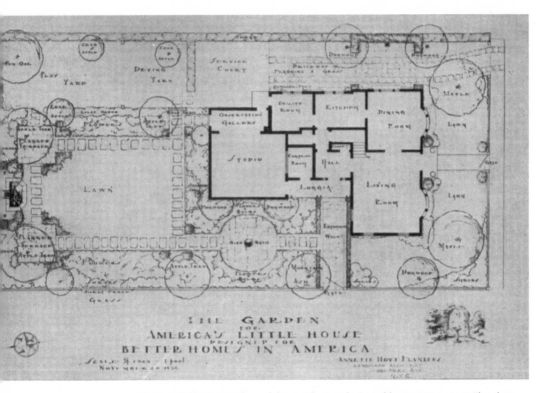

America's Little House, plan of the garden as designed by Annette Hoyt Flanders for the Better Homes campaign, ca. 1934. (Better Homes in America Collection, Box 39, folder 1, Hoover Institution Archives)

spatial character was more like that of the *Good Housekeeping* garden than of a cottage garden, although this garden did have space for flower beds. A water feature served as a focal point in the middle of the primary garden room, which was surrounded by young cypress trees that appeared very small in scale, compared to the skyscrapers in the background. The garden's character, indeed, was in many respects the antithesis of its urban setting. Its apple trees harkened back to rural life, when the garden was both productive and a source of pleasure. The functional separations too were more contemporary, as were the garden's connections to the house. The drying yard, the service court, and the play area were off the kitchen and utility room, tucked in the back, out of view of the sidewalk. Not quite a modern garden and not quite a traditional landscape, this model garden was a source of wonder for many.

A year later, to the amazement of the public, the *New York Times* announced, "Little House Gets Crop of 36 Apples." The garden and house were widely hailed as an important effort in "the movement for improving the standards of dwellings in America."[33] The garden, with its fragrant flowers and productive, beautiful, magical apple trees, was also critical, suggesting that a garden was not just an extension of a house's architecture but rather a space defined by distinct seasonality, temporality, and aesthetics in a way that only a garden can be.

This house and garden modeled an image of the ideal American family dwelling, within an urban context of towers and industry. Flanders used her design in her lectures to illustrate "An Average City Lot." By thus bringing the scale of the single-family home and its cottage garden to the urban landscape of skyscrapers and towers, Flanders and the model-home promoters advocated a very specific American Dream that might transform the urban landscape. And Pearl Buck did not suggest that this house was out of place, but rather that it might hold its ground, even though "above it stand the tall towers of New York, the towers where so much business and pleasure are carried on. But this little house stands unperturbed and unfrightened."[34]

With model homes being built across the nation, promoters suggested a shared American ideal for the home and garden, even if the details differed slightly. The typical model home could be viewed as a standard of dwelling for the masses. As Calvin Coolidge suggested, home ownership and care were to be viewed as patriotic duties and evidence of the national character. Flanders's interest in model gardens likewise revealed her commitment to teaching the average home owner the art and craft of landscape design. It was not likely that these projects were necessary to promote her practice, as she was well-established by the time she created them. In each of these model gardens, Flanders's likely intention was to introduce the public to new ideas, drawing them into acquiring taste by designing modest gardens they might imitate and emulate. In these projects, as well as her essays for popular magazines, she emphasized the

"An oasis among the towering skyscrapers": America's Little House, placed on Park Avenue, New York City. (Better Homes in America Collection, Box 39, folder 1, Hoover Institution Archives)

average American's ability to design a garden that would in turn modernize and improve their daily lives. Thus, while Hutcheson was most concerned with bringing beauty to each home and garden, Flanders sought more broadly to promote a modern life and aesthetic. Modern gardens might, she suggested, improve the home's tranquility, ease, and privacy, while providing a suitable setting for a modern family, without excessive investment. Such living would in turn improve the community life of the nation.

Flanders's decision to design these model gardens was not just chance, but most likely in response to her position as both a woman and a landscape architect. Flanders was thus able to deftly present herself as both Mrs. Flanders, a married woman of the upper classes, and as Flanders, ASLA, an established practitioner with offices in New York and the Midwest. The former established her expertise in domestic and residential spaces, while the latter lent an authority to her designs and her critique of designed landscapes.

America's little garden with one of the four apple trees that produced fruit the following spring. While the urban context is acknowledged in the views and setting, the garden was about country living, expressed by the miniature apple orchard, cottage style flower beds, bird bath, and bench. (Better Homes in America Collection, Box 39, folder 1, Hoover Institution Archives)

Landscapes of the Future

World's fairs, regional exhibits, and model homes are potent examples of
the ways in which the public was shown what the future might hold, with
the assumption that good taste would prevail. The Better Homes Campaign drew on traditional images of homes and gardens, while promoting the models as vital to the collective future. The Century of Progress
exhibits celebrated a past while imagining a future. Women were a part
of this movement, serving in a variety of roles—as architects, interior designers, and efficiency engineers; as writers, editors, and publicists; and as
consumers, readers, and visitors. Helen Elise Bullard (1896–1987), for example, helped design the 1939 New York World's Fair. Born in Schuylerville,
New York, she had graduated from Cornell University in 1918, receiving a
bachelor's degree in landscape architecture from the College of Agriculture. After being briefly employed by the Wagner Park Nursery Company
in Sidney, Ohio (lecturing and advising on small home grounds), Bullard
was hired by Warren H. Manning to work in his office.

Warren H. Manning (1860–1938), a critical mentor and teacher for wom-
en in the profession, was probably the most well-known practitioner at
the turn of the century, aside from the Olmsted firm. After initially working for Olmsted Sr., Manning had launched his practice as an independent landscape designer in 1896. Manning's office (variously in Boston,
Billerica, and Cambridge) provided training to over forty-five women between 1910 and the 1930s. Kathleen Cutting noted Manning's influence
to Cautley, on hearing that she was coming to work in Manning's office:
"There is no place I am sure where one could find more interesting work
nor gain wider experience for here one sees and does all kinds of landscape work. Mr. Manning is the most wonderful of men to work for and
with and we are to be congratulated on the opportunity we have in being
here."[35] As one of the larger firms, Manning's was an established firm
that could teach an apprentice both the business and the art of practice.
Bullard and Cautley were just two of many women Manning trained.

Manning hired many women specifically to assist in the leadership of
what he termed "Community Days." "Community Days," organized within a town, generally involved communitywide participation in restoring
or revitalizing an outdoor public space, such as a park or "commons"
area, in conjunction with a celebration of the town's history, residents,
or other notable attributes. Good taste and positive values were the hall-
marks of these events, as they were meant to demonstrate the best of what
a community had to offer. This venue provided an ideal place for women
to assume leadership, as the public was comfortable crediting women
with social organizational skills and the ability to model good values.

From 1921 to 1925, Bullard worked in the Manning office as a plants
expert, planting designer, and supervisor of projects including both private estates and community pageants. She thus acquired skills in office

management, client relations, and organizing. By 1929 she was employed in Flanders's office, supervising a number of estate projects, chiefly on Long Island, including the Simmonds and Kisor estates. After ten years working in private offices, Bullard was employed in 1930 by the New York State Civil Service, responsible for the state's parks, under the direction of Robert Moses. Here she was responsible for designing and supervising projects for the Long Island State Park Commission, Rye Beach Park, and the Southern State Parkway. In 1937, as noted, Bullard was appointed as a landscape architect for the 1939 New York World's Fair and was featured in an article in the *New York Sun* as one of five women working for the fair. Later she recalled that this article caused some resentment in her office, as she was in fact one of a team of eight landscape architects.[36] The World's Fair, held in Flushing from April to October 1939 and again in the summer of 1940, was a giant pageant, its grounds excavated, planted, and landscaped from swampland that had been a trash dump and would afterward become a city park. This fair hosted "Building the World of Tomorrow" and featured the first television. It also introduced many Americans to the streamlined modernism of Europe. Thus, Bullard and the team of landscape architects, under the direction of Robert Moses, created a landscape that would eventually bring over forty-five million visitors to see the "future," the fairgrounds, like the model homes and gardens, exhibiting trends in design and a vision of what leaders at least imagined to be the future of the American home and landscape.

Bullard was named a junior landscape architect for the New York State Department of Public Works in 1938, remaining employed there until she retired in 1964.[37] She had established herself within the male-dominated world of public landscape architects, though did not see herself as paving a new path for other women; instead, she believed, she was "merely" taking advantage of opportunities. Nonetheless, Bullard and her colleagues had taken opportunities open to women as housekeepers of the community and turned them into professional pursuits that positioned women in a place of authority.

Women's Authority

Hiring women to write about, promote, and design residential landscapes, the editors and publishers of popular magazines understood the authority women held in the public eye, as did practitioners and leaders in the field, such as Manning, Frost, and Pray. A woman was an empathic messenger to other women, who would trust her to know what would work. She would also know how to talk with other women, many of whom controlled domestic space, including the home landscape. As practitioners they were professional advocates; as women they were seen as especially knowledgeable. Women filled these roles in diverse ways—as writers, lecturers, and designers, all expanding women's sphere of influence, as well as that of the profession as a whole.

Late in the twentieth century, when women were commonly being commissioned to design public projects, it was frequently suggested that this was new territory for women, that women had not previously been able to practice in these venues. In fact, however, women's practice in landscape architecture had rarely been bounded by the strict assumptions and conventions many assumed. This is not to say that women did not confront stereotypes or gendered limitations. But just as men in the profession often invented ways to practice as the profession evolved, women likewise created opportunities and constructed foundations upon which future generations might build. Women, involved in the profession from its earliest days, were able to grow with the profession, constantly forging new routes and addressing new challenges.

Of course, certain venues or routes were particularly suitable for such new ventures and experiments—homes and gardens, public facilities for families. Both of these areas of practice could be traced to earlier associations between women and the family, and between women and nature and the well-being of society. As more women entered the profession of landscape architecture, they did so through doors already opened but simultaneously uncovered new opportunities.

Again, it is not the individual stories that are remarkable here so much as the cumulative history that emerges from these stories. Annette Hoyt Flanders drew on traditions and histories to establish a successful career, to teach her audiences about design, and to introduce the public to some of the newer ideas and experiments emerging in the practice of landscape architecture. Similarly, and significantly, while Marjorie Sewell Cautley's work in designing landscapes for housing projects reflects the unbounded nature of practice, it more importantly reveals how she drew on her experience as a woman, a mother, and a professional to inscribe her designs with a concern for the quality of life of women, children, and families living in housing projects. Her story furnishes the last major narrative of this history.

8

New Projects and New Horizons

From Housing to the Government and Beyond

A Woman's Home Garden: Private and Public Space

With all this interest in homes, women were clearly not alone in their interest in residential landscapes. Many women, however, viewed the home garden and landscape from a different perspective than their male colleagues. While male practitioners generally considered residential landscapes integral to efforts to improve society, they typically believed that the best solutions to contemporary problems came through the implementation of modern, efficient, and streamlined design and construction. Gardens, in this view, were an ornamentation of the landscape, serving as the setting for the house rather than as an integral part of the domestic life lived in and on the landscape. While they thus might focus on the garden's appearance and maintenance, they did not address the day-to-day activities that might occur within the home garden—what we might call its utilitarian functions.

On the other hand, women viewed the home and its garden as the primary place for the family, requiring much more than just economic and physical efficiencies. The home ground needed to function in the family's daily lives, providing a setting within the larger community—both a private, domestic space and a public space for viewing, entertainment, and engagement. It was this dual role that challenged designers and reformers, as well as home owners. Privacy was crucial to modern living, while civic responsibility simultaneously emphasized citizens' obligations to display good taste in the public eye. The home ground was at the heart of these debates.

The home garden and landscape were (and are) expected to function within two inherently conflicting constructions: the private and the public. The constructive distinction between private and public has been the subject of lengthy debates focused on how such spheres significantly frame social and cultural values and definitions.[1] The roles of the private sphere of the home (the family, the house, and its domestic life and economy) and the public sphere of the people and the government have been frequent topics of contention in the planning of modern cities, towns, and communities, although not as much attention is commonly given to the design of home grounds within these constructions. For women understanding the home in these terms is particularly potent. Women have increasingly transgressed the boundaries between these two realms, specifically as they moved from within the family into the public worlds of employment, advocacy, and leadership. The home thus remained both a signifier of traditional values and an agent of potential change.

It is critical to briefly explore how the home garden served constructions of the private and the public. The residential landscape and, in turn, the domestic space outdoors were, first, private. Whether the home was owned by the family was particularly significant, as home ownership was viewed as both the dream of every American and the social expectation of all who succeeded. If a home was rented, the property would still reflect the family's taste and manners—in turn likely to determine the likelihood of their eventually owning a home.

Private family activities took place in the home, which was in particular the realm of the woman, the mother and housekeeper, who oversaw the raising of children and the care of the family. Traditionally, she was to provide a home to which the father/man could return for respite, comfort, and warmth, all in privacy. The home space was thus sacred to family life, both in its daily form and in the more social form it held within contemporary culture. In the late nineteenth century, as families became smaller, the nuclear family turned inward, into the home and the home garden. The private backyard gained popularity, as did the back porch and the family den.

The home was also the site of domestic duties, from cleaning to food production. These duties were to be done, traditionally, out of view of the public eye. Laundry lines were not to be hung where they could be seen, and children were increasingly moved into the backyard, where they too could not be seen by passersby. Fences became an important addition to the home, hiding family life yet further. No longer did women gather in public washing areas, or to raise a barn, or to attend sewing groups—except as special occasions. Such activities were now performed out of sight, within the privacy of the family.

The home landscape, however, was also public, by virtue of two related characteristics. First, the home was considered a reflection of the values and morals of its residents. Second, the residential environment was believed to guide the behavior of individuals, who in turn made up the public. As George Eliot had suggested, "There is no private life which is not determined by a wider public life."[2] Both of these ways of viewing residential landscapes as part of the public landscape frame the approach of women landscape designers in the early twentieth century.

Progressives were convinced that environment shaped behavior. In this way, it was argued, families residing in aesthetically flat, neglected, and overcrowded spaces risked their moral character.[3] If this were true, then it was a public responsibility to ensure that American citizens were growing up in the appropriate environment. Progressive reformers saw it as their duty to help and guide families, particularly mothers, to make sure they provided a tasteful and healthy environment for children and family. Mary Ritter Beard reported in 1915 that much of reform work was meant to arouse "the nation to a knowledge of the deadly peril of low standard homes and to a sense of the immediate urgency of reform." She continued, "Women have . . . learned that to swat disease they must swat poor housing, evil labor conditions, ignorance, and vicious interests."[4] While Beard's comments focus on urban places, there was similar concern for the blight of the rural home landscape, and professional interests also turned to the design of housing projects and middle-income residential plans. Landscape architects and architects thus became both critics of homes and generators of alternatives and models.

Residential spaces were also understood as a part of the public landscape because the public looked inside them, literally. Mariana Van Rensselaer commented on the improved public views of residential landscapes, which, she argued, had come in response to efforts to improve living conditions, as well as the increased visual access allowed by the automobile. She believed that residential landscapes should be improved so as to please the tourist and "attract his custom."[5] Residential landscapes were most obviously open to the public who chose to walk or drive by. Rehmann suggested, in her 1918 book, that the designer or home owner should consider it "a duty to the outsider and a duty to oneself" to create an appropriate garden picture for the public gaze.[6]

Domestic space was supposed to be hidden in designed residential landscapes, while it was less obscured in poorer, less privileged, and more rural landscapes. In modern suburbia laundry lines, vegetable gardens, and work areas were often either unavailable or placed behind hedges or fences. For some this was done to spare the viewer the ugly scene of laundry hanging or of productive rather than ornamental gardens. A barbecue area might be visible as a family gathering space, but not anywhere to wash or even store outdoor dishes. The implication was in part that in a modern home efficiencies might render these activities unnecessary—that is, with the electric dryer there was no need for a laundry line, with the grocery store there was no need for a vegetable garden. Barbecues were a pleasure for Dad and the children, and women could thus manage to run back and forth between kitchen and garden.

Nevertheless, these assumptions were not true for all families, or necessarily even most. Some designers understood this and designed domestic spaces in a way that might provide privacy for the mother as she did her work and watched her children. For those concerned with the public view, it sufficed to put up a hedge or fence that would hide the scene. For those concerned with the daily life of the mother and children, outdoor domestic spaces were designed to be within easy access of the kitchen and indoor domestic spaces. These concerns, as well as those regarding child-care centers and recreational facilities, are reflected in the work and advocacy of women like Catherine Bauer and Edith Elmer Wood, as well as landscape architects Annette Hoyt Flanders, Martha Brookes Brown Hutcheson, and Marjorie Sewell Cautley.

These influences worked in a circular manner. In many respects, increased attention to the public appearance of private homes was a case of civic values shaping private landscapes. Yet these civic values had been shaped by the ideals of municipal housekeeping, which had arisen from domestic standards and values being placed on public spaces. This circular nature of public and private spaces would be critical in landscape architects' work on home gardens, model gardens, and housing projects. Women's design of residential and domestic landscapes and their efforts to educate the female public can be viewed as both an interpretation of Progressive Era politics and ideals and an inscription of women's own experience as wives, mothers, and daughters.

While early twentieth-century model homes and gardens such as those described earlier were important, particularly those set within urban landscapes like New York or Chicago, it was essential to also create homes for the masses of individuals moving to larger cities. Beginning in the mid-nineteenth century, then, the notion of planned communities was explored. While they were in part investment projects, these planned communities were also viewed as having the potential to establish standards of taste in residential landscapes. Although landscape architects were not always successful in establishing themselves as part of the design teams for such large-scale projects, a few, such as Marjorie Louisa Sewell Cautley, were able to develop long-term relationships with architects and planners. Cautley in particular, as a result, expanded the sphere of influence for landscape architecture and proposed a feminist perspective on residential spaces for the wider public.

Housing and the Garden City

By the mid-nineteenth century there was already debate as to how planning might help officials meet the needs of an increasingly urban and industrial society. The dilemma in part rested on individuals' conflicting desires: to reside in urban areas but to retain the amenities of the country. Garden suburbs were one solution. The first American garden suburb was created in Llewellyn Park in Orange, New Jersey (just outside New York City). In 1857 Llewellyn Solomon Haskell hired the architect Alexander Jackson Davis to lay out the development of this suburb, according to the principles outlined by Andrew Jackson Downing. The resulting planned community, focused on addressing both the function and the aesthetics of the landscape, included a fifty-acre central park and "villa" sites of from one to twenty acres each. By requiring joint ownership of the central park area, discouraging fences, and instituting collective decision-making procedures, Haskell intended "the fortunate purchaser of two or three acres [to become] a virtual owner of the whole five hundred; a plan by which a poor man, for a few thousands of dollars, may buy a country seat that challenges comparison with the Duke of Devonshire."[7]

Olmsted and Vaux similarly designed Riverside, Illinois (just outside Chicago), in 1869 for the Riverside Improvement Company. Individual houses, set within spacious landscapes, were sited back from the street, looking inward toward an interior community-owned park. Olmsted firmly believed that such new suburbs, if well done, would prove "the most refined and the most soundly wholesome forms of domestic life, and the best application of the arts of civilization to which mankind has yet attained."[8] Riverside, then, was not merely another development for Olmsted, instead representing what he believed to be a significant social project to improve American culture, allowing those otherwise unlikely to live in the country to be surrounded by nature. While such suburbs did not necessarily address the needs of middle-class families—they became popular upper-class communities—they did set the standard for the smaller home landscape.

The landscapes of such communities were important not only for their explorations of the nature of planned communities but also for their emphasis on nature within the larger housing project. Unlike urban housing, suburban homes were built within the landscape, with the goal of allowing residents to commune with nature in a more natural state than found in city and urban parks. The landscape, then, was a critical element of the larger design, often a raison d'être for the entire suburban development.

Few women, however, were commissioned to design the landscapes for suburban housing projects: generally, the contracts for this work were given to larger firms led by men such as Olmsted Sr., John Nolen, the Olmsted Brothers, and Charles Mumford. Marjorie Sewell Cautley was an early exception, with others following in the 1940s and 1950s. Cautley, indeed, was an active member of a team of designers that created four important housing landscapes, both suburban and urban: Sunnyside, Radburn, the Phipps Garden Apartments, and Hillside Housing.

MARJORIE LOUISA SEWELL CAUTLEY (1891–1954)

Marjorie Louisa Sewell Cautley was able to take advantage of both expanding opportunities for women and the increased focus by landscape architects on housing development and city planning. She had been born in 1891 near San Francisco to a U.S. Navy family, which traveled extensively, taking long trips by ship to Japan and the East. She spent time in between trips with her extended family, either on California's Mare Island or in Brooklyn, New York, absorbing the Victorian education deemed appropriate for a middle-class woman. This meant learning to draw and paint, to garden, and to read and write, among other skills. When she was just nine, her mother died, and her father became the governor of Guam, where, he believed, he could effectively raise his three daughters.[9] However, two years later he too died. Orphaned, the girls were sent to live with relatives in New York and New Jersey, spending summers with the family at its Lake George campground, discovering a nature very different from Guam's in the Adirondack wilderness. Each of the three girls went on to establish careers, Barbara as a nurse, Helen as a book illustrator, and Marjorie as a landscape architect. Marjorie, who attended the Pratt Institute from 1904 to 1908, enrolled at the Packer Collegiate Institute, graduating in 1911.

Cautley, like Flanders, then took advantage of the opportunities provided by a land-grant university. At the age of twenty-three she enrolled in the landscape design program at Cornell University, Professor E. Gorton Davis writing her that "young ladies are admitted to our courses on the same basis as young men." "The day is past," Davis continued, "when people are supposed to do landscape work by means of native genius instead of academic training."[10]

While at Cornell Cautley established lifelong friendships with Russell Van Nest Black and Helen Spalding, both of whom later also became successful landscape architects. The Cornell program further provided Cautley with a formal education in the art of landscape architecture, training in the technical skills needed to lead a professional practice, and key networks within the professional community. Cautley graduated from Cornell in 1917. Shortly afterward she went to work, first for the Boston-based landscape architect Warren Manning and then for Julia Morgan, a California architect, working on war-housing projects under the auspices of the YWCA.

Cautley led a productive and successful practice for almost twenty years. Sadly, at the height of her success, her career was cut short by a nervous breakdown. In 1937 her husband committed Cautley to Greystone Park, a New Jersey state hospital for the mentally ill. She was only paroled in 1942, with help from her friends and professional colleagues, MIT's Dean William Emerson and the architects Robert Kohn and Russell Van Nest Black. Upon release Cautley divorced her husband, reclaimed the name Marjorie L. Sewell, and enrolled in the M.F.A. program at the University of Pennsylvania. She received her degree in the city planning program, with honors, in 1943. Her thesis, focused on transforming blighted areas of Philadelphia, suggested familiar reconstruction themes through superblocks, community space, and parks.[11] Her only major project at this time was done with Van Nest Black, developing Meuser Park, in Wilson Borough, Pennsylvania. During this time she also completed a course in

Portrait of Marjorie Sewell as a student at Cornell University. (Marjorie Sewell Cautley Papers, #4908, Division of Rare and Manuscript Collections, Cornell University Library)

industrial camouflage. Unfortunately, however, by 1946 she had returned to a sanitarium, dying there in 1954.

A Practice Focused on the Public Realm

Cautley opened her first office in Paterson, New Jersey, in 1920, establishing contacts through family friends, including her uncle John Sewell, a local judge. She specialized in public projects, including the grounds of Bamburger Ideal Home, a hospital in Newark; the Town Park for Bolton, on Lake George; the Pierce Arrow Service Station off Bloomfield Avenue and the Ellis Motor Car Co., both in Newark; and the Studio for the Ethical Culture School, Riverdale on Hudson, New York. In 1922, after marrying a Cornell engineer, Randolph Cautley, she moved her office to their home, Cricket's Hearth, in Glen Wood, New Jersey.

By 1924, Cautley was working on public and private projects with a staff of at least three female employees. Cautley also established herself as a writer and speaker, publishing articles and photographic essays for professional and popular magazines including *Landscape Architecture Magazine*, the *Planners' Journal*, and *Architecture*. She also lectured for garden clubs and civic associations and was a guest instructor for the landscape architecture programs at MIT and Columbia.

Cautley, elected to membership in the ASLA in 1925, was regularly included in the annual exhibits of both the larger association and the ASLA's New York chapter. Her work was also featured as part of a traveling show sponsored by the Cambridge School. Indeed, Cautley was adept at promoting her work through professional circles. Like Coffin, she understood the importance of being visible to the professional community, although Cautley was never elected a fellow of the ASLA.

The breadth of Cautley's practice was remarkable both for its diversity and for her ability to address problems in new ways. The Roosevelt Memorial Common, in Tenafly, New Jersey, was Cautley's first significant project, establishing her reputation for park design. It was also the beginning of longer friendships with a number of individuals important to the emerging garden city movement, in particular Mrs. John Hawes, a social activist and patron. Cautley's interest in housing and its relationship to landscape led her to travel in Europe in 1929, visiting planned communities. She later incorporated impressions of these European housing projects into her own work, especially their integration of the landscape into the houses' overall siting and design.

As noted earlier, Cautley's best-known work was done with Clarence Stein (1882–1975) and Henry Wright (1878–1936) for four garden city projects, all within the New York metropolitan area: Sunnyside, Radburn, the Phipps Garden Apartments, and Hillside Housing. Cautley is likely to have first met Stein through Robert D. Kohn (1870–1953), when she worked with both architects on a design for the Society of Ethical Culture School/Fieldstone in the Bronx (completed 1926). Stein and Kohn were members of the Society for Ethical Culture, Kohn serving as its president.

In 1933 Cautley was appointed as a landscape architectural consultant for New Hampshire, overseeing Civilian Conservations Corps (CCC) projects in ten state parks, designing the parks and supervising their construction and planting. In 1935 Cautley's book, *Garden Design: The Principles of Abstract Design as Applied to Landscape Composition,* was published, subsequently recommended by Lewis Mumford, Henry Wright, the *New York Times,* and the *American City Magazine,* among others. She was invited to serve as an instructor at MIT (1934–37) and in Columbia's Department of Architecture (1935–37), lecturing to Carl Feiss's design classes on the relationship of landscape architecture to architecture and site planning.

Cautley, like many of her colleagues, had her office in her home. She had worked with an architect to design this home and office, in Glen Rock (near Ridgewood), New Jersey, and it featured an attached office space at the center of the living area. While Cautley thus folded her professional space into her domestic setting, unlike her contemporaries she did not limit professional activities to this office space. Her practice, rather, encompassed the entire house, the drawing board often set up in the dining room, overlooking the gardens. The garden, where her daughter Patricia (born 1925) played, featured a stone pool, surrounded by a patio and shaded by trees that Cautley regularly photographed for display. The house and garden, then, simultaneously served as an office space, design laboratory, and family territory, although this overlap was not especially evident to her clients, since project meetings were generally held at the site to be designed, rather than at her office.

Cautley hired women to work in her office, including Katherine Cole Church and Alice Recknagel Ireys, both of whom later opened practices of their own. Like Farrand and Flanders, Cautley had the reputation of being demanding, overtaxing the staff with requests and projects. However, she was described not as haughty or arrogant, but as disorganized and overwhelmed. She often corresponded with staff by writing quick notes on scraps of paper—often described as indecipherable—as she was too busy to write them out carefully. Generally, without a secretary or an office manager, Cautley's practice was more informal than Flanders's, Farrand's, or Coffin's. Cautley also lacked an upper-class support network and depended on her practice for the family's income for many years. Further, as an essentially single mother for much of her career, she certainly faced pressures unknown to many of her professional colleagues.

Teaching Design

Cautley's legacy is most evident in her book, her garden city landscapes, and her published articles. Of these her book, *Garden Design,* remains an important work on design as an art, embracing contemporary theories of composition and color, as well as the social agendas of reformers and advocates. *Garden Design* focused on the principles of design—specifically composition, using plants as the primary materials—in a language accessible to the layperson and the young student. Cautley described the design process as an aesthetic project requiring an artist's eye, her broad intent to apply the principles of composition developed by Arthur Wesley Dow to the designed landscape.

Arthur Wesley Dow (1857–1922), author of the 1899 book *Composition: A Series of Exercises Selected from a New System of Art Education,* was an early proponent of the American Arts and Crafts Movement and a specialist in East Asian art. He advocated for and taught beauty and balance in composition, not solely the replication of nature. His approach to the design of crafts, then, was to seek both beauty and utility. Dow's principles focused on the use of line, value, and color, and his book on artistic composition was standard in many art programs.

Cautley, as a student at the Pratt Institute, took courses based on Dow's book. She kept a copy of Dow throughout her career, specifically interested in applying his principles of abstract design to gardens, "no matter how informal or picturesque the effect."[12] Her book, then, was her translation of Dow's principles into the language of landscape architecture.

Cautley also applied Albert H. Munsell's contemporary color theory to garden design, including an intricate color wheel in her book. Munsell (1858–1918), the author of *A Color Notation* (1905) and the *Atlas of the Munsell Color System* (1915), had developed the first widely accepted color-order system to create accurate descriptions of color that might be used in art classes. He had also introduced an order of colors, grouped around a "naturally grown" central, vertical gray-scale—also known as a "color tree," because of its irregular outer profile. In 1917 he founded the Munsell Color Company, which in 1942 formed the Munsell Color Foundation to promote the advancement of the science of color. Cautley presented Munsell's theories as central to landscape architects, and a primary portion of her book is devoted to a series of color pages.

Cautley was clearly interested in landscape architecture as a design problem. Her book did not address botanical collections, rock gardens, or other plant or horticultural issues, although she did include plant lists at the end of each chapter, as well as an index of plant names. Her chapters were arranged by design themes, including principles of design, ornament, form, texture, and color. To illustrate her ideas, she used line cuts by Dirk J. Luykx—generally simple sketches illustrating one particular idea. Cautley also included illustrations and photographs of design projects by other practitioners, including Catherine Koch, Henry Wright, and Ruth Dean, and she frequently began her chapters with a quote from a well-known artist or landscape designer. Her bibliography was divided into themes: art, color, architecture, horticulture, ecology, and flower arranging.

Cautley sought to distinguish her book from works by amateur garden designers and writers, without sacrificing her desire to educate the public. Maintaining this balance, however, was a struggle. On the one hand, Cautley tried to explain the principles of design in simple, lay language. At the same time, as noted earlier, she was careful to reference the work of well-known artists and landscape designers. She included several quotations in French, as well as references to designers who would be unfamiliar to amateurs but well-known to educated practitioners and students. For example, her definition of "scale" read simply: "Scale may be defined as the relation of a unit of accepted size to its surroundings, such as the length of a pace or the average height of a human being." On the other hand, this section ends with a quote from Julien Guadet: "C'est la consideration du voisinage, du milieu . . . On dit parfois que le plein air devore les objets. Cette expression figure est just; il en est de meme de la distance."[13] The average gardener would be unlikely to translate such quotes, although he or she might be impressed by their cultural connotations. Despite Cautley's wish to educate the public, then, her book was likely intended for an educated and literate audience of young designers. And indeed, *Garden Design* was regularly recommended as a student textbook by professors including MIT's Dean Emerson, who had written its introduction. While the book went through only one printing, it was nonetheless listed among recommended reading at MIT, Cornell, and similar institutions.

While Cautley's book may have been geared toward the principles of design and composition, it also emphasized the need for designers to address the needs of families, children, wives, and mothers. Cautley carefully considered the placement of service areas, specifically laundry yards, in her designs, articulating the role of the mother at home and her need for an efficient landscape. Her book, like the essays she wrote for popular magazines, also went beyond the image of the typical suburban family, considering tenement and low-income-housing residents.[14] Indeed, Cautley at several points included housing projects as illustrations of design principles, with a focus on the work of Henry Wright and Clarence Stein, her collaborators. She further included a section on designing city lots and city plans, acknowledging the semipublic nature of city lots, which served both the resident and all those who viewed the landscape from outside. In her book and her essays, then, Cautley addressed the middle class, the working class, and the professionals who, she believed, should serve both of these constituencies.

Cautley was recognized for her interest in social issues, in particular for her attention to housing and garden design for middle-income families. Her work emphasized community participation and the importance of landscape to children and mothers. She also provided consultation on several community projects pro bono, signifying her dedication to efforts to improve the social standing of the poor and the unemployed. Cautley's social agenda infused all that she did, much more overtly than for many other professionals.

Cautley's landscape designs reveal her strong social agenda, making a feminist inscription vividly evident. Historians and designers who have credited Cautley with little more than planting some native trees and shrubs between houses have generally ignored this inscription, but a closer look at her landscapes, in conjunction with her written work, exposes a critical characteristic of her designs—her specific attention to improving the lives of women and children.

Cautley designed small city parks, suburban parks, park systems, and large-scale state parks. Her first known public landscape work was the Roosevelt Memorial Common in Tenafly, New Jersey, a project funded by the Hawes Foundation. From 1921 through 1930 Cautley oversaw the design and construction of the thirty-acre park, its playground, and a memorial to Theodore Roosevelt's conservation efforts. She collaborated closely with the sculptor Trygve Hammer (1878–1947) to integrate his monument into her landscape. Surrounded by trees, this monument to-day remains one of the only tributes to Roosevelt's conservation efforts.

The Roosevelt Memorial Common design reflected Cautley's attention to both the existing site and the need for families and children to have specific places where they might come to recreate. She described the project as "a first-class athletic field with quarter mile track, football, and baseball diamond, an outdoor theatre, skating lake, game grounds, school gardens, picnic grove, woodlot for the boy scouts, and demonstration center for the girl scouts. The park will also serve as an arboretum of native plants."[15] Her design drew on the site's rolling topography, defining functional spaces through the use of plant materials. A creek was dammed to create the small pond and skating rink for teenagers. She used existing trees to edge spaces and opened pathways that followed the contours of the landscape, providing access for mothers and strollers.

Cautley wrote that well-designed public spaces should "provide whole-some recreation, to offset anti-social gangs and to furnish relaxation areas for apartment or tenement house dwellers right in their own neighborhoods." She was careful to note the different publics that might use the park, from "very low-brow" couples walking aimlessly through the park to "high speed health enthusiasts."[16] Her parks generally addressed the range of activities in which a city's contemporary—that is, modern—residents might wish to engage.

Further reflecting her social concerns, Cautley encouraged the city to hire "needy men" to plant and construct the park, along with local volunteers (particularly children), writing an article for the 1928 issue of *New Jersey Gardens* titled "Landscape Gardening for the Unemployed." While a school was built in part of Tenafly park, its building intruding on the open spaces, its placement here is certainly appropriate to Cautley's broad vision of the role of public landscapes.

Cautley also designed and oversaw construction of ten state parks for the New Hampshire State Park Department in the 1930s. (See color plate 10.) Her designs, as seen in the plan for Kingston, embraced a dynamic integration of traditional and modern approaches. As she had at Roosevelt Memorial Commons, here she applied a traditional Olmstedian approach to the overall layout of roads and to the placement of views and scenery and a more modernist approach to the park's functional spaces and areas.

Like Garrett Eckbo and Thomas Church, who also focused on landscapes for living, Cautley sought to create outdoor spaces in which individuals and communities could live. She added to the park's restorative character, emphasizing facilities for active sports and recreation, including playgrounds and athletic fields and gathering spaces for adolescents. Cautley's modern park design encouraged sports, nature walks, and bird

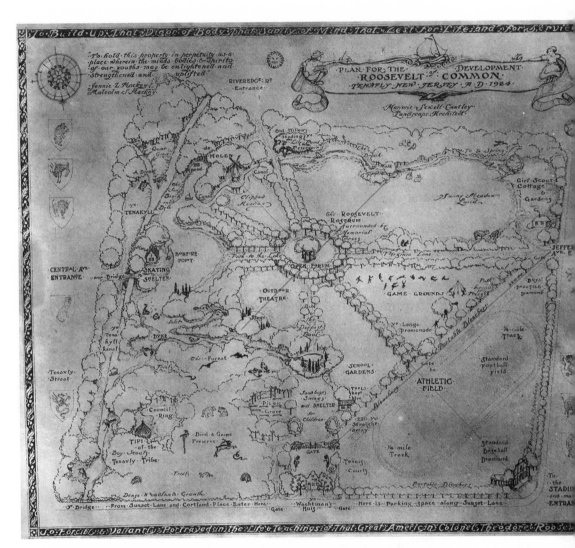

Roosevelt Common, Tenafly, New Jersey, as designed and planned by Marjorie Sewell Cautley. The park served the neighborhood as a gathering place, as well as a space for organized groups such as the Boy Scouts and the Girl Scouts. Unemployed workers were hired to help build the project, and children helped with the plantings. The park represented growing interest in functional spaces for recreation rather than passive scenery. This park brought Cautley significant recognition among designers and park advocates. (The Architectural Archives, University of Pennsylvania)

watching—an altogether more active relationship to the land and community than was common at the time.[17] The specific needs of a variety of users were of central concern to Cautley. Girl Scouts, for example, were offered a space where they might safely meet to learn camping skills. Families were encouraged to take nature walks through the natural areas and the bird preserve, which provided access to much of the landscape and its natural character. Other areas were designed to host pageants or athletic activities. The park thus helped to build and support communities of many types and constituencies.

These early projects established Cautley's design process. She began the design of each park by creating a framework within which she might respond to specific local requests. The site's topography and its genius loci were her first considerations, her designs highlighting the natural landscape and native plants and using the existing landscape to frame her designs, inventoried through photographs and sketches. She took advantage of natural topography, creating high spots for views and intimate valleys for isolated activities, thus both emphasizing vistas and creating secluded, private areas. Cautley argued that a park must fit its context and serve the community. She thus integrated a site's topographical diversity and natural landscapes with geometrically oriented and defined-use spaces, considering road systems, parking, and functional architecture in her plans rather than later imposing them on a picturesque design. After she had established her designs, Cautley frequently supervised park construction by WPA workers or volunteer groups, who helped by planting trees and shrubs. Park projects were individually addressed through inventories of existing landscape elements and the community of potential users.

Cautley used images and scenes made familiar by Olmsted's parks, while simultaneously meeting the needs and wishes of contemporary users in ways that earlier designers rarely did. An athletic field was not just an open meadow but included tennis courts, a baseball diamond, a handball court, and an archery field. A bird preserve would include paths and feeding areas, as well as specific sites for viewing the birds. An outdoor theater might be planned for one corner of the park, while different types of camping sites were designed for the woodlands and meadows. All of these spaces were distinctly defined, Cautley's design revealing the function of each through the different ordering of plant materials and architectural elements, rendering a recreational area visibly distinct from a natural preserve.

Again, community participation played an important role in Cautley's approach. While she did not advocate participation of the type promoted today by practitioners such as Randy Hester, Walter Hood, and Cheryl Doble, Cautley did consistently write of incorporating the ideas and wishes of the public into her designs. She thought potential users should be invited to comment on her design and then to realize it through planting and construction. In an essay published in *American City* in 1944, Cautley argued that a park was a "practical asset and laboratory for the development of good citizenship and human character."

She suggested that the landscape designer invite "groups of citizens both young and old to help plant and develop the small city park (even if your own workmen could do it faster and better)," noting that the design would "benefit by their personal interest and protection in its after care."[18] She further noted:

> One aspect of planning which cannot be too strongly impressed upon your mind is that you must have your community with you, step by step, even though it means a lot of extra time devoted to publicity and to arousing interest and cooperation. Yes, you are a public servant and therefore open to attack in spite of your college background and ethical standards. So be a good sport and play the game, and make sure you understand what the public needs, which is often very different from what it thinks it wants or even from what you think it ought to want.[19]

Cautley's belief in the power of community participation is clearly evident in the films she made of community work days for projects such as Sunnyside and the Phipps Garden Apartments.[20] Her promotional films demonstrated how the communities of Radburn, Sunnyside, and Phipps used their landscapes to gather family, enjoy recreational activities, and engage in nature. Through her park designs she advocated for the conservation of open spaces for community recreation and enjoyment. While many of her colleagues, including Warren Manning, Sarah Orme Jewett, Jens Jensen, Genevieve Gillette, Elsa Rehmann, Wilhelm Miller, and Kate Sessions, also advocated for preserving and conserving open landscapes throughout the nation, Cautley was one of only a handful of practitioners focused on bringing such landscapes into the daily lives of the working class, in particular women, mothers, and children.

Communities and Housing

Cautley's particular interest in housing issues can be traced to her early descriptions of the streets and houses of Guam, from the time she spent there as a young girl. Her first professional positions, first in Manning's and then in Morgan's practice, were focused on landscape designs for army housing projects. In 1922 *Architecture* published Cautley's photographic essay "A City Garden," which addressed the need for a city dweller to have both physical and visual access to nature.[21] In the same year she collaborated with her sister Helen, as illustrator, and the architect Charles Cutler to produce a seven-part series for the popular magazine *Country Life in America,* titled "New Houses of Old Flavor." These plans emphasized the environment, sunlight and air circulation, access to views, issues of privacy versus public access, and recreational space.

Significant priority was given to the ease and efficiency of the home and garden in the mother's daily life. Cautley's focus on such issues mirrors contemporary architectural and landscape practice, with specific notice given to the life of the woman and mother at home. Already here Cautley evidenced concern for the "vigilant eye of the mother [who] may supervise the children . . . while she sets the table or hangs out the table linen."[22] Amenities such as laundry yards and herb gardens were carefully integrated with the design of the functional elements of the house, imagining a lifestyle that would later be actively promoted by the planners for Radburn and Sunnyside.

Cautley did her first project in housing and planned communities in the 1920s, when she was hired to design Oak Croft, a small residential landscape in Ridgewood, New Jersey. Funded by the Hawes Foundation, Cautley created the plans for Oak Croft, while the architect Thomas C. Rogers designed the houses, beginning in 1921. The Hawes Foundation funded Oak Croft because Mrs. Henrietta (John) Hawes, who lived in Ridgewood and was active in a number of women's civic groups, had a particular interest in housing for the working class.[23] Oak Croft was one of the foundation's first housing projects. L. Porter Moore, an editorial staff member of the *New York Tribune* and the president of the Home Owner's Service Bureau, asked that the Oak Croft homes be considered demonstration homes in the "Better Homes Campaign," crediting both Mrs. Hawes and Cautley for their innovative thinking and design, and in 1923 the *Tribune* noted the opening of Oak Croft—or "Tribune Demonstration Houses." The project's details were later also published by *House Beautiful*, described as "A Group of Houses Planned and Planted as a Unit."[24]

Oak Croft was designed on a relatively small scale and modestly laid out. The houses were sited on the outside of the common garden court, owned in part by each resident, all of whom had access to it. This shared park space gave Oak Croft the character, if not the scale, of an English park, rather than a middle-income housing development. Further, the landscape was dominated by large preexisting oak trees surrounding the open lawn, which lent an air of age and maturity to the site and shaded its residents. Small, private terrace gardens formed the transition area between the common park and the individual homes. To enter the community development, one ascended a stairway in the middle of a long stone wall at the southern end of the park. Oak Croft remains today as it was designed.

Cautley was clearly aware of the new town planning ideas being developed by practitioners such as Henry Wright and Frederick Ackerman, as these were discussed at Cornell, where she had studied, and were known to her colleagues Robert Kohn and William Emerson at MIT. Oak Croft, however, was an early implementation of this new approach in an American suburb.

A GROUP OF HOUSES PLANNED AND PLANTED AS A UNIT

MARJORIE SEWALL CAUTLEY, LANDSCAPE ARCHITECT

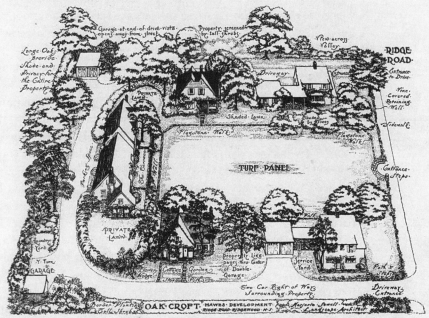

AN UNUSUAL *suburban development, in contrast to the more usual one which consists of houses placed in a row with uniform setbacks, exposed lawns, and a large proportion of land wasted by long drives. Here at Ridgewood, New Jersey, a group of six houses built by Mrs. John Hawes are placed on three sides of a common lawn and served by a single drive which runs behind them*

Oak Croft development, as featured in *House Beautiful*, January 1929. This development, funded by Mrs. John Hawes, was an early example of the type of planning that would appear at Radburn, featuring the central commons, open to residents but not necessarily to the public. With a drive circulating behind the houses, the focus of each home was the open commons.

Fascinated with the potential of planned developments, Cautley traveled to Sweden, Latvia, Czechoslovakia, France, England, Yugoslavia, and Hungary, visiting housing projects in 1929 and again in the 1930s. Her book for children, *Building a House in Sweden,* tells the story of a young family moving to one of the housing projects in the government's garden suburbs of Stockholm. This story represented an ideal Cautley believed Americans should emulate, and she often used the book to advance her ideas.[25] During her travels she also befriended Sir Raymond Unwin, an influential urban planner, a founding member of the Town Planning Institute, and the president of the International Federation for Housing and Town Planning (after Ebenezer Howard's death). Sir Unwin and Lady Unwin maintained their friendship with Cautley, visiting her in New Jersey in 1936, while he was lecturing at Columbia University, where Cautley was teaching.

As Cautley was developing her design approach, the Garden City Movement was simultaneously gaining momentum throughout the United States, Clarence Stein and Henry Wright acting as two of its key leaders and thinkers. Stein had grown up in New York City, where he attended the Ethical Culture School and trained as an architect at Columbia University and the École des Beaux-Arts. He worked in the office of Bertram Grosvenor Goodhue and assisted in the planning of the San Diego World's Fair (1915). He later led design teams for many projects: Sunnyside Gardens, Queens; Radburn, New Jersey; Greenbelt, Maryland; Greendale, Wisconsin; Greenhills, Ohio; and Baldwin Hills Village, Los Angeles. Stein eventually received the Gold Medal of the American Institute of Architects (1956); the Distinguished Service Award of the American Institute of Planners (1958); and the Ebenezer Howard Memorial Medal, honoring the well-known British advocate of garden cities. Stein's *Toward New Towns for America* (1951), based on his experiences, reflected on the development of garden cities.

Henry Wright, a landscape architect and community planner who had studied architecture at the University of Pennsylvania, served as the town planner for the Housing Division of the U.S. Emergency Fleet Corporation (1918) and was a consultant to the New York State Commission on Housing and Regional Planning during the 1920s and, later, to the Public Works Administration. Wright also taught at Columbia University during the 1930s. His book, *Rehousing Urban America* (1935), was long an important resource for architects and planners.

In 1923 Stein and Wright together formed the Regional Planning Association of America (RPAA), a group of acknowledged experts in architecture, regional planning, community building, real estate development, and housing. Members included Edith Elmer Wood, Frederick Ackerman, Henry Wright, Lewis Mumford, Alexander M. Bing, and later Catherine Bauer. Among other projects, the group discussed how it might develop plans for an American garden city, or "New Town," based on the ideas of Ebenezer Howard, whose broad principles had been described in his book *Tomorrow: A Peaceful Path to Real Reform* (1898).[26]

As a group these designers, professionals, and advocates "recognized the need to think holistically, conceiving a total environment in which physical design strove to preserve, enhance, and render visible the vitality of natural systems, as well as the individual and social lives of residents."[27] They combined this larger vision with the need to address tangible, specific urban problems: the shortage of affordable housing, overcrowding in metropolitan areas, the impact of the automobile, and the need for more efficient land-use policies. Plans and projects were developed over the years in locations as far apart as New Jersey and California. While a number of the RPAA's towns met with relative success, Stein and Wright's most lasting legacy remains Radburn, for which Cautley designed the landscape.

Stein, Wright, Bing, and others established the City Housing Corporation to develop model neighborhoods and towns based on garden city principles, its members including Felix Adler (the founder of the Society for Ethical Culture) and Eleanor Roosevelt. Cautley was brought into this team to serve as a landscape architect for its first projects, her designs, as noted earlier, including four projects within the larger New York metropolitan area: Sunnyside, Radburn, the Phipps Garden Apartments, and Hillside Housing.

The first collaboration enacted under the auspices of the City Housing Corporation was Sunnyside (1924–28). On an eighty-acre site a mix of single- and two-family houses and apartment buildings was sited along a perimeter of twelve contiguous city blocks, housing 1,202 families. Sunnyside's plans also called for common ownership of shared courtyards or inner park areas, an innovation that would continue to be at the center of each of Cautley and Stein's projects. Surrounding these common parks were small private gardens for the community's residents, each planned as a horticulturally distinct garden court.

With the success of Sunnyside, the design team planned a community even closer to the garden city ideal: Radburn (1928–30). Henriette Hawes, who had been instrumental to the development of Oak Croft, was an original advocate of Radburn, along with Alexander Bing, and she was most likely also involved in the Sunnyside project. Indeed, Bing, Hawes, and others frequently served on boards and other organizations in pursuit of civic and economic improvements in the community and region. Due to the Depression, however, Radburn was never completed.

In planning Radburn, the developers did not have to address an existing road grid or the politics of a landscape already within city limits. Instead, they were able to start with open, expansive farmland, allowing them to create a plan based on their ideals, without restrictions. The plans for Radburn developed five important themes, which became collectively known as the "Radburn idea": the superblock, designed as the core framework of the development; houses with two entrances, one facing the interior park and the other an alley/street; alleys and streets that were reduced to a minimalist scale, creating a system of dedicated streets and lanes; the separation of pedestrian and vehicular traffic; and a continuous park that ran throughout the community.[28] The park in particular created an environment conducive to children, and the development was immediately recognized as a child-oriented new town.

Then, in 1931, the Society of Phipps Houses supported the addition of an affordably priced apartment complex adjacent to Sunnyside: the Phipps Garden Apartments. This was the fourth in a series of model housing projects supported by Phipps Houses, a foundation instituted in 1905 by Henry Phipps. Phipps, a partner with Andrew Carnegie in the

Men planting large, mature trees at Radburn, their expense emphasizing the importance of the landscape in the plan's development. African American men were frequently photographed by Cautley working on the Stein/Cautley projects. (The Architectural Archives, University of Pennsylvania)

steel business, had become a major philanthropist in his later years, with working-class housing one of his primary causes. The first three Phipps projects, in fact, had been built under his direction, including housing "for colored people" in Manhattan.[29] These housing projects featured modern amenities, including hot water, steam heat, public laundry facilities, garbage disposal, electric lights, and roof gardens. Outdoor areas for children were also provided in all of these projects. Another Phipps project, a hotel for working women, was later planned, but it was cancelled because of the Depression. Alexander Bing, a Phipps Houses trustee, helped to shape plans for the Phipps Garden Apartments.

By the time the Phipps Garden Apartment project got under way, Henry Phipps had died, and Howard Phipps had been elected president of Phipps Houses (1919). Howard was an avid gardener, and this may well be reflected in the extensive attention given to the landscape of the Phipps Garden Apartments, the first major new housing project under his leadership. He was likely also responsible for the decision to approve Cautley's request to drill a well for water and to plant large elm trees in the development's courtyards.

Toddlers at Radburn riding bicycles on the paths running around the communal park. The small home gardens are evident, as is the expanse of space allotted to play and recreation. Photograph by Gretchen Van Tassell. (Clarence Stein Papers, #3600, Division of Rare and Manuscript Collections, Cornell University Library)

This project remains remarkable for the elaborate garden courts at the core of the complex—a model of outstanding housing in an urban environment. The apartments provided housing for 340 families in four- and six-story-high buildings that covered only 43 percent of the land, leaving 57 percent for gardens and outdoor space. On awarding the New York chapter of the AIA's Medal of Honor for large-scale planning to the design, the architectural critic Lewis Mumford wrote: "This apartment group shows what can be done in the way of commodious planning when the unit of design is no longer a few building lots on the regulation street layout. . . . The enormous inner court is landscaped with trees and shrubs that have plenty of sunlight for growth; here Mrs. Marjorie S. Cautley has done an excellent job."[30]

Although private space for individual families was minimal, the garden courts provided intimate areas for a variety of activities, supplementing related public spaces within the buildings. To emphasize the permanency and importance of the garden areas, Cautley persuaded the Phipps Foundation to purchase large trees and move them by crane into the gardens prior to the apartment buildings' completion.[31] In 1935 an addition was made to the complex, and Cautley was again brought in as the landscape architect. As at Sunnyside, here Cautley's landscape design defined the community, today remaining a distinct element of the development.

Hillside Homes in the Bronx (now known as Eastchester Heights) was the last project Cautley worked on with Clarence Stein (1932–37). With only 40 percent of the land here dedicated to the building, the remaining portion of the sloped site provided the maximum amount of open space for its residents. The largest of the Public Works Administration's limited-dividend projects, Hillside Homes eventually hosted 1,416 apartments, in addition to spaces for commercial use, recreation, and resident programming. In planning it, Stein worked with Louise Blackham, who later undertook an extensive assessment of the community's facilities after it opened. The project had many admirers, including Catherine Bauer, who used Hillside Homes as an exemplar of housing development with government assistance.[32]

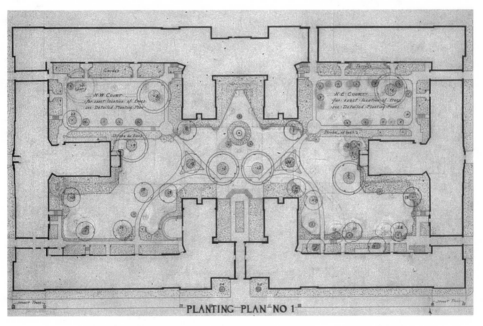

Landscape design for Phipps Garden Apartments, 1931, as designed by Marjorie Sewell Cautley. Note that the large circles represent the elm trees that were transplanted into the landscape prior to completion of the building. The courtyards each featured a plant theme and thus became a part of the residents' immediate community, each courtyard distinguishable from the others. (Avery Architectural and Fine Arts Library, Columbia University)

A resident enjoying her small courtyard garden at Hillside Housing, one of the gardens provided for each of the basement-level apartments. These were the only private gardens in the community. Photograph by Samuel Gottscho. (Clarence Stein Papers, #3600, Division of Rare and Manuscript Collections, Cornell University Library)

As in Cautley's other designs, the Hillside landscape is primarily defined by lawns and hedges, using trees as vertical accents. With more space Cautley was able to dedicate the park's perimeter to private gardens opening out from the first-floor apartments. Each of these was bounded by flowering hedges that allowed a sense of ownership yet were not tall enough to block views into and out of the spaces. The site was also large enough for Cautley to establish separate landscape spaces for different uses: children's playgrounds, walkways for mothers and young children, game grounds for older children, and larger open spaces for community activities.

Both Cautley's essays and her garden city landscape designs illustrate her interest in nature, families, and the community as critical elements of the design process. Her designs did not merely frame a site's architecture but actively engaged the community in an experience of nature and landscape. Her work also reflected the growing movement to use native and regional plants in designed landscapes, promoted by practitioners including Rehmann and Dean, who encouraged gardeners to carefully consider the existing landscape and native plant materials before importing any exotic plants. Dean wrote that "any naturalistic planting should express the character of the land where the border is being planted, so as to bring out the individuality of different parts of the country."[33] She believed one should never mix native and nonnative plants, even if tempted by similarities of growth habit, color, or other characteristics.[34] Dean thus believed in integrity and honesty in the use of native plants and naturalistic planting. Cautley would suggest a looser approach, while still supporting the inherent values of the native plant movement.

Cautley began her design for Radburn where the community landscape bordered the 1928 natural landscape: a mix of farmland, meadows,

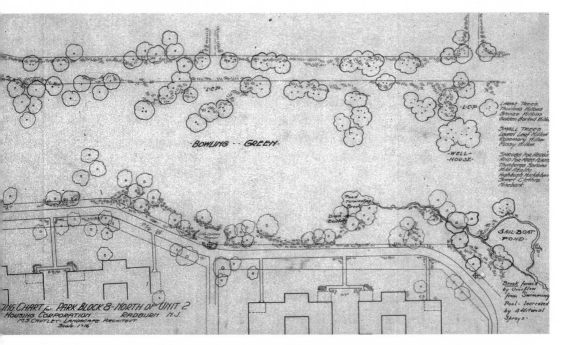

Planting plan for Radburn, Park Block 8. Cautley used the natural stream to create a landscape feature incorporating local plants to transition into the park landscape. Other elements such as the topography of the previous farmland and local vegetation (transplanted from streams and farms) were used throughout the designed landscape. (Avery Architectural and Fine Arts Library, Columbia University)

and waterways. She incorporated pieces of this original landscape into her residential design, actively engaging residents in the land and nature. The edge of the community landscape was designed to appear "natural," with an extensive use of native or naturalized plants in an informal layout, arranged with an outward show of randomness. Describing her work, Cautley wrote, "It was the desire of the landscape designer to preserve for Radburn a part of the beautiful natural growth that is being destroyed so rapidly throughout northern New Jersey."[35] In the southern park she preserved a meadow of wild asters and also planted a grove of native cedars, so that "when Radburn is a city of twenty-five thousand souls there will still be an echo of the woods and meadows upon which it was built."[36] These areas could be viewed from the homes and parks or enjoyed on foot or bicycle.

For the interior parks Cautley integrated existing trees, landscape forms, and waterways with a designed landscape of lawn, shrubs, and trees. These areas, such as Ashburn and Berkeley parks, resembled both picturesque urban spaces and the more "wild" natural areas that were increasingly popular as the backpacking movement gained momentum. In one park Cautley designed a gazebo with a natural garden surrounding it, as if she had left a piece of nature remaining within the larger designed community, although even this feature was completely designed, planted, and constructed. Clumps of birch, viburnum, wild azalea, and highbush blueberries (all considered native) were transplanted from the neighboring woods to the new landscape, softening the transition between the natural lands and the domestic gardens. These areas celebrated local and native trees and shrubs, while clearly designed and maintained. Although Cautley was recognized for her use of native plants, she did not limit her palette to botanical natives, instead including plants that "naturally" blended into the landscape, aesthetically and ecologically.

Cautley thus developed a repertoire of appropriate plant materials and horticultural approaches. She used native plants both to articulate her respect for the local landscape and to economize her planting plan. Indeed, using flora that might survive the local climate and the city atmosphere, use little water, and require minimal care was a significant component of her plans, focused on creating low-maintenance, and thereby affordable and viable, landscape designs, in keeping with the goal of such housing developments and garden cities. This approach extended to her park designs for the state of New Hampshire. "Property," she noted, "has been developed to utilize existing features, & to conserve natural character & beauty. Buildings located at strategic points to control use & simplify maintenance."[37] She wanted landscapes that children and families could enjoy and explore.

One might accurately describe Cautley's approach as fostering ecologically sustainable design, exhibiting her concern for economic responsibility, functionality, and accessibility and providing visual and physi-

A gazebo set in the park and surrounded by local plants, many transplanted from nearby woods and fields. Photograph likely taken by Clara Sipprell. (Radburn Association)

cal pleasure. Cautley here was following in the steps of other designers, including Hutcheson, in promoting native plants and design principles grounded in natural cycles. Cautley, however, was applying these principles to middle-class housing projects, as other designers rarely did.

Cautley's landscape designs further specifically addressed the issues of economy and efficiency, focusing on the role of the mother in the home. The aforementioned "vigilant eye of the mother," for example, would be significantly aided by open views between the private and the community spaces. The mother's ability to monitor the landscape of daily life was critical to her role in the family and the community, and Cautley's designs acknowledged her needs.

Thus, while the views at Radburn are often described in aesthetic terms as open and expansive, they were first and foremost functional. Shrubs and trees rarely blocked the view from inside the house to the private yard area or the larger common spaces. Residents understood the logic behind this and early in the town's history enacted a rule that fences could not exceed two and a half feet. Ample seating was also provided in the parks, allowing mothers, elderly residents, and children to safely socialize.

Yet the space was not merely open, as open space can be difficult to oversee and supervise. Rather, the landscape was designed for specific activities. For younger children Cautley created designated play areas (noted in her plans as "LCP": little children's playground) where mothers might visit with friends while paying close attention to their young ones. For older children she featured dedicated game fields. Cautley valued such a communal emphasis and, indeed, often brought her own daughter along when she was performing on-site work. Indeed, years later her daughter, Patricia Cautley, recalled how seriously her mother had considered Radburn's design. As Michael David Martin has noted, "Radburn's landscape protected children, not just from cars but from the uncertain dangers inherent in the very publicness of the community street."[38] These articulated spaces, visually accessible landscapes, and identifiable circulation systems were in the interior of the community, thus acting as private-community places. As designed, then, Cautley's landscapes were clearly and easily defensible: residents knew who should and should not be present and what types of activities were appropriate and acceptable.

Children playing in the Hillside courtyard were always visible from the apartment buildings. They enjoyed open space defined by landscape and architecture. Photograph by Samuel Gottscho. (Clarence Stein Papers, #3600, Division of Rare and Manuscript Collections, Cornell University Library)

Mother with a carriage strolling in the Phipps courtyard. The courtyards were large enough for strolling but small enough for residents to see all corners. Winding paths and varied plant material provided the character of an extensive garden, one not generally accessible to families of low or middle incomes in New York City. Photograph by Samuel Gottscho. (Clarence Stein Papers, #3600, Division of Rare and Manuscript Collections, Cornell University Library)

By making her spaces "surveyable," Cautley rendered the boundaries of private and community space visually ambiguous. This ambiguity can be read within the context of utopian community developments, particularly those designed by early urban feminists, whose designs and ideals for modern communities, according to Dolores Hayden, endeavored to merge the public and the private in conjunction with respective male and female spaces.[39] Cautley's spaces similarly encouraged movement between what was private and public, between domestic and nondomestic spaces, thereby expanding "usable" space for women, extending it from within the house and its immediate landscape to the entire community. Her landscapes challenged what was in private, unseen, and in public, and thus viewed. This is particularly meaningful in view of how small contemporary middle-class houses were and how little domestic interiors reflected the various aspects of women's lives.

Cautley's designs addressed the daily activities of domestic life, including such necessities as laundry yards and herb gardens close to the house. At other projects, such as Port Sunlight, constructed by the manufacturers of Lever Soap, developers were frustrated to see housewives hanging laundry on the fences, as there was no appropriate area designated for laundry.[40] At Radburn, in contrast, laundry yards were placed near kitchens, out of sight of the community at large—in keeping with Cautley's recommendation in *Garden Design*.[41] Privacy was provided to benefit the mother, rather than to meet social norms established by city planners. Fruit orchards were planted across neighboring gardens, easily accessible to everyone. "To pluck a sprig of parsley," Cautley wrote, "or to sample one's grapes . . . is to know the richness of simple living."[42] The landscape was thus functional, aesthetically enjoyable, and instrumental in building community, especially for women and children.

The family-friendly features Cautley stressed were the ones most often noted by Stein and other male critics. The designs' functional attributes, however, were rarely described in a convincingly specific manner, beyond general statements that the communities were ideal for families. Stein, for example, emphasized Radburn's family-friendliness by noting that children could ride their bicycles throughout the community, but he never fully articulated which features of the landscape made it appropriate and safe for children and their mothers, in spite of devoting a considerable percentage of his book to the plan's landscape.

This negligence is also evident in the design of the houses themselves, where obviously less care was taken to ease modern daily life, particularly in the spaces designated for family living. Radburn's small houses allowed for few improvements or amenities and as a result have often been severely altered, while the gardens and open spaces have been largely retained. Thus, while Stein and Wright focused on the architecture's economy, Cautley designed economically feasible landscapes that would further encourage the success of such affordable housing.[43] Similarly, she

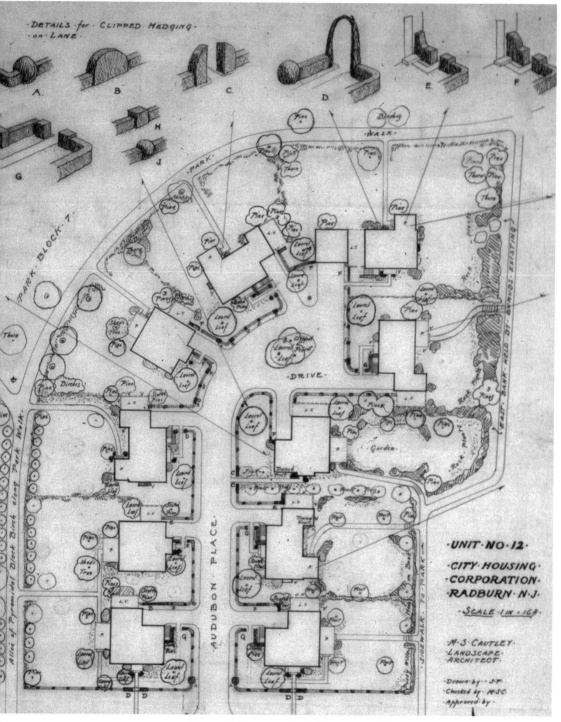

Plan for Audubon neighborhood of Radburn. Note Cautley's specification for trimmed hedges to define garden spaces. The plan responded to the needs of mothers watching children while doing household chores while creating the impression of an elegant garden park. (Avery Architectural and Fine Arts Library, Columbia University)

Sunnyside Courtyard, the pergola and laundry area demonstrating the overlapping spaces in this hybrid of private and semipublic landscape space. Photograph by the Brown Brothers. (Clarence Stein Papers, #3600, Division of Rare and Manuscript Collections, Cornell University Library)

promoted the oversight of a dividend corporation, such as the City Housing Corporation, in such designed communities, because she believed that "the limited dividend corporation [as an agency was] committed to good construction, durable pavements, community recreation, and planting which, when mature, should increase in value as the buildings depreciate."[44]

Cautley was adamant that planning should pay careful attention to construction costs and forecast appropriate maintenance plans and expenses. At least 5 percent of the buildings' cost, she argued, should be dedicated to the landscape: "If the development of . . . the land is considered as a permanent installation of definite sales' value, why should it receive an allotment which is equal only to such incidentals as radio outlets and awnings."[45] As for the architecture itself, Cautley, in the *Planners' Journal,* suggested that a typical Radburn house "hardly function[s] as a house," specifically in light of the kind of lifestyle modern Americans desired and expected. She argued that the provision of a "soundly built dwelling . . . at moderate cost is a problem that the planner and the architect have not yet solved."[46]

Housing nationally was shifting at the same time as Cautley, Stein, and others were trying to move forward. The emerging profession of city planning had begun to distance the work of planners from housing per se, identifying planning as a public effort and housing, increasingly, as a private issue. As early as 1912 the National Conference on City Planning, born of the Congestion Committee's 1909 city planning exhibit, had almost completely dropped the question of housing from its agenda. Instead, its focus was on transportation, traffic, streets, and civic/public buildings. Raymond Unwin and Thomas Adams, after attending the 1913 National Conference on City Planning, complained that U.S. planners showed no concern whatsoever for housing matters.[47]

However, the "houser"—the advocate for better housing for low-income families—did not entirely disappear. Simkohvitch and Kelly, for example, continued to focus on housing from the perspective of real urban housing conditions and potential improvements, while the more mainstream professional community emphasized availability and affordability. The federal government also retained an interest in housing issues. Herbert Hoover oversaw the national Housing and Homeownership Committee, promoting private initiatives such as the "Own Your Own Home" movement. With the 1930s a renewed interest in housing policy emerged at the federal level, various housing experts lending their opinions as the U.S. government developed new programs. Catherine Bauer, for example, was instrumental in the Labor Housing Conference, a significant force behind the establishment of the first permanent public housing program. Still, Bauer was in many ways a lone voice among her professional colleagues.[48] By the 1940s, then, interest in quality housing as a means of improving the lives of low-income families had been almost entirely marginalized. Solutions proposed in the following decades instead focused on urban renewal, even though renewal clearly did not successfully address the need for high-quality housing for low-income and disadvantaged families.

This turn away from a focus on the design of domestic landscapes was also evident academically. For example, while the "Cambridge School of Domestic Architecture and Landscape Architecture" had been so titled in 1918 because its name underscored the importance Frost and his students placed on domestic design, the word "domestic" was dropped in the early 1930s, becoming a limiting framework rather than a valued asset. This change in many ways reflected general national trends away from housing issues and domestic landscapes. Frost, like others of his time, had to respond to such trends in order to remain within the mainstream of the profession; clearly, whatever his personal views, associating his school with domestic work came to be seen as having a limiting rather than a visionary effect.

New Opportunities and a New Generation

While housing did not remain at the forefront of the profession of landscape architecture, as it grew, opportunities for women expanded, particularly in government and public administration, and yet another generation of practitioners began to shape the profession. While women did not find work in governmental agencies in the numbers that men did, they were still able to build practices relying on such commissions. These women, like their male counterparts, generally combined governmental and public work with private commissions.

Clara Stimson Coffey (1894–1982) was one professional whose practice reflected contemporary opportunities and challenges. With a bachelor's degree (1917) and a master's degree in landscape design (1919), both from the University of Michigan, Coffey initially worked for Aubrey Tealdi (1919–21) and then for Warren Manning, in his Cleveland office. In Manning's office she was responsible for creating topographic surveys, road-building designs, and designs and plans for large estates (1921–22). She then worked in Coffin's office off and on until 1957 (1923–25, 1926–28, 1945–57). In 1925 she worked briefly for Shipman, designing estate plans (1925–26). In the 1930s she opened a small office at 41 Union Square, Gramercy, in New York City, while she continued to work on commission for Coffin and other landscape architects.

Coffey networked among landscape architects, planners, and social activists and contributed to a Housing Study Group sponsored by Clarence Stein and Henry Churchill (1939–41). In 1936 she was appointed the chief of tree plantings for the New York City Park Department, supervising, in this capacity, several prominent landscaping projects throughout the city, including planting designs for the Hutchinson River and Belt parkways (1941) and the redesign of the Park Avenue Malls (1970). Coffey was also frequently asked to design parks, including Clement Clarke Moore and Haffen parks in Manhattan (1968–69) and Yellowstone Park in Queens (1970). In 1977 New York mayor Abraham Beame appointed Coffey to the Art Commission as its professional landscape architect. She was the only woman to have served in this position.

In the mid-1940s Coffey had collaborated with W. Earle Andrews, Cynthia Wiley, and Alice Ireys on designing New York City playgrounds, contract drawings, and housing projects. In or around 1945 Coffey launched a partnership with the architectural firm of Levin & Blumberg P.C., with offices at 386 Park Avenue South. During this period Coffey was noted for her work with Albert Mayer, a colleague of Stein and Churchill, collaborating with him on the initial plans for India's Chandigarh, prior to Le Corbusier's involvement.

Coffey's professional involvement centered on her membership in the New York chapter of the ASLA; she was elected to national membership in 1958 and chosen as a fellow in 1978. She served on the ASLA's Exhibition Committee in 1965 and on the organization's New York City Examining Board for two years, from 1967 until 1969. Her awards included an ASLA Award for the 139th Street Playground (1972); the Queens Chamber of Commerce Award for Yellowstone Park and Bayswater Park (1970, 1972); the Chelsea-Clinton News Award for Clement Moore Park (1969); the New York City Association of Architects/AIA Award; and a citation from the City Club of New York Bard Awards Program (1972). Coffey, in many ways, served as a link between the generation of Coffin and Cautley and future practitioners.

Another woman who forged new paths and created new opportunities was Ruth Patricia Shellhorn (1909–2005), who worked in Southern California beginning in the mid-twentieth century. She was born in Los Angeles in 1909, her parents advocates of the Progressive movement. They encouraged her to identify a career that would not only draw on her talents but make a difference. After learning of the work of Florence Yoch, Shellhorn decided to pursue landscape architecture. She enrolled at the Oregon State College (University) School of Landscape Architecture in 1927 and then later at Cornell University. (She left Cornell without finishing her degree, although the university, upon reviewing her records, awarded her the degree in 2005.) Shellhorn launched her own practice at the height of the Depression, after working briefly for Ralph Cornell and then for the firm of Yoch & Council.

Like Yoch's clients, Shellhorn's included well-known motion picture stars, including Spencer Tracy, Gene Autry, and Barbara Stanwyck, and Ben Goetz, MGM's superintendent of producers. Shellhorn was commissioned for a number of commercial projects, including the Western Home Office for the Prudential Insurance Company, the John Tracy Clinic, the Santa Monica Civic Auditorium, Vroman's Book Depository in Pasadena, and the Segerstrom Center in Santa Ana. During World War II Shellhorn began working on the Shoreline Development Study for the Greater Los Angeles Citizens Committee, a group of businessmen interested in making sure that public funding was used to create recreational landscapes and spaces. This project included plans for the area's first sewage-treatment plant, which would eventually support efforts to establish the California Coastal Act.[49]

Shopping areas were a hallmark of Shellhorn's practice. First hired by Bullock's department store in 1945, Shellhorn designed the landscape for the midcentury modernist building, designed by the Los Angeles architect Welton Becket. Having established a new look for the typical shopping mall, she went on to design the landscapes for Bullock's Wilshire, Bullock's Palm Springs, Bullock's Lakewood, a remodel of Bullock's Westwood, and the Fashion Square Malls in Santa Ana, Sherman Oaks, Del Amo, and La Habra. Department stores were a new landscape development, and it was important to create for their shoppers an overall experience of elegance and luxury. Shellhorn's landscape designs thus celebrated the arrival of customers by car, her designs for parking lots as part of the entrance sequence an important part of the shopping experience.

Walt Disney hired Shellhorn to work on the redesign of Disneyland in 1955. She designed the pedestrian circulation plan for the entire park, as well as the Plaza and Main Street. In April 1956 Shellhorn recounted her experience in *Landscape Architecture Magazine,* publishing "Disneyland: Dream Built in One Year through Teamwork of Many Artists." Recreational planning had become a significant area of practice for landscape architects, Shellhorn's role in Disneyland one example of this.

In 1956 Shellhorn was hired as the supervising and executive landscape architect for the University of California at Riverside. Holding this position for eight years, she completed a campuswide master landscape plan and detailed plans for many of the campus's building projects. Like Farrand she also held other executive and consulting landscape architect positions for such academic institutions as the Marlborough School for Girls (1968-93), El Camino College (1970-78), and the Harvard School (1974-90).

Shellhorn's practice, clearly broad, comprised a variety of design types, much more diverse than those of the first women-led West Coast firms (Yoch & Council, and Lord & Schryver). Shellhorn was widely acknowledged for her designs, receiving several National Industrial Landscape Awards from the American Association of Nurserymen, as well as civic beautification awards. In 1955 Shellhorn was named Woman of the Year by the *Los Angeles Times* and the South Pasadena, San Marino Business and Professional Women's Club. She was elected a fellow of the ASLA in 1971 and honored as Horticulturist of the Year by the Southern California Horticultural Institute in 1986.

Other women also benefited from the doors opened by earlier practitioners and the multiplying opportunities in the corporate, government, and commercial realms. Alice I. Bourquin and Genevieve Gillette worked for the Michigan Highway Department, Helen E. Bullard was employed by the Division of Architecture in Albany, and Iris Ashwell and Beatrice Horneman were both on the staff of the Public Buildings Administration in Washington, D.C. Another practitioner, Harriet Rodes Bakewell (1904-1988), worked extensively in Missouri. She attended Smith College in the early 1920s, enrolled in Harvard's Graduate School of Design summer program in 1929, and attended the Washington University School of Architecture from 1929 to 1934 and again in 1946-47. During the course of her career she was involved in site planning and landscape development for the McDonnell-Douglas Engineering Campus and Space Center in Saint Louis; Westport Plaza, in Saint Louis County; the Maritz headquarters, in Fenton; and the Missouri Botanical Garden, where her archives remain.

Yet another prominent practitioner, Alice M. Bauhan (1902-1962), graduated from Cornell University in 1928. She worked briefly for George

F. Pentecost Jr., Farrand, and Flanders. Unlike many others, however, Bauhan did not open her own practice but instead remained employed, as Helen Bullard had. During the Depression years she worked for the Long Island Park Commission and in 1942 was appointed to the New York City Department of Public Works. In 1952 she came to the City Park Department as a landscape architect, addressing all scales of park design in this capacity. During her career her projects included the Lindsay Park addition, the Jacob Riis Park addition, a park at Clason Point, and the athletic fields at Kissena Corridor Park. She was also a member of the design team addressing a large beach development at Plum Beach, part of Marine Beach, and the Perkins Garden in Riverdale—one of her last projects before she retired.

At the same time as these women were practicing, women in England, Sweden, and Italy were also gaining recognition. At the opening of the first International Conference in Landscape Architecture, held in London in 1948, which led to the foundation of the International Federation of Landscape Architects, eight landscape architects sat on the podium: four men and four women, including an Italian (Maria Teresa Parpagliolo Shephard), a German (Herta Hammerbacher), an Englishwoman (Sylvia Crowe), and an American (Edith Schryver). Ulla Bodorff, also an active member of the International Federation of Landscape Architects, belonged to the Swedish Society of Landscape Architects. In England, Brenda Colvin, Lady Allen of Hurtwood, Nan Fairbrother, and Sylvia Crowe wrote many important books, including Crowe's *The Landscape of Power* and Fairbrother's *The Nature of Landscape Design*. As the profession thus expanded to other countries and cultures, it appeared to retain some of the porous nature evident in the United States in the first half of the twentieth century.

Women as a Force

Women since the time of the Progressive Era have served as volunteers, advocates, and professionals, framing plans for the reconstruction of American society and culture: "Thrust into the global violence which marks our age is the dynamism of women who, with men, have set the world on fire and helped to frame plans for its reconstruction."[50] Women in landscape architecture were actively engaged in such reconstruction efforts. They advocated for improvements in the home and garden—some revolutionary, some based on traditional values. Their work was linked closely with efforts to transform relationships between men and women, giving the latter a stronger place in the public realm, as municipal housekeepers, mothers, and educators, as well as professionals, leaders, and advocates.

A later generation of practitioners positioned their work in the public and governmental domains. Some, such as Coffey, were leaders and advocates, while others, such as Bullard, acted more as team members. These women built on the foundations of earlier constellations, both by taking advantage of the doors opened to them and by developing the perseverance to open new doors. They influenced the public discourse on landscape, its designs, its functions, and its role in society, by writing, lecturing, and designing. In 1973 an ASLA report stated that few were aware of the presence or influence of women in the profession, but not for lack of presence—only for lack of memory and acknowledgment.

Conclusion

What We Have Learned, We Can Learn Anew

In 1928 Henry A. Frost and William R. Sears wrote that women "have become a power to be reckoned with."[1] Addressing the Garden Club of America in the 1930s, Martha Brookes Brown Hutcheson told the women gathered, "We, who first lit the way for women in the profession, would beg of those who are following, on a far easier and smoother path, to hold the torch higher and higher until the world in general learns that Landscape Architects are to be reckoned with and that the profession ranks in importance with those of the other Fine Arts."[2] For many the path to professional status was indeed, as Hutcheson claimed, "far easier and smoother" than it had been for their predecessors, and women had in fact become a force to be reckoned with—a force that both signified contemporary practice and served as an agent of change in the profession.

Throughout this book, stories of individuals have focused on the variety of paths and means by which women accessed and shaped the practice of landscape architecture. As this narrative draws to a close and its lessons are synthesized, a new set of questions and challenges arises. Perhaps most important, why, if women have been so involved in landscape architecture, do they remain often hidden in the profession and its history?

Landscape architecture was not confined initially to one normative state. As it developed into a full-fledged profession, it was shaped by a rich breadth of practitioners from distinct backgrounds. The founding members of the ASLA included a woman, Beatrix Jones Farrand, and within weeks the organization had also elected a second woman, Elizabeth Bullard, to membership. In 1916 Marian Cruger Coffin was named the ASLA's third female fellow, and during the 1920s several more women were elected members. The 1924 dinner held in honor of the ASLA's twenty-fifth anniversary, held at the Biltmore, was attended by Coffin, Ruth Dean, Farrand, Annette Hoyt Flanders, and Hutcheson, and the guest attendees included Ellen Biddle Shipman, Theodora Kimball (Hubbard), Helen Swift Jones, Mrs. William Lockwood, Helena Burnham, and

Mabel Parsons. Theodora Kimball was named a corresponding member of the ASLA in 1919 and Mariana Van Rensselaer an honorary member in 1926. The 1927 dinner included Marjorie Sewell Cautley, Farrand, Dean, Eleanor Roche, Coffin, and Mary Parson Cunningham. Women were also named to a variety of committees and task forces; Rose Ishbel Greely, for example, served on the task force for Williamsburg. In the 1930s Hutcheson, Katherine Bashford, and Greely were elected fellows of the ASLA, with Flanders so named in 1942 and nine more women joining her over the next thirty-six years.

Women also served in leadership positions in the ASLA, although not in numbers reflecting their role as practitioners. Katherine Bashford, for example, served as the chapter secretary in Southern California in the 1930s. In 1953 Dorothea Harrison was elected president of the ASLA's Boston chapter and also served as the organization's first woman trustee. Cary Mullholland Parker, Jane Silverstein Ries, Helene B. Warner, and Karen Anderson all followed in Harrison's path. It was not, however, until 1971 that the first woman was elected the vice president of the ASLA, Edith Henderson in fact becoming the group's first national woman officer.

Academies and educational institutions also included women, but again in unrepresentatively small numbers. While women such as Florence Bell Robinson, Geraldine Knight, Mae Arbegast, Elizabeth May McAdams, and Theodora Kimball Hubbard had opened doors for women in academia, few seemed to follow them. Only nine women were employed as full-time faculty members in all of the landscape architecture programs across the country in the 1980s, according to a report by the Council of Educators in Landscape Architecture.[3] Anne Whiston Spirn was a notable exception: she joined the Harvard faculty in 1979 and served as the director of the Landscape Architecture Program from 1984 to 1986. In 1986 she was named chair of the University of Pennsylvania's Department of Landscape Architecture and Regional Planning, serving in this capacity until 1993, and in 1996 she became codirector of the Urban Studies Program at the University of Pennsylvania. What is apparent here is that despite their numbers, women have indeed participated in shaping and professionalizing the field.

The first generations of women in landscape architecture would recognize many of the roles and positions women held in the latter half of the twentieth century. They would appreciate Genevieve Gillette as an advocate of state and national parks and reserves. They would be inspired by the environmentally responsible work of Cornelia Hahn Oberlander and the success of Harriet Barnhart Wimmer's commercial practice. They would recognize the success of Geraldine Knight's work in California, which has won recognition from landscape architects and architects alike. All of these women clearly built on the successes of earlier constellations, expanding the profession and exploring new areas of practice.

The first women practitioners believed in the power of the landscape in public and private life. While women in the profession today might come to it with a different set of priorities, they share with earlier women a vision of a sustainable and better future. Early practitioners might marvel at Martha Schwartz's status in the profession, at her teaching at Harvard University; at Kathryn Gustafson's ability to lead an international practice; at the recognition awarded Andrea Cochran; and at Diane Dale's role as landscape planner for the architecture firm of William McDonough and Partners. Nonetheless, while their successes might be notable to the first women, their ambitions would certainly be familiar.

Still, while the profession has thus embraced a breadth of women in practice, their role has remained invisible in its histories, remaining an enigma. In the 1970s the ASLA issued a report noting that two-thirds of the women surveyed had experienced discrimination in the field, despite the long history of women's participation.[4] However, while this report discussed possible solutions, it did little to consider the root of the disparity between women's numeric and imaginative presence and their impact on the field.

Changes in the Practice, the Profession, and Personalities

This professional invisibility is notably tied to those who chose alternative paths of practice. Why did women's practice differ from men's? First, the standardization of educational requirements for practice, which valued the architectural rather than the agricultural roots of the profession, limited those who could practice. Second, the rise of the corporate office, and the related limited opportunities for alternative practices, led to similar limitations. Third, the rise of modernism as a style eventually negated the relationship between landscape architecture and landscape gardening. While these factors deserve in-depth research, below I attempt to synthesize how they together forced most women to the margins of the discipline and the profession.

Modern Education

Landscape architectural education, as noted earlier, had been launched in the nineteenth century within agricultural schools (land-grant colleges). In 1921 no professional landscape architecture programs were housed in a school of architecture; three were within horticulture programs, one was in a forestry program, one was part of an arts and sciences college, and nine fell under agriculture programs.[5] By the 1940s, however, many programs were either within schools of architecture or art or otherwise associated with the arts rather than with agriculture. As the profession matured, many landscape architects became concerned that landscape design, when taught as part of a scientific curriculum rather than as a fine art, would lead to landscape gardening rather than landscape architecture. James Sturgis Pray, for example, wrote of Harvard's program in 1909:

> In view of the professional standards upheld by [the ASLA] which recognizes Landscape Architecture as a fine art, co-ordinate with that of architecture,—in short, as an art of Design—this approach from the side of Agriculture or Horticulture, or even Engineering, is a left-handed approach to the subject, and is not so likely ever to develop in the students a high power of artistic creation. . . . [It was] a very decided advantage that our work began and continued in such close association with the instruction in Architecture.[6]

The ASLA Committee on Education, on which Pray served, thus recommended that landscape programs emphasize courses in the arts, including architecture, painting, sculpture, and music, rather than courses in the sciences. The education of young landscape architects increasingly focused, then, on elements of design, engineering, and planning, unlike earlier programs, which had emphasized horticulture, botany, and ecology. This architectural and technical viewpoint eventually dominated the profession, marginalizing those who practiced in alternate ways, particularly those who had come to the practice via gardening, horticulture, agriculture, and/or farming.

Frederick Law Olmsted and Beatrix Farrand, for example, would have had difficulty launching professional practices in the last half of the twentieth century, when it was substantially harder to become a professional without matriculating from an accredited institution of higher learning. In the 1920s there was an informal list of acknowledged schools, considered rigorous enough to educate landscape architects (Harvard University, the University of Illinois, Iowa State University, the University of Michigan, Ohio State University, and the University of California, Berkeley). As schools for women did not grant degrees, they were not awarded this recognition, although they nevertheless remained an option, since accreditation was not required for professional education. In the 1940s, however, these schools closed, and in 1958 the ASLA accepted the National Commission on Accrediting as an official agency for reviewing professional curricula; it accredited seventeen schools. Accreditation thus became standard. While the recognition accorded helped to establish educational and pedagogical standards, it also limited the opportunities for young men and women to pursue a professional education, alternative programs and approaches rendered ineligible.

After education, licensing or registration was the next professional hurdle. Since the formation of the ASLA in 1899, landscape architects have struggled to be recognized as professionals alongside doctors, lawyers, and architects. Many believed the best path to such recognition was alignment with architecture, which had implemented professional registration by the 1940s. The AIA's Committee on Education made its standards clear: "An architect we defined as one ranking in the class of men of culture, learning and refinement, differentiated from the others of his class solely by his function as a creator of pure beauty."[7] While this community would seem appropriate to landscape architects, the alignment was more complicated from a public perspective. With increased calls to protect public health and safety from inexperienced architects and builders, the state of Illinois passed the first licensing law for architects in 1897. Many architects subsequently took offense, and the AIA initially tried to prevent such licensing laws. Eventually, then, registration replaced licensing: it seemed less "sinister," requiring the practitioner simply to take an exam in order to practice.[8] This licensing of practitioners further narrowed the field.

After decades of debate the ASLA too endorsed the process of licensing and registration by state. The laws were meant to protect the health, safety, and welfare of the public by establishing standards for professional practice, and the initial concern for landscape architects was to limit the number of florists, nurserymen, and gardeners who might also call themselves landscape architects. California passed the first licensing standards in 1951, and other states soon followed. Licensing requirements included an accredited degree and a minimum number of years as an apprentice, followed by an exam. By requiring licensing or registration, landscape architecture was finally officially aligning itself with architecture and engineering, medicine and law, instead of with the sciences of horticulture or the fine arts. Access, then, had been narrowly proscribed to those holding the rank of professional landscape architect.

Modern Practice

In addition to these public transformations, a more internal, professional change was also taking place: the expansion of offices from individual practices to partnerships reflected a concomitant move from private to corporate and governmental clients. A significant portion of the client base of the Olmsted Brothers firm, for example, was made up of corporate and/or government agencies. Landscape architects thus joined professional architects and engineers, working as team members on larger building projects. They found positions in government offices and served in the National Park Service and state agencies. New Deal projects briefly provided a way to establish landscape architecture as a powerful force in the American landscape, a number of landscape architects employed under national and statewide projects. For such public positions, however, women were at a disadvantage: public sympathy was geared toward jobless men, assumed to be heads of households. With limited commissions and professional standing, women were thus seen as competing with men for positions, and in the post–World War II era this was not a positive circumstance.

Women did surmount each of these obstacles. As noted earlier, women attended Harvard, taught at the University of California, opened offices, worked for the government, participated on city planning teams, and actively engaged in the professional community. Women were not, however, given a strong voice in the profession. Rather than acknowledging women, the professional community appeared to distance them, isolating their practices and, in professional historical narratives, portraying a lineage that disregarded their contributions. Rediscovering the influence and leadership of many women in the early twentieth century thus creates a new framework for exploring the century's second half. For example, once we know that Maud Sargent hired landscape architects under Robert Moses, we know to search out whom she employed and for what projects. Once we know that Cautley was intimately involved in the design of Stein and Wright's garden cities, we know to look more carefully at plans for later developments. Once we know that Ruth Shellhorn was the designer of Disneyland and some of the earliest department store landscapes, we can question the apparent lack of women in the later planning of commercial centers and urban projects. Contemporary women are thus placed within the context of a richer and more dynamic lineage.

Modern Landscapes

Modernism changed not only the predominant design style of landscape architecture but also the value system that guided its assessment. While initial interest in modernism was focused on the concept as praxis, outcome was more stylistically defined. Drawing on the work of Fletcher Steele, Garrett Eckbo, James Rose, Daniel Urban Kiley, and Thomas Church, some practitioners became known for their modernist style of garden design, exhibiting a multiplicity of views; a lack of a major and/or central axis; a love of asymmetry; and above all an individual, often even playful approach. Modernist landscape architects focused their attention on contemporary technologies and materials in the landscape, ways in which the garden might respond to modern architecture and contemporary living. Plants were a source for materials, and many designs sacrificed the dimensions of time and growth to the immediacy of an artistic message.

While early modernists did understand the importance of environmental and ecological approaches to design, the academic exploration of the environmental sciences was eventually separated from landscape programs, as were conservation, natural resources, forestry, and other fields focused on nature and the natural environment. These areas of study, once integrated into agriculture schools and offices, became distinct domains, individuals rarely collaborating across their boundaries. Landscape architects thus became known as "beauty doctors" to foresters and ecologists.[9]

Landscape architecture continued to struggle to clarify its position as a profession. For example, *Landscape Architecture Magazine* has published many suggested definitions of the profession and even proposed a change in its name. By shifting the profession into a closer alignment with engineering and architecture, practitioners believed that landscape architecture would be reinvigorated and become more professionally sound. In essence, then, the profession chose to pair itself with architecture as nature is paired with culture, woman with man, and art with science. This pairing is not benign, for such binary pairs hold a powerful implication—that an implicit, inherent hierarchy exists between the two members of the pair. Culture dominates nature, man dominates woman, and architecture dominates landscape architecture. This process of alignment and pairing thus essentially marginalized the craft of gardening, the science of horticulture, and the art of painting with plants, in the process defining these activities as feminine inscriptions and thus of less importance. This process marginalized many, not only women. In the late 1930s, for example, Jensen, after resigning from the ASLA, wrote a friend that there was a "strong tendency by the American Landscaper to get away from gardening, as if that word smelled of cabbage. He has a fear of being classed with the craftsman instead of the professional, and today the art is practically killed, because of his efforts to make a profession of it."[10]

An approach such as Jensen's—based on the use of native plants and an appreciation for native landscapes—was apparently too akin to gardening and thus not professional enough. Jensen's colleague Frank Waugh wrote in 1938 that the "problem of preserving and improving the native landscape is the greatest one before the profession of landscape architecture and one of the greatest questions anywhere in the nation. Unfortunately the American Society of Landscape Architects has heard nothing about it, and of course will do nothing about it."[11] Waugh's and Jensen's belief in the possibility of an American style of design, based in the local landscape and native plants, was no longer shared with the professional community. As Ann E. Komara has eloquently pointed out, "Landscape Architecture positioned itself as an equal counterpart to architecture by asserting its parallel role in culturalizing nature; gardening was relegated to horticultural and decorative status."[12] The discussion thus turned from describing landscape architecture in its breadth and depth to comparing its practice and practitioners within the confines of the profession of architecture.

With these increased associations with architecture and engineering, and the related distancing of the practice from landscape gardening, horticulture, and the craft of gardening, not only did a diversity of practice become invisible, but a substantial cohort of practitioners were essentially erased in the history of landscape architecture as a practice and a profession. No longer was a knowledge or love of gardening relevant to a career in landscape architecture. No longer was landscape architecture described as an art, an artist like Olmsted or Shipman described as painting with nature. No longer were early modernist designs said to play with the seasonality, temporality, layering, and spatiality of landscape materials, in particular the plants and the land.

The narrative of the profession's history as a linear progression, from Olmsted to Harvard, remains in the mainstream of the professional community. For example, a post on the "Land Arch" listserv recently stated: "If we think back to the Harvard Three: Dan Kiley, James Rose and Garrett Eckbo, what were they rebelling against? It was the fact that [landscape architects] had, to that point, been categorically applying one method, and one method only, to professional practice." This misunderstanding of history is pervasive in the profession, among practitioners, teachers, and students.

Looking Ahead

I have sought here to recover the stories of women practitioners; to redescribe a breadth of practice that, in turn, shaped the emerging praxis of landscape architecture; and to consider the possibility of reading history through an alternative lens. This description of a group of successful female landscape architects, within the context of larger constellations of women practicing in the first half of the twentieth century, illustrates the importance of women in the development of the profession, providing a gendered analysis in which gender is considered as a category rather than an essential characteristic. They were agents of change and signifiers of culture. Their work merits a close reading, inviting a better understanding of the history of landscape architectural praxis and providing role models for young men and women today. By looking at how women have practiced, we gain a more holistic view of the profession and of how landscape architects have chosen to redefine practice in their own terms, using their own vocabularies—both rooted in and distinct from those who came before them, as individuals and as members of a community.

Women in landscape architecture in the mid-twentieth century, from 1950 to 1980, built on the foundations established by earlier constellations, emerging as influential leaders and as advocates for landscape, landscape architecture, and architecture as focused on providing places for living. They trained and worked in the offices of practitioners of earlier generations, bringing with them the skills to address new challenges. In turn, today's practitioners are building on the work of previous individuals and communities. While monographs frequently suggest a false autonomy of individual stars, a more in-depth consideration of contemporary landscape architecture requires a deeper understanding of its background and setting.

Learning the history of the profession encourages us to understand our world in a different way. We begin to more fully understand how landscape shapes our values and culture, how it underlies our view of the local and global environment. As landscape historians expand narratives to reflect the breadth of practice, questions will arise that will in turn engender further discussion, encouraging intellectual curiosity about the landscape in which society and culture exist. The lesson of the importance originally accorded residential design is one from which people living now, in the twenty-first century, could benefit. By reinvigorating the practice of addressing residential design, we might thus provide better, safer, and healthier places in which people can live their daily lives. Annette Hoyt Flanders, Martha Brookes Brown Hutcheson, and Marjorie L. Sewell Cautley have much to teach us.

Contemporary practitioners and thinkers, from Walter Hood to Andrea Cochran, from James Corner to Dianne Harris, are challenging us to expand our horizons and reconsider our sources so that we might design a more enticing, responsive, and livable landscape. Cautley's work at Radburn and Hillside is certainly a resource to which we can turn.

Landscape architecture, further, is more broadly important on a global level. Again and again we are told that we must change the way we live if we are going to truly affect the course of global warming, and landscape architecture can powerfully support the necessary changes. As population density increases and environmental problems plague us at local and global levels, landscape architects can offer critical expertise in the design of our environment, leading to greater ecological responsibility and more sustainable development. The writings and work of Ruth Dean and Elsa Rehmann clearly have something to communicate here.

Social agendas might once again become essential parts of practice, for it is when the public is served that change becomes real. Through explorations of community design in the work of a variety of practitioners in landscape architecture and architecture, much can be learned about how to listen and respond to people of different cultures, embracing diverse visions. Cautley and Hutcheson, along with a myriad of other writers in the early twentieth century, can certainly contribute to this discourse.

I do not mean to imply that all the answers can be found by reexploring the practices of early designers; it has been shown, for example, that a simple return to native plants cannot solve the problem of ecological health. The solutions to contemporary problems are surely complex. We can, however, reclaim the depth of knowledge of these early practitioners and combine that knowledge with what we have learned since, enabling a potent response to future challenges. We can, in other words, become a force "to be reckoned with."

Introduction

1. Spirn, *Language of Landscape,* 54.
2. Meyer, "Expanded Field of Landscape Architecture," 48–49.
3. Hartt, "Women and the Art," 695.
4. As quoted in a letter: Jens Jensen to Mr. and Mrs. Boardman, n.d., in Grese, *Jens Jensen,* 61.
5. Newton, *Design on the Land,* 445.
6. Gwendolyn Wright, "Partnership," 185.
7. Meyer, "Expanded Field of Landscape Architecture," 50.

1. Landscape Architecture Emerges as a Profession

1. Jefferson, *Thomas Jefferson's Garden Book,* 303–4.
2. Cooper, *Rural Hours,* 23.
3. This landscape was subsequently altered under the 1901 McMillan Plan (O'Malley, "'Public Museum of Trees,'" 72).
4. As quoted in Major, *To Live in the New World,* 7.
5. Downing, "American versus British Horticulture."
6. Schuyler, *Apostle of Taste,* 206–7.
7. Ibid., 203.
8. As quoted in Newton, *Design on the Land,* 368 (my emphasis).
9. Gruber, "McCrea, Annette E." and "Annette E. Maxson McCrea."
10. "Mrs. Annette E. McCrea, Pioneer Woman Landscape Architect Dies at 64 Years," *New York Times,* Sept. 22, 1928, p. 13.
11. "Woman Landscape Architect, Notable Work Done by Mrs McCrea of Chicago," *Christian Science Monitor,* Jan. 16, 1913, p. 6.
12. McCrea, "Color Harmony and Discord" and "Railroad Station Improvement"; Frances Copley Seavey, "Women in Business," *Los Angeles Times,* Sept. 22, 1901.
13. As quoted in Gruber, "Annette E. Maxson McCrea," 559.
14. Krall, "Illusive Miss Bullard."
15. Ibid., 118.

16. Frederick Law Olmsted Sr. to Mr. Noble, 1892, Papers of Frederick Law Olmsted, all 340–41.

17. Krall, "Illusive Miss Bullard," 118.

18. "Bullard Died at Home, 472 Park Avenue, Bridgeport," *Bridgeport Telegram*, Aug. 16, 1916; Bullard, "Letter."

19. Seavey, "Women in Business."

20. Corbin, "No 'Gross Offenses,'" 158.

21. Sargent and Stiles, "Art and Nature in Landscape Gardening," 192.

22. Van Rensselaer, "Art of Gardening" and "Landscape Gardening—A Definition."

23. Van Rensselaer, *Art Out-of-Doors,* 3 (my emphasis).

24. Robbins, "Park-Making as a National Art," 86–98.

25. Bledstein, *Culture of Professionalism,* 87.

26. Prieto, *At Home in the Studio,* 14.

27. See Woods, *From Craft to Profession.*

28. Newton, *Design on the Land,* 2.

29. Caparn, "Founding of the American Society of Landscape Architects," 22.

30. "American Park and Outdoor Art Association."

31. Maybeck and Maybeck, "Programme for the Development of a Hillside Community."

32. Van Rensselaer, "Art of Gardening," 7–8.

33. Records of the ASLA, Feb. 2, 1914. (Number of votes in parenthesis.)

34. Vernon, "Toward Defining the Profession."

2. Learning a Craft

1. Tusser, *Five Hundredth Points of Good Husbandry.*

2. Bell, "Women Create Gardens."

3. As quoted and discussed in Shteir, *Cultivating Women,* 117 (my emphasis).

4. As quoted in Schnare, "Women Garden Writers," 87.

5. Loudon and Downing, *Gardening for Ladies,* iii–iv, 16–17.

6. Catherine Parr Traill, *The Female Emigrant's Guide,* 1854, quoted in Guttman, *Women Writing Gardens,* 6–7.

7. Earle, *Old Time Gardens,* 20.

8. Spicer, "Gardening Women in Our Town."

9. Cynthia, "Parable of Planting."

10. Albee, *Hardy Plants,* 24.

11. Harris, "Cultivating Power."

12. Beatrix Farrand, *Bulletins of Reef Point Gardens.*

13. "Woman Landscape Gardener: Miss Beatrix Jones Has Attained Her Eminence in the Profession by Hard Study and by Travel," *New York Times,* Dec. 31, 1899.

14. Patterson, Bliss, and Roper, *Beatrix Jones Farrand.*

15. Beatrix Farrand to Dorothy Elmhirst, Oct. 22, 1943, Beatrix Jones Farrand papers.

16. Fowler, "Women in Landscape Architecture," 2.

17. Sargent, "Taste Indoors and Out."

18. Robbins, "Some Questions about Taste."

19. Sargent, "Taste Indoors and Out, Response" (my emphasis).

20. Sargent, "New Botany Program."

21. "Beatrix Farrand, 1872–1959," in Farrand, *Bulletins of Reef Point Gardens.*

22. Patterson, Bliss, and Roper, *Beatrix Jones Farrand.*

23. Sargent, "Taste Indoors and Out," 373.

24. Frost and Sears, *Women in Architecture,* 18 (my emphasis).

25. Mary Cadwalader Jones, *European Travel for Women.*

26. "Woman Landscape Gardener."

27. André wrote her a letter in Dec. 1900 in which he noted that "the most curious is to see women entering also into career" (Beatrix Jones Farrand Collection; letter translated by author).

28. "Landscape Architecture"; "Miss Beatrix Jones' Vocation: She Does Landscape Gardening of All Kinds, from the Ground Up," *New York Sun,* Oct. 31, 1897.

29. Beatrix Jones, "Nature's Landscape-Gardening in Maine."

30. Beatrix Jones, "Bridge over the Kent" and "Garden in Relation to the House."

31. Beatrix Jones, "Le Notre and His Gardens."

32. "New York Society Girl a Landscape Gardener," *New York World,* ca. 1900.

33. Klaus, "All in the Family."

34. As quoted in Klaus, "All in the Family," 86.

35. As quoted in Beveridge, Rocheleau, and Larkin, *Frederick Law Olmsted,* 37.

36. Child, "Two Decades of Landscape Architecture," 269.

37. Beatrix Jones, "Book of Gardening."

38. "Miss Beatrix Jones' Vocation."

39. "Woman Landscape Gardener."

40. Beatrix Jones, "City Parks."

41. As quoted in Balmori, McGuire, and McPeck, *Beatrix Farrand's American Landscapes,* 146.

42. Beatrix Jones Farrand, "Talk to a Garden Club."

43. "New York Society Girl."

44. "Woman Landscape Gardener."

45. Beatrix Farrand to Thomas Farnam, Oct. 18, 1922, Yale University Archives.

46. "Woman Landscape Gardener."

47. "Miss Beatrix Jones' Vocation."

48. "Woman Landscape Gardener."

49. As quoted in a letter: Beatrix Jones Farrand to Robert Milliken, director of the Institute, 1932, in Balmori, McGuire, and McPeck, *Beatrix Farrand's American Landscapes,* 148.

50. Balmori, McGuire, and McPeck, *Beatrix Farrand's American Landscapes,* 148.

51. Records of the ASLA, Jan. 24, 1900, box 33, folder 5.

52. Records of the ASLA, box 1, 1900–15 folder.

53. Beatrix Jones, *Garden in Relation to the House,* 133.

54. "New York Society Girl."

55. Patterson, Bliss, and Roper, *Beatrix Jones Farrand,* 2.

56. Ibid., 6.

57. Beatrix Farrand, "The Oaks," 2–6.

58. "Miss Beatrix Jones' Vocation."

59. Beatrix Jones, "Garden as a Picture," 2, 10.

60. Farrand and McGuire, *Beatrix Farrand's Plant Book,* 31.

61. Beatrix Farrand to J. Thacher, June 27, 1944, Beatrix Jones Farrand papers.

62. B. J. Farrand to John S. Thacher, Oct. 1, 1946, Beatrix Jones Farrand papers.

63. Beatrix Farrand, *Bulletins of Reef Point Gardens,* 2.

64. Ibid., 3.

65. Ibid.

66. Beatrix Farrand, "Contemplated Landscape Changes," 43.

67. Robinson, "From the Ground Up," 19.

3. From Garden Craft to Landscape Architecture

1. As quoted in Cole, *From Tipi to Skyscraper,* 54.

2. Leichtle, "Gibson Girl on the Farm?" 143.

3. Haines, "Where Practical Gardening May Be Learned," 54.

4. Eliot, "Open Letter."

5. MacPhail, *Kate Sessions.*

6. Hines, *Irving Gill,* 56, 84, 159.

7. Bertha H. Smith, "Western Personalities," 702.

8. Two important works on Shipman are Meador, "Making of a Landscape Architect," and Tankard and Library of American Landscape History, *Ellen Biddle Shipman.*

9. Shelton, *Beautiful Gardens in America,* 23.

10. Shipman, "Garden—Notebook."

11. Davidson, "Italian Garden."

12. Her books were donated to the Avery Library at Columbia University, while her office and professional files were donated to Cornell University.

13. Dona E. Caldwell, interviews with the author, June 12, Aug. 9, 2003.

14. "House on Beekman Place."

15. Shipman, "Garden—Notebook."

16. Ibid., preface.

17. Caldwell, interviews with the author, June 12, Aug. 9, 2003.

18. E. B. Shipman to Mrs. Willis G. Wilmot, June 28, 1945, Ellen Shipman Archives, box 8, folder 35.

19. Shipman, "Garden—Notebook," 2.

20. Ibid., 2-4.

21. E. B. Shipman to Mr. and Mrs. William G. Mather, Nov. 15, 1945, Ellen McGowan Biddle Shipman papers, #1259, box 8, folder 54.

22. Shipman, "Garden—Notebook," foreword.

23. Ibid.

24. Ibid., 1.

25. Howe, *American Country Houses of To-Day,* 223.

26. Davidson, "Italian Garden."

27. Auwaerter, "Cultural Landscape Report."

28. Anne Peterson, "Women Take Lead in Landscape Art," *New York Times,* Mar. 13, 1938.

29. Deck, "Interpreting Classic Signature Elements."

30. Quoted in Helphand and Rottle, "Cultivating Charm," 29.

31. Quoted in Helphand and Rottle, "Cultivating Charm," 29.

32. Yoch, *Landscaping the American Dream*. See also Streatfield, *California Gardens*.

33. Dobyns, *California Gardens*.

34. Tankard and Library of American Landscape History, *Ellen Biddle Shipman*, 3; W. H. Manning to Frank Seiberling, Akron, Ohio, July 20, 1917, Stan Hywet Archives.

35. Richardson Wright, "House & Gardens Own Hall of Fame."

4. The New Woman and a New Education

1. Prieto, *At Home in the Studio*, 27–28.

2. American Landscape School, "Advertisement for Correspondence School," *Horticulture*, July 1924, 413.

3. Filzen, "Garden Designs," 43.

4. Glave, "'Garden So Brilliant,'" 5.

5. Records of the ASLA, box 2.

6. Lois Page Poinier, interviews with the author, Mar. 10, June 8, 2003.

7. As quoted in Corbin, "No 'Gross Offenses,'" 162.

8. Solomon, *In the Company of Educated Women*, 79.

9. Frost and Sears, *Women in Architecture*, 18.

10. Robinette, *Landscape Architectural Education*, 2:265.

11. Filzen, "Garden Designs," 30.

12. Bever, "Women of MIT."

13. Krall, "One Hundred Years of Outdoor Art," 8.

14. Filene, *Careers for Women*, 50.

15. Ibid., 53.

16. Records of the ASLA, box 1, 1920 folder.

17. Pattee, "Landscape Architecture in American Colleges" (which includes charts summarizing the research).

18. Evans, "Report of Committee on Co-Education"; Hubbard, "Report of the Committee on Graduate and Undergraduate Instruction."

19. Evans, "Report of Committee on Co-Education," 3.

20. Kimball, "Little Visit to Lowthorpe."

21. "Catalogue for Lowthorpe School of Landscape Architecture," 1903, n.p.

22. "Catalogue for the Lowthorpe School," 1911, 6.

23. "Lowthorpe School," in Robinette, *Landscape Architectural Education*, 1:118–28.

24. "Women in Landscaping."

25. E. B. Shipman to Mrs. Conoley, Oct. 9, 1945, Ellen McGowan Biddle Shipman papers, #1259, box 8, folder 54.

26. Libby, "Jane Haines' Vision."

27. See Anderson, *Women*.

28. Frost, "History of the Cambridge School."

29. Frost, "The Cambridge School."

30. Ibid.

31. Furr, "Academic Program of the Cambridge School," 23.

5. Professional Legitimacy

1. Harris, "Women as Gardeners," 1448.

2. Hohmann, "Theodora Kimball Hubbard."

3. Rehmann and Rehmann Perrett, *Garden-Making,* vii.

4. Rehmann, "Ecological Approach," 239.

5. Filene, *Careers for Women,* 66.

6. I am indebted to the scholarship of Valencia Libby in these discussions of Marian Cruger Coffin (Libby, "Henry Francis du Pont" and "Marian Cruger Coffin").

7. Fowler, "Three Women in Landscape Architecture."

8. Ibid.

9. Fowler, "Women in Landscape Architecture," 7–8.

10. Ibid., 8.

11. M. C. Coffin to H. F. du Pont, May 7, 1948, Marian Cruger Coffin papers, 1903–1990.

12. Coffin, "Where East Meets West."

13. Fowler, "Three Women in Landscape Architecture."

14. Coffin, *Trees and Shrubs for Landscape Effects,* xviii–xix.

15. Warren Hunting Smith, "Museum Exhibit: Gardens."

16. M. C. Coffin to H. F. du Pont, Sept. 22, 1919, Marian Cruger Coffin papers, 1903–1990.

17. See Marian Cruger Coffin papers, 1903–1990, box 2, Connecticut College folder.

18. M. C. Coffin to H. F. du Pont, Dec. 17, 1925, du Pont/Coffin correspondence folder, Marian Cruger Coffin papers, 1903–1990.

19. See Marian Cruger Coffin papers, 1903–1990, box 3, Smith Correspondence folder.

20. Elizabeth F. Colwell to H. F. du Pont, Apr. 5, Apr. 12, 1912, Marian Cruger Coffin papers, 1903–1990, box 642, Du Pont/Coffin Correspondence folder.

21. Coffin, "Suburban Garden Six Years Old."

22. Coffin, "Method of Practice."

23. See Marian Cruger Coffin papers, 1903–1990, box 1, Byer folder.

24. Coffin, *Trees and Shrubs,* xx.

25. There are a number of references to her paintings in Coffin's correspondence with du Pont, Smith, and Scheiner. For example, see H. F. du Pont to Marian Cruger Coffin, Dec. 27, 1954: "Dear Marian, Thank you so much for the charming little oil painting which I love having. It will be an important addition to my gallery of Coffins" (Henry F. du Pont papers, box HF632, Coffin, Marian, 1931–47, 1952–54).

26. Warren Hunting Smith, "Museum Exhibit: Gardens," 3.

27. Coffin, "Method of Practice."

28. Coffin to du Pont, Dec. 17, 1925, du Pont/Coffin correspondence folder, Marian Cruger Coffin papers, 1903–1990.

29. Coffin, *Trees and Shrubs,* xviii.

30. Coffin, "Method of Practice."

31. "Pioneer among Women Landscape Architects."

32. Coffin, "General Plan for Layout."

33. Ibid.

34. Coffin, *Trees and Shrubs,* 14.

35. Ibid., xvii.

36. "Pioneer among Women Landscape Architects."

37. Coffin, *Trees and Shrubs,* xx–xxi.

38. Henry F. du Pont asked her to join him on the committee, and they were, for a short while, its only members. See Henry F. du Pont papers, box HF632, Coffin, Marian, 1931–47.

39. Coffin, "Suburban Garden," 20.

40. "Landscape Architect—a New Vocation for Women," *Christian Science Monitor,* May 23, 1916.

41. "The Woman Landscape Architect Speaks," *Christian Science Monitor,* Jan. 20, 1917.

42. Dean, "War Tax on Beauty," 48.

43. Dean, "Landscape Architecture on a House-Top," 18.

44. Lee, "Three Gardens at Grosse Pointe," 509.

45. This was recalled by Dona Caldwell, who worked for Smith (interview, June 12, 2003).

46. Filzen, "Garden Designs," 76.

47. Poinier, interview, June 8, 2003.

48. Filzen, "Garden Designs," 78.

49. Cautley, "The Black Cat," Marjorie Sewell Cautley papers, #4908, box 1, folder 126.

50. Filzen, "Garden Designs," 75.

51. Miller, "What Alumnae Are Doing," 31.

6. Designing a Social Agenda

1. Rodgers, *Atlantic Crossings,* 160.

2. Wolschke-Bulmahn, "From the War-Garden," 53.

3. Manning, "History of Village Improvement," 429.

4. Beard, *Woman's Work in Municipalities,* v.

5. Robbins, "Village Improvement Societies," 212.

6. Waring, *Village Improvements and Farm Villages,* 20.

7. Ibid., 16.

8. Robbins, "Art of Public Improvement," 742.

9. Ibid., 743.

10. Robbins, "Village Improvement Societies," 222.

11. Ibid., 212–13.

12. Manning, "History of Village Improvement," 430.

13. Recently, the records of the Negro Garden Clubs of Virginia were donated to Hampton University as a result of a garden documentation project. Thank you to Ann Pierce for bringing this to my attention.

14. Battles and Dickey, *Fifty Blooming Years,* 23.

15. Dillon, "Municipal Landscaping for Women."

16. Farrand gave this lecture to a number of groups, including a publication on vocations for girls (Beatrix Jones Farrand, "Landscape Gardening for Women").

17. *Woman's National Farm and Garden Association Bulletin* 4, no. 5 (October 1917), 4.

18. Mrs. Francis King to Mrs. J. Willis Martin, n.d., Beatrix Jones Farrand papers, folder 11-36.

19. Mary Rutherfurd Jay, "Garden Architecture as a Career," *Christian Science Monitor,* Dec. 30, 1924, 8.

20. Beard, *Woman's Work in Municipalities,* x.

21. Ibid., 294–302.

22. Ibid., 217.

23. Ibid., 294.

24. Beatrix Jones, "City Parks."

25. Hutcheson and Library of American Landscape History, *Spirit of the Garden;* Davidson, "Spirit of the American Garden." Additional scholarship critical to my analysis was done by Jean Marie Hartmann, Landscape Architecture Department, Rutgers University.

26. Martha Brookes Hutcheson, quoted in Davidson, "Introduction," ix.

27. Fowler, "Women in Landscape Architecture," 4; Hutcheson and Library of American Landscape History, *Spirit of the Garden,* ix.

28. Davidson, "Introduction," vii.

29. "Landscape Gardening: A Conversation."

30. Brown, "Statement Regarding Professional Methods and Charges."

31. Hutcheson, *Spirit of the Garden,* 50–51.

32. Ibid., foreword, ix.

33. See Davidson, "Italian Garden."

34. Hartt, "Women and the Art," 699.

35. Hutcheson, "Lecture—The Fine Art of Landscape Architecture."

36. "Landscape Gardening: A Conversation," 728.

37. Hutcheson, "Co-Operation of Citizens." Other manuscripts can be found in Martha Brookes Brown Hutcheson papers, Papers and Photographs.

38. Martha Brookes Hutcheson, "Trees for School Yards," *New York Sun,* July 9, 1934.

39. Hutcheson, "Wider Program for Garden Clubs," 5.

40. Ibid., 36.

41. Beatrix Farrand, "Talk to a Garden Club."

42. Mrs. Francis King to Mrs. J. Willis Martin, n.d., Beatrix Jones Farrand papers, folder 11-36.

43. Hutcheson, "Wider Program for Garden Clubs," 8.

44. Ibid., 1.

45. Ibid., 2.

46. Ibid., 12.

47. Iannacone, "Open Space for the Underclass."

48. Hutcheson, "Native Tree and Shrub Group," 40.

49. Hutcheson, "One of Our National Blights."

50. Hutcheson, "Possible Inspiration through Garden Clubs," 118.

51. Ely, *Woman's Hardy Garden,* 98.

52. Hutcheson, "Wider Program for Garden Clubs," 6, 14.

7. Model Gardens

1. Major, *To Live in the New World,* 17.
2. Waugh, "Landscape Architecture in North America," 421.
3. "Design," in Shipman, "Garden—Notebook," chap. 1.
4. Peters and Morgan, "Country Life Commission," abstract.
5. Beveridge, Rocheleau, and Larkin, *Frederick Law Olmsted,* 115.
6. Records of the ASLA, box 1, folder 23, 1925.
7. Frost, "Cambridge School Bulletin, 1940."
8. Peterson, "Women Take Lead."
9. See, e.g., Flanders, "Value of Vistas."
10. "Annette Hoyt Flanders: A Biographical Minute," 30.
11. A graduate of Smith College, Jones opened her own office around 1926. She was elected a member of the ASLA in 1930.
12. "Gardener's Calendar for July."
13. Richardson Wright, "House & Garden's Own Hall of Fame."
14. First names for Watson and Clark are not identified.
15. Gertrude Sawyer to Natalie Alpert, n.d., Annette Hoyt Flanders papers.
16. Alice Upham Smith to Natalie B. Alpert, Jan. 3, 1977, Annette Hoyt Flanders papers, 1920s-1950s.
17. A. H. Flanders to Miss Bullard, 1929, Helen Bullard papers.
18. Flanders, "Modern Garden."
19. For attendees see the references in the brochure; see also women who mentioned her courses in their interviews with Patricia Filzen ("Garden Designs").
20. A. H. Flanders to Senator Lawrence C. Phipps, Dec. 21, 1935, Phipps/ Flanders Correspondence.
21. Filzen, "Garden Designs," 111.
22. Henry, "Notes," 123.
23. Flanders, "Landscape Architecture."
24. Virginia Pope and Mattie Edwards Hewitt, "Little Gardens That Hide in New York," *New York Times,* June 8, 1920.
25. Flanders, *Exhibition of Landscape Architecture.*
26. Walter Rendell Storey, "Fitting the Terrace for All-Year Play," *New York Times,* Oct. 16, 1932.
27. Storey, "Fitting the Terrace."
28. Koues, "Good Housekeeping Exhibition."
29. "Letters from Flanders to the Phipps Concerning the Landscape Design of the Estate," House and Garden Archives.
30. Meloney, *Better Homes in America,* 1.
31. "Little House Gets Crop of 36 Apples," *New York Times,* July 20, 1935.
32. *America's Little House.*
33. "Little House Gets Crop."
34. *America's Little House.*
35. Letter of May 29, 1917, Marjorie Sewell Cautley papers, box 1, folder 136.
36. "Leading Women in the Big Performance of Building a World's Fair on Flushing Meadows," *New York Sun,* Oct. 19, 1937.

37. David Bullard, "Obituary of Helen Bullard," Helen Bullard Papers, #6501, box 1, folder 24.

8. New Projects and New Horizons

1. Arendt, *Human Condition.*
2. George Eliot, as quoted in Hayden, *Redesigning the American Dream,* 79.
3. For how this argument fits into a larger view of nature and gardening as important to the nation's moral and patriotic character, see Norwood, *Made from This Earth,* 121.
4. Beard, *Woman's Work in Municipalities,* 221.
5. Van Rensselaer, *Art Out-of-Doors,* 403-6.
6. Rehmann, *Small Place,* 64.
7. Henderson, "Llewellyn Park, Suburban Idyll," 221-43.
8. Klaus, Olmsted, and Library of American Landscape History, *Modern Arcadia,* 58n.4.
9. Sewell, "Magic of Guam," 649-52.
10. Letter of Jan. 30, 1915, Marjorie Sewell Cautley papers.
11. Sewell, "How Blighted Areas in Philadelphia and Boston" and "Small City Parks for Community Use."
12. Cautley, *Garden Design.*
13. Ibid., 2, 3.
14. Cautley, "Landscaping the Housing Project" and "Potted Plants?"
15. Letter to *Cornell Alumni News,* Feb. 23, 1925, Marjorie Sewell Cautley papers.
16. Sewell, "Small City Parks for Community Use," 63.
17. For a good discussion of this change, see Rainey and Miller, *Modern Public Gardens.*
18. Sewell, "Small City Parks for Community Use," 66.
19. Ibid.
20. "Cautley Films," Marjorie Sewell Cautley papers.
21. Sewell, "City Garden."
22. Cautley, Sewell, and Cutler, "New Houses of Old Flavor."
23. Ascher, "Remarks on the Designation of Radburn."
24. Cautley, "Group of Houses Planned."
25. Cautley, *Building a House in Sweden.*
26. Howard, *Garden Cities of To-Morrow.*
27. Howett, "Ecological Values," 87.
28. For good descriptions see Cautley, "Landscape Gardening for the Unemployed"; Girling and Helphand, *Yard, Street, Park,* 54-64.
29. Fox, *Housing for the Working Classes.*
30. Mumford, "Sky Line."
31. Stein, *Toward New Towns for America,* 87-88.
32. Larsen, "Visionary and Pragmatist," 6-7.
33. Dean, *Livable House, Its Garden,* 59-60.
34. Ibid., 59-64.
35. Cautley, "Planting at Radburn," 24.
36. Ibid.

37. See plans for Kingston Park and Dorrs Pond Park, 1934, Marjorie Sewell Cautley papers, #4908.

38. Martin, "Returning to Radburn," 158.

39. Hayden, *Grand Domestic Revolution,* 7.

40. Greed, *Women and Planning,* 95.

41. Cautley, *Garden Design,* 58–62.

42. Cautley, Sewell, and Cutler, "New Houses of Old Flavor."

43. See "Landscape Artists Help to Reduce Property Costs," *New York Herald Tribune,* June 29, 1930.

44. Cautley, "Potted Plants?" 52.

45. Ibid.

46. Cautley, "Effects of the American Standard of Living."

47. Rodgers, *Atlantic Crossings,* 195–96.

48. Thank you to Professor Kristin Larsen, of the University of Florida, for pointing this out to me.

49. Comas, "Ruth Patricia Shellhorn."

50. Beard and Lane, *Making Women's History,* 174.

Conclusion

1. Frost and Sears, *Women in Architecture.*

2. Fowler, "Women in Landscape Architecture," 8.

3. Rutz, "Women in Landscape Architectural Education."

4. Neal, "Women in Landscape Architecture."

5. Hubbard, "Report of the Committee on Graduate and Undergraduate Instruction."

6. ASLA et al., *Transactions,* presentation at the annual meeting in Boston, Feb. 1909.

7. Grossman and Reitzes, "Caught in the Crossfire," 30–31.

8. Woods, *From Craft to Profession,* 44–45.

9. Simo, *Forest and Garden;* McHarg and American Museum of Natural History, *Design with Nature.*

10. As quoted in a letter: Jensen to Mr. and Mrs. Boardman, n.d., Morton Arboretum Archives; Grese, *Jens Jensen,* 61.

11. As quoted in Grese, *Jens Jensen.*

12. Komara, "Glass Wall," 24.

Archives

Records of the American Society of Landscape Architects (ASLA). Library of Congress, Washington, D.C.

Archives of American Gardens (AAG). The Smithsonian Institute. Washington, D.C.

Helen Bullard Papers, #6501. Division of Rare Book and Manuscript Collections. Cornell University Library, Ithaca, N.Y.

Cambridge School Collection. Smith College Archives. Northampton, Mass.

Marjorie Sewell Cautley papers, #4908. Division of Rare Book and Manuscript Collections. Cornell University Library.

Century of Progress Archives. University of Illinois, Chicago.

Marian Cruger Coffin papers, 1903–1990. Winterthur Archives. Winterthur Library. Wilmington, Del.

Henry Francis du Pont papers. Winterthur Archives. Wilmington, Del.

Beatrix Jones Farrand Collection, 1866–1959. Environmental Design Archives. University of California, Berkeley.

Beatrix Jones Farrand papers. Dumbarton Oaks, Research Library and Collections. Washington, D.C.

Annette Hoyt Flanders papers. Sophia Smith Collection. Smith College Archives.

House and Garden Archives. Lawrence C. Phipps Memorial Conference Center. Denver, Colo.

Martha Brookes Brown Hutcheson papers. Morris County Park Commission. Morristown, N.J.

Mary Rutherfurd Jay Collection, 1872–1953. Environmental Design Archives. University of California, Berkeley.

Maybeck Archive. Environmental Design Archives. University of California, Berkeley.

Morton Arboretum Archives. Sterling Morton Library, Lisle, Ill.

Papers of Frederick Law Olmsted. Library of Congress. Washington, D.C.

Phipps/Flanders Correspondence. University of Denver Library.

Radburn Archives and Collections. Radburn Association. Radburn, N.J.

Ellen McGowan Biddle Shipman papers, #1259. Division of Rare Book and Manuscript Collections. Cornell University Library.

Sophia Smith Collection. Smith College Archives.

Stan Hywet Archives. Akron, Ohio.

University of Delaware Archives. Winterthur Archives.

Women Working, 1890–1930. Open Collections. Harvard University. Cambridge, Mass.

Print and Manuscript Sources

Albee, Helen Rickey. *Hardy Plants for Cottage Gardens*. New York: H. Holt and Company, 1910.

American Landscape School. "Advertisement for Correspondence School." *Horticulture*, July 1924, 413.

"The American Park and Outdoor Art Association." *American Gardening*, June 3, 1899, 396.

American Society of Landscape Architects (ASLA), Carl Rust Parker, Bremer Whidden Pond, and Theodora Kimball Hubbard. *Transactions of the American Society of Landscape Architects, 1909–1921*. Amsterdam, N.Y.: Recorder Press, 1922.

America's Little House. New York: New York Better Homes in America, 1934.

Anderson, Dorothy May. *Women, Design, and the Cambridge School*. West Lafayette, Ind.: PDA Publishers, 1980.

"Annette Hoyt Flanders: A Biographical Minute." *Landscape Architecture Magazine* 38, no. 1 (1946): 29–30.

Arendt, Hannah. *The Human Condition*. Charles R. Walgreen Foundation Lectures. [Chicago]: University of Chicago Press, 1958.

Ascher, Charles S. "Remarks on the Designation of Radburn as a Historic Landmark." 1975. Radburn Archives and Collections.

Auwaerter, John E. "Cultural Landscape Report for the Mansion Grounds, Marsh-Billings-Rockefeller National Historical Park, Volume 1: Site History." Boston: National Park Service, Olmsted Center for Landscape Preservation, 2005.

Balmori, Diana, Diane Kostial McGuire, and Eleanor M. McPeck. *Beatrix Farrand's American Landscapes: Her Gardens and Campuses*. Sagaponack, N.Y.: Sagapress, 1985.

Battles, Marjorie Gibbon, and Catherine Colt Dickey. *Fifty Blooming Years, 1913–1963*. New York: Garden Club of America, 1963.

Beard, Mary R. *Woman's Work in Municipalities*. New York: D. Appleton, 1915.

Beard, Mary R., and Ann J. Lane. *Making Women's History: The Essential Mary Ritter Beard*. 1st ed. New York: Feminist Press at the City University of New York, 2000.

"Beatrix Farrand, 1872–1959." In *The Bulletins of Reef Point Gardens*, by Beatrix Farrand, 112–14. Bar Harbor, N.Y: Island Foundation, dist. Sagapress, 1997.

Bell, Susan Groag. "Women Create Gardens in Male Landscapes: A Revisionist Approach to Eighteenth-Century English Garden History." *Feminist Studies* 16, no. 3 (1990): 471–91.

Bever, Marilyn A. "The Women of MIT, 1871 to 1941: Who They Were, What They Achieved." Boston: Massachusetts Institute of Technology, 1976.

Beveridge, Charles E., Paul Rocheleau, and David Larkin. *Frederick Law Olmsted: Designing the American Landscape.* Rev. ed. New York: Universe Publishing, 1998.

Bledstein, Burton J. *The Culture of Professionalism: The Middle Class and the Development of Higher Education in America.* 1st ed. New York: W. W. Norton, 1976.

Brown, Martha Brookes. "Statement Regarding Professional Methods and Charges, 1905." Martha Brookes Brown Hutcheson papers.

Bullard, Elizabeth. "Letter." *Garden and Forest,* Sept. 9, 1891. Archives of American Gardens, Bullard file.

Caparn, Harold A. "The Founding of the American Society of Landscape Architects." *American Landscape Architect* (1931): 20-23.

"Catalogue for the Lowthorpe School of Landscape Architecture, Gardening, and Horticulture for Women." Women Working, 1890-1930.

Cautley, Marjorie Sewell. *Building a House in Sweden.* New York: Macmillan, 1931.

———. "Effects of the American Standard of Living on Planning." *Planner's Journal* 88 (July 1937).

———. *Garden Design: The Principles of Abstract Design as Applied to Landscape Composition.* New York: Dodd Mead & Company, 1935.

———. "A Group of Houses Planned and Planted as a Unit." *House Beautiful* 65, no. 1 (1929): 68-69.

———. "Landscape Gardening for the Unemployed." *New Jersey Gardens* (February 1928).

———. "Landscaping the Housing Project." *Architecture* 72, no. 4 (1935): 182-86.

———. "Planting at Radburn." *Landscape Architecture Magazine* 21, no. 1 (1930): 23-29.

———. "Potted Plants? or, Adequate Landscaping for Community Projects?" *American City* 50, no. 8 (1935): 51-52.

Cautley, Marjorie, Helen Sewell, and Charles Cutler. "New Houses of Old Flavor." *Country Life* 49, nos. 1-6 (1922).

Child, Stephen. "Two Decades of Landscape Architecture in Retrospect, 1910-1930." *Landscape Architecture Magazine* 20 (July 1930): 267-75.

Coffin, Marian Cruger. "General Plan for Layout of Delaware College at Newark, Delaware and Descriptive Report for the Proposed Layout of the State College of Delaware, 1919." University of Delaware Archives.

———. "Method of Practice." Henry F. du Pont papers, Du Pont/Coffin Correspondence, box HF632, Coffin, Marian, 1919-1930.

———. "A Suburban Garden Six Years Old." *Country Life in America,* February 15, 1912, 19-22.

———. *Trees and Shrubs for Landscape Effects.* New York: C. Scribner's Sons, 1940.

———. "Where East Meets West: Visit to Picturesque Dalmatia, Montenegro and Bosnia." *National Geographic* 19, no. 5 (1908): 309-44.

Cole, Doris. *From Tipi to Skyscraper: A History of Women in Architecture.* Boston: i Press, dist. George Braziller, 1973.

Comas, Kelly. "Ruth Patricia Shellhorn—Landscape Architect: A Short Biography." 2007. Unpublished manuscript, private collection.

Cooper, Susan Fenimore. *Rural Hours.* 1st ed. Syracuse: Syracuse University Press, 1968.

Corbin, Carla. "No 'Gross Offenses against Good Taste in Landscape Art': The Pre-Professional Era in *Garden and Forest.*" *Landscape Journal* 25, no. 2 (2006): 158–68.

Cynthia. "A Parable of Planting." *House Beautiful* 62, no. 4 (1927): 384.

Davidson, Rebecca Warren. "Introduction." In *The Spirit of the Garden,* by Martha Brookes Hutcheson and Library of American Landscape History, 3:221. Amherst: University of Massachusetts Press, 2001.

———. "The Italian Garden." In "American Landscape Design: Its History, Significance, and Manifestation in the Villa Vizcaya." Master's thesis, Cornell University, 1989.

———. "The Spirit of the American Garden: Landscape and Cultural Expression in the Work of Martha Brookes Hutcheson." *Journal of the New England Garden History Society* 4 (Spring 1996): 22–29.

Dean, Ruth. "Landscape Architecture on a House-Top." *American Landscape Architect* (May 1931): 18–20.

———. *The Livable House, Its Garden.* New York: Moffat Yard and Co., 1917.

———. "The War Tax on Beauty." *New Country Life* (April 1918): 48–49.

Deck, Liz. "Interpreting Classic Signature Elements for Garden Design: Rediscovering Pacific Northwest Landscape Architects Lord & Schryver, Salem, Oregon." Master's thesis, University of Oregon, 2005.

Dillon, Julia Lester. "Municipal Landscaping for Women." *Farm and Garden* 10, no. 3 (1922): 3–6.

Dobyns, Winifred Starr. *California Gardens.* New York: Macmillan, 1931.

Downing, A. J. "American versus British Horticulture." *Horticulturist and Journal of Rural Art and Rural Taste* 7 (1852): 249–52.

Earle, Alice. *Old Time Gardens, Newly Set Forth.* New York, London: Macmillan, 1901.

Eliot, Charles. "Open Letter." *Landscape Architecture Magazine* 15, no. 4 (1925): 265.

Ely, Helena Rutherford. *A Woman's Hardy Garden.* New York, London: Macmillan, 1903.

Evans, Frederick N. "Report of Committee on Co-Education." 1921. Appendix 10a: National Conference on Instruction in Landscape Architecture.

Farrand, Beatrix. *The Bulletins of Reef Point Gardens.* Bar Harbor, N.Y.: Island Foundation, dist. Sagapress, 1997.

———. "Contemplated Landscape Changes at the Arnold Arboretum." *Arnoldia: The Magazine of the Arnold Arboretum* 6, no. 10 (1949): 45–48.

———. "The Oaks, Report for Mrs. Robert Woods Bliss, June 24, 25, 1922." 1922. Beatrix Jones Farrand papers.

Farrand, Beatrix, and Diane Kostial McGuire. *Beatrix Farrand's Plant Book for Dumbarton Oaks.* Washington: Dumbarton Oaks Trustees for Harvard University, 1980.

Farrand, Beatrix Jones. "Landscape Gardening for Women." 1916. Beatrix Jones Farrand Collection, 1866–1959, "Professional Papers," box 2, folder 29.

———. "A Talk to a Garden Club: Sewickley." 1916. Beatrix Jones Farrand Collection, 1866–1959, "Professional Papers," box 2, folder 25.

Filene, Catherine, ed. *Careers for Women.* Boston, New York: Houghton Mifflin Company, 1920.

Filzen, Patricia Louise. "Garden Designs for the Western Great Lakes Region: Annette Hoyt Flanders and Early Twentieth Century Women Landscape Architects." Master's thesis, University of Wisconsin, 1988.

Flanders, Annette Hoyt. *An Exhibition of Landscape Architecture.* N.p., 1932.

——. "Landscape Architecture: Photographs and Models." *Bulletin of the Milwaukee Art Institute* 5 (April 1932): 1-10.

——. "Modern Garden." Century of Progress Archives.

——. "The Value of Vistas in the Small Garden." *Good Housekeeping* 98 (1935): 76-77, 154, 156.

Fowler, Clarence. "Three Women in Landscape Architecture." *Cambridge School of Architecture and Landscape Architecture Alumnae Review* 4 (April 1932).

——. "Women in Landscape Architecture, Annotated by Martha Brookes Hutcheson." Martha Brookes Brown Hutcheson papers.

Fox, John L. *Housing for the Working Classes.* Larchmont, N.Y.: Memorystone Publishing, 2007.

Frost, Henry Atherton. "The Cambridge School: Domestic Architecture, Landscape Architecture, the Faculty and Courses for the Year 1930-31." Cambridge School Collection.

——. "Cambridge School Bulletin, 1940." Sophia Smith Collection.

——. "History of the Cambridge School of Architecture and Landscape Architecture for Women." Sophia Smith Collection.

Frost, Henry Atherton, and William R Sears. *Women in Architecture and Landscape Architecture.* Ed. Ethel P. Howes. Bulletin 7, Institute for the Co-Ordination of Women's Interests. Northhampton, Mass.: Smith College, 1928.

Furr, Mary Pope. "The Academic Program of the Cambridge School of Architecture and Landscape Architecture, 1915-1942." Master's thesis, University of Virginia, 1995.

"The Gardener's Calendar for July." *House & Garden,* July 1923, 76.

Girling, Cynthia L., and Kenneth I. Helphand. *Yard, Street, Park: The Design of Suburban Open Space.* New York: J. Wiley, 1994.

Glave, Dianne D. "'A Garden So Brilliant with Colors, So Original in Its Design': Rural African American Women, Gardening, Progressive Reform, and the Foundation of an African American Environmental Perspective." *Environmental History,* no. 3 (2003), at http://www.historycooperative.org/journals/eh/8.3/glave.html.

Greed, Clara. *Women and Planning: Creating Gendered Realities.* London, New York: Routledge, 1994.

Grese, Robert E. *Jens Jensen: Maker of Natural Parks and Gardens, Creating the North American Landscape.* Baltimore: Johns Hopkins University Press, 1992.

Grossman, Elizabeth G, and Lisa B. Reitzes. "Caught in the Crossfire: Women and Architectural Education 1880-1910." In *Architecture: A Place for Women,* ed. Ellen Perry Berkeley and Matilda McQuaid, 27-39. Washington: Smithsonian Institution Press, 1989.

Gruber, John. "Annette E. Maxson McCrea." In *Women Building Chicago 1790-1990: A Biographical Dictionary,* ed. Rima Lunin Schultz and Adele Hast, 558-60. Bloomington: Indiana University Press, 2001.

——. "McCrea, Annette E." In *Pioneers of American Landscape Design,* ed. Charles A. Birnbaum and Robin S. Karson, 248–49. New York: McGraw-Hill, 2000.

Guttman, Naomi Ellen. "Women Writing Gardens: Nature, Spirituality and Politics in Women's Garden Writing." Ph.D. diss., University of Southern California, 1999.

Haines, Ella Wister. "Where Practical Gardening May be Learned." *House & Garden* 41, no. 3 (March 1922): 54, 86.

Harris, Dianne. "Cultivating Power: The Language of Feminism in Women's Garden Literature, 1870–1920." *Landscape Journal* 13, no. 2 (1994): 113–23.

——. "Women as Gardeners." In *Encyclopedia of Gardens: History and Design,* ed. Candice A. Shoemaker and Chicago Botanic Garden, 1447–50. Chicago: Fitzroy Dearborn, 2001.

Hartt, Mary Bronson. "Women and the Art of Landscape Gardening." *Outlook,* March 28, 1908, 695–704.

Hayden, Dolores. *The Grand Domestic Revolution: A History of Feminist Designs for American Homes, Neighborhoods, and Cities.* Cambridge: MIT Press, 1981.

——. *Redesigning the American Dream: The Future of Housing, Work, and Family Life.* Rev. and expanded ed. New York: W. W. Norton, 2002.

Helphand, Kenneth I., and Nancy D. Rottle. "Cultivating Charm: The Northwest's First Female Landscape Architecture Firm Created a Lasting Legacy at Deepwood Gardens." *Garden Design* 7, no. 3 (1988): 26–33, 88.

Henderson, Susan. "Llewellyn Park, Suburban Idyll." *Journal of Garden History* 7, no. 3 (1987): 221–43.

Henry, Marianne Morgan. "Notes: A Practical Course in Landscape Architecture." *Bulletin of the Garden Club of America* (1938): 122–25.

Hines, Thomas S. *Irving Gill and the Architecture of Reform: A Study in Modernist Architectural Culture.* New York: Monacelli Press, 2000.

Hohmann, Heidi. "Theodora Kimball Hubbard and the 'Intellectualization' of Landscape Architecture, 1911–1935." *Landscape Journal* 25, no. 2 (2006): 169–86.

"A House on Beekman Place, New York." *House Beautiful* 62, no. 5 (1927): 513–16, 568–69.

Howard, Ebenezer. *Garden Cities of To-Morrow (Being the Third Edition of "To Morrow: A Peaceful Path to Real Reform").* London: S. Sonnenschein & Co., 1902.

Howe, Samuel. *American Country Houses of To-Day: An Illustrated Account of Some Excellent Houses Built and Gardens Planted During the Last Few Years Showing Unmistakable Influence of the Modern Trend in Ideals Architectural.* New York: The Architectural Book Publishing Company, 1915.

Howett, Catherine. "Ecological Values in Twentieth-Century Landscape Design: A History and Hermeneutics." *Landscape Journal* 17, no. 2 (1998): 80–98.

Hubbard, Henry Vincent. "Report of the Committee on Graduate and Undergraduate Instruction." 1921. Appendix 3: National Conference on Instruction in Landscape Architecture.

Hutcheson, Martha Brookes. "Co-Operation of Citizens, Trained and Untrained in Beautifying Our Rural Towns, Paper Presented to Annual Meeting of the American Civic Association." Martha Brookes Brown Hutcheson papers.

———. "Lecture—The Fine Art of Landscape Architecture." Martha Brookes Brown Hutcheson papers.

———. "A Native Tree and Shrub Group." *Garden Club of America Bulletin* (1936): 36–40.

———. "One of Our National Blights." *Garden Club of America Bulletin* (1926): 30–31.

———. "Possible Inspiration through Garden Clubs toward Wiser and More Beautiful Plantings." *Garden Club of America Bulletin* (1931): 117–21.

———. *The Spirit of the Garden.* Boston: Atlantic Monthly Press, 1923.

———. "A Wider Program for Garden Clubs." Martha Brookes Brown Hutcheson papers.

Hutcheson, Martha Brookes Brown, and Library of American Landscape History. *The Spirit of the Garden.* Amherst: University of Massachusetts Press, 2001.

Iannacone, Rachel. "Open Space for the Underclass: New York City's Small Parks (1885–1915)." Ph.D. diss., University of Philadelphia, 2005.

Jefferson, Thomas. *Thomas Jefferson's Garden Book, 1766–1824, With Relevant Extracts from His Other Writings.* Ed. Edwin M. Betts. Philadelphia: American Philosophical Society, 1944 (Charlottesville: Thomas Jefferson Memorial Foundation, 1999).

Jones, Beatrix. "Book of Gardening." Beatrix Jones Farrand Collection, 1866–1959.

———. "Bridge over the Kent at Levens Hall." *Garden and Forest* 9, no. 412 (1896): 22.

———. "City Parks." *Journal of the Committee on Municipal Administration: Municipal Affairs* (1899): 687–90.

———. "The Garden as a Picture." *Scribner's Magazine* 42, no. 1 (1907): 2–11.

———. "The Garden in Relation to the House." *Garden and Forest* 10, no. 476 (1897): 132–33.

———. "Le Notre and His Gardens." *Scribner's Magazine* 38 (July 1905): 43–55.

———. "Nature's Landscape—Gardening in Maine." *Garden and Forest* 6, no. 289 (1893): 378–79.

Jones, Mary Cadwalader. *European Travel for Women: Notes and Suggestions.* New York: MacMillan, 1900.

Kimball, Richard B. "A Little Visit to Lowthorpe." *House Beautiful* 39, no. 3 (1916): 111–13.

Klaus, Susan. "All in the Family: The Olmsted Office and the Business of Landscape Architecture." *Landscape Journal* 16, no. 1 (1997): 80–95.

Klaus, Susan, Frederick Law Olmsted, and Library of American Landscape History. *A Modern Arcadia: Frederick Law Olmsted, Jr. & the Plan for Forest Hills Gardens.* Amherst: University of Massachusetts Press, 2002.

Komara, Ann E. "The Glass Wall: Gendering the American Society of Landscape Architects." *Studies in the Decorative Arts* 8, no. 1 (2000): 22–30.

Koues, Helen. "Good Housekeeping Exhibition: Classic Modern Garden and Pavilion at a Century of Progress—Chicago." *Good Housekeeping* 99, no. 2 (1934): 54, 55, 56, 132.

Krall, Daniel. "The Illusive Miss Bullard: First Professional Woman Landscape Architect." *Landscape Journal* 21, no. 1 (2002): 116–21.

———. "One Hundred Years of Outdoor Art at Cornell University." Unpublished manuscript, private collection.

"Landscape Architecture." *New York Journal*[?], February 11, 1900.

"Landscape Gardening: A Conversation." *Outlook,* July 1909, 726–39.

Larsen, Kristin. "Visionary and Pragmatist—Stein and Federal Housing Policy." Paper presented at the Association of Collegiate Schools of Planning conference, Baltimore, November 21–24, 2002.

Lee, Anne. "Three Gardens at Grosse Pointe, Mich.: Ruth Dean, Landscape Architect." *Architectural Forum* (1929): 505–12.

Leichtle, Kurt E. "The Gibson Girl on the Farm? The View of the Role of Women in Popular Farm Literature at the Turn of the Twentieth Century." Paper presented at the Harvesting New Rural History conference, Indianapolis, Fall 1989.

Libby, Valencia. "Henry Francis du Pont and the Early Development of Winterthur Gardens, 1880–1927." Master's thesis, University of Delaware, 1984.

———. "Jane Haines' Vision: The Pennsylvania School of Horticulture for Women." *Journal of the New England Garden History Society* 10 (2002): 44–52.

———. "Marian Cruger Coffin: Landscape Architect of Distinction." Preservation League of New York State. *Newsletter* 16, no. 2 (1990): 4–5.

Loudon, Jane, and A. J. Downing. *Gardening for Ladies and Companion to the Flower-Garden.* 1st U.S. ed., from the 3rd British ed. New York: Wiley & Putnam, 1843.

Lowell, Guy. *American Gardens.* Boston: Bates and Guild, 1902.

MacPhail, Elizabeth C. *Kate Sessions: Pioneer Horticulturist.* San Diego: San Diego Historical Society, 1976.

Major, Judith K. *To Live in the New World: A. J. Downing and American Landscape Gardening.* Cambridge, London: MIT Press, 1997.

Manning, Warren H. "The History of Village Improvement in the United States." *Craftsman* 5, no. 5 (1904): 423–32.

Martin, Michael David. "Returning to Radburn." *Landscape Journal* 20, no. 2 (2001): 156–73.

Maybeck, Bernard, and Annie Maybeck. "Program for the Development of a Hillside Community." Berkeley Hillside Club. Maybeck Archive.

McCrea, Annette E. "Color Harmony and Discord." *Suburban Life* 4 (1907): 311–12.

——— [Mrs. A. E. McCrea]. "Railroad Station Improvement." *Chautauquan* 34, no. 4 (1904): 868.

McHarg, Ian L., and American Museum of Natural History. *Design with Nature.* 1st ed. Garden City, N.Y.: Published for the American Museum of Natural History by the Natural History Press, 1969.

Meador, Deborah Kay. "The Making of a Landscape Architect: Ellen Biddle Shipman and Her Years at the Cornish Art Colony." Master's thesis, Cornell University, 1989.

Meloney, Mrs. W. B. *Better Homes in America: Plan Book for Demonstration Week October 9 to 14, 1922.* New York: Advisory Council for Better Homes Campaign, 1922.

Meyer, Elizabeth. "The Expanded Field of Landscape Architecture." In *Ecological Design and Planning,* ed. George F. Thompson, 45–79. New York: John Wiley, 1997.

Miller, Julia. "What Alumnae Are Doing: The Fascination of Landscape Architecture." *Smith Alumnae Quarterly* (1921): 30–32.

Mumford, Lewis. "The Sky Line." *New Yorker,* April 16, 1932, 36.

Neal, Darwina L. "Women in Landscape Architecture." *ASLA Bulletin* (July 1973).

Newton, Norman T. *Design on the Land: The Development of Landscape Architecture.* Cambridge: Belknap Press of Harvard University Press, 1971.

Norwood, Vera. *Made from This Earth: American Women and Nature, Gender and American Culture.* Chapel Hill: University of North Carolina Press, 1993.

O'Malley, Therese. "'A Public Museum of Trees': Mid-Nineteenth Century Plans for the Mall." *Studies in the History of Art* 30 (1991): [60]–76.

Pattee, Sarah Lewis. "Landscape Architecture in American Colleges." *Landscape Architecture Magazine* 14, no. 4 (1924): 171–77.

Patterson, Robert W., Mildred Bliss, and Lanning Roper. *Beatrix Jones Farrand, 1872–1959: An Appreciation of a Great Landscape Gardener.* [Washington]: R. W. Bliss, 1960.

Peters, Scott J., and Paul A. Morgan. "The Country Life Commission: Reconsidering a Milestone in American Agricultural History." *Agricultural History* 78, no. 3 (2004): 289–316.

"Pioneer among Women Landscape Architects." 1929. Source unknown. Personal collection.

Prieto, Laura R. *At Home in the Studio: The Professionalization of Women Artists in America.* Cambridge: Harvard University Press, 2001.

Rainey, Reuben, and J. C. Miller. *Modern Public Gardens: Robert Royston and the Suburban Park.* Ed. Marc Treib. San Francisco: William Stout Publishers, 2006.

Rehmann, Elsa. "An Ecological Approach." *Landscape Architecture Magazine* 23, no. 4 (1933): 239–45.

———. *The Small Place: Its Landscape Architecture.* New York, London: G. P. Putnam's Sons, 1918.

Rehmann, Elsa, and Antoinette Rehmann Perrett. *Garden-Making.* Boston, New York: Houghton Mifflin Company, 1926.

Robbins, Mary Caroline. "The Art of Public Improvement." *Atlantic Monthly* 78, no. 470 (1896): 742–51.

———. "Park-Making as a National Art." *Atlantic Monthly* 79, no. 471 (1897): 86–98.

———. "Some Questions about Taste." *Garden and Forest* 5, no. 235 (1892): 405.

———. "Village Improvement Societies." *Atlantic Monthly* 79, no. 472 (1897): 212–22.

Robinette, Gary O. *Landscape Architectural Education.* 2 vols. Dubuque: Kendall/ Hunt Publishing Company, 1973.

Robinson, Selma. "From the Ground Up." *Collier's* 91 (1933): 19–20.

Rodgers, Daniel T. *Atlantic Crossings: Social Politics in a Progressive Age.* Cambridge: Belknap Press of Harvard University Press, 1998.

Rutz, Miriam. "Women in Landscape Architectural Education." *ASLA Bulletin* (December 1975).

Sargent, Charles Sprague. "New Botany Program at Barnard College." *Garden and Forest* 4, no. 191 (1892): 494.

———. "Taste Indoors and Out." *Garden and Forest* 5, no. 233 (1892): 373.

———. "Taste Indoors and Out, Response." *Garden and Forest* 5, no. 238 (1892): 433.

Sargent, Charles Sprague, and William A. Stiles. "Art and Nature in Landscape Gardening." *Garden and Forest* 10, no. 482 (1897): 191–92.

Schnare, Susan E. "Women Garden Writers." Paper presented at the the the Influence of Women on the Southern Landscape conference, Old Salem, N.C., October 5–7, 1995.

Schuyler, David. *Apostle of Taste: Andrew Jackson Downing, 1815–1852*. Baltimore: Center for American Places, Johns Hopkins University Press, 1996.

Sewell, Marjorie. "A City Garden." *Architecture* 45, no. 4 (1922): 125–26.

———. "How Blighted Areas in Philadelphia and Boston Might Be Transformed." *American City* 58, no. 10 (1943): 47–48.

———. "The Magic of Guam." *Atlantic Monthly* 3, no. 5 (1913): 649–52.

———. "Small City Parks for Community Use: How Neighborhood Parks Meet Public Needs." *American City* 59, no. 5 (1944): 63–66.

Shelton, Louise. *Beautiful Gardens in America*. Rev. ed. New York: C. Scribner, 1924.

Shipman, Ellen Biddle. "Garden–Notebook." Ellen McGowan Biddle Shipman papers, #1259, box 1.

Shteir, Ann B. *Cultivating Women, Cultivating Science: Flora's Daughters and Botany in England, 1760–1860*. Baltimore: Johns Hopkins University Press, 1996.

Simo, Melanie Louise. *Forest and Garden: Traces of Wildness in a Modernizing Land, 1897–1949*. Charlottesville: University of Virginia Press, 2003.

Smith, Bertha H. "Western Personalities: The Lady of the Christmas Flower, Miss Kate Sessions." *Sunset: The Pacific Monthly* (1912): 699–702.

Smith, Warren Hunting. "Museum Exhibit: Gardens Designed by Marian Cruger Coffin: Landscape Architect 1876-1957, Memorial Exhibition of Photographs of 17 Gardens." Hobart College Arts Building, Geneva, N.Y.

Solomon, Barbara Miller. *In the Company of Educated Women: A History of Women and Higher Education in America*. New Haven, London: Yale University Press, 1985.

Spicer, Anne Higginson. "The Gardening Women in Our Town." *House Beautiful* 33, no. 3 (1913): 103–4.

Spirn, Anne Whiston. *The Language of Landscape*. New Haven: Yale University Press, 1998.

Stein, Clarence S. *Toward New Towns for America*. 3rd ed. Cambridge: MIT Press, 1969.

Streatfield, David. *California Gardens: Creating a New Eden*. New York: Abbeville Press, 1994.

Tankard, Judith B., and Library of American Landscape History. *The Gardens of Ellen Biddle Shipman*. Sagaponack, N.Y.: Sagapress, in association with the Library of American Landscape History, dist. H. N. Abrams, 1996.

Tusser, Thomas. "Five Hundredth Points of Good Husbandry." 1557.

Van Rensselaer, Mariana (Mrs. Schuyler). "The Art of Gardening—A Historical Sketch" (series of seven essays). *Garden and Forest* 2–3 (1889–90).

———. *Art Out-of-Doors: Hints on Good Taste in Gardening*. New York: C. Scribner's Sons, 1893.

———. "Landscape Gardening—A Definition." *Garden and Forest* 1, no. 1 (1888): 2.

Vernon, Noël Dorsey. "Toward Defining the Profession." *Landscape Journal* 6, no. 1 (1987): 13–20.

Waring, George E. *Village Improvements and Farm Villages*. Boston: J. R. Osgood and Company, 1877.

Waugh, Frank A. "Landscape Architecture in North America." In *A History of Garden Art: With over Six Hundred Illustrations*, ed. Marie Luise Schroeter Gothein and Walter P. Wright, 421. London, New York: J. M. Dent, E. P. Dutton, 1928.

Way, Thaïsa. "Designing Garden City Landscapes: Works by Marjorie L. Sewell Cautley, 1922–1937." *Studies in the History of Gardens and Designed Landscapes* 25, no. 4 (2005): 297–316.

——. "Early Social Agendas of Women in Landscape Architecture." *Landscape Journal* 25, no. 2 (2006): 187–204.

Wolschke-Bulmahn, Joachim. "From the War-Garden to the Victory Garden: Political Aspects of Garden Culture in the United States during World War I " *Landscape Journal* 11, no. 1 (1992): 51–57.

"Women in Landscaping: Professional Standing Is Developed by Thorough Training at Lowthorpe School." *House & Garden*, January 1939, 28–29.

Woods, Mary N. *From Craft to Profession: The Practice of Architecture in Nineteenth-Century America*. Berkeley, London: University of California Press, 1999.

Wright, Gwendolyn. "A Partnership: Catherine Bauer and William Wurster." In *An Everyday Modernism: The Houses of William Wurster*, ed. Marc Treib, 184–203. San Francisco, Berkeley: San Francisco Museum of Modern Art, University of California Press, 1995.

Wright, Richardson. "House & Garden's Own Hall of Fame." *House & Garden*, June 1933, 50.

Yoch, James J. *Landscaping the American Dream: The Gardens and Film Sets of Florence Yoch, 1890–1972*. New York: H. N. Abrams/Sagapress, 1989.

INDEX

Italicized page numbers refer to illustrations.